Peterson's

Master the

Officer

Candidate Tests

8th Edition

Scott A. Ostrow,
Lt. Col., USAF (Ret.)

PETERSON'S

A **nelnet** COMPANY

About Peterson's, a Nelnet company

To succeed on your lifelong educational journey, you will need accurate, dependable, and practical tools and resources. That is why Peterson's is everywhere education happens. Because whenever and however you need education content delivered, you can rely on Peterson's to provide the information, know-how, and guidance to help you reach your goals. Tools to match the right students with the right school. It's here. Personalized resources and expert guidance. It's here. Comprehensive and dependable education content—delivered whenever and however you need it. It's all here.

Petersons.com/publishing

Check out our Web site at www.petersons.com/publishing to see if there is any new information regarding the test and any revisions or corrections to the content of this book. We've made sure the information in this book is accurate and up-to-date; however, the test format or content may have changed since the time of publication.

For more information, contact Peterson's, 2000 Lenox Drive, Lawrenceville, NJ 08648; 800-338-3282; or find us on the World Wide Web at www.petersons.com.

Stephen Clemente, President; Bernadette Webster, Director of Publishing; Roger S. Williams, Sales and Marketing; Mark D. Snider, Editor; Ray Golaszewski, Manufacturing Manager; Linda M. Williams, Composition Manager

ISBN-13: 978-0-7689-2794-8
ISBN-10: 0-7689-2794-3

Printed in the United States of America

10 9 8 7 6 5 4 3 2 1   11 10 09

Eighth Edition

By producing this book on recycled paper (40% post consumer waste) 133 trees were saved.

Acknowledgments

Much of the information and statistics in the chapter on women in the military were taken, with permission, from *Women in the Military: Where They Stand* (2005), provided by the Women's Research & Education Institute.

Contents

Before You Begin

HOW THIS BOOK IS ORGANIZED

Taking any of the officer candidate tests involves serious preparation. Test taking shares some aspects with other endeavors, such as competing in athletics. It requires discipline and practice to succeed.

These are skills that can be improved through coaching, but, ultimately, improvement also requires practice. This book gives you both.

- **Part I** provides essential information on career opportunities in the military. Potential occupations, officer rank structure, pay and benefits, and general commissioning requirements are covered in detail. You'll also learn about opportunities for women in the military, including information about pay equity, being a single parent in the military, and job restrictions for servicewomen.

- **Part II** contains information about branch-specific commissioning requirements, including a chapter on each branch of the armed services. Each chapter details the history of the respective officer candidate or officer training school, what to expect there, career fields available, and requirements and qualifications for admittance.

- **Parts III–V** contain information about the structure and content of the officer candidate tests. Tips and strategies for preparing for test day are listed, along with the basic info about each test. There are also sections about every question type you are likely to encounter and plenty of examples and sample test items.

- **Part VI** consists of nine practice tests, with detailed answer explanations for each question. The answer explanations are invaluable for helping you learn from your mistakes.

- **Part VII** contains three officer candidate tests, with detailed answer explanations for each question. These tests are similar in format and structure to the actual officer candidate tests; however, they are not meant to be comprehensive. These tests are a useful approximation of essential sections from actual exams.

SPECIAL STUDY FEATURES

Peterson's Master the Officer Candidate Tests 8th Edition was designed to be as user friendly as it is complete. To this end, it includes a couple features to make your preparation more efficient.

Overview

Each chapter begins with a bulleted overview listing the topics covered in the chapter. This will allow you to quickly target the areas in which you are most interested.

Summing It Up

Most of the chapters end with a point-by-point summary that reviews the most important items. The summaries offer a convenient way to review key points.

YOU'RE WELL ON YOUR WAY TO SUCCESS

You've made the decision to apply to become an officer. *Peterson's Master the Officer Candidate Tests* will help prepare you for the steps you'll need to take to achieve your goal—from scoring high on the exam to being admitted to the Officer Candidate School or Officer Training School of your choice. Good luck!

GIVE US YOUR FEEDBACK

Peterson's publishes a full line of resources to help guide you through the Officer Candidate School or Officer Training School admission process. Peterson's publications can be found at your local bookstore or library and you can access us online at www. petersons.com.

We welcome any comments or suggestions you may have about this publication and invite you to complete our online survey at www.petersons.com/booksurvey. Or you can fill out the survey at the back of this book, tear it out, and mail it to us at:

    Publishing Department
    Peterson's, a Nelnet company
    2000 Lenox Drive
    Lawrenceville, NJ 08648

Your feedback will help us make your educational dreams possible.

PART I
CAREER OPPORTUNITIES FOR COMMISSIONED OFFICERS

Career Opportunities for Officers in the Military

OVERVIEW

- Military officer occupations
- Officer rank structure
- Pay and benefits
- General commissioning requirements
- How to become an officer
- Reserve and guard opportunities
- Branch-specific commissioning information
- Summing it up

If you are reading this book you have decided to or at least are considering applying for a commission as an officer in the U.S. military. This book will help you prepare for the officer candidate test that will be used to determine, in part, your eligibility for a commissioning program. In addition to being a study guide, *Peterson's Master the Officer Candidate Tests* provides helpful information on choosing the best commissioning path for you.

As a commissioned officer you will join the ranks of thousands who have come before you and will become part of the rich history and heritage of the U.S. military.

Serving as a commissioned officer in the U.S. military has its benefits. Among these benefits are:

- Competitive pay
- $400,000 life insurance at a very low cost (as well as life insurance for family)
- 30 vacation days each year
- Retirement after twenty years
- Educational benefits for advanced degrees
- Thrift Savings Plan (for additional retirement funds)
- Responsibility and leadership positions at an early age
- Tax-free shopping at base stores and commissary

chapter 1

As with most occupations, there are also some negative aspects and, as you can probably imagine, serving in the military has its share of disadvantages, including:

- Working hours that may not always be constant
- Working in hazardous conditions (and locations)
- Family separations due to assignments and/or deployments
- Family moves
- Job locations that may not be desirable to you

MILITARY OFFICER OCCUPATIONS

Military officers work in many different types of occupations that fall into nine broad categories:

① Combat specialty officers
② Engineering, science, and technical officers
③ Executive, administrative, and managerial officers
④ Health care officers
⑤ Human resource development officers
⑥ Media and public affairs officers
⑦ Protective service officers
⑧ Support services officers
⑨ Transportation officers

The table below illustrates the breakdown of the number of personnel, by service branch, in each occupational category (according to 2007 U.S. Department of Labor statistics).

Military Officer Personnel by Broad Occupational Category and Branch of Service (January 2007)

Occupational Group—Officer	Army	Air Force	Coast Guard	Marine Corps	Navy	Total (all Services)
Combat specialty occupations	19,421	2,861	81	4,684	1,260	28,307
Engineering, science, and technical occupations	20,189	19,852	1,057	3,639	7,873	52,610
Executive, administrative, and managerial occupations	11,262	9,013	231	2,572	5,437	28,515
Health care occupations	9,953	8,970	5	—	7,737	26,665
Human resource development occupations	2,151	2,275	184	293	643	5,546
Media and public affairs occupations	237	408	19	170	265	1,099
Protective service occupations	2,611	1,229	96	327	275	4,538
Support services occupations	1,596	768	—	38	884	3,286
Transportation occupations	13,112	23,540	1,736	7,188	27,049	72,625
Total, by service*	**82,884**	**69,284**	**7,853**	**18,998**	**51,558**	**230,577**

*Occupational employment does not sum to totals because occupational information is not available for all personnel.

Combat specialty officers plan and direct military operations, oversee combat activities, and serve as combat leaders. This category includes officers in charge of tanks and other armored assault vehicles, artillery systems, Special Forces, and infantry. Combat specialty officers normally specialize by the type of unit that they lead. Within the unit, they may specialize by type of weapon system. Artillery and missile system officers, for example, direct personnel as they target, launch, test, and maintain various types of missiles and artillery. Special operations officers lead their units in offensive raids, demolitions, intelligence gathering, and search-and-rescue missions.

Engineering, science, and technical officers have a wide range of responsibilities based on their area of expertise. They lead or perform activities in areas such as space operations, environmental health and safety, and engineering. These officers may direct the operations of communications centers or the development of complex computer systems. Environmental health and safety officers study the air, ground, and water to identify and analyze sources of pollution and its effects. They also direct programs to control safety and health hazards in the workplace. Other personnel work as aerospace engineers to design and direct the development of military aircraft, missiles, and spacecraft.

Executive, administrative, and managerial officers oversee and direct military activities in key functional areas such as finance, accounting, health administration, international relations, and supply. Health services administrators, for instance, are responsible for the overall quality of care provided at the hospitals and clinics they operate. They must ensure that each department works together. As another example, purchasing and contracting managers negotiate and monitor contracts for the purchase of the billions of dollars' worth of equipment, supplies, and services that the military buys from private industry each year.

Health care officers provide health services at military facilities, on the basis of their area of specialization. Officers who examine, diagnose, and treat patients with illness, injury, or disease include physicians, registered nurses, and dentists. Other health care officers provide therapy, rehabilitative treatment, and additional services for patients. Physical and occupational therapists plan and administer therapy to help patients adjust to disabilities, regain independence, and return to work. Speech therapists evaluate and treat patients with hearing and speech problems. Dietitians manage food service facilities and plan meals for hospital patients and for outpatients who need special diets. Pharmacists manage the purchase, storage, and dispensing of drugs and medicines. Physicians and surgeons in this occupational group provide the majority of medical services to the military and their families. Dentists treat diseases, disorders, and injuries of the mouth. Optometrists treat vision problems by prescribing eyeglasses or contact lenses. Psychologists provide mental health care and also conduct research on behavior and emotions.

Human resource development officers manage recruitment, placement, and training strategies and programs in the military. Recruiting managers direct recruiting efforts and provide information about military careers to young people, parents, schools, and local communities. Personnel managers direct military personnel functions such as job assignment, staff promotion, and career counseling. Training and education directors identify training needs and develop and manage educational programs designed to keep military personnel current in the skills they need.

Media and public affairs officers oversee the development, production, and presentation of information or events for the public. These officers may produce and direct motion pictures, videos, and television and radio broadcasts that are used for training, news, and entertainment. Some plan, develop, and direct the activities of military bands. Public information officers respond to inquiries about military activities and prepare news releases and reports to keep the public informed.

Protective service officers are responsible for the safety and protection of individuals and property on military bases and vessels. Emergency management officers plan and prepare for all types of natural and human-made disasters. They develop warning, control, and evacuation plans to be used in the event of a disaster. Law enforcement and security officers enforce all applicable laws on military bases and investigate crimes when the law has been broken.

Support services officers manage food service activities and perform services in support of the morale and well-being of military personnel and their families. Food services managers oversee the preparation and delivery of food services within dining facilities located on military installations and vessels. Social workers focus on improving conditions that cause social problems such as drug and alcohol abuse, racism, and sexism. Chaplains conduct worship services for military personnel and perform other spiritual duties according to the beliefs and practices of all religious faiths.

Transportation officers manage and perform activities related to the safe transport of military personnel and material by air and water. These officers normally specialize by mode of transportation or area of expertise because, in many cases, they must meet licensing and certification requirements. Pilots in the military fly various types of specialized airplanes and helicopters to carry troops and equipment and to execute combat missions. Navigators use radar, radio, and other navigation equipment to determine their position and plan their route of travel. Officers on ships and submarines work as a team to manage the various departments aboard their vessels. Ship engineers direct engineering departments aboard ships and submarines, including engine operations, maintenance, repair, heating, and power generation.

Figure 1 further illustrates the distribution of officers by occupational group.

Figure 1: DISTRIBUTION OF OFFICERS BY OCCUPATIONAL GROUP

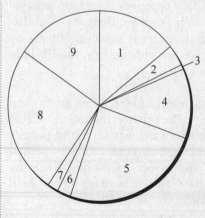

1. Executive, administrative, and managerial (12.37%)

2. Human resource development (2.4%)

3. Media and public affairs (0.47%)

4. Health care (11.56%)

5. Engineering, science, and technical (22.82%)

6. Protective services (1.97%)

7. Support services (1.43%)

8. Transportation (31.5%)

9. Combat specialty (12.28%)

The nine categories above can be further divided into specific occupations. The table that follows lists those specific occupations under their respective categories. Although most occupations are common to all the services, some are not. An "X" is placed under each branch if that specific occupation pertains to that branch of service.

OFFICER OCCUPATIONAL AREAS					
Officer Occupations	**Army**	**Navy**	**Air Force**	**Marine Corps**	**Coast Guard**
Executive, administrative, and managerial occupations					
Administrative officers		X	X	X	X
Finance and accounting managers	X	X	X	X	X
Health services administrators	X	X	X		X
International relations officers	X	X	X	X	X
Logisticians	X	X	X	X	
Management analysts and planners	X	X	X	X	X
Purchasing and contracting managers	X	X	X	X	X
Recruiting managers	X	X	X	X	X
Store managers	X	X	X	X	X
Supply and warehousing managers	X	X	X	X	X
Human resource development occupations					
Personnel managers	X	X	X	X	X
Recruiting managers	X	X	X	X	X
Teachers and instructors	X	X	X	X	X
Training and education directors	X	X	X	X	X
Support services occupations					
Chaplains	X	X	X		
Food service managers	X	X	X		X
Social workers	X	X	X		
Media and public affairs occupations					
Audiovisual and broadcast directors	X	X	X	X	
Music directors	X	X	X	X	X
Public information officers	X	X	X	X	X
Health care occupations					
Dentists	X	X	X		X
Dietitians	X	X	X		
Optometrists	X	X	X		
Pharmacists	X	X	X		X
Physical and occupational therapists	X	X	X		X
Physician assistants	X	X	X		X
Physicians and surgeons	X	X	X		X
Psychologists	X	X	X		
Registered nurses	X	X	X		X
Speech therapists	X	X	X		X
Engineering, science, and technical occupations					
Aerospace engineers		X	X	X	X
Civil engineers	X	X	X	X	X
Communications managers	X	X	X	X	X
Computer systems officers	X	X	X	X	X
Electrical and electronics engineers	X	X	X	X	X
Environmental health and safety officers	X	X	X	X	X
Industrial engineers	X	X	X	X	X

Intelligence officers	X	X	X	X	X
Lawyers and judges	X	X	X	X	X
Life scientists	X	X	X		
Marine engineers		X			X
Nuclear engineers	X	X		X	
Ordnance officers	X	X	X	X	X
Physical scientists	X	X	X	X	X
Space operations officers	X	X	X	X	
Protective service occupations					
Emergency management officers	X	X	X	X	X
Law enforcement and security officers	X	X	X	X	X
Transportation occupations					
Air traffic control managers	X	X	X	X	
Airplane navigators	X	X	X	X	X
Airplane pilots	X	X	X	X	X
Helicopter pilots	X	X	X	X	X
Ship and submarine officers	X	X			X
Ship engineers	X	X			X
Transportation maintenance managers	X	X	X	X	X
Transportation managers	X	X	X	X	X
Combat specialty occupations					
Armored assault vehicle officers	X			X	
Artillery and missile officers	X	X	X	X	
Combat mission support officers	X	X	X	X	
Infantry officers	X	X			
Special officers	X	X	X	X	

OFFICER RANK STRUCTURE

Most officers begin their careers as an O-1. What does that mean? When referring to military rank, the terms "pay grade" and "rank" are often used interchangeably; however, they are not the same.

Pay grade refers to the number classification of an officer and is linked to how much that officer is paid. All officer pay grades begin with the letter "O," while enlisted members' pay grades begin with the letter "E." Officers in all branches of the military serve in pay grades of O-1 through O-10. The corresponding ranks linked to those number designators are called by different names depending on the branch of service. For instance, an O-3 in the Navy is called a lieutenant, while an O-3 in the Air Force is a captain. Therefore, a member of the Air Force can have the pay grade of O-3 and the rank of captain and be equivalent in rank to a member of the Navy who has the pay grade of O-3 and the rank of lieutenant.

Although most military officers start out as an O-1 and then progress upward through the ranks, very few make it to O-10. Figure 2 on page 10 shows the pay grades and their ranks and insignia for each military branch. You will notice that the rank insignia for the top pay grade (O-10) is four stars; so what about the five-star generals we always hear about in the movies? Well, there have been only a handful of officers to hold the rank of five-star general (or General of the Army) in modern times. The last to hold this rank was Gen. Omar Bradley in 1950.

PAY AND BENEFITS

In the past, military officer pay has seriously lagged behind the pay of their civilian counterparts. Today, however, this is not the case. In addition to an officer's basic pay, military officers receive additional pay that is often tax-exempt. These tax-exempt monies help to create a pay scale in which military pay often surpasses corresponding civilian pay. In addition to raises based on promotion, military members receive longevity raises based on the number of years they have served. Furthermore, they usually receive an annual cost-of-living increase.

Incentive Pay

Military officers may be entitled to other monetary compensation in addition to their basic pay. Depending on the duty being performed, this may be in the form of "incentive pay." Personnel with flying status may receive *flight pay,* individuals assigned to a submarine receive *submarine pay,* and personnel assigned to ships receive *sea pay.* Other incentive pay may be received, for example, by those serving in a hazardous environment, on an explosives demolition team, or as a diver.

In addition, many health profession officers receive additional incentive pay as well as annual bonuses, which put their total salaries on par with their civilian contemporaries.

Allowances

Some of the pay military officers receive is in the form of allowances (which are usually tax-exempt). For instance, officers living off-base receive a tax-exempt monthly housing allowance. This allowance is based on marital status, rank, and location. In 2008, monthly housing allowances for officers ranged from $500 to $4,000. Officers also receive a monthly allowance for food, called the Basic Allowance for Subsistence (BAS), currently set at $202.76.

The table on page 11 is the most current officer monthly basic pay table (as of January 1, 2009). As previously mentioned, most military officers begin their careers as an O-1 (second lieutenant in the Army, Air Force, and Marine Corps; ensign in the Navy and Coast Guard). Some professionals, such as doctors and nurses, may enter at a higher rank.

For up-to-date, and more detailed, information about military pay and allowances, visit the Defense Finance and Accounting Service (DFAS) Web site at www.dfas.mil. This Web site is an excellent tool not only now, while you are researching opportunities as a military officer, but in the future to manage and understand your pay and allowances.

Retirement Benefits

Military members are eligible for retirement after serving twenty years. Active-duty retirees receive 50 percent of their base pay at the time of their retirement, and National Guard and Reserve retirees receive a percentage of their base pay based on the number of "points" they have accumulated. (National Guard officers and reservists earn points during their careers that can greatly affect their retirement pay.) In addition, they may not start receiving retirement pay (pension) until the age of 60 (although there are bills now being drafted that would lower that age). The

Figure 2: OFFICER PAY GRADES

SERVICE PAY GRADE	ARMY	NAVY	AIR FORCE	MARINE CORPS	COAST GUARD
O-10	GENERAL	ADMIRAL	GENERAL	GENERAL	ADMIRAL
O-9	LIEUTENANT GENERAL	VICE ADMIRAL	LIEUTENANT GENERAL	LIEUTENANT GENERAL	VICE ADMIRAL
O-8	MAJOR GENERAL	REAR ADMIRAL (UPPER HALF)	MAJOR GENERAL	MAJOR GENERAL	REAR ADMIRAL (UPPER HALF)
O-7	BRIGADIER GENERAL	REAR ADMIRAL (LOWER HALF)	BRIGADIER GENERAL	BRIGADIER GENERAL	REAR ADMIRAL (LOWER HALF)
O-6	COLONEL	CAPTAIN	COLONEL	COLONEL	CAPTAIN
O-5	LIEUTENANT COLONEL	COMMANDER	LIEUTENANT COLONEL	LIEUTENANT COLONEL	COMMANDER
O-4	MAJOR	LIEUTENANT COMMANDER	MAJOR	MAJOR	LIEUTENANT COMMANDER
O-3	CAPTAIN	LIEUTENANT	CAPTAIN	CAPTAIN	LIEUTENANT
O-2	FIRST LIEUTENANT	LIEUTENANT JUNIOR GRADE	FIRST LIEUTENANT	FIRST LIEUTENANT	LIEUTENANT JUNIOR GRADE
O-1	SECOND LIEUTENANT	ENSIGN	SECOND LIEUTENANT	SECOND LIEUTENANT	ENSIGN

MONTHLY BASIC PAY TABLE
EFFECTIVE 1 JANUARY 2009

YEARS OF SERVICE

COMMISSIONED OFFICERS

PAY GRADE	<2	2	3	4	6	8	10	12	14	16	18	20	22	24	26	28	30	32	34	36	38	40
O-10	0.00	0.00	0.00	0.00	0.00	0.00	0.00	0.00	0.00	0.00	0.00	14688.60	14750.10	14750.10	14750.10	14750.10	14750.10	14750.10	14750.10	14750.10	14750.10	14750.10
O-9	0.00	0.00	0.00	0.00	0.00	0.00	0.00	0.00	0.00	0.00	0.00	12846.90	13032.00	13299.30	13765.80	13765.80	14454.60	14454.60	14454.60	14454.60	14454.60	14454.60
O-8	9090.00	9387.60	9585.30	9640.50	9887.10	10299.00	10395.00	10786.20	10898.10	11235.30	11722.20	12172.20	12472.50	12472.50	12472.50	12784.50	13104.30	13104.30	13104.30	13104.30	13104.30	13104.30
O-7	7553.10	7904.10	8066.40	8195.40	8429.10	8660.70	8926.80	9192.90	9460.20	10299.00	11007.30	11007.30	11007.30	11007.30	11063.10	11063.10	11284.50	11284.50	11284.50	11284.50	11284.50	11284.50
O-6	5598.30	6150.30	6553.80	6553.80	6578.70	6860.70	6897.90	6897.90	7290.00	7983.30	8390.10	8796.60	9027.90	9262.20	9716.70	9716.70	9910.80	9910.80	9910.80	9910.80	9910.80	9910.80
O-5	4666.80	5257.20	5621.40	5689.80	5916.60	6052.80	6351.60	6570.60	6853.80	7287.30	7493.40	7697.40	7928.70	7928.70	7928.70	7928.70	7928.70	7928.70	7928.70	7928.70	7928.70	7928.70
O-4	4026.90	4661.40	4972.20	5041.80	5330.40	5640.00	6025.20	6325.50	6534.90	6654.00	6723.30	6723.30	6723.30	6723.30	6723.30	6723.30	6723.30	6723.30	6723.30	6723.30	6723.30	6723.30
O-3	3540.30	4013.40	4332.00	4722.90	4948.80	5197.20	5358.00	5622.30	5759.70	5759.70	5759.70	5759.70	5759.70	5759.70	5759.70	5759.70	5759.70	5759.70	5759.70	5759.70	5759.70	5759.70
O-2	3058.80	3483.90	4012.50	4148.10	4233.30	4233.30	4233.30	4233.30	4233.30	4233.30	4233.30	4233.30	4233.30	4233.30	4233.30	4233.30	4233.30	4233.30	4233.30	4233.30	4233.30	4233.30
O-1	2655.30	2763.60	3340.50	3340.50	3340.50	3340.50	3340.50	3340.50	3340.50	3340.50	3340.50	3340.50	3340.50	3340.50	3340.50	3340.50	3340.50	3340.50	3340.50	3340.50	3340.50	3340.50

COMMISSIONED OFFICERS WITH OVER 4 YEARS ACTIVE DUTY SERVICE AS AN ENLISTED MEMBER OR WARRANT OFFICER

PAY GRADE	<2	2	3	4	6	8	10	12	14	16	18	20	22	24	26	28	30	32	34	36	38	40
O-3E	0.00	0.00	0.00	4722.90	4948.80	5197.20	5358.00	5622.30	5844.90	5972.70	6146.70	6146.70	6146.70	6146.70	6146.70	6146.70	6146.70	6146.70	6146.70	6146.70	6146.70	6146.70
O-2E	0.00	0.00	0.00	4148.10	4233.30	4368.30	4595.70	4771.50	4902.30	4902.30	4902.30	4902.30	4902.30	4902.30	4902.30	4902.30	4902.30	4902.30	4902.30	4902.30	4902.30	4902.30
O-1E	0.00	0.00	0.00	3340.50	3567.60	3699.30	3834.30	3966.60	4148.10	4148.10	4148.10	4148.10	4148.10	4148.10	4148.10	4148.10	4148.10	4148.10	4148.10	4148.10	4148.10	4148.10

NOTE—BASIC PAY FOR O7-O10 IS LIMITED TO LEVEL II OF THE EXECUTIVE SCHEDULE ($14,750.10)

NOTE—BASIC PAY FOR O6 AND BELOW IS LIMITED TO LEVEL V OF THE EXECUTIVE SCHEDULE ($11,958.30)

FY2009, 3.9% Pay Raise Increase. Public Law No 110-417 National Defense Auth Act, signed into law on October 14, 2008.

Level II and Level V of the Executive Schedule increased by 2.8%.

major drawback of the military pension is that once a veteran dies, the pension dies with him or her, unless the veteran was enrolled in an insurance program called the Survivors Benefit Plan.

Many military officers choose to remain in the military longer than twenty years. In that case, active-duty members' retirement pay is increased by 2.5 percent of their base pay for every year past twenty (usually up to a total of thirty years, depending on pay grade). Therefore, an active-duty member retiring with thirty years will receive a pension of 75 percent of their base pay.

In recent years, another plan has been offered to military members that were previously only available to civil servants, called the Thrift Savings Plan. This plan allows military members to contribute to the plan using pre-tax dollars.

Another benefit of military retirement is the continuation of health care benefits at little to no cost (depending on the level of insurance selected), as well as the continuation of privileges at base stores and facilities.

Educational Benefits

Numerous educational benefits are available for military officers wishing to pursue a degree beyond the undergraduate level. Military members can use the Tuition Assistance Program while serving on active duty or in the National Guard or Reserve. This program helps defray the cost of a large percentage of tuition. Military members usually incur a commitment if they use the Tuition Assistance Program. This means that you must commit to serve a longer term (compare it to extending your cell phone contract because you were allowed to upgrade to a new phone at a discounted price). The military will help pay your tuition if you agree to extend your contract.

Another source of money for college is the Montgomery GI Bill (MGIB). Currently there are two versions of the bill. The original MGIB required a servicemember to contribute $1,200 in pre-tax dollars. In exchange, the government would pay the servicemember monthly as long as he or she could prove full-time student status. For the 2008–09 school year, the monthly amount was raised to $1,324. That amount would be paid for a total of thirty-six months as long as the servicemember continued to attend school. If the servicemember stopped being a full-time student, the payments would stop (although they could be restarted if the servicemember once again became a full-time student). The other stipulation of the old MGIB is that the benefit must be used within ten years of the servicemember's release from service.

In July 2008, a new MGIB was approved. In this new program, named the "Post 9/11 MGIB," payment is capped at the highest amount of established tuition and fees for the most expensive in-state public colleges; however, this does not mean that a servicemember must attend a public college. The servicemember makes no contribution to this program and the benefit must be used within fifteen years of the member's release from service. In addition, the Post 9/11 MGIB will pay up to $1,000 per month to help cover housing costs for students enrolled in a traditional "brick and mortar" college program (i.e., not an online program) and will also pay $1,000 per year for books and equipment.

In addition, the amount of benefits received by the servicemember is linked to the amount of time served in the military. The other major change to the MGIB is that the benefits now are transferable to the spouse and children of the servicemember.

Although the MGIB is funded by the Department of Defense (DoD), it is administered by the Department of Veterans Affairs (VA). For the most up-to-date information about the MGIB, visit the VA Web site at www.gibill.va.gov.

Although not related to education, another benefit offered by the VA is a guaranteed home loan. The VA is not in the business of providing mortgages; however, they will provide guarantees of payment to mortgage companies and banks that allow them to grant mortgages to military individuals with no down payment. There is a funding fee involved, but that fee can be worked into the mortgage. In addition, the VA guarantees that Private Mortgage Insurance (PMI) (usually associated with mortgages) is unnecessary with a down payment of less than 20 percent. VA-guaranteed loans have been helping veterans realize their dreams of home ownership since the end of World War II.

GENERAL COMMISSIONING REQUIREMENTS

Each branch of the military sets its own qualification standards for commissioned officers. Those standards, however, may exceed DoD standards but may not be less stringent. The following qualifications provide a general overview of commissioning requirements (specific requirements are contained in each branch's section). Note that requirements can change from time to time, so check with recruiting officials or admissions counselors to ensure that you meet the most up-to-date requirements.

Age

Must be between 19 and 29 years for OCS/OTS, 17 and 21 years for ROTC, 17 and 22 years for the service academies.

Citizenship Status

Must be a U.S. citizen.

Physical Condition

Must meet minimum physical standards listed below. (Some occupations have additional physical standards.)

- **Height:** Men must be between 5′ and 6′ 5″. Women must be between 4′ 10″ and 6′ 5″.
- **Weight:** There are minimum and maximum weights, according to age and height, for males and females.
- **Vision:** There are minimum vision standards.
- **Overall Health:** Must be in good health and pass a medical exam. Certain diseases or conditions may exclude persons from enlistment, such as diabetes, severe allergies, epilepsy, alcoholism, and drug addiction.

Education

Must have a four-year college degree from an accredited institution. Some occupations require advanced degrees or four-year degrees in a particular field.

Aptitude

Must achieve the minimum entry score on an officer qualification test (or SAT, ACT, or Armed Services Vocational Aptitude Battery [ASVAB], depending on service).

Moral Character

Must meet standards designed to screen out persons unlikely to become successful officers. Standards cover court convictions, juvenile delinquency, arrests, and drug use.

Marital Status and Dependents

May be either single or married for ROTC, OCS/OTS, and direct appointment pathways. Must be single to enter and graduate from service academies. The number of dependents allowable varies by the branch of service.

Waivers

On a case-by-case basis, exceptions (waivers) are granted by individual services for some of the above qualification requirements.

HOW TO BECOME AN OFFICER

Now that you've learned about what military officers do, the qualifications necessary to become a commissioned officer, and the benefits of being an officer, let's find out about the different commissioning sources available.

There are four basic avenues to becoming an officer:

1. Reserve Officers' Training Corps (ROTC)
2. Officer Candidate School (OCS)/Officer Training School (OTS)
3. Service academies
4. Direct appointments

Figure 3 illustrates the portion of personnel who become officers through these avenues. Note that, by far, the greatest percentage of officers (approximately 40 percent) are commissioned through ROTC.

Figure 3: PATHWAYS TO NEWLY COMMISSIONED OFFICERS

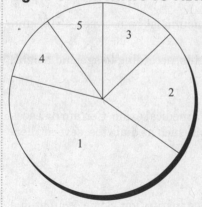

1. Reserve Officers' Training Corps (ROTC)
2. Officer Candidate School (OCS) and Officer Training School (OTS)
3. Service academies
4. Direct appointments
5. Other

Reserve Officers' Training Corps (ROTC)

Reserve Officers' Training Corps (ROTC) program is active at many U.S. public and private colleges and universities. Despite its name, this program's primary purpose is to educate and then commission individuals for active-duty service (they receive what is called a reserve commission). Although most graduates of ROTC programs go directly to active duty, some individuals go on to serve in the National Guard or Reserve.

ROTC is taken as an elective course with mandatory participation in additional activities (such as physical fitness training) in order to receive a commission upon graduation. Depending on the branch of service, students may participate in ROTC for two to four years in order to qualify for partial or full scholarships. Also, many colleges offer ROTC scholarship recipients additional scholarships and grants that may cover any tuition above the ROTC "cap" and may also cover room and board.

In addition to help with tuition, ROTC scholarship recipients receive a monthly stipend, as well as monies to help defray the cost of books. As the old saying goes, "There's no such thing as a free lunch." Such is the case here. In return for receiving an ROTC scholarship, the student must agree to serve in the military upon graduation. However, students may also take ROTC classes as an elective with no scholarship, and therefore no military commitment.

ROTC scholarships are competitive, and students must meet not only academic requirements but moral and physical standards as well. Most ROTC scholarships are awarded to graduating high school seniors; however, scholarships are also awarded to current college students and active-duty enlisted personnel.

For more information about ROTC scholarships, college students should contact the ROTC unit at their school. High school students may contact the ROTC program for the branch of their choice by visiting the corresponding Web site (see below). It's a good idea to apply to two or more services to keep your options open. The Coast Guard does not offer an ROTC program, and although there is a Marine Corps option, Marine Corps ROTC students participate in the Naval ROTC program. Active-duty enlisted members should contact their base/post education office for information.

- **Air Force:** www.afrotc.com
- **Army:** www.armyrotc.com
- **Navy:** www.navy.com/careers/nrotc
- **Marine Corps:** www.officer.marines.com

Officer Candidate School (OCS)/Officer Training School (OTS)

The military services offer programs for individuals who already hold a bachelor's degree and who desire to earn a commission. These programs are referred to either as Officer Candidate School (OCS) or Officer Training School (OTS) depending on the branch of service.

Approximately 20 percent of all newly commissioned officers receive their commissions through OCS/OTS annually. The competition for OCS/OTS slots is keen, and individuals need to meet not only high academic and physical standards, but high moral standards as well.

OCS/OTS is, in essence, basic training for officers, but because the roles of junior officers differ from those of junior enlisted members, more emphasis is placed on leadership training. Individuals attending OCS/OTS will also learn military history and basic drill (marching), and will participate in physical fitness training.

Many factors play a part in the selection process for OCS/OTS, including the student's major, GPA, and officer candidate test scores. Each of the military branches has its own eligibility requirements. You should contact them directly for more information and current requirements. Detailed information concerning OCS/OTS programs for specific military branches follows later in this book.

Service Academies

Undoubtedly, the most competitive of all the pathways to earning a commission are the service academies. The Army, Navy, Coast Guard, and Air Force, as well as the U.S. Merchant Marine, all offer a high-quality, no-cost, four-year education to highly qualified individuals in the form of the service academies.

To be accepted for attendance, an individual must meet the following standards:

- Be a U.S. citizen (a requirement of all commissioning programs)
- Be at least 17 years old
- Be of "good moral character"
- Meet minimum SAT/ACT scores
- Be physically qualified
- Be able to pass a physical fitness exam
- Meet minimum high school GPA requirements
- Obtain a congressional nomination (not required for the Coast Guard Academy)
- Be single (and remain unmarried for the duration of his/her attendance)

Note that qualifying does not guarantee acceptance. In addition to the qualifications listed above, the following qualifications, though not mandatory, enhance an applicant's chances for acceptance:

- Be a member of at least one high school team sport
- Hold an office in student government
- Have a history of community service
- Participate in an organization such as the Boy Scouts/Girl Scouts
- Be a member of an honor society (such as the National Honor Society)
- Complete high school Junior Reserve Officers' Training Corps (JROTC)

Students at any of the service academies receive an education equal to that of civilian Ivy League schools. In addition to high academic standards, students are introduced to a highly structured and disciplined environment. They participate in leadership courses, drill (marching), and daily physical fitness exercises. Graduates of the service academies incur a commitment to serve on active duty.

Those who persevere and graduate after a rigorous four years will join a long roster of distinguished service academy graduates, such as Gen. Ulysses S. Grant, Gen. Douglas MacArthur, Gen. Robert E. Lee, and Adm. Chester Nimitz, who have helped change the course of history.

Because the Armed Forces realize that not everyone has had the opportunity to receive a high-quality high school education that would help prepare them for acceptance to a service academy, many also offer "preparatory schools" to prepare otherwise qualified individuals for entrance.

Although most applicants for service academies are high school students, programs are also available for highly qualified enlisted servicemembers. Enlisted members should contact their base/post education office for more details. High school students should contact the service academies directly (beginning in their junior year). As with ROTC scholarships, you are encouraged to apply to more than one academy.

The four military service academies are:

1. U.S. Military Academy (Army), West Point, New York, www.usma.edu
2. U.S. Naval Academy (Navy and Marine Corps), Annapolis, Maryland, www.usna.edu
3. U.S. Air Force Academy (Air Force), Colorado Springs, Colorado, www.usafa.edu
4. U.S. Coast Guard Academy (Coast Guard), New London, Connecticut, www.cga.edu

The U.S. Merchant Marine also operates a service academy, and all of the rules above also apply, with the exception of the active-duty service commitment. Graduates of the Merchant Marine Academy are committed only to serving in the Naval Reserve, although many graduates choose to go on active duty upon graduation.

The Merchant Marine Academy is in King's Point, New York. You can contact the Academy on its Web site at www.usmma.edu.

Direct Appointments

Annually, 11 percent of all new officers receive their commission through direct appointment. This pathway for commissioning is reserved for professionals such as doctors (and other health care professionals), lawyers, and clergy. These individuals receive abbreviated officer training and are then commissioned, typically at a rank commensurate with their experience.

RESERVE AND GUARD OPPORTUNITIES

Although most positions in the National Guard and Reserve are filled with fully qualified individuals separating from active duty, opportunities still exist for individuals to earn a commission. Many states have programs that allow an individual to attend school at state expense and then earn a commission in the National Guard. Although highly competitive, the opportunity also exists for highly qualified enlisted personnel to earn a commission, providing they first earn a bachelor's degree.

National Guard and Reserve officers enjoy many of the same privileges as their active-duty counterparts, except that they serve on a part-time basis. Typically, reservists and guardsmen serve one weekend each month and a two-week active-duty tour each year. Because of current operations, however, many guard members and reservists have found themselves on extended active-duty tours (typically overseas).

For more information about National Guard and Reserve opportunities, contact a local recruiter, go to these Web sites, or use the toll-free numbers below.

Air Force
www.afreserve.com
(800) 257-1212

Navy
www.navalreserve.com
(800) 872-8767

Army
www.goarmy.com
(888) 550-2769

Air National Guard
www.goang.com
(800) 864-6264

Coast Guard
www.uscg.mil/reserve
(800) 883-8724

Army National Guard
www.1800goguard.com
(800) 464-8273

Marine Corps
www.marforres.usmc.mil
(800) 627-4637

BRANCH-SPECIFIC COMMISSIONING INFORMATION

The chapters that follow contain specific commissioning information for each military branch. This is the most current data available at the time of publication, but information and requirements do change from time to time. Check with your recruiter or admissions officer for the most up-to-date information. In addition, the Web is an invaluable tool for getting information.

SUMMING IT UP

- Military officers work in many different types of occupations, including as combat specialty officers; engineering, science, and technical officers; executive, administrative, and managerial officers; health care officers; human resource development officers; media and public affairs officers; protective service officers; support services officers; and transportation officers.

- Most officers begin their careers at the O-1 pay grade. Pay grade refers to the number classification of an officer and is linked to how much that officer is paid. Officers in all branches of the military earn pay grades between O-1 and O-10; only a handful of soldiers attain the O-10 pay grade.

- In addition to basic pay, military officers may also receive tax-exempt pay, making their salaries commensurate with their civilian counterparts. Some of the pay received by military officers is in the form of allowances based on marital status, rank, and location.

- Military members are eligible for retirement pay based on years of service, pay grade, type of duty, and the number of "points" accumulated.

- Several financial resources are available for military officers who wish to pursue a degree beyond the undergraduate level.

- Each branch of the military sets its own qualification standards for commissioned officers. Check with recruiting officials (or admissions counselors) to ensure that you meet current requirements.

- Four basic avenues are available to becoming an officer: service academies, Officer Candidate School (OCS) and Officer Training School (OTS), Reserve Officers' Training Corps (ROTC), and direct appointment. The greatest percentage of officers (approximately 40 percent) is commissioned through ROTC. OCS/OTS is, in essence, basic training for officers.

- Although most positions in the National Guard and Reserve are filled with fully qualified individuals separating from active duty, opportunities do exist for individuals seeking to earn a commission.

Officer Opportunities for Women in the Military

OVERVIEW

- In the beginning
- By the numbers
- Women in the service academies
- Pay equity in the military
- Being a single parent and a soldier
- Job restrictions for servicewomen
- Fighting mistreatment
- A few words about DACOWITS
- For more information
- Summing it up

Most people reading this book would probably agree that today the gender gap is becoming smaller. However, gender equality in general has not always been the norm in America, and women have had to struggle to be recognized in society. The U.S. military has been a leader in promoting equality between the sexes and is proud of its commitment to creating opportunities for women in the Armed Services.

This chapter will address three separate issues. First, it will outline women's roles in the military today compared to the military of the past. Second, this chapter will detail some of the education, career, and health care realities in the military and dispel some of the common misconceptions and stereotypes about women who serve their country. Third, it will provide several resources where you can find detailed information about women in the military.

IN THE BEGINNING

Since the beginning of our nation's military, women have found ways to serve. As early as the American Revolution, women masquerading as men served beside their male counterparts—often undetected by fellow soldiers.

Not until the Spanish-American War did women receive a quasi-official role in the U.S. military. Women were allowed to serve in the Army as nurses (although not as regular Army members). Keep in mind that at this time, women were decades away from having the right to vote in elections.

chapter 2

By the 1940s, the tide was turning for women in the military. Although they were not fully integrated with male servicemembers, women were finally given official military status. Most served as nurses and in administrative and support roles; however, some women were trained to fly and to transport airplanes in non-combat missions.

The 1970s ushered in a revolution of sorts for military women. Many nontraditional jobs opened up to them, and the barriers to certain types of work started to crumble. By the onset of the first Gulf War in 1990, women had become an integral part of the country's Armed Forces.

BY THE NUMBERS

The percentage of women serving in the U.S. Armed Forces since 1973, when the draft (compulsory military service) ended, has increased tremendously. In 1973, women made up only 1.6 percent of active-duty forces. As of September 2007, 14 percent (approximately 196,000 women) were on active duty in the military. Women also make up 14.3 percent of all active-duty officers today and more than 4,900 women are on active duty with the U.S. Coast Guard (which is part of the Department of Homeland Security in peacetime; in wartime it reports directly to the Department of the Navy).

The following Active-Duty Women Officers chart shows the number and percentage of active-duty women officers listed by military service:

ACTIVE-DUTY WOMEN OFFICERS

	Total Number of Women	Women as a Percentage of Total Personnel
Total DoD	33,567	15.1
Army	12,983	15.3
Navy	7,611	14.8
Marine Corps	1,138	5.8
Air Force	11,835	18.0
Coast Guard*	1,160	14.4

*The U.S. Coast Guard is part of the Department of Homeland Security in peacetime; in wartime it reports directly to the Department of the Navy.

Women make up an even greater percentage of total personnel for the National Guard and Reserve components of the military than they do for active duty, as the following Women in the National Guard and Reserve chart shows:

WOMEN IN THE NATIONAL GUARD AND RESERVE

	Total Number of Women	Women as a Percentage of Total Personnel
Total Reserve & Guard	22,131	18.0
Army Reserve	8,476	23.5
Navy Reserve	2,493	15.8
Marine Corps Reserve	205	6.2
Air Force Reserve	4,295	26.3
Coast Guard Reserve*	264	20.1
Army National Guard	4,338	11.6
Air National Guard	2,324	16.6

*The U.S. Coast Guard is part of the Department of Homeland Security in peacetime; in wartime it reports directly to the Department of the Navy.

WOMEN IN THE SERVICE ACADEMIES

On October 7, 1975, President Gerald Ford signed Public Law 94-106, thereby opening the doors of the nation's service academies (the U.S. Military Academy at West Point, New York; the U.S. Naval Academy at Annapolis, Maryland; the U.S. Air Force Academy in Colorado Springs, Colorado; the U.S. Coast Guard Academy in New London, Connecticut; and the U.S. Merchant Marine Academy in King's Point, New York) to women for the first time in the country's history. In 1976, when the classes of 1980 entered the academies, 300 women were among those matriculating.

The law, which passed by a 303-to-96 vote in the House of Representatives, did not come easily. The Department of Defense fought hard to keep the service academies a "men's club." Ultimately, however, advocates for women's admission to the academies prevailed.

Sixty-six percent of the women who entered U.S. military academies in 1976 graduated as part of the class of 1980, compared with 70 percent of the men who started at the same time. An interesting note, however, is that men dropped out for academic reasons at twice the rate that women did.

Today, less than 30 years since that first class, it is hard to imagine a service academy without female students.

In addition to the service academies, all other military commissioning pathways are now open to women and, as with the academies, the opportunities for women are now practically equal to those of their male counterparts.

PAY EQUITY IN THE MILITARY

Even today, women often receive lower pay than men for performing the same work. Although we'd like to believe that gender equality exists throughout corporate America, the sad fact is that this is often not the case.

But did you know that the military actually outpaces the civilian sector in terms of equality and introductory career opportunities for women? You may remember seeing the Monthly Basic Pay Table in the first chapter of this book. The table does not divide pay grades into gender, since men and women who serve in the military receive equal pay. The same goes for promotion opportunities: Military promotions continue to be based on job performance rather than gender.

Although civilian women often find themselves fighting to receive employer-based health care for their children, military women and their families receive health care and child support automatically, including low-cost child care and maternity leave.

BEING A SINGLE PARENT AND A SOLDIER

It is possible to be a single mother and a soldier (sailor, marine, etc.). Thousands of servicewomen do just that. They manage to juggle the long hours of military work and the equally long hours of motherhood. Of course, it's difficult to do this alone; women in the military must have a plan in place in case they are deployed away from home, or are required to work shifts that interfere with child care and their children's schooling. Many single parents rely on family and friends to care for their children in these situations.

Some women become single parents while they are serving in the military (by divorce, or the death of a spouse, for example). In the past, such situations would have qualified women for an immediate discharge from the military—but not in today's military.

Becoming a military officer as a single parent is difficult, and in most cases it requires a waiver. Because being a single parent and undergoing officer training is so hard, the single parent who is interested in becoming an officer must agree to temporarily relinquish custody of his or her children. Usually, an immediate family member takes custody during this period and returns the child to the parent when he or she finishes training.

Make no mistake about it: Being a single parent in the military is not easy and requires enormous life adjustments. If your goal is a career in the military, however, you need to know what you will be asked to do.

JOB RESTRICTIONS FOR SERVICEWOMEN

Although women have come a long way in terms of equality with men in the military, several military jobs remain restricted to male servicemembers. Special Forces units, such as the Navy SEALs and the Army Green Berets, are comprised entirely of men, as are the crews of all Navy submarines and Army tanks.

Yet, the numbers of women in positions once thought of as "male only" have increased over the years. Women now fly combat aircraft, and they serve in combat units that have direct contact with opposing forces. They are no longer restricted to being in the rearguard of battle. It is clear that women can perform jobs once thought too difficult or too dangerous for them.

The following Military Occupations Open to Women chart illustrates, by branch of service, the percentages of military occupations available to women. Note that the chart includes all occupations without breaking down enlisted and officer positions.

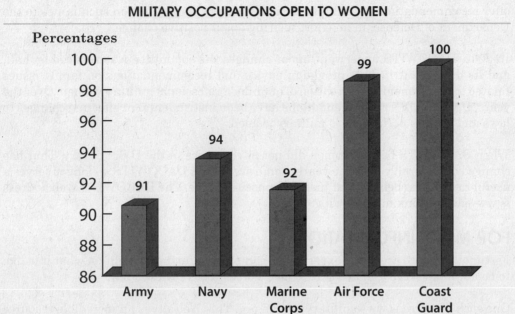

MILITARY OCCUPATIONS OPEN TO WOMEN

FIGHTING MISTREATMENT

The military has always been closely watched for allegations of sexual harassment or abuse. In the past decade or so, reports of rape of female personnel surfaced at the Air Force Academy, and in 1997, the Army investigated its top enlisted soldier on reports that he sexually assaulted another soldier. That same year, the Army investigated instances of alleged sexual harassment at its Ordnance School in Aberdeen, Maryland. Some years earlier, in 1991, the Navy was immersed in a similar scandal when charges of sexual assault arose after the Las Vegas, Nevada, meeting of the Tailhook Association, a fraternal, nonprofit organization formed by active-duty naval aviators.

All of these incidents have one thing in common: They were fully investigated, and in cases where it was warranted, high-ranking officials lost their jobs over the failure to maintain proper respect and discipline. More recent incidents of alleged sexual assault and harassment of female military personnel have continued to draw public scrutiny, including allegations of such occurrences in military operations in Iraq—where one in seven U.S. military service personnel is female—and in Afghanistan.

The U.S. military and its members are understandably held to higher standards than civilians. The U.S. Armed Forces claim zero tolerance for sexual assault and harassment. As with the cases described above, proven cases of assault or harassment can and do end the careers of military servicepeople.

A FEW WORDS ABOUT DACOWITS

The Defense Department Advisory Committee on Women in the Services (DACOWITS), initiated in 1951, is composed of civilian and retired military women and men. These committee members have been appointed by the Secretary of Defense to provide advice and recommendations on matters and policies relating to the recruitment and retention, treatment, employment, integration, and well-being of qualified professional women in the U.S. Armed Forces. They travel to military installations to provide advice and offer recommendations on military women's issues. They report on such issues to the Department of Defense, in an effort to bring about positive change.

In 2002, DACOWITS underwent major changes. Its committee was reduced by half, and its duties now include providing advice and recommendations on family issues related to recruitment and retention of qualified professional military women. Over the years, DACOWITS's recommendations have been instrumental in effecting changes to laws and policies pertaining to military women.

When DACOWITS began, women did not have a voice in the U.S. military. That has changed considerably over the years. Some argue that DACOWITS no longer serves a useful role; others believe that just the opposite is true. The DACOWITS Web address is www.defenselink.mil/dacowits/.

FOR MORE INFORMATION

Fortunately, there are many experts who can provide further insight on what it is like to be a woman serving in the U.S. Armed Forces. Let's review a few.

One such resource is www.militarywoman.org. This Web site is an incredible resource for information on a broad array of issues relating to women serving in the military. It also provides a discussion forum for women who have served, are now serving, or are considering serving. The site is run by two retired female veterans, an Air Force officer and an Army senior enlisted member, who manage it in their spare time. Their only compensation is the satisfaction of knowing that they are helping others. This is a site you'll want to keep on your browser's "favorites" list even after you join the military.

Another fantastic resource is the book *Women in the Military: An Unfinished Revolution* (1993) by Jeanne Holm, Maj. Gen., USAF (Ret.). The book covers women's roles in the military through the first Gulf War.

If you are into statistics and want to learn more about the "numbers" relating to women serving in the military, check out the booklet *Women in the Military: Where They Stand* (2005) by Lory Manning, Capt., USN (Ret.). The booklet is available from the Women's Research and Education Institute (WREI) at www.wrei.org/Publications.htm. This 37-page booklet contains statistics on women in the services as well as a chronology of milestones dealing with women in the military. In addition to Capt. Manning's book, the WREI Web site also lists several other titles for purchase on the subject of women in the U.S. military.

Another interesting and amusing Web site is that of Barbara A. Wilson, Capt., USAF (Ret.). The site is chock-full of history, news, and opinion on women in the military. The Web address is http://userpages.aug.com/captbarb/.

Below are a few more Web sites that deal with military women's issues.

Alliance for National Defense (AND): www.4militarywomen.org
Alliance for National Defense (AND) is a nonprofit, educational organization that offers a monthly newsletter about issues relating to military women; a resource for

speakers of educational events; and a library of publications by and about women. It also monitors U.S. legislation relating to women and alerts members to issues relevant to their situations. The organization will offer two $2,500 scholarships to current and future military women in 2009.

Center for Women Veterans, U.S. Department of Veterans Affairs: www.va.gov/womenvet

The Center for Women Veterans assures that female veterans receive benefits on par with male veterans. The site offers female veterans information about their Veterans Affairs entitlements, health care programs, and sexual abuse/harassment counseling. It also posts links to other sites that may be of interest to female veterans.

Defense Equal Opportunity Management Institute (DEOMI): www.deomi.org

Defense Equal Opportunity Management Institute (DEOMI) provides education and training in human relations and equal opportunity/equal employment opportunity for military active-duty personnel, reservists, and civilians. It offers thirteen different core education/training courses, as well as service-specific training. Many courses are offered as both resident and nonresident. DEOMI also publishes an online magazine and a video catalog, in addition to other resources available on its site.

African-Americans in Military History: www.au.af.mil/au/aul/bibs/afhist/afwom.htm

The African-Americans in Military History Web site is a bibliography of readings on the role of African Americans in the U.S. military, with a lengthy section on women in the military. The bibliography was created and maintained by Diana Simpson, bibliographer of the Air University Library at Maxwell-Gunter Air Force Base, Montgomery, Alabama.

Of course, many other resources are available online, in your local library, and in bookstores.

> The Women in Military Service for America Memorial is the only major national memorial to honor the approximately 2 million uniformed women who have served in the nation's defense. Located at the Ceremonial Entrance to Arlington National Cemetery, the memorial and its 33,000 square-foot Education Center chronicles the history and showcases individual stories of U.S. servicewomen. To learn more about the memorial, its programs and activities, membership eligibility and how to join, visit the site at www.womensmemorial.org or call 800-222-2294 (toll-free).

SUMMING IT UP

- On the whole, the U.S. military has been ahead of the civilian world in promoting gender equality, and has been a leader in creating equal pay and job opportunities for women.

- Today, women make up 14.3 percent of all active-duty officers. In addition, more than 4,900 women serve on active duty with the U.S. Coast Guard (which is part of the Department of Homeland Security in peacetime; in wartime it reports to the Department of the Navy).

- U.S. service academies have been open to women since 1975, when President Gerald Ford signed Public Law 94-106. In addition, other military commissioning pathways are now available to women, and the opportunities for women in the military are now practically equal to those of their male counterparts.

- Becoming a military officer as a single parent is difficult, and in most cases it requires a waiver. The single parent who is interested in becoming an officer must agree to temporarily relinquish custody of his or her children—usually to an immediate family member, who then returns custody to the parent when he or she finishes training.

- Several military jobs remain restricted to men only. Special Forces units are comprised entirely of men, as are the crews of all Navy submarines and Army tanks. Yet the numbers of women in positions once thought of as "male only" have increased over the years. Women now fly combat aircraft, and they serve in combat units that have direct contact with opposing forces.

- The military has always been closely watched for allegations of sexual harassment or abuse, and its members are understandably held to higher standards than civilians. The U.S. Armed Forces claims zero tolerance for sexual abuse or harassment. Proven cases of assault or harassment can and do end the careers of military servicepeople.

- The Defense Advisory Committee on Women in the Services (DACOWITS) is composed of committee members who have been appointed by the Secretary of Defense to provide advice on the recruitment and retention, treatment, employment, integration, and well-being of qualified professional women in the U.S. Armed Forces. In 2002, DACOWITS underwent major changes; its duties now include providing advice on family issues related to recruitment and retention of qualified professional military women.

- For more advice on female officers in the military, check out the resources listed at the end of this chapter.

PART II

BRANCH-SPECIFIC COMMISSIONING REQUIREMENTS

Becoming an Army Officer

OVERVIEW

- A brief history of Army Officer Candidate School (OCS)
- What to expect in OCS
- Career fields
- Requirements and qualifications
- The U.S. Military Academy at West Point
- Summing it up

In the sections that follow, you will find specific information on commissioning programs for each branch of the military. Use these sections as a guide rather than a rule book.

They contain information about Officer Candidate School/Officer Training School (OCS/OTS) programs as well as facts about each service academy. (You can find information on ROTC programs in Chapter 1.) Contact the specific service branch in which you're interested for more detailed information.

If you're interested in a flight career with the U.S. military, you may want to check out *Peterson's Master the Military Flight Aptitude Tests*. The book helps prepare you to take any flight aptitude test offered by U.S. military branches; it also provides useful information about the flight training programs for each branch.

A BRIEF HISTORY OF ARMY OFFICER CANDIDATE SCHOOL (OCS)

Brig. Gen. Asa L. Singleton, Commandant of the Infantry School at Fort Benning, Georgia, conceived the idea for the modern OCS for Infantry in June 1938. His plan was later revised by Brig. Gen. Courtney Hodges, Assistant Commandant of the Infantry School. It went into effect in July 1941 as the Infantry, Field Artillery, and Coastal Artillery Officer Candidate Schools. Other branches of the military followed with corresponding OCSs. The first Infantry OCS class included 204 candidates, of which 171 second lieutenants graduated on September 27, 1941.

Gen. Omar Bradley, former Commandant of the Infantry School, is credited with establishing the foundation of training that is still used in OCS today. Gen. Bradley emphasized rigorous training, strict discipline, and efficient

chapter 3

31

organization. These tenets remain the base values of today's OCS. After World War II, Infantry OCS was transferred to Fort Riley, Kansas, as part of the Ground General School. Subsequently, all other OCSs were discontinued, including the Infantry OCS, which was eliminated in 1947.

A shortage of officers during the Korean War caused the Department of the Army to reopen Infantry OCS at Fort Benning in 1951, and to lengthen the course from seventeen to twenty-two weeks. The Infantry OCS became the First Officer Candidate Battalion, Second Student Regiment. The strength of OCS increased rapidly. As one of eight branch programs, Infantry OCS included as many as twenty-nine companies, with a class graduating every week. During the Korean War, OCS commissioned approximately 7,000 infantry officers.

In 1953, the Army reduced OCS from eight to three programs: Infantry, Artillery, and Engineer. With the onset of the Vietnam War, the Army eliminated the Engineer program and kept just Infantry and Field Artillery. At the height of the Vietnam War, Infantry OCS produced 7,000 officers annually from five battalions. As the war appeared to be drawing to a close, Female OCS was established at Fort McClellan, Alabama. A Branch Immaterial OCS was established at Fort Benning in 1973; these programs merged in 1976 to become a program very similar to the modern OCS, which consists of a fourteen-week training cycle.

In 1998, to further integrate the total force, the Army National Guard OCS Phase III candidates began training with their active-duty counterparts at Fort Benning. OCS currently trains approximately 100 future Reserve component officers annually.

OCS has grown and adapted to meet the needs of the Army. The addition of C Company in 2000 and D Company shortly after increased the Army's battalion strength to four companies. The most recent addition, E Company, was activated in 2005 and began training in 2006.

Each company trains up to 160 officer candidates during each class and conducts as many as three classes each year. This increased operational structure reflects OCS's ability to transform and execute its mission according to the needs of a fast-paced and changing Army. The mission of OCS remains constant: to train selected personnel in the fundamentals of leadership and basic military skills, instill professional ethics, evaluate leadership potential, and commission those who qualify as second lieutenants in all basic branches of the Army.

WHAT TO EXPECT IN OCS

OCS is a twelve-week program that consists of Basic and Senior Officer Candidate Phases. To successfully complete OCS, you will be required to:

- pass two standard Record Army Physical Fitness Tests (no alternate test is authorized) with a minimum score of 60 points for each event
- complete a 3-, 4-, and 5-mile release run
- complete foot marches between 5–10 miles long
- attempt to complete the Combat Water Survival Test and a confidence obstacle course

- successfully complete separate day and night land navigation courses while finding the correct number of points
- receive academic instruction in ten areas, pass ten academic tests, and successfully complete training on seventy-one pre-commissioning common core tasks (you must score 70 percent or higher on all academic tests)
- serve in numerous evaluated leadership positions in both garrison and field environments while attaining a successful rating
- meet the standards of conduct and discipline as outlined in Army Regulations and the OCS Standing Operating Procedures

After an individual successfully completes OCS and is commissioned as a second lieutenant, he or she is then assigned to training in one of the sixteen basic Army branches.

CAREER FIELDS

Those who successfully complete OCS attend an officer basic course in the Army branch in which they were commissioned. These basic courses are about four months in length and prepare newly commissioned officers for their first assignment. OCS provides commissioned officers for all sixteen basic branches of the Army:

1. Adjutant General Corps
2. Air Defense Artillery
3. Armor/Cavalry
4. Aviation
5. Chemical Corps
6. Corps of Engineers
7. Field Artillery
8. Finance
9. Infantry
10. Medical Service Corps
11. Military Intelligence
12. Military Police
13. Ordnance
14. Quartermaster
15. Signal Corps
16. Transportation

REQUIREMENTS AND QUALIFICATIONS

Age

Applicants must be at least 19½ years and not more than 29 years of age at time of enrollment (a waiver may be granted for persons up to 32 years of age).

Citizenship

Applicants must be citizens of the United States.

Character

Applicants must be of high moral character. Persons who have been convicted by a military or civilian court for an offense involving a fine or forfeiture of $100 or more are ineligible (a waiver may be granted in certain instances).

Physical

Vision: Individuals being initially appointed or assigned as officers in Armor, Field Artillery, Infantry, Corps of Engineers, Military Intelligence, Military Police, and Signal Corps must possess uncorrected distance visual acuity of any degree that corrects with spectacle lenses to at least 20/20 in one eye and 20/100 in the other eye within 8 diopters of plus or minus refractive error, and must be able to identify without confusion the colors vivid red and vivid green.

Height: Male applicants must be 5' to 6' 10" tall. Female applicants must be 4' 10" to 6' 10" tall.

Weight: Weight must be proportional to height and within standards for age.

Dental: Teeth must be in good condition without excessive cavities.

General: Applicants must be in good health with no abnormalities or chronic illnesses.

The maximum Weight for Height table (also appearing in Army Regulation 600-9), used by the Army in screening individuals for physical fitness for military duty, may serve as a useful guide.

If a servicemember does not meet the initial weight for height requirements, the Army uses a calculation based on his or her abdominal and neck measurements to determine body fat percentage. The following chart shows the maximum allowable body fat percentages:

ARMY BODY FAT STANDARDS			
Male		Female	
Age Range	Body Fat (%)	Age Range	Body Fat (%)
17–20	20	17–20	30
21–27	22	21–27	32
40+	26	40+	36

The Army, like the other services, uses the following weight charts for initial screening:

ARMY WEIGHT FOR HEIGHT REQUIREMENTS

Height (in inches)	Male Age 17-20	21-27	28-39	40+	Female Age 17-20	21-27	28-39	40+
58	—	—	—	—	109	112	115	119
59	—	—	—	—	113	116	119	123
60	132	136	139	141	116	120	123	127
61	136	140	144	146	120	124	132	137
62	141	144	148	150	125	129	132	137
63	145	149	153	155	129	133	137	141
64	150	154	158	160	133	137	141	145
65	155	159	163	165	137	141	145	149
66	160	163	168	170	141	146	150	154
67	165	169	174	176	145	149	154	158
68	170	174	179	181	150	154	159	164
69	175	179	184	186	154	158	163	168
70	180	185	189	192	158	163	168	173
71	185	189	194	197	163	167	172	177
72	190	195	200	203	167	172	177	183
73	195	200	205	208	172	177	182	188
74	201	206	211	214	178	183	188	194
75	208	212	217	220	183	188	194	200
76	212	217	223	226	189	194	200	206
77	215	223	229	232	193	199	206	211
78	223	229	235	238	198	204	210	216
79	229	235	241	244	203	209	215	222
80	234	240	247	250	208	214	220	227

Notes:

1. The height will be measured in stocking feet (without shoes), standing on a flat surface with the chin parallel to the floor. The body should be straight but not rigid, similar to the position of attention. The measurement will be rounded to the nearest inch with the following guidelines:

   a. If the height fraction is less than ½ inch, round down to the nearest whole number in inches.

   b. If the height fraction is ½ inch or greater, round up to the next highest whole number in inches.

2. The weight should be measured and recorded to the nearest pound within the following guidelines:

   a. If the weight fraction is less than ½ pound, round down to the nearest pound.

   b. If the weight fraction is ½ pound or greater, round up to the next highest pound.

3. All measurements will be in a standard PT uniform (gym shorts and T-shirt, without shoes).

4. If the circumstances preclude weighing soldiers during the APFT, they should be weighed within 30 days of the APFT.

5. Add 6 pounds per inch for males over 80 inches and 5 pounds for females for each inch over 80 inches.

Academic

College option enlistees must have a baccalaureate degree from an accredited college or university.

Active-duty soldiers must have completed two years of a four-year college degree program or have a two-year college equivalency evaluation. In addition, both male and female applicants must obtain an aptitude area General Technical (GT) score of 110 or higher on the Armed Services Vocational Aptitude Battery (ASVAB). The GT aptitude area consists of arithmetic reasoning, word knowledge, and paragraph comprehension. It is derived from the academic ability composite on the Armed Services Vocational Aptitude Battery (ASVAB). They must also have a score of 850 on the SAT or 19 on the ACT.

Those interested in flight training are encouraged to study *Peterson's Military Flight Aptitude Tests*.

Service Commitment

A three-year service obligation from the date of graduation and commission is required of all Army officers.

Additional information and guidance regarding a commission in the U.S. Army may be obtained by contacting any Army recruiting office, company commander, battalion commander, or by contacting www.goarmy.com or by calling 800-USA-ARMY.

For more detailed and up-to-date information about Army OCS, visit the Web site at https://www.benning.army.mil/infantry.

THE U.S. MILITARY ACADEMY AT WEST POINT

Since its founding two centuries ago, the U.S. Military Academy, also known simply as West Point, has successfully trained cadets in four critical areas of life: intellectual, physical, military, and moral/ethical.

The challenging academic program at West Point consists of a core of thirty-one courses that provide a balanced education in the arts and sciences. This core curriculum is the foundation for elective courses, which permit cadets to explore a particular field of study or an optional major in greater depth. All cadets receive a Bachelor of Science degree, which is specifically designed to meet the intellectual requirements of a commissioned officer in the Army.

The physical program at West Point includes physical education classes and competitive athletics. Every cadet participates in an intercollegiate, club, or intramural sport each semester. This rigorous physical program contributes to the mental and physical fitness required for service as an officer in the Army.

Cadets also learn basic military skills, including leadership, in a demanding military program that begins on their first day at West Point. Most military training occurs during the summer, as new cadets undergo Cadet Basic Training—nicknamed "Beast Barracks"—during their first year. This is followed by Cadet Field Training at nearby Camp Buckner during the second year. Cadets spend their third and fourth summers serving in active Army units anywhere in the world; attending advanced training courses such as airborne, air assault, or northern warfare; or training first- and second-year cadets as members of the leadership cadre. Military training is combined with science instruction to provide a solid military foundation for officership.

Moral/ethical development is taught and encouraged throughout each of the formal programs, and throughout a host of activities and experiences available at the Academy.

- Formal instruction in the values of the military profession
- Opportunities in the voluntary religious programs
- Interaction with staff and faculty role models
- Attending a vigorous guest speaker program

The foundation of the ethical code at West Point is clear in the Academy's motto: "Duty, Honor, Country." Cadets also develop mature ethical standards by adhering to the Cadet Honor Code, which states that "A cadet will not lie, cheat, steal, or tolerate those who do."

Admission is open to all young men and women in the United States, but admission is extremely competitive. Candidates must be nominated by a member of Congress or by the Department of the Army. Each one is then evaluated on his or her academic, physical, and leadership potential. Only those who are considered fully qualified will receive appointments to the Academy.

The life of a cadet is demanding, but the Academy affords leisure time as well. Cadets can participate in recreational activities such as golf, skiing, sailing, and ice skating. Intramural clubs include a cadet radio station, orienteering, rock climbing, and Big Brother/Big Sister programs. A wide variety of religious activities is available to cadets, who come from virtually all religious backgrounds.

From the day of its founding on March 16, 1802, West Point has grown in size and stature, but it remains committed to the task of producing commissioned leaders of character for the U.S. Army. Today, the Academy graduates more than 900 new officers each year, representing approximately 25 percent of the new lieutenants acquired annually by the Army. The student body, or Corps of Cadets, numbers 4,000, of whom approximately 15 percent are women.

SUMMING IT UP

- The mission of OCS remains constant: train selected personnel in the fundamentals of leadership and basic military skills, instill professional ethics, evaluate leadership potential, and commission those who qualify as second lieutenants in all basic branches of the Army.

- To successfully complete OCS, you are required to pass two standard Record Army Physical Fitness Tests; complete a 3-, 4-, and 5-mile release run; complete foot marches between 5–10 miles long; attempt to complete the Combat Water Survival Test and a confidence obstacle course; successfully complete separate day and night land navigation courses; receive academic instruction in ten areas, pass ten academic tests, and successfully complete training on seventy-one pre-commissioning common core tasks; serve in numerous evaluated leadership positions; and meet the OCS standards of conduct and discipline.

- OCS provides commissioned officers for all sixteen basic branches of the Army: Adjutant General Corps, Air Defense Artillery, Armor/Cavalry, Aviation, Chemical Corps, Corps of Engineers, Field Artillery, Finance, Infantry, Medical Service Corps, Military Intelligence, Military Police, Ordnance, Quartermaster, Signal Corps, and Transportation.

- OCS applicants must have a bachelor's degree. Active-duty soldiers must have completed two years of a four-year college degree or have a two-year college equivalency evaluation. Army officers are required to serve three years from the date of graduation.

- West Point aims to develop cadets in four critical life areas: intellectual, physical, military, and moral/ethical. A core of thirty-one academic courses, a rigorous physical program, and a demanding program of basic military skills and science instruction fulfill the first three areas. The ethical code of the Academy is clear: "Duty, Honor, Country." Cadets are expected to adhere to the Cadet Honor Code: "A cadet will not lie, cheat, steal, or tolerate those who do."

- Candidates for West Point must first receive a nomination from a member of Congress or from the Department of the Army to be considered. They are then evaluated on their academic, physical, and leadership potential. Only those who are deemed fully qualified receive appointments to the Academy.

Becoming a Naval Officer

chapter 4

OVERVIEW

- A brief history of Navy Officer Candidate School (OCS)
- What to expect in OCS
- Career fields
- Requirements and qualifications
- The U.S. Naval Academy at Annapolis
- Summing it up

A BRIEF HISTORY OF NAVY OFFICER CANDIDATE SCHOOL (OCS)

Officer Candidate School (OCS) is one of five officer training schools located at Naval Station Newport in Rhode Island. The twelve-week OCS course is designed to provide a working knowledge of the Navy (afloat and ashore), prepare individuals to assume the responsibilities of a naval officer, and help candidates achieve their fullest potential. OCS is morally, mentally, and physically demanding. Those who attend OCS will have their sense of honor, courage, and commitment tested, and they will be challenged to live up to the highest standards of these core values.

The school's curriculum reflects these standards. Mental training involves memorization of military knowledge, success in academic courses, and passing multiple inspections. Physical training (PT) begins immediately upon arrival at OCS; it consists of running programs augmented by calisthenics, and aquatic programs. Even before they arrive at OCS attendees must be committed to the goal of earning a commission as an ensign in the Navy.

Military training at OCS is comprised of five broad categories:

1. **Physical Training:** OCS includes three Physical Fitness Assessments (PFA): the Indoctrination PFA, the Mid-PFA, and the Out-PFA. The passing requirements are Satisfactory-Medium for the IN-PFA, Satisfactory-High for the Mid-PFA, and Good-Low for the Out-PFA.

2. **Room and Locker Inspection (RLP):** A candidate's room is subject to inspection at any time. To ensure cleanliness and maintain standards, room inspections occur at regular intervals in lieu of zone inspections. Rooms must be maintained according to the daily room standards. Racks (beds) are to be made between 0500–2200 hours (5:00 a.m.–10:00 p.m.).

❸ **Personnel Inspection (PI):** Each candidate will be inspected for proper uniform, haircut, shave, knowledge, hygiene, and general military appearance.

❹ **Drill:** Approximately 40 hours of initial training are spent learning and practicing drill. Officer candidates also march as they move between different areas in the school.

❺ **Graduation/Commissioning Ceremony:** This is the final exercise as an officer candidate. It is the ultimate goal at Officer Candidate School: a commission as an ensign in the U.S. Navy.

WHAT TO EXPECT IN OCS

At OCS, the highest standards of personal and military appearance are maintained at all times. This includes strict regulations regarding one's appearance in the following three areas:

❶ **Haircuts:** Upon arrival, all candidates will receive haircuts. Men will have their heads shaved. Women's hair is not to be longer than an imaginary line level with the lower edge of the back of the collar, and no hair on the head may be longer than two inches. Hair may not extend below eyebrows when headgear is removed, show under front of headgear, or interfere with proper wearing of military headgear.

❷ **Grooming Standards:** Personal hygiene and cleanliness in all OCS facilities is paramount. Daily showers and regular hand washing is required. All candidates must keep fingernails clean and neatly trimmed. For male candidates, the face must be clean-shaven. For women, conservative makeup in moderation is acceptable while on leave or liberty. Cosmetics colors must blend with natural skin tone.

❸ **Jewelry:** Other than the following exceptions, no jewelry can be worn on any part of the body while training at OCS. Body piercings are not authorized. Jewelry exceptions include:

- a wedding band
- one religious medallion, no larger than a dog tag and worn on a large dog tag chain
- a wristwatch (authorized for officer candidates, watchstanders, section leaders, and possibly for the class team for certain training sessions)
- for female candidates, a gold ball or pearl earrings measuring 6 mm (approximately ¼ inch), to be worn on leave or liberty

Navy OCS hosts an excellent Web site filled with information, including a video outlining the Academy's physical fitness standards. There is also information about applying for OCS and about what to expect once you get there. The Navy's Officer Training Command has recently undergone a major overhaul, which is reflected in its Web site. You can visit the site at https://www.netc.navy.mil/nstc/otcn/Schoolhouses/OCS/index.htm.

CAREER FIELDS

Those who successfully complete Navy OCS have access to a wide variety of employment opportunities. Career fields are listed under the following categories of Officer Careers and Health Care Careers.

Officer Careers:
- Aviation
- Civil Engineering
- Chaplain Corps
- Information Warfare
- Intelligence
- Law
- Nuclear Power
- Public Affairs
- Science
- Special Operations
- Submarine
- Supply, Transportation, and Logistics
- Surface Warfare

Health Care Careers:
- Dentist
- Health Care Sciences, and Clinical Care Providers
- Medical Service Corps: Health Care Administration,
- Nurse
- Physician

REQUIREMENTS AND QUALIFICATIONS

Age

Non-aviation applicants must generally be at least 19 and no more than 29 years of age on the date of appointment to commissioned grade. Stricter age requirements apply for several naval occupations, such as nuclear propulsion officer, who must be 19 to 27 years of age at the time of commissioning.

The age requirement for Civil Engineer Corps officer, cryptology officer, intelligence officer, and oceanography officer is 19 to 35 years at time of commissioning.

Citizenship

Applicants must be citizens of the United States.

Character

Applicants must be of good moral character.

Physical

Vision:
- *Correctable to 20/20 with normal color vision:*

> Engineering duty officer
> Nuclear propulsion officer
> Special warfare officer
> Submarine warfare officer
> Surface warfare officer

- *Correctable to 20/20 with normal color vision and depth perception:*
  Intelligence officer
- *82 percent Binocular Vision Efficiency; spherical not more than 8.0; cylindrical not more than 3.0:*
  Civil Engineering Corps officer
  Cryptology officer
  Oceanography officer (also normal color vision)
  Supply Corps officer
- *Correctable to 20/20:*
  Most other non-aviation officers

Height: Non-aviation male officers—4'10" to 6'6". For non-aviation female officers—4'10" to 6'6"

Dental: Teeth must be in good condition without excessive cavities.

General: Applicants must be in good health with no abnormalities or chronic illnesses.

The Navy's Body Composition Assessment (BCA) is based on the maximum weight for height screening and body fat percentage estimation. The Body Fat Standards estimations are based on circumference measurements. Only servicemembers not meeting the Navy weight standard for their height will be measured for body fat percentage. The following chart shows the maximum allowable body fat percentages:

NAVY BODY FAT STANDARDS			
Male		**Female**	
Age Range	*Body Fat (%)*	*Age Range*	*Body Fat (%)*
17–39	22	17–39	33
40+	23	40+	34

The Navy, like the other services, uses the following weight charts for initial screening:

NAVY WEIGHT FOR HEIGHT REQUIREMENTS		
Height (inches)	Male Maximum Weight Standard (pounds)	Female Maximum Weight Standard (pounds)
58	131	131
59	136	136
60	141	141
61	145	145
62	150	149
63	155	152
64	160	156
65	165	160
66	170	163
67	175	167
68	181	170
69	186	174
70	191	177
71	196	181
72	201	185
73	206	189
74	211	194
75	216	200
76	221	205
77	226	211
78	231	216

Note: Due to muscle mass and other factors, exceeding the weight indicated on the chart doesn't necessarily mean a servicemember is considered overweight. It means that the Navy needs to perform a body fat measurement to determine if he or she falls within the prescribed Navy's Body Fat Standards.

Academic

Applicants must have a baccalaureate degree to qualify for the Officer Candidate School. However, for the more highly specialized naval occupations, there are additional educational requirements.

Engineering duty officer: A baccalaureate degree in engineering or science is required.

Nuclear power instructor: A baccalaureate degree in engineering, physics, mathematics, or chemistry, including one year of calculus, is required.

Nuclear propulsion officer: A baccalaureate degree with a minimum of one year of college physics and mathematics through integral calculus is required.

Oceanography geophysics officer: A baccalaureate degree in meteorology, oceanography, or other field of earth science, physical science, or engineering is required.

All Staff Corps officers require a professional, scientific, or highly technical background.

In addition to needing a college degree to qualify for the Officer Candidate Schools, applicants must also achieve a qualifying score on the Officer Aptitude Rating (OAR), a composite exam formed from the following two tests of the U.S. Navy and Marine Corps Aviation Selection Test Battery: the Math Skills Test, Reading Skills Test, and the Mechanical Comprehension Test.

The Math Skills Test and the Reading Skills Test measure quantitative aptitude (arithmetic reasoning, general mathematics, algebra, and plane geometry) and reading aptitude (paragraph comprehension).

The Mechanical Comprehension Test measures mechanical aptitude (understanding of the principles involved in the operation of mechanical devices, basic physics, and so on).

The complete U.S. Navy and Marine Corps Aviation Selection Test Battery must be taken by those applying for flight training. Scores on the six tests comprising this battery are used to construct four composite ratings that are used in evaluating aviation candidates.

Those interested in flight training are encouraged to study *Peterson's Military Flight Aptitude Tests*.

Service Commitment

Service Commitment varies with the program applied for and the training received. Nuclear propulsion officers incur a five-year active-duty obligation upon commissioning. Non-aviation officers generally incur a four-year active-duty obligation upon commissioning.

Additional information and guidance regarding a commission in the U.S. Navy may be obtained by contacting www.navy.com or by calling 800-USA-NAVY.

THE U.S. NAVAL ACADEMY AT ANNAPOLIS

The Naval Academy was founded in 1845 by the Secretary of the Navy, George Bancroft, in what is now Annapolis, Maryland. The history of the Academy has often reflected the history of the United States itself. As the U.S. Navy moved from a fleet of sail- and steam-powered ships to a high-tech fleet of nuclear-powered submarines and surface ships, and supersonic aircraft, the Academy has changed also. Still it continues to give young men and women the most current academic and professional training they need to become effective naval and marine officers after graduation.

Moral and ethical development is a fundamental element of the Naval Academy experience. As future officers in the Navy or Marine Corps, midshipmen will someday be responsible for the lives of many men and women and for the maintenance of multimillion-dollar equipment. From Plebe Summer, a summer training program required of all incoming freshmen to the U.S. Naval Academy, through graduation, the four-year Naval Academy's Officer Development Program focuses on the attributes of integrity, honor, and mutual respect.

One of the goals of the program is to develop midshipmen who possess a clear sense of their own moral beliefs and have the ability to articulate them and act on them. Honor is emphasized through the Honor Concept of the Brigade of Midshipmen based on respect for human dignity, honesty, and the property of others. The Honor Concept of the Brigade of Midshipmen states the following:

> Midshipmen are persons of integrity: they stand for that which is right. They tell the truth and ensure that the full truth is known. They do not lie. They embrace fairness in all actions. They ensure that work submitted as their own is their own, and that assistance received from any source is authorized and properly documented. They don't cheat. They respect the property of others and ensure that others are able to benefit from the use of their property. They do not steal.

Brigade Honor Committees composed of elected upper-class midshipmen are responsible for implementing the Honor Concept. Midshipmen who violate the Honor Concept—as judged by their peers—may be expelled from the Naval Academy.

Every midshipman's academic program begins with a core curriculum that includes courses in engineering, science, mathematics, humanities, and social sciences. This is designed to provide a broad-based education that will qualify the midshipmen for practically any career field in the Navy or Marine Corps. At the same time, the Academy's majors program allows midshipmen to develop a particular area of academic interest. The Academy also offers challenging honors programs and opportunities to start work on a postgraduate degree while still enrolled at the Academy.

The Academy also provides professional and leadership training. After four years at the Naval Academy, the life and customs of naval service should be second nature. At first, midshipmen are required to take orders from practically everyone. Before long, they earn the responsibility for making decisions that affect hundreds of other midshipmen. Classroom studies are backed by many hours of practical experience in leadership and naval operations, including assignments with actual Navy and Marine Corps units.

Just as the Naval Academy aims to promote the moral and intellectual development of midshipmen, it also aims to help each midshipman reach top physical form. The Naval Academy athletic program, as part of the Academy's education mission, has a much higher priority than physical education programs at civilian schools. Academy athletic teams are an integral part of the overall education of midshipmen. Athletics provides leadership opportunities and the experiences of team play, cooperative effort, commitment, and individual sacrifice. A physical education program is required, but each person has a wide variety of elective athletics from which to choose. The primary goal of the physical education curriculum is top fitness, which is vital for midshipmen health, personal appearance, and well-being.

SUMMING IT UP

- The twelve-week OCS course is designed to give a working knowledge of the Navy (afloat and ashore), prepare individuals to assume the responsibilities of a Naval officer, and begin developing them to their fullest potential.

- Military training at Officer Candidate School is comprised of five broad categories: Physical Training, Room and Locker Inspection (RLP), Personnel Inspections (PI), Drill, and Graduation/Commissioning Ceremony.

- Career fields in the Navy can be divided into operations and management positions and scientific and technical positions. Other positions are designated as unrestricted line officers, restricted line officers, and staff corps officers.

- Non-aviation applicants for OCS must be between 19½ and 29 years old at the time of appointment (some positions have stricter or broader age requirements), citizens of the United States, and of high moral character. Each candidate must have excellent sight, a height between 4′ 10″ and 6′ 6″ tall, have weight proportional to height, have teeth in good condition, and be in good overall health.

- Applicants must have a bachelor's degree. Additional educational requirements may apply for more highly specialized naval occupations. Service obligations vary according to the program applied for and the training received.

- The Naval Academy's Officer Development Program is a four-year integrated continuum that focuses on the attributes of integrity, honor, and mutual respect. One of the goals of this program is to develop midshipmen who possess a clear sense of their own moral beliefs and the ability to articulate them.

- Every midshipman's academic program begins with a core curriculum that includes courses in engineering, science, mathematics, humanities, and social sciences. First, midshipmen learn to take orders. Before long, they earn the responsibility for making decisions that affect hundreds of other midshipmen.

- The Academy athletic program is higher in priority than physical education programs are at civilian schools. Athletics provide leadership opportunities and the experiences of team play, cooperative effort, commitment, and individual sacrifice. The primary goal of the physical education curriculum is top fitness, which is vital for midshipmen's health, personal appearance, and well-being.

Becoming an Air Force Officer

OVERVIEW

- A brief history of Air Force Officer Training School (OTS)
- What to expect in OTS
- Career fields
- Requirements and qualifications
- The U.S. Air Force Academy
- Summing it up

A BRIEF HISTORY OF AIR FORCE OFFICER TRAINING SCHOOL (OTS)

A staff of 114 active-duty members including 75 officers, 41 enlisted personnel, and 9 civilian personnel, make up the Air Force Officer Training School (OTS). The organization has three squadrons who trained 1,650 students in 2006: 560 in Basic Officer Training (BOT) and 1,090 in Commissioned Officer Training (COT). Students include Air Force active-duty, Air Force Reserve, and Air National Guard members.

The Air Force's OTS was organized at Medina Annex, Lackland Air Force Base (AFB), Texas, in 1959. Its predecessor, the Officer Candidate School (OCS), was established in 1942 in Miami Beach, Florida, to train and commission members from the enlisted ranks. OCS moved to Lackland AFB in 1944, and it gained the additional mission of training officers directly from civilian status in 1951. OCS closed after its last graduation in 1963.

The first OTS class was comprised of 89 trainees, including 11 women. Since then, graduation numbers have varied, from 323 that first year to 7,894 in 1967. The school moved to Maxwell AFB, Alabama, in 1993 as part of the Air Force Chief of Staff's vision to align all officer education/training programs under Air University.

WHAT TO EXPECT IN OTS

At OTS, Basic Officer Training (BOT) is for college graduates pursuing commissions as second lieutenants for active-duty Air Force and Air Force Reserve in partnership with the U.S. Air Force Academy and the Air Force Reserve Officer Training Corps (the two other members of the Air Force officer training triad). BOT graduation numbers fluctuate in response to variations between projected and actual Air Force Academy and Air Force ROTC officer accessions, and the Air Force end strength projections that refer to the number of uniformed personnel at the end of a fiscal year and the total size of active forces.

The BOT program consists of twelve weeks of military instruction for college graduates leading to commissions as second lieutenants. The goal is to instill a high standard of conduct and to provide officer candidates with the essential military knowledge and skills they need to perform their duties effectively.

To ensure that this happens, OTS staff members provide instruction and guidance in these five areas:

1. Leadership studies
2. Professional knowledge
3. Communication skills
4. Military studies and international and security studies
5. Leadership instruction and application

OTS presents these areas concurrently, emphasizing team-building, followership, and knowledge during the first half of training and leadership applications during the second half. Lectures, readings, guided discussions, classroom exercises, field leadership exercises, and after-hours training activities provide graduates with a broad, in-depth understanding of their role as commissioned officers in the U.S. Air Force.

OTS is, above all, a leadership laboratory. Among the highlights are:

- **Leadership Reaction Course:** A field exercise using a specialized obstacle course in which small groups of students practice under stressful situations. This exercise is designed to test students' ability to reason quickly and lead effectively.

- **Air Expeditionary Force Exercise:** A capstone field leadership assessment exercise in which students demonstrate their ability to integrate and apply communication and leadership skills they have learned throughout the course.

The OTS's motto is "Always With Honor," which is reflected in the students' honor code: "I will not lie, cheat, or steal, nor tolerate among us anyone who does." The code is a standard of personal conduct for each officer trainee. OTS expects each graduate to adopt the code as his or her minimum ethical standard to be adhered to throughout one's career.

OTS trainees also receive instruction in the following fundamentals in leadership studies:

- Leadership and team building
- Leadership styles
- Management principles
- Time management
- Goal setting
- Scientific problem solving
- Group dynamics

- Counseling skills
- Accountability
- Ethics

Threaded throughout the leadership studies program are lectures and exercises that introduce and reinforce the principles of officership, authority and responsibility of officers, the Honor Code, standards of conduct, and the Air Force Core Values.

The professional knowledge curriculum teaches the skills and knowledge sets that are unique to commissioned service. Topics include:

- Dress and appearance
- Customs and courtesies
- Special and additional duties
- Military law
- Professional and unprofessional relationships
- Educational opportunities
- Pay and allowances
- Survivor and retirement benefits
- Officer evaluations and career progression
- Social actions issues (e.g., managing diversity, equal opportunity and treatment, sexual harassment/assault, substance abuse)

Communication skills classes are designed to develop the prospective officer's ability to speak more effectively, write more clearly, and listen more efficiently. The communication curriculum includes:

- Communication skills foundations
- Writing for results
- Briefing techniques
- Air Force publications and staff work

Every officer is required to have a broad knowledge of the workings of the Air Force. This includes information on the Air Force's origin and development, mission and purpose, doctrine, organization, position in the national military establishment, customs, and more. The military studies and international security studies curriculum area is designed to provide students with a broad and basic knowledge of the following:

- Air Force history and heritage
- The nature and laws of armed conflict
- U.S. internal and foreign policies and national security issues
- The organization and function of the Department of Defense
- The organization and function of the Air Force
- Employment of aerospace forces
- Strategic issues for the twenty-first century

Each trainee is given the opportunity to apply leadership theory and techniques throughout the program. The leadership instruction and application area of study provides practical application in three subjects:

1. Leadership training
2. Military discipline
3. Physical conditioning

This is accomplished through field leadership activities, including the Air Expeditionary Force Exercise, teaching drill and ceremonies, uniform standards and military customs, and courtesies classes. Physical fitness is assessed through a series of tests. Trainees prepare for the tests by daily participation in organized fitness training.

Once BOT trainees complete all OTS requirements, they are administered the Oath of Office and are commissioned (on extended active duty) as second lieutenants in the Air Force. Most newly commissioned lieutenants will attend a technical school after OTS. Technical training subject areas include flying, navigation, or air battle management; space and missile operations; and several support career fields. The length of these courses varies according to the specialty.

Commissioned Officer Training (COT) is a four-and-a-half-week program that provides initial officership training for Air Force judge advocates, chaplains, medical officers (including doctors, nurses, dentists, biomedical science corps officers, and hospital administrators), and medical scholarship recipients. COT is located on the OTS campus at Maxwell AFB.

The program, which began in 1996, combines three courses:

1. Air Force Officer Orientation Course
2. Health Professions Officer Indoctrination Course
3. Military Indoctrination for Medical Services Officers Course

The COT program covers the same subject areas as BOT. However, the curriculum is more compact and the program is shorter than that of BOT.

In this program, students are commissioned before training. Military rank is awarded to COT students based on their professional credentials in their respective fields. COT student ranks typically range from second lieutenant to lieutenant colonel. COT provides military training for approximately 1,300 officers annually.

Upon completion of COT, judge advocate and chaplain students typically attend career specialty schools offered at Maxwell AFB. Medical scholarship recipients report to various medical schools located throughout the country, and most medical service officers report to their operational units throughout the world. Some medical officers attend specialized training before reporting to their units. COT conducts training for Air Force active-duty, National Guard, and Reserve components.

Construction began in 1998 on a $75-million OTS campus. The current campus has two academic buildings with two auditoriums, four dormitories, a dining facility, and a fitness center. Adjacent to the campus are a running track, parade field, volleyball courts, and flickerball fields.

FOR MORE INFORMATION

For more information on the Air Force OTS, visit the OTS Web site at www.au.af.mil/au/holmcenter/. Find information about the Air Force OTS and the application process via the Air Force recruiting home page at www.airforce.com.

CAREER FIELDS

Those who successfully complete OTS have access to a wide variety of employment opportunities. Only 4 percent of servicemembers in the Air Force are pilots. There are many other careers available. Opportunities for OTS officers fall into the following four categories:

1. Flight careers
2. Nontechnical careers
3. Specialty careers
4. Technical careers

REQUIREMENTS AND QUALIFICATIONS

Age

Applicants must be at least 18 years of age at the time of commissioning and not have reached age 30 by the initial selection board convening date. Applicants should be commissioned before reaching age 30, though this requirement may be waived to allow commissioning up to age 35 in outstanding and deserving cases based on the needs of the Air Force.

Citizenship

Applicants must be citizens of the United States.

Character

Applicants must be of good moral character. All offenses or infractions pertaining to character are evaluated on a case-by-case basis.

Physical

Physical requirements are more stringent for rated (pilot or navigator) applicants.

Vision: Correctable with glasses to 20/20 in one eye and 20/30 in the other eye. Normal color vision is required for some technical job skills.

Height: 5'0" to 6'8"

Weight: Weight must be proportional to height. Applicants must meet the weight standards specified in Air Force Instruction 40-502.

Dental: Teeth must be in good condition without excessive cavities.

General: Applicants must be in good health with no abnormalities or chronic illness.

Weight and body fat determinations, decided at Military Entrance Processing Stations (MEPS) or other point of entry to service, remain part of accession physical standards and may also be used as entry criteria for accession training programs. The following chart shows the maximum allowable body fat percentages:

AIR FORCE BODY FAT STANDARDS			
Male		Female	
Age Range	Body Fat (%)	Age Range	Body Fat (%)
<30	20	<30	28
>30	24	>30	32

The Air Force, like the other services, uses the following weight charts for initial screening:

AIR FORCE WEIGHT FOR HEIGHT REQUIREMENTS		
Height (inches)	Minimum Weight (pounds)	Maximum Weight (pounds)
58	91	131
59	94	136
60	97	141
61	100	145
62	104	150
63	107	155
64	110	160
65	114	165
66	117	170
67	121	175
68	125	180
69	128	186
70	132	191
71	136	197
72	140	202
73	144	208
74	148	214
75	152	220
76	156	225
77	160	231
78	164	237
79	168	244
80	173	250

Notes: Weight requirements are now exactly the same for males and females.

Academic

Applicants must possess a baccalaureate degree to enroll in the OTS program. In addition, applicants must complete the Air Force Officer Qualifying Test (AFOQT).

The AFOQT measures aptitudes used in selecting candidates for officer commissioning programs and specific commissioned officer training programs. The AFOQT consists of twelve subtests. Subtest scores are combined to generate one or more composite scores used to help predict success in certain types of Air Force training programs.

The Pilot composite measures some of the knowledge and abilities considered necessary for successful completion of pilot training.

The Navigator-Technical composite measures some of the knowledge and abilities considered necessary for successful completion of navigator training.

The Academic Aptitude composite measures verbal and quantitative knowledge and abilities. The verbal subtests measure the ability to reason and recognize relationships among words, the ability to read and understand paragraphs on diverse topics, and the ability to understand synonyms. The quantitative subtests measure the ability to understand and reason with arithmetic relationships, interpret data from graphs and charts, and to use mathematical terms, formulas, and relationships. The Academic Aptitude composite measures some of the knowledge and abilities considered necessary for successful completion of training to become an Air Force officer.

The Air Force uses the Academic Aptitude composite score as one of the factors in selecting applicants for OTS. Those interested in flight training are encouraged to study *Peterson's Military Flight Aptitude Tests*.

Service Commitment

Non-rated officers incur a four-year active-duty obligation from the date of commission.

Pilots incur eight-year active duty terms of service and navigators, six. Additional information and guidance regarding a commission in the U.S. Air Force can be obtained by contacting any Air Force recruiting office or by contacting www.afoats.af.mil or by calling 800-423-USAF.

THE U.S. AIR FORCE ACADEMY

The following is a brief description of the U.S. Air Force Academy. The information contained in this section is provided by the Air Force Academy as general information only.

The U.S. Air Force Academy campus boasts state-of-the-art facilities, including laboratories, observatories, and a library. Other landmarks include the cadet chapel with its seventeen spires that soar 150 feet toward the Colorado sky. Spanning 18,000 acres in the Rocky Mountains, the Academy annually draws thousands of visitors from around the world.

The Air Force Academy Mission is to educate, train, and inspire men and women to become officers of character, motivated to lead the U.S. Air Force in service to the country. At the Air Force Academy, enlightened leadership is inspired through a wide variety of subjects. Students can choose from more than thirty available majors. Air Force Academy faculty and staff members take education seriously, and they expect the same of their cadets. Grading is strict, and expectations are high.

The core curriculum will arm each cadet with the knowledge he or she needs to succeed in a military career, with more than thirty courses in the following disciplines:

- Aeronautical engineering
- Astronautical engineering
- Behavioral sciences
- Biology
- Chemistry
- Civil engineering
- Computer science
- Economics
- Electrical engineering
- Engineering mechanics
- English
- Foreign languages
- History
- Law
- Management
- Mathematics
- Philosophy
- Physics
- Political science

Cadets at the Air Force Academy may choose from the following specific majors:

- Aeronautical engineering
- Astronautical engineering
- Basic science
- Behavioral sciences
- Biology
- Chemistry
- Civil engineering
- Computer engineering
- Computer science
- Economics
- Electrical engineering
- Engineering mechanics
- English

- Environmental engineering
- Foreign area studies
- General engineering
- Geospatial science
- History
- Humanities
- Legal studies
- Management
- Mathematical sciences
- Mechanical engineering
- Meteorology
- Military strategic studies
- Operations research
- Physics
- Political science
- Social sciences
- Space operations
- Systems engineering
- Systems engineering management

For the most up-to-date and accurate information, visit the Air Force Academy Web site at www.usafa.edu.

SUMMING IT UP

- The purpose of Basic Officer Training (BOT) is to train and commission second lieutenants in response to active-duty Air Force and Air Force Reserve requirements, in partnership with the U.S. Air Force Academy and Air Force Reserve Officer Training Corps.

- OTS staff members provide instruction and guidance in leadership studies, professional knowledge, communication skills, military studies and international and security studies, and leadership instruction and application.

- Trainees receive instruction on the fundamentals in leadership studies: leadership and team building, leadership styles, management principles, time management, goal setting, scientific problem solving, group dynamics, counseling skills, accountability, and ethics.

- Professional knowledge curriculum teaches the skills and knowledge sets unique to commissioned service, including dress and appearance, customs and courtesies, special and additional duties, military law, professional and unprofessional relationships, educational opportunities, pay and allowances, survivor and retirement benefits, officer evaluations and career progression, and social actions issues.

- The military studies and international security studies curriculum area is designed to provide students basic knowledge of Air Force history and heritage, the nature and laws of armed conflict, U.S. internal and foreign policies and national security issues, the organization and function of the Department of Defense and the Air Force, employment of aerospace forces, and strategic issues for the twenty-first century.

- Commissioned Officer Training (COT) combines three courses: Air Force Orientation Course, Health Professions Officer Indoctrination Course, and Military Indoctrination for Medical Services Officers Course.

- Applicants for OTS must be between 18 and 30 years old at the time of enrollment, citizens of the United States, and of high moral character. Each candidate must have excellent sight, a height between 5' and 6' 8" tall, have weight proportional to height, have teeth in good condition, and be in good overall health.

- Applicants must have a bachelor's degree to enroll in the OTS program and must complete the Air Force Qualifying Test (AFOQT). Non-rated officers must serve four years of active duty. Pilots must serve eight years of active duty; navigators, six years.

Becoming a Marine Corps Officer

OVERVIEW

- A brief history of Marine Corps Officer Candidate School (OCS)

- What to expect in OCS

- Career fields

- Requirements and qualifications

- Summing it up

As we discussed earlier in this book, the path to becoming a Marine Corps officer are through Naval Reserve Officers Training Corps (NROTC), the Naval Academy, and the Marine Corps Officer Candidate School (OCS). This chapter will review OCS.

Marine Corps OCS lasts up to twelve weeks, depending on the attendees' status. Training takes place at the Marine Corps Base at Quantico, Virginia.

A BRIEF HISTORY OF MARINE CORPS OFFICER CANDIDATE SCHOOL (OCS)

Before World War I, Marine officers primarily came from the Naval Academy or from enlisted ranks. The first officer's training school at Quantico traces its beginnings to 1891, when Marine Corps General Order No. 1 established the first formal resident school for Marine Officers, the School of Application at Marine Barracks, Washington, DC. In 1909, the school moved to the Marine Barracks at Annapolis, Maryland, and was renamed the Marine Officers' School; the following year it moved to Norfolk, Virginia.

U.S. involvement in World War I led to an increase in the sizes of all the Armed Services branches, and the Marine Corps was no exception. To meet the growing need for qualified officers for the American Expeditionary Forces in Europe, the military moved its instructional efforts to Quantico, where individual replacements and new units were being formed for the war. All new officers were moved to Quantico, where they received training at the Officers Camp of Instruction, organized in 1917.

The Marine Corps Officers Training School and the Marine Officers Infantry School were established at Quantico in 1919 and later became Marine Officers

Training School. In the 1920s, the Corps began recruiting potential officers from colleges and universities through the Naval Reserve Officer Training Corps (NROTC) program, with lieutenants commissioned from the U.S. Naval Academy, NROTC units, and enlisted, commissioned Marines reporting to The Basic School (TBS) for instruction.

In 1934, the Marine Corps established the Platoon Leaders Course (PLC), selecting students from colleges that did not have ROTC. Under this new program, college graduates became second lieutenants in the Marine Corps Reserve after two six-week training periods and received further training at TBS. In 1940, a special unit tasked with training additional officer candidates, called Officer Candidate Class, was instituted to train potential officers in the fundamentals of military discipline, and in the school of the soldier, squad, and platoon to select those qualified for commission to provide capable and well-fitted officers for the Marine Corps Reserve. Thus, shortly after the onset of World War II, the entire Corps' junior officer training, excluding aviators, was conducted at Quantico, including TBS functions that had been performed in Philadelphia before the war.

During the war, the commandant established temporary candidate detachments at Camp Elliot, California, and Camp Lejuene, North Carolina. In 1944, the PLC was reestablished and combined with the Officer Candidate Class to become the Officer Candidate School (OCS).

During World War II, potential Marine Corps Reserve women officers were trained at Mount Holyoke College and Smith College, both in Massachusetts. The passage of the Women's Armed Service Integration Act in 1948 enabled women marines to serve for the first time as members of the regular military establishment. In 1949, to accommodate this new requirement for women officers, the Women Officer Training Course was established under the cognizance of TBS.

After TBS headquarters left Brown Field and moved to Camp Upshur, Virginia, TBS was no longer responsible for training female officers, NROTC midshipmen, and PLC candidates. The Training and Test Regiment at Brown Field assumed these responsibilities and was redesignated under the OCS. The last reorganization occurred in 1977, when training of female officers was placed under the cognizance of the commanding officer of OCS.

WHAT TO EXPECT IN OCS

The mission of the Marine OCS is to educate, train, evaluate, and screen officer candidates to ensure that they possess the moral, intellectual, and physical qualities for commissioning and the leadership potential to serve successfully as company-grade officers in the Marine Corps. If you're considering officership with the Corps, here are the qualities OCS offers to candidates:

- **Firmness:** Candidates are required to meet Marine Corps standards; they can expect to be held accountable for their actions.
- **Fairness:** OCS evaluation is mentally and physically challenging. Each candidate is provided every opportunity to prove his or her potential, because OCS wants candidates to succeed.
- **Respect:** Every candidate is treated with respect because each one has volunteered to enter OCS. Accepting of the challenge to prove oneself as a leader is the first step in earning one's commission as a second lieutenant in the Marine Corps.

Likewise, you need the following elements to succeed in Marine Corps OCS:

- A commitment to be a leader in the Marines
- Mental and physical preparation. Physical preparation includes both strength and endurance
- Belief in yourself
- A clear understanding of the OCS program
- An understanding of OCS standards and expectations
- The ability to learn from mistakes
- The ability to progress from focus on oneself to focus on the team to which you belong

Each candidate at the Marine Corps OCS is evaluated according to three categories:

1. **Leadership:** 50 percent
2. **Academics:** 25 percent
3. **Physical Fitness:** 25 percent

A candidate's leadership grade is based on practical application events, staff observation, and classroom instruction. OCS teaches eleven courses, including instruction on fundamental and intermediate leadership (core values classes) and on Marine Corps/Department of Defense policies. Leadership is also evaluated in the following courses:

- Leadership Opportunities
- Leadership Billets
- Drill
- Leadership Reaction Course
- Fire Team in the Offense
- Squad in the Offense
- Small Unit Leadership Evaluation I
- Small Unit Leadership Evaluation II

Officer candidates receive instruction on Marine Corps history, tactics, operations and organization, land navigation, and other military subjects. They are evaluated on their knowledge of this material through written exams and practical application.

The physical training program at OCS consists of teaching, then testing and evaluating, a very high level of physical fitness in a short time. It is built on principles that test physical courage, willpower, and determination, while preparing candidates for the rigors of future Marine Corps duty. The physical evaluations are designed to assess each individual's general strength and endurance under varying field and tactical conditions.

Physical training consists of the following activities:

- **UBDs:** Upper Body Development Course
- **Run Circuit:** A circular course along which are exercise stations; the course is designed to build endurance and overall body strength

- **Fartlek Course:** A 3- to 4-mile trail, along which are several exercise stations; the course is designed to build endurance
- **Obstacle Course:** A 100-meter series of obstacles that must be negotiated in a prescribed amount of time
- **Confidence and Tarzan Courses:** A series of high obstacles aimed at building candidates' self-confidence while teaching them physical military skills
- **Combat Readiness Test:** Consists of physical events one is likely to face in combat situations
- **Conditioning Hikes:** Ranges from 3 to 15 miles; candidates must navigate with combat gear
- **Pugil Sticks:** Exercise using these sticks, which simulates close combat fighting
- **Combat Course:** A 1.5-mile course that simulates a combat environment by stressing all-around security and noise discipline, as candidates negotiate a series of obstacles
- **Endurance Course:** A 3.5-mile course testing candidates' physical endurance and ability to traverse and negotiate various obstacles

Acceptable physical performances greatly increase an individual's self-confidence and positively influence his or her leadership ability. A candidate's desire and motivation to become an officer in the U.S. Marine Corps is a major factor in determining whether he or she will be successful.

When candidates report to OCS, they are first physically evaluated with the initial Physical Fitness Test (PFT). This consists of pull-ups for men, flex-arm hangs for women, abdominal crunches, and a 3-mile run. Candidates must achieve a score of 225 out of 300 points on the initial PFT to begin the training session. Exceptional performance in one category can offset poor performance in another category—but only to a certain extent. A candidate, for example, who can perform twenty pull-ups but cannot complete a 3-mile run in less than 30 minutes is viewed as not having the physical stamina necessary for success as an officer.

CAREER FIELDS

Those who successfully complete Marine Corps OCS have access to a wide variety of employment opportunities. Career fields are listed below under the categories of Ground Careers, Air Careers, and Law Career.

Ground Careers:
- Infantry
- Field Artillery
- Tank
- Combat Engineer
- Assault Amphibian Vehicle
- Light Armored Vehicle
- Ground Intelligence
- Communications Systems
- Military Police

- Logistics
- Financial Management
- Human Source Intelligence
- Signals Intelligence
- Public Affairs
- Ground Supply
- Adjutant
- Aviation Intelligence
- Aviation Maintenance
- Air Support Control
- Air Defense Control
- Air Traffic Control
- Aviation Supply

Air Careers:
- Pilot
- Naval Flight

Law Career:
- Judge Advocate

REQUIREMENTS AND QUALIFICATIONS

Age

Ground applicants must be at least 18 years and younger than 30 years of age on the date of appointment to commissioned grade.

Citizenship

Applicants must be citizens of the United States.

Character

Applicants must be of high moral character. Persons convicted of any felony or misdemeanor involving moral turpitude are disqualified. Addiction to narcotics or history of such addiction is disqualifying. All other offenses or infractions pertaining to character are evaluated on a case-by-case basis.

Physical

Vision: Applicants must be correctable to 20/20 with glasses (waiver may be granted up to 20/400).

Height: Male applicants—5′6″ to 6′6″ (waiver may be granted down to 5′4″); female applicants—5′1″ to 6′0″ (waiver may be granted down to 4′10″ and up to 6′1″)

Weight: Weight must be proportional to height, as shown in the Weight Standards for Marines table.

Dental: Teeth must be in good condition without excessive cavities.

General: Applicants must be in good health with no abnormalities or chronic illness.

Male applicants must pass a physical fitness test that consists of pull-ups or chin-ups, bent-knee crunches, and a 3-mile run. Female applicants must pass a physical fitness test that consists of the flexed arm hang, bent-knee crunches, and a 3-mile run.

The following chart reflects the Marine Corps Body Fat Standards for both male and female marines:

MARINE CORPS BODY FAT STANDARDS			
Male		**Female**	
Age Range	*Body Fat (%)*	*Age Range*	*Body Fat (%)*
17–26	18	17–26	26
27–39	19	27–39	27
40–45	20	40–45	28
46+	21	46+	29

The following charts reflect the Marine Corps weight requirements for both male and female marines:

MARINE CORPS WEIGHT FOR HEIGHT REQUIREMENTS (MALE)		
Height (inches)	**Maximum Weight (pounds)**	**Minimum Weight (pounds)**
58	132	91
59	136	94
60	141	97
61	146	100
62	150	104
63	155	107
64	160	110
65	165	114
66	170	117
67	176	121
68	181	125
69	186	128
70	192	132
71	197	136
72	203	140
73	208	144
74	214	148
75	220	152
76	226	156
77	232	160
78	238	164
79	244	168
80	250	173

MARINE CORPS WEIGHT FOR HEIGHT REQUIREMENTS (FEMALE)		
Height (inches)	Maximum Weight (pounds)	Minimum Weight (pounds)
58	120	91
59	124	94
60	128	97
61	132	100
62	137	104
63	141	107
64	146	110
65	150	114
66	155	117
67	160	121
68	164	125
69	169	128
70	174	132
71	179	136
72	184	140
73	189	144
74	195	148
75	200	152
76	205	156
77	211	160
78	216	164
79	222	168
80	228	173

Academic

Applicants must be full-time students or college graduates to qualify for the Officer Candidates Class (OCC) or the Platoon Leaders Class (PLC). A bachelor's degree is required for a commission.

Marine Corps officer applicants are no longer required to take a specific officer candidate test. Instead, applicants must have a minimum combined score of 1000 on the Critical Reading (verbal) and Math sections of the SAT or a minimum combined Math and English score of 45 on the ACT, or must obtain an acceptable score on the Armed Services Vocational Aptitude Battery (ASVAB).

The complete U.S. Navy and Marine Corps Aviation Selection Test Battery (ASTB) must be taken by those applying for flight training. Scores on the six tests comprising this battery are used to construct four composite ratings that are used in evaluating aviation candidates.

Those interested in flight training are encouraged to study the *Peterson's Military Flight Aptitude Tests*.

Service Commitment

For non-aviation officers there is a 3½-year active-duty obligation from commencement of active duty after commissioning.

Additional information and guidance regarding a commission in the Marine Corps can be obtained by contacting any of the Marine Corps officer selection officers who travel the college circuit on a regular basis, any Marine Corps recruiting office, any major Marine Corps installation, or by contacting www.marines.com/officer or by calling 800-MARINES.

For more detailed and up-to-date information, visit the official Marine Corps OCS Web site at www.ocs.usmc.mil. The site provides a comprehensive survey of Marine Corps OCS and is an exceptionally rich resource.

SUMMING IT UP

- One can become a Marine Corps officer through the Naval Reserve Officers Training Corps (NROTC), the Naval Academy, or the Marine Corps OCS.

- The first officer's training school at Quantico was established in 1891. The first formal resident school for Marine Officers was the School of Application at Marine Barracks, Washington, DC. In 1918, the school was formalized and titled the Officers Training Camp (OTC).

- The Corps developed the Platoon Leaders Course (PLC) in 1934 for students from colleges that did not have a Reserve Officers Training Corps. During World War II, Officer Candidate Class was established. When the revived PLC program was incorporated into officer candidate training, the combination became the Officer Candidate School.

- The passage of the Women's Armed Service Integration Act in 1948 enabled women marines to serve for the first time as members of the regular establishment.

- In 1955, the training of women officers, NROTC midshipmen, and PLC candidates was removed from TBS responsibility and shifted to the newly formed Training and Test Regiment. Training of female officers came under the cognizance of the commanding officer of OCS in 1977.

- In return, OCS demands a commitment to be a leader in the Marines, mental and physical preparation, belief in oneself, a clear understanding of the OCS program and its standards and expectations, the ability to learn from mistakes, and the ability to progress from a focus on the self to a focus on the team.

- Each officer candidate is evaluated for leadership qualities, academics, and physical fitness. The leadership grade is based on practical application events, staff observation, and classroom instruction.

- Those who complete training at TBS are selected for various career paths based on the needs of the Marine Corps, class standing, company commander's recommendation, and personal preference. A special law option allows law school students and graduates to postpone active duty until they are admitted to the bar.

- Applicants for OCS must be between 18 and 30 years old at the time of appointment, citizens of the United States, and of high moral character. Each candidate must have excellent sight, a height between 5′ 6″ and 6′ 6″ (male) or 5′ 1″ and 6′ (women), have weight proportional to height, have teeth in good condition, and be in good overall health.

- OCS applicants must have a bachelor's degree. Marine Corps officer applicants must have particular SAT, ACT, and ASVAB scores. Those applying for flight training must take the U.S. Navy and Marine Corps ASTB. Non-aviation officers are required to serve 3½ years of active duty.

Becoming a Coast Guard Officer

OVERVIEW

- A brief history of Coast Guard Officer Candidate School (OCS)
- What to Expect in OCS
- Career fields
- Requirements and qualifications
- The U.S. Coast Guard Academy
- Summing it up

A BRIEF HISTORY OF COAST GUARD OFFICER CANDIDATE SCHOOL (OCS)

The Coast Guard is considered one of the military branches, but, in fact, it now falls under the direction of the U.S. Department of Homeland Security. However, in times of war, the Coast Guard may be placed under the control of the Department of Defense.

The Coast Guard's missions are varied, but its primary mission is maritime law enforcement. It also carries out search-and-rescue missions and is responsible for maintaining a worldwide network of navigational aids. The Coast Guard collects and analyzes oceanographic and meteorological data, clears ice-blocked shipping lanes, and administers a merchant marine safety program. In addition, it enforces maritime conservation laws and patrols America's 200-mile fisheries zone.

WHAT TO EXPECT IN OCS

Coast Guard Officer Candidate School (OCS) provides a rigorous seventeen-week course of instruction at the Leadership Development Center of the Coast Guard Academy in New London, Connecticut. In addition to introducing students to a military lifestyle, Coast Guard OCS also teaches a wide range of highly technical information that candidates need to perform the duties of a Coast Guard officer. Graduates of the program receive a commission in the Coast Guard at the rank of ensign and are required to serve a minimum of three years on active duty. Graduates may be assigned to a ship, flight training, a staff job, or an operations ashore billet. Although personal desires and performance at OCS are considered, first assignments are based primarily on the needs of the U.S. Coast Guard. All graduates must be available for assignment anywhere in the world.

chapter 7

Applicants for OCS must be between 21 and 26 years old, but they may exceed this age limit by the number of months (up to sixty) served on active duty in any Armed Forces branch. To apply to the Coast Guard Academy, one must be a college senior or must hold at least a bachelor's degree from an accredited college or university.

Applicants must pass a physical exam and meet Coast Guard weight standards. Applicants are also required to pass extensive swimming tests.

CAREER FIELDS

Those who successfully complete Coast Guard OCS have access to a wide variety of employment opportunities. Career fields are listed below under the thirteen categories.

1. Aviation
2. Command, Control, Communications, and Computers
3. Engineering Logistics
4. Civil Engineering
5. Naval Engineering
6. Financial Resource Management
7. Human Resource Management
8. Health Services
9. Legal
10. Marine Safety
11. Operations
    - Afloat
    - Ashore
    - Law Enforcement
    - Intelligence
12. Reserve Program Management
13. Selected Reserve

REQUIREMENTS AND QUALIFICATIONS

Age

Applicants must be at least 21 years and under 26 years of age at the convening date of the Officer Candidate School class for which application is made (a waiver may be granted in certain instances).

Citizenship

Applicants must be citizens of the United States.

Character

Applicants must be of good moral character. Persons who have been convicted of a felony are ineligible.

Dependents

Applicants may not have more than three dependents. Any single individual who has sole/primary custody of another individual or relinquishes custody of another individual solely for the purpose of applying for appointment may not apply.

Swimming

Applicants are required to pass extensive swimming tests.

Physical

Vision: Applicants must have a minimum distant visual acuity of 20/400 or better, corrected to 20/20. Color vision must be normal.

Height: 5'0" to 6'6" for both male and female applicants.

Weight: Weight must be proportional to height. The weight-height standards used are available at U.S. Coast Guard recruiting offices.

Dental: Teeth must be in good condition without excessive cavities.

General: Applicants must be in good health with no abnormalities or chronic illnesses.

All servicemembers are screened against the height and weight standards every October and April. The Coast Guard weight standards are based on the height and frame size of the servicemember, which is determined by measuring the wrist. Since wrist size and height do not tend to change over time, they generally need to be determined at the beginning of a servicemember's career. The Coast Guard will use this measurement as the basis for all future weight screenings.

If a servicemember fails the weight screening, then the Coast Guard will measure his or her body fat percentage. If the servicemember's body fat exceeds the standards, he or she will be placed on probation, during which time he or she must lose the excess weight or body fat. The following chart shows the maximum allowable body fat percentages:

COAST GUARD BODY FAT STANDARDS			
Male		Female	
Age Range	Body Fat (%)	Age Range	Body Fat (%)
<30	23	<30	33
30–39	25	30–39	35
>39	27	>39	37

Academic

Applicants must have a baccalaureate degree to qualify for Officer Candidate School. Applicants are no longer required to take the Officer Aptitude Rating (OAR). However, SAT Reasoning Test or ACT scores are considered in the "whole person" application concept.

All applicants must provide a qualifying score on the SAT, ACT, or ASVAB. No waivers are considered. Minimum qualifying scores are as follows:

- **SAT:** combined 1000 on Critical Reading (Verbal) and Mathematics
- **ACT:** at least 23
- **ASVAB:** 109 on ASVAB General Technical aptitude area after July 1, 2004; 110 before July 1, 2004.

The complete U.S. Navy and Marine Corps Aviation Selection Test Battery (ASTB) must be taken by those applying for flight training. Scores on the six tests comprising this battery are used to construct four composite ratings that are used in evaluating aviation candidates.

Those interested in flight training are encouraged to study *Peterson's Military Flight Aptitude Tests*.

Service Commitment

Graduates of OCS have a three-year active-duty obligation from the date of commission.

Additional information and guidance regarding a commission in the Coast Guard can be obtained by contacting the military recruiting officer at any major Coast Guard installation or by contacting www.cga.edu (Once online, select LDC [Leadership Development Center] for OCS information.) or by calling 800-438-8724.

THE U.S. COAST GUARD ACADEMY

The smallest of the five U.S. service academies, the Coast Guard Academy in New London, Connecticut, offers elite higher education, rigorous professional development, and the honor and tradition of a military academy with a more personalized approach.

The Coast Guard Academy offers an integrated life experience emphasizing academics, physical fitness, and character and leadership with the goal of graduating officers of the highest caliber. The Academy also features an impressive 8:1 student-to-faculty ratio.

As with those in other military branches, Coast Guard cadets follow a code of honor and go on to careers at sea, on land, in the air, and even in space. Many also pursue graduate-level study, some of which is funded by the Coast Guard.

Students at the Coast Guard Academy may concentrate on one of the following eight available majors:

1. Civil engineering
2. Electrical engineering
3. Government
4. Management
5. Marine and environmental science

⑥ Mechanical engineering

⑦ Naval architecture and marine engineering

⑧ Operations research and computer analysis (applied mathematics)

For additional information about Coast Guard OCS, visit its Web site at www.cga.edu. For more information about joining the Coast Guard, visit its Web site at www.gocoastguard.com/officerindex.html or call 800-GET-USCG (toll-free).

SUMMING IT UP

- The Coast Guard falls under the direction of the U.S. Department of Homeland Security, but in times of war it may be placed under the control of the Department of Defense.

- The Coast Guard's primary mission is maritime law enforcement; it also carries out search-and-rescue missions and is responsible for maintaining a worldwide network of navigational aids.

- The Coast Guard OCS consists of a rigorous seventeen-week course of instruction at the Coast Guard Academy in New London, Connecticut. In addition to introducing students to a military lifestyle, Coast Guard OCS also teaches a wide range of highly technical information that candidates need to perform the duties of a Coast Guard officer.

- Applicants for the OCS must be between 21 and 26 years old, but they may exceed this age limit by the number of months (up to sixty) served on active duty in any Armed Forces branch.

- All applicants must provide a qualifying score on the SAT, ACT, or ASVAB. Minimum qualifying scores are a combined 1100 on Critical Reading (Verbal) and Mathematics on the SAT, at least 23 on the ACT, and 110 on ASVAB General Technical aptitude area on the ASVAB.

- Applicants must pass a physical exam and meet Coast Guard weight standards. Applicants are also required to pass extensive swimming tests.

- Coast Guard cadets follow a code of honor and graduate to careers at sea, on land, in the air, and in space.

- Coast Guard Academy cadets concentrate on one of the following eight majors: civil engineering, electrical engineering, government, management, marine and environmental science, mechanical engineering, naval architecture and marine engineering, and operations research and computer analysis (applied mathematics).

PART III
MILITARY TESTS AND TRAINING

CHAPTER 8   Introduction to Military Testing

Introduction to Military Testing

OVERVIEW

- **Armed Services Vocational Aptitude Battery (ASVAB)**
- **SAT**
- **ACT**
- **Air Force Officer Qualifying Test (AFOQT)**
- **Aviation Selection Test Battery (ASTB)**
- **Summing it up**

Can one exam determine your suitability for service as a commissioned military officer? It may not be a foolproof method, but you will largely be evaluated based on how well you do on a single exam. Of course, exceptions allow you to retest if necessary, but just as your suitability to enter college was based in part on the results of a standardized test you took (either the SAT or ACT), the military will use such a test in determining whether you are suitable for military life. These tests—in addition to being part of the initial qualification process for commissioning—may also determine whether you will attain certain officer occupations.

The actual test you take varies by service; some services may accept your SAT or ACT scores in lieu of a specific officer candidate test. For acceptance into some officer candidate programs, you may not actually take a standardized test until you have already been accepted into the program. Such is the case with the Air Force ROTC (AFROTC): Cadets are accepted based on other criteria (including SAT or ACT scores), but they must later take the Air Force Officer Qualifying Test (AFOQT) while attending college. The following information explains the Officer Candidate or Officer Training School requirements.

Army Officer Candidate School

All applicants for OCS must achieve a qualifying score on the ASVAB General Technical (GT) aptitude area and a qualifying score on the SAT or ACT. Minimum qualifying scores are as follows:

- ASVAB GT: 110 or higher
- SAT: 850
- ACT: 19

SAT/ACT scores must be dated within six years of the application. A soldier who wishes to retake either test will do so at his/her own expense. Retaking the ACT requires a sixty-day waiting period; the SAT can be retaken only once during any fiscal year.

Navy Officer Candidate School

The Navy and Marine Corps Aviation Selection Test Battery (ASTB) is used by Bureau of Naval Personnel (BUPERS) and Commandment Marine Corps to select candidates for the Navy and Marine Corps pilot and flight officer programs. The selection test is also used by the naval community for aviation maintenance and intelligence officer selection.

Air Force Officer Candidate School

The Air Force Officer Qualifying Test (AFOQT) is used to select applicants for officer commissioning programs, such as Officer Training School (OTS) or Air Force Reserve Officer Training Corps (AFROTC). It is also used for selection into specific training programs such as pilot and navigator training.

Marine Corps Officer Candidate School

There is no longer a specific officer candidate academic test for Marine Corps officer applicants. Those wishing to apply for a commission in the Marine Corps must achieve *one* of the following minimums:
* combined score of 1000 on the Critical Reading (Verbal) and Math sections of the SAT
* combined Math and English (Verbal) score of 45 on the ACT
* score of 120 (can be waivered to 115) on the composite score of the ASVAB (derived from the General Science, Arithmetic Reasoning, Mathematics Knowledge, and Electronics Information subtests)

Pilot and flight officer applicants must also take the ASTB.

Coast Guard Officer Candidate School

All applicants for OCS must provide a qualifying score on the SAT, ACT, or ASVAB. No waivers will be considered. Minimum qualifying scores are as follows:
* SAT: combined score 1000 on Critical Reading (Verbal) and Math
* ACT: 23
* ASVAB: 109 on ASVAB General Technical (GT) aptitude area after July 1, 2004; 110 before July 1, 2004.

Pilot candidates in the Coast Guard must also take the ASTB.

If you are an AFROTC cadet using this book to prepare for the AFOQT, you may also want to check out *Peterson's Master the Military Flight Aptitude Tests,* which contains more extensive information and test preparation for those seeking to become military pilots.

In this chapter, we'll examine the various exams administered to potential officer candidates. As with any such information, remember to check with your recruiter or admissions officer before committing any time to studying so that you're certain you're using the right material.

ARMED SERVICES VOCATIONAL APTITUDE BATTERY (ASVAB)

The ASVAB began as the Armed Forces Qualification Test (AFQT) at the end of World War II, and all the armed services currently use some version of it to determine candidates' suitability for enlistment and training. The military also uses the nine separate subtests of the ASVAB to determine the proper vocation for enlisted military members, and the Army and Marine Corps use it as their officer candidate test (although the Marine Corps will also accept SAT or ACT scores in lieu of ASVAB scores).

Although the ASVAB administered for commissioning programs is the same as the version administered for enlisted programs, the military branches use the test scores differently.

The table below describes the nine ASVAB subtests. The time allotment is 149 minutes with a total number of 225 items.

Test	Time Allowed (Minutes)	Items	Description
General Science	11	25	Covers material typically taught in high school science courses, including life sciences (basic biology, human nutrition, health), physical sciences (elementary chemistry, physics), and earth sciences (geology, meteorology, astronomy).
Arithmetic Reasoning	36	30	Covers basic mathematical problems. Questions are designed to measure general reasoning and the ability to solve mathematical problems.
Word Knowledge	11	35	Tests the ability to understand the meaning of words through synonyms. In synonym questions, a key word may appear in the stem and be followed by the phrase "most nearly means," or the key word may be used in a sentence.
Paragraph Comprehension	13	15	Measures the ability to obtain information from written material. Reading passages are one to several paragraphs long and each is followed by one or more questions.
Mathematics Knowledge	24	25	Tests the ability to solve problems using high school–level mathematics, including algebra and basic geometry.

Electronics Information	9	20	Tests knowledge of electrical principles, radio principles, and electronics.
Auto and Shop Information	11	25	Tests knowledge of material typically taught in automobile mechanics class at the high school or vocational school level.
Mechanical Comprehension	19	25	Tests understanding of mechanical and physical principles using drawings or illustrations.
Assembling Objects	15	25	Measures test-taker's spatial aptitude (the ability to perceive spatial relations). Questions focus on a series of five drawings and require identification of an assembled puzzle or correctly coupled objects.

ASVAB results are reported by three academic composite scores—Academic Ability, Verbal Ability, and Math Ability—and the nine test scores in the test battery.

Academic Ability measures how well you did on the Verbal Ability and Math Ability sections combined. Verbal Ability measures how well you did on the Word Knowledge and Paragraph Comprehension tests combined. Math Ability measures how well you did on the Arithmetic Reasoning and Mathematics Knowledge tests combined.

The nine ASVAB test scores, as well as the three composite scores, are reported as percentiles. Percentile scores show how well you did in relation to others. Two types of percentile scores are reported: same grade/same sex and same grade/opposite sex scores.

The Arithmetic Reasoning, Word Knowledge, and Paragraph Comprehension tests are used to construct the aptitude area General Technical (GT) used by the Army in screening applicants for its OCS program. The General Science, Arithmetic Reasoning, Mathematics Knowledge, and Electronics Information tests are used by the Marine Corps as one of the methods of meeting the academic requirement for its Officer Candidates Class and Women Officer Candidates program.

SAT

If you are a college graduate, are attending college, or are preparing to attend college, you're likely to be quite familiar with the SAT. This test has been the standard assessment test required by virtually every college in the United States. The SAT is administered by the nonprofit College Board. The SAT comprises three subject areas.

Subject Area	Time Allowed	Question Type	Score Range
Critical Reading	70 minutes (two 25-minute sections and one 20-minute section)	Passage-based reading and sentence completion	200–800
Mathematics	70 minutes (two 25-minute sections and one 20-minute section)	Multiple-choice questions and student-produced responses	200–800
Writing	60 minutes (two 25-minute sections and one 10-minute section)	Multiple-choice questions (35 minutes) and student-written essay (25 minutes)	200–800

Critical Reading: Tests reading comprehension, vocabulary, and understanding of sentence structure. In one type of question, test takers read passages and answer multiple-choice questions based on information in the passage. In a second question type, test takers answer sentence completion questions.

Mathematics: Consists of two types of questions: multiple-choice and response. Test takers fill in responses on an answer sheet.

Writing: Consists of writing an essay on a specific issue and answering three types of multiple-choice questions: improving sentences, identifying sentence errors, and improving paragraphs.

ACT

The ACT, like the SAT, is primarily used to determine suitability for college enrollment. Although not as widely used as the SAT, the ACT is gaining in popularity and acceptability by colleges. The ACT consists of four to five parts.

Subject Area	Number of Questions	Time Allowed (Minutes)	Measures
English	75	45	Standard written English and rhetorical skills
Mathematics	60	60	Math skills students usually acquire by the beginning of twelfth grade
Reading	40	35	Reading comprehension
Science	40	35	The interpretation, analysis, evaluation, reasoning, and problem-solving skills in the natural sciences
Writing Test (Optional)	1 Writing Prompt	30	Writing skills developed in high school English and entry-level college composition courses

AIR FORCE OFFICER QUALIFYING TEST (AFOQT)

The Air Force Officer Qualifying Test (AFOQT) is a standardized test similar to the SAT and ACT, designed to measure aptitudes and used to select applicants for officer commissioning programs. The military also uses it to determine which applicants are selected for specific training programs, such as piloting and navigator training.

The AFOQT contains eleven cognitive subtests and a recently added Self-Description section: 250 cognitive test questions and 220 Self-Description questions in all. The entire AFOQT takes approximately 3½ hours.

Subtest	Number of Questions	Time Allowed (Minutes)	Measures
Verbal Analogies	25	8	Ability to reason and to see relationships between words
Arithmetic Reasoning	25	29	Ability to use arithmetic to solve problems
Word Knowledge	25	5	Basic word definition (synonyms)
Math Knowledge	25	22	Knowledge of mathematical terms and principles
Instrument Comprehension	20	6	Ability to determine position of an airplane from reading instruments
Block Counting	20	3	Ability to look at a three-dimensional stack of blocks and determine how many pieces are touched by certain numbered blocks
Table Reading	40	7	Ability to read tables quickly and accurately
Aviation Information	20	8	Knowledge of general aviation concepts and terminology
General Science	20	10	Knowledge of high school science
Rotated Blocks	15	13	The ability to visualize and manipulate objects
Hidden Figures	15	8	Ability to see a simple figure in a complex drawing, also known as template matching
Self-Description Inventory	220	40	Personal traits and attitudes (there are no "right" or "wrong" answers)

AFOQT Test Results

AFOQT tests are scored in five areas:

① Pilot
② Navigator
③ Academic Aptitude
④ Verbal
⑤ Quantitative (Math)

The AFOQT may be taken more than once under the following guidelines:

- Only one retest is permitted. (Waivers may be granted, but exceptions are not guaranteed.)
- Examinees must wait 180 days before retesting.
- The most recent AFOQT test score is accepted. (AFOQT scores do not expire.)

Army Officer Candidate Tests

In the past the Army administered its own version of the AFOQT called the Army Officer Candidate Test (OCT). Instead, the Army now utilizes SAT, ACT, or ASVAB results to determine eligibility.

Although the Army no longer administers its own officer candidate test, it does administer a separate test for individuals desiring to become Army helicopter pilots called the Alternate Flight Aptitude Selection Test (AFAST). The contents of the AFAST fall outside the scope of this book and, therefore, readers wishing to become Army pilots are advised to study *Peterson's Master the Military Flight Aptitude Tests.*

AVIATION SELECTION TEST BATTERY (ASTB)

The ASTB is administered by the Navy, Marine Corps, and Coast Guard to help determine suitability of aviation officer candidates. The Navy and Coast Guard also use portions of the ASTB for evaluating potential candidates for their OCS programs. Applicants may choose to take only the Officer Aptitude Rating (OAR) portion of the exam, which includes the Math Skills Test (MST), Reading Skills Test (RST), and Mechanical Comprehension Test (MCT), if they do not wish to be considered for pilot training.

The ASTB takes approximately 2½ hours to administer and consists of six subtests.

Subtest	Number of Questions	Time Allowed (Minutes)	Measures
Math Skills Test (MST)	30	25	Math skills including arithmetic, algebra, and some geometry
Reading Skills Test (RST)	27	25	Ability to extract information from text passages

Mechanical Comprehension Test (MCT)	30	15	Knowledge of information usually covered in an introductory high school physics course
Spatial Apperception Test (SAT)	25	10	Ability to match external and internal views of an aircraft regarding its direction and orientation relative to the ground
Aviation and Nautical Information Test (ANIT)	30	15	Knowledge of aviation history, nautical terminology, and knowledge of aircraft components, aerodynamic principles and flight rules and regulations
Aviation Supplemental Test (AST)	34*	25	Contains a variety of items similar to those found in the other subtests

*Number of items in the AST varies

The following section provides more detailed information about each one of the six subtests:

① **Math Skills Test (MST):** Tests both equations and word problems. Requires solving for variables, time and distance problems, and the estimation of simple probabilities. Assesses ability to understand basic arithmetic operations, variables, fractions, roots, exponentiation, and the calculation of angles, area, and perimeter of geometric shapes.

② **Reading Skills Test (RST):** Test takers determine which response options can be inferred from the passage itself. It is important that test takers remember that incorrect response options may still appear to be "true," even though only one answer can be correct.

③ **Mechanical Comprehension Test (MCT):** Gauges test takers' knowledge of principles related to gases and liquids, and their understanding of the ways in which these properties affect pressure, volume, and velocity. Tests understanding of the components and performance of engines, principles of electricity, gears, weight distribution, and the operation of simple machines, such as pulleys and fulcrums.

④ **Spatial Apperception Test (SAT):** Consists of a view from inside the cockpit, which the test takers must match to one of five external views. Captures the ability to visualize the orientation of objects in three-dimensional space.

⑤ **Aviation and Nautical Information Test (ANIT):** Of all the ASTB subtests, ANIT scores are the most easily improved by study because it is largely a test of knowledge, rather than aptitude.

⑥ **Aviation Supplemental Test (AST):** The final subtest of the ASTB, it will typically contain a variety of items that are similar in format and content to the items in the preceding subtests.

Testing Policies

Examinees who wish to improve their scores on the ASTB must wait until the thirty-first day following their initial attempt before taking different versions of the test. For example, an individual who takes Form 3 during his or her first administration must take Form 4 or Form 5 during the second testing session (form numbers refer to different versions of the test). A third and final attempt at Form 3, 4, or 5 is authorized on the ninety-first day following the first retest. These test interval requirements cannot be waived, so it is important that examinees are aware of the forms they have taken during previous administrations and the amount of time that has passed between administrations.

A major change regarding the administration of the ASTB was the establishment in July 2004 of a three-test lifetime limit. An examinee may take each version of the test (Form 3, Form 4, and Form 5) only once, which means that an individual will be allowed to take the ASTB only three times during his or her lifetime. Examinees must take a different form during each retest, but the forms can be taken in any order. This limit applies only to Forms 3, 4, and 5. If an individual took a previous version of the test (Forms 1 and 2, which are no longer in use), it is not counted against this limit.

Illegal Testing

An examinee who retests too early or retests using a form that he or she has already taken will generate an illegal test. This means that the individual will not receive valid scores for that administration. However, the illegal test is still counted against the individual's lifetime limit.

SUMMING IT UP

- The military will judge your suitability, at least in part, by the outcome of a standardized test. This test may also serve to determine your suitability for certain officer occupations. Depending on which commissioning program you apply to, you might not take an officer candidate test until after you have been accepted.

- The Armed Services Vocational Aptitude Battery (ASVAB) is used by every branch of the Armed Services to determine suitability for enlistment and training. The Army and the Marine Corps use the ASVAB as an officer candidate test. There are nine ASVAB subtests: General Science, Arithmetic Reasoning, Word Knowledge, Paragraph Comprehension, Mathematics Knowledge, Electronics Information, Auto and Shop Information, Mechanical Comprehension, and Assembling Objects.

- Some service branches accept SAT or ACT scores in lieu of a specific officer candidate test.

- The Air Force Officer Qualifying Test (AFOQT) is used to evaluate applicants for officer commissioning programs, such as Officer Training School (OTS) or Air Force Reserve Officer Training Corps (Air Force ROTC), and for selection into specific training programs, such as pilot and navigator training.

- The complete AFOQT takes approximately 3½ hours to administer and contains 250 cognitive test questions and 220 Self-Description questions. The AFOQT is divided into twelve subtests: Verbal Analogies, Arithmetic Reasoning, Word Knowledge, Math Knowledge, Instrument Comprehension, Block Counting, Table Reading, Aviation Information, General Science, Rotated Blocks, Hidden Figures, and the Self-Description Inventory. Test results are given in these five areas: Pilot, Navigator, Academic Aptitude, Verbal, Quantitative (Math).

- In the past the Army administered its own version of the AFOQT called the Army Officer Candidate Test (OCT). It now accepts SAT, ACT, or ASVAB results to determine eligibility.

- For those desiring to become Army helicopter pilots, the Army administers the Alternate Flight Aptitude Selection Test (AFAST).

- The Aviation Selection Test Battery (ASTB) is administered by the Navy, Marine Corps, and Coast Guard to help determine suitability for aviation officer candidates. The Navy and Coast Guard also use portions of the ASTB to evaluate candidates for the Navy and Coast Guard OCS programs.

- The ASTB takes approximately 2½ hours to administer and consists of six subtests: Math Skills Test, Reading Skills Test, Mechanical Comprehension Test, Spatial Apperception Test, Aviation and Nautical Information Test, and Aviation Supplemental Test. Applicants may choose to take only the Officer Aptitude Rating (OAR) portion of the exam which includes the Math Skills Test, Reading Skills Test, and Mechanical Comprehension Test, if they do not wish to be considered for pilot training.

- Examinees who wish to improve their scores on the ASTB must wait until the thirty-first day following their initial attempt, before taking a different version of the test. An examinee may take each version of the test (Form 3, Form 4, and Form 5) only once.

PART IV

PREPARING FOR AND TAKING THE OFFICER CANDIDATE TESTS

Preparing to Take the Officer Candidate Tests

chapter 9

OVERVIEW

- **About multiple-choice tests**
- **Tips for taking computer-adaptive tests**
- **Get ready for test day**
- **Seven strategies for taking the officer candidate test**
- **Summing it up**

Chances are if you are reading this book you have already begun the application process for a commissioning program. If you haven't done so already, now would be a good time to contact a recruiter or admissions counselor. It is important that you understand the requirements of the service and commissioning program for which you wish to apply. Also make sure that you know the test requirements, so you do not waste time studying material that will not be on your test.

Following the instructions of your recruiter or admissions counselor will help you ensure that everything goes smoothly on the test day. You may be required to produce identifying documents, such as your Social Security card, a copy of your birth certificate, your driver's license, and so on.

ABOUT MULTIPLE-CHOICE TESTS

Millions of people take multiple-choice exams every year. You have probably taken at least one, such as the SAT® or ACT®. Educational institutions, government agencies, industry, and the military all use multiple-choice exams to measure candidate aptitude, achievement, specific knowledge, and essential skills. Test scores are used to determine eligibility for school exams and admissions, scholarships, employment in public and private sectors, and suitability for military service.

Because multiple-choice tests are extremely versatile and can be easily and reliably scored, and because test results are highly suitable for statistical analysis, research, and development, they are widely used throughout U.S. military branches.

Most multiple-choice tests administered by the military contain four or five options per question, although some may include fewer options. Examples of two-option test items are true/false, right/wrong, agree/disagree, like/dislike, or yes/no questions. This type is commonly used to determine characteristics or traits, such as opinions or preferences.

The following is an example of a typical multiple-choice question with four options:

The U.S. president's place of residence in Washington, D.C., is called
_____

(A) the President's Mansion.

(B) the House of Representatives.

(C) the Washington Monument.

(D) the White House.

The Stem of a test item either asks a question or states a problem. In the above example, the stem is the phrase "The U.S. president's place of residence in Washington, D.C., is called."

The Choices (options) represent all available answer choices or solutions to a question. In the example above, choices (A), (B), (C), and (D) are all answer choices.

The Distracters (foils) are incorrect answer choices. Often they are worded in such a way as to make you think that they may be the correct answer, even if you know that another one is correct. Do you know which of the answer choices in the above example are distracters?

The Key (correct answer) is, obviously, the only correct answer to the stem. In this example, the key is choice (D). That means that the distracters—the answer choices that are incorrect—are choices (A), (B), and (C).

TIPS FOR TAKING COMPUTER-ADAPTIVE TESTS

If you'll be taking the Armed Services Vocational Aptitude Battery (ASVAB), you may be taking the computerized version, called the CAT-ASVAB, rather than the paper-and-pencil version. In the paper-and-pencil ASVAB, all test-takers, regardless of their ability, take the same questions. Although the content of the test varies only slightly between this format and the CAT-ASVAB—the Automotive and Shop Information subject test is split into two separate tests in the CAT-ASVAB—the main difference is that the CAT-ASVAB is adaptive, which means that it tailors questions to the ability level of each test taker.

For example, the first test question is in the middle ability range—not too difficult and not too easy. If you answer it correctly, the next question will be more difficult. If you answer it incorrectly, the next question is less difficult. The CAT-ASVAB continues this way until your proficiency level is determined. You will answer questions that are appropriate for your ability level, so you will not waste time answering questions that are too easy or too difficult for you. However, you will not be able to skip a question or go back to check your answers, as you might do on a paper-and-pencil ASVAB.

Advantages of Computer-Adaptive Tests:

- Length of the test session is reduced.
- The test can be scored immediately.
- Scoring errors are reduced, and score accuracy is increased.

- Test security is higher.
- Periodic review and refinement of test items is readily and easily conducted.
- Administration is more flexible; you do not need to wait for the next scheduled test administration to take your test.

Disadvantages of Computer-Adaptive Tests:

- Test takers cannot skip around or go back to an earlier part of the exam to change or check an answer.
- Test takers cannot review their answers at the end of the test.

Unlike the paper-and-pencil subtest raw scores, computer-adaptive subtest raw scores are not equal to the total number of correct answers. Computer-adaptive test scores are computed using formulas that take into account the difficulty of each test item and the correctness of the answer. Both paper-and-pencil raw scores and computer-adaptive raw scores are calculated so that they are equivalent to one another.

It is up to you to decide which version of the exam you want to take. Be sure that you choose the one you feel more comfortable with, so you can increase your chances of scoring high on test day.

GET READY FOR TEST DAY

The Night Before the Test:

- Get plenty of sleep.
- Avoid alcohol, caffeine, or any substance that may prevent your getting a good night's sleep.

On Test Day:

- Eat a light breakfast if testing in the morning or a light lunch if testing in the afternoon.
- Make sure you know exactly where to report for the test and how you will get there. If the area is unfamiliar to you, you may want to consider taking a "dry run" a few days before test day.
- Leave home in plenty of time to arrive at least 15 minutes before you're scheduled to report to the test center. Remember to take into account traffic delays and/or problems with your vehicle or other transportation.
- Be sure to bring everything you need for the exam: Number 2 pencils (with good erasers), proof of identification, a watch, and anything else you were instructed to take to the test. (Usually, pencils and scratch paper are provided at the test center.)
- If you do not feel well on the day of the test, try to reschedule if possible. You want to do your best on the officer candidate exam, so you should be feeling your best.
- Drink sparingly; you do not want the distraction of having to use the rest room during the test. Besides wasting valuable testing time, you may lose your momentum, which may adversely affect your score.
- Try to prepare for the unexpected. For example, if you wear contact lenses, bring a backup pair of eyeglasses.

- If you are given a choice of where you can sit in the testing room, find a seat where you will be most comfortable and least distracted. If you are left-handed and taking a paper-and-pencil exam, for example, seek a desk or table with a left return or ask whether any are available.

- Dress in layers so that you can adjust to the room temperature and stay comfortable. If the room is too cold or too hot, alert the test proctor.

- Keep track of the time—but don't spend too much time looking at your watch or the clock.

- Listen carefully to all instructions given by the test proctor. If you don't understand something, don't be embarrassed to ask for clarification.

- If you're taking a paper-and-pencil exam, go back and check your answers if you have spare time, and make sure you have not skipped any questions. Be aware, however, that your first response is generally your best, so only change your answer if you're absolutely sure that you answered incorrectly the first time. If you are only second-guessing, chances are you're better off leaving your answer choice as it is.

- Use all the time allotted for each section. If you finish a section early (on paper-and-pencil exams), review all of your answers in that section.

Try to relax. If you've properly prepared, you will do well—so don't stress out.

SEVEN STRATEGIES FOR TAKING THE OFFICER CANDIDATE TEST

Let's review some general strategies for taking your officer candidate test. Even if you've read these elsewhere or they seem like common sense to you, it's a good idea to reinforce them in your mind. Please review the following seven strategies:

❶ **Know your optimal pace and stay at it.** Time is definitely a factor in multiple-choice exams. On certain sections, you may find that to complete all the questions, you need to work at a quicker pace than is comfortable for you. Check your pace after every few questions and adjust it accordingly so that you have time to at least consider every question. The best way to avoid the time squeeze is to practice under timed conditions before you take the actual exam. This will give you a sense of what your optimal pace should be.

❷ **If you're not sure about an answer, don't dwell on it—move on.** This follows logically from the first tip. You might find yourself reluctant to leave a question until you're sure your answer is correct. While this is admirable, doing this under the time conditions of the test will only defeat you. Remember: You can miss *some* questions and still earn a high score.

❸ **Make educated guesses—but avoid random guesswork if possible.** Some multiple-choice exams levy penalty points or fractions of points on questions you answer incorrectly. In those cases, guessing at an answer could hurt your overall score. The officer candidate tests do not assess penalty points—so it makes sense to make an educated guess rather than leaving the question unanswered. This means that you should always try to eliminate obvious wrong-answer choices first; then go with your hunch. On multiple-choice questions, eliminating even one possible answer improves your odds of answering correctly. If you're out of time and haven't answered every available question, though, there's no advantage to making random guesses at the remaining questions.

❹ **Read each question in its entirety.** Beware: Some multiple-choice questions offer wrong-answer choices that may seem correct if you haven't read the entire question and all the answer choices thoroughly. Unless you're running out of time, make sure you read every question from start to finish, and never confirm an answer unless you've first compared it with all the other answer choices for that question.

⑤ **Maintain an active mindset.** When taking an exam such as the officer candidate test, it's easy to fall into a "passive" mode in which you scan answer choices and hope that the correct answer "jumps out" at you as you do so. Fight this tendency by keeping your mind engaged while reading each question. Remember, each question on the officer candidate test is designed to measure a specific ability or skill. Try to adopt an active, investigative approach to answering the questions. Ask yourself: What skill is the question measuring? What is the most direct thought process for determining the correct response? How might I be tripped up on this type of question if I'm not careful?

⑥ **Use your pencil and scratch paper.** Scratch work helps keep your mind in active mode. Make brief notes, draw simple diagrams and flow charts, and scribble equations and geometry figures. All of this will help you think clearly.

⑦ **Know the test directions thoroughly.** It bears repeating: *Always* read directions for each test section completely and thoroughly before answering any questions in that section.

SUMMING IT UP

- If you've already begun the application process for a commissioning program, make sure to contact a recruiter or admissions counselor to confirm the requirements of the service and commissioning program in which you're interested. Find out what your test requirements are so you do not waste time studying material that will not be on your test.

- Educational institutions, government agencies, industry, and the military use multiple-choice exams to measure candidate aptitude, achievement, specific knowledge, and essential skills. Test scores determine eligibility for school exams and admissions, scholarships, employment in public and private sectors, and suitability for military service.

- Multiple-choice tests are widely used throughout U.S. military branches. Most multiple-choice tests administered by the military contain four or five options per question, although some may include fewer options. Examples of two-option test items are true/false, right/wrong, agree/disagree, like/dislike, or yes/no questions, commonly used to determine characteristics or traits, such as opinions or preferences.

- A typical multiple-choice question includes a stem, which asks a question or states a problem; the choices, which represent all available answer choices or solutions to the question; distracters, which are incorrect answer choices; and the key, which is the only correct answer to the stem.

- If you're taking the Armed Services Vocational Aptitude Battery (ASVAB), you have a choice of taking the computerized version, called the CAT-ASVAB, or the paper-and-pencil version. The CAT-ASVAB is adaptive: It tailors questions to the ability level of each test-taker. Among the advantages of taking the CAT-ASVAB: the length of the test session is reduced; the test can be scored immediately; scoring errors are reduced and score accuracy is increased; test security is higher; and periodic review and refinement of test items is readily and easily conducted. Among the drawbacks: Test takers cannot skip around or go back to an earlier part of the exam to change or check an answer, and test takers cannot review their answers at the end of the test.

- To be at your best on test day, follow the tips in this chapter, such as planning out your route to the test center ahead of time and getting plenty of sleep the night before exam day.

- Follow the commonsense strategies listed in this chapter for taking the officer candidate exam: Know your optimal pace and stay at it; don't dwell on an answer if you're not sure about it; make educated guesses but avoid random guesswork; read each question in its entirety; maintain an active mindset; use your pencil and scratch paper; and thoroughly familiarize yourself with all test directions.

Types of Questions Used for Selecting Officer Candidates

chapter 10

OVERVIEW

- Synonyms
- Verbal Analogies
- Reading Comprehension
- Arithmetic Reasoning
- Math Knowledge
- General Science
- Electronics Information
- Mechanical Comprehension
- Summing it up

SYNONYMS

Synonym questions appear as five-option items in the Word Knowledge subtest of the Air Force Officer Qualifying Test (AFOQT). They also appear as four-option items in the Word Knowledge subtest of the Armed Services Vocational Aptitude Battery (ASVAB).

Synonyms are commonly used to measure breadth of vocabulary or word knowledge. For each word given (they are usually capitalized, underlined, or italicized), you are required to select from the available options the choice that is the same or most nearly the same in meaning. The usual dictionary definition is required only if the word is presented alone. If the word appears in a sentence, then the contextual meaning of the word is required.

Consider all options before answering the question. Although several options might have some connection with the key word, the closest in meaning to the key word is the correct answer.

Sample Items (five options)

S1. SUCCUMB means most nearly to
   (A) aid
   (B) be discouraged
   (C) check
   (D) oppose
   (E) yield

The correct answer is (E). To *succumb* means "to cease to resist before a superior strength or overpowering desire or force." Choice (E) is the only one that means almost the same as *succumb*.

S2. SUBSUME means most nearly to

(A) belong

(B) cover

(C) include

(D) obliterate

(E) understate

The correct answer is (C). To *subsume* is "to include within a larger class or category." Of all of the options given, choice (C) is closest in meaning to *subsume*.

Sample Items (four options)

S3. DEFICIENT means most nearly

(A) sufficient

(B) outstanding

(C) inadequate

(D) bizarre

The correct answer is (C). Of the options given, *inadequate* is the only one that is synonymous with *deficient*.

S4. "The *rear* compartment is locked." The word *rear* as used in the sentence means most nearly

(A) raised

(B) upright

(C) high

(D) back

The correct answer is (D). As used in the sentence, the word *rear* most nearly means *back*.

VERBAL ANALOGIES

Verbal analogy questions appear as five-option items in the Verbal Analogies subtest of the AFOQT.

Verbal Analogy questions test not only your knowledge of word meanings and your vocabulary level, but also your ability to reason; that is, to see the relationships between words and the ideas they represent. To determine such relationships, you must know the meaning of each word in the first given pair and figure out the precise relationship between these two words. Then you must complete the analogy by selecting the pair of words that best expresses a relationship similar to that expressed by the first two paired words.

Two forms of verbal analogy questions are in general use:

1. The first pair of words and the first word of the second pair are provided. Of the given options, only one best expresses a relationship to the third word that is similar to that expressed between the first two words.
   MAN is to BOY as WOMAN is to

   (A) baby

   (B) bride

   (C) child

   (D) girl

   (E) lad

2. Only the first pair of words is provided. Answer choices each consist of a pair of words.
   MAN is to BOY as

   (A) adult is to girl

   (B) bride is to groom

   (C) lass is to child

   (D) woman is to youth

   (E) woman is to girl

Let's analyze the first analogy form given above. What is the relationship of the first two paired words?

MAN: member of the human race, male, mature
BOY: member of the human race, male, young

Both are male members of the human race. MAN is mature; BOY is young.

What is the meaning of the word WOMAN and each of the words appearing in the options?

WOMAN: member of the human race, female, mature

baby: member of the human race, either male or female, very young
bride: member of the human race, female, about to be married or newly married
child: member of the human race, either male or female, young
girl: member of the human race, female, young
lad: member of the human race, male, young

To complete the analogy with WOMAN as the first word, we need a term denoting a young female member of the human race.

Choice (A) is incorrect because *baby* can be male or female and is very young. Choice (B) is incorrect because *bride* is a special kind of female—one about to be married or newly married. If GROOM had been substituted for BOY in the first half of the analogy, then *bride* would have been the proper choice. Choice (C) is incorrect because *child* might be male or female. Choice (E) is incorrect because *lad* is a male.

Choice (D) is the correct choice because *girl* denotes a young female member of the human race.

The correct answer is (E). Analyzing the second analogy form given above, again we find that the relationship of MAN is to BOY, is that both are male members of the human race: MAN is mature; and BOY is young. Of the choices given, the only similar relationship is WOMAN (member of the human race, female, and mature) to GIRL (member of the human race, female, and young).

Relationships commonly found in verbal analogies are as follows:

RELATIONSHIP	EXAMPLE
synonyms	brochure : pamphlet
antonyms	victory : defeat
homonyms	hale : hail
measurement (time, distance, weight, volume, etc.)	distance : mile
location (in, at, near)	Boston : Massachusetts
numerical	ten : dime
cause : effect	burn : blister
whole : part	ship : keel
object : purpose or function	pencil : write
object : user	saw : carpenter
creator : creation	composer : opera
raw material : final product	cotton : dress
female : male	goose : gander
general : specific	fruit : apple
larger : smaller	river : stream
more : less (degree)	hot : warm
early stage : later stage	larva : pupa

Grammatical Relationships

Noun

singular : plural	child : children

Pronoun

singular : plural	she : they
nominative : objective	he : him
first person : third person	we : they

Verb

tense	fly : flown

Adjective

comparative	bad : worse
superlative	little : least

Different Parts of Speech

noun : adjective	dog : canine
adjective : adverb	good : well

Be careful! The order of the two words in the second pair must be in the same sequence as the order of words in the first pair. As in mathematical proportions, reversing the sequence of the second pair of words breaks the relationship between the two and makes it no longer analogous. The following example demonstrates the importance of the order of the words:

2 is to 5 as 4 is to 10 (correct)
2 is to 5 as 10 is to 4 (incorrect)

MAN is to BOY as WOMAN is to GIRL (correct)
MAN is to BOY as GIRL is to WOMAN (incorrect)

Sample Items (five options)

Each of the following sample items consists of an incomplete analogy. Select the answer that best completes the analogy developed at the beginning of each question.

S1. BOTANY is to PLANTS as ENTOMOLOGY is to

   (A) animals

   (B) climate

   (C) diseases

   (D) languages

   (E) insects

The correct answer is (E). *Botany* is the study of *plants*; *entomology* is the study of *insects*.

S2. EPILOGUE is to PROLOGUE as

   (A) appendix is to index

   (B) appendix is to preface

   (C) preface is to footnote

   (D) preface is to table of contents

   (E) table of contents is to index

The correct answer is (B). *Epilogue* is a closing section added to a novel or a play; *prologue* is an introduction to a novel or a play. *Appendix* is material added after the end of a book; *preface* is an introduction to a book.

S3. OCTAGON is to SQUARE as HEXAGON is to

   (A) cube

   (B) military

   (C) pyramid

   (D) rectangle

   (E) triangle

The correct answer is (E). *Octagon* is an eight-sided figure; *square* is a four-sided figure (one-half of eight). *Hexagon* is a six-sided figure; *triangle* is a three-sided figure (one-half of six).

S4. GLOW is to BLAZE as

   (A) compact is to sprawling

   (B) eager is to reluctant

   (C) glance is to stare

   (D) hint is to clue

   (E) wicked is to naughty

The correct answer is (C). *Glow* is steady subdued light; *blaze* is intensely bright light. *Glance* is to look briefly; *stare* is to gaze intently.

S5. WATER is to THIRST as FOOD is to

(A) famine

(B) grief

(C) hunger

(D) indigestion

(E) Scarcity

The correct answer is (C). *Water* satisfies *thirst*; *food* satisfies *hunger*.

READING COMPREHENSION

Paragraph comprehension questions appear as four-option items in the Reading Skills Test subtest of the ASVAB.

Sentence comprehension questions appear in the Reading Skills Test of the Navy and Marine Corps Aviation Selection Test Battery.

The ability to read and understand written or printed material is an important skill. Reading comprehension tests present passages that vary in length from one sentence to several paragraphs, followed by one or more questions about each passage. The reading selections are usually samples of the type of material that you would be required to read, whether at military school or on the job.

The following six examples are some of the common types of reading comprehension items:

1. Finding specific information or directly stated detail in the reading passage.

   Although this type is commonly found in elementary-level tests, it is also found in intermediate-level tests such as the Armed Services Vocational Aptitude Battery. At the intermediate levels, the vocabulary is more difficult, the reading passages are of greater complexity, and the questions posed are much more complicated.

Samples:

Helping to prevent accidents is the responsibility of _____.
The principal reason for issuing traffic summonses is to _____.
The reason for maintaining ongoing safety education is that _____.

2. Recognizing the central theme, the main idea, or concept expressed in the passage.

   Although questions of this type may be phrased differently, they generally require that you summarize or otherwise ascertain the principal purpose or idea expressed in the reading passage. In addition to reading and understanding, the ability to analyze and interpret written material is necessary. Some questions require the ability to combine separate ideas or concepts found in the reading passage to reach the correct answer. Other questions merely require drawing a conclusion that is equivalent to a restatement of the main idea or concept expressed in the passage.

Samples:

The most appropriate title for the above passage is _____.
The best title for this paragraph would be _____.
This paragraph is mainly about _____.
The passage best supports the statement that _____.
The passage means most nearly that _____.

3. Determining the meaning of certain words as used in context.

   The particular meaning of a word as used in the passage requires an understanding of the central or main theme of the reading passage, as well as the idea being conveyed by the sentence containing the word.

Samples:

The word ...... as used in this passage means _____.
The expression ...... as used in the passage means _____.

4. Finding implications or drawing inferences from a stated idea.

   This type of item requires the ability to understand the stated idea and then to reason by logical thinking to the implied or inferred idea. *Implied* means not exactly stated but merely suggested; *inferred* means derived by reasoning. Although the terms are somewhat similar in meaning, *inferred* implies being further removed from the stated idea. Much greater reasoning ability is required to arrive at the proper inference.

Samples:

Which of the following is implied by the above passage?
Of the following, the most valid implication of the above paragraph is _____.
The author probably believes that _____.
It can be inferred from the above passage that _____.
The best of the following inferences that can be made is that _____.

5. Sentence completion items.

   Sentence completion items are considered to be both vocabulary items and reading comprehension items. They are considered to be vocabulary items as they test the ability to understand and use words. However, they also measure an important aspect of reading comprehension: the ability to understand the implications of a sentence or a paragraph.

   Sentence completion items consist of a sentence or paragraph in which one or two words are missing. The omissions are indicated by a blank underlined space _____. You must read and understand the sentence or paragraph as given and then select the option that best completes the idea of the reading passage. Your choice must also be consistent in style and logic with other elements in the sentence.

Sample:

Select the lettered option that best completes the thought expressed in the sentence.

6. Word substitution items.

   Word substitution items are very similar to sentence completion items and are also considered both vocabulary and reading comprehension items. These items consist of a sentence or paragraph in which a key word has been changed. The changed word is incorrect, and it is not in keeping with the meaning that the sentence is intended to convey. Determine which word is used incorrectly. Then select from the choices that, when substituted for the incorrectly used word, would best convey the meaning of the sentence or paragraph.

Eight General Suggestions for Answering Reading Comprehension Questions:

❶ Scan the passage to determine the general intent of the reading selection.

❷ Reread the passage carefully to understand the main idea and any related ideas. If necessary for comprehension, reread the passage again.

❸ Read each question carefully and base your answer only on the material in the reading passage. Be careful to base your answer on what is stated, implied, or inferred. Do not be influenced by your opinions, personal feelings, or any information not expressed or implied in the reading passage.

❹ Options that are partly true and partly false are incorrect.

❺ Be very observant for such words as *least, greatest, first, not,* etc., appearing in the preamble of the question.

❻ Be suspicious of options containing words such as *all, always, every, forever, never, none, wholly,* and so on.

❼ Be sure to consider all answer choices before selecting the one you believe is correct.

❽ Speed is an important consideration in answering reading comprehension questions. Try to proceed as rapidly as you can without sacrificing careful thinking or reasoning.

Paragraph Comprehension
Sample Items (five options)

For each of the following sample five-option questions, select the option that best completes the statement or answers the question.

S1. The rates of vibration perceived by the ears as musical tones lie between fairly well-defined limits. In the ear, as in the eye, there are individual variations. However, variations are more marked in the ear, because its range of perception is greater.

The paragraph best supports the statement that the ear

(A) is limited by the nature of its variations.

(B) is the most sensitive of the auditory organs.

(C) differs from the eye in its broader range of perception.

(D) is sensitive to a great range of musical tones.

(E) depends for its sense on the rate of vibration of a limited range of sound waves.

The correct answer is (C). The passage makes the point that individual differences in auditory range are greater than individual differences in visual range because the total range of auditory perception is greater. Although the statements made by choices (D) and (E) are both correct, neither expresses the main point of the reading passage.

S2. The propaganda of a nation at war is designed to stimulate the energy of its citizens and their will to win, and to imbue them with an overwhelming sense of the justice of their cause. Directed abroad, its purpose is to create precisely contrary effects among citizens of enemy nations and to assure to nationals of allied or subjugated countries full and unwavering assistance.

The title below that best expresses the ideas of this passage is

(A) "Propaganda's Failure."

(B) "Designs for Waging War."

(C) "Influencing Opinion in Wartime."

(D) "The Propaganda of Other Nations."

(E) "Citizens of Enemy Nations and Their Allies."

The correct answer is (C). The theme of this passage is influencing opinion in wartime, both at home and abroad.

Answer the following two sample questions on the basis of the information contained in the passage below.

I have heard it suggested that the "upper class" English accent has been of value in maintaining the British Empire and Commonwealth. The argument runs that all manner of folk in distant places, understanding the English language, will catch in this accent the notes of tradition, pride, and authority and so will be suitably impressed. This might have been the case some nine or ten decades ago, but it is certainly not true now. The accent is more likely to be a liability than an asset.

S3. The title below that best expresses the ideas of this passage is

(A) "Changed Effects of a 'British Accent'."

(B) "Prevention of the Spread of Cockney."

(C) "The Affected Language of Royalty."

(D) "The Decline of the British Empire."

(E) "The 'King's English'."

S4. According to the author, the "upper class" English accent

(A) has been imitated all over the world.

(B) has been inspired by British royalty.

(C) has brought about the destruction of the British Commonwealth.

(D) might have caused arguments among the folk in distant corners of the Empire.

(E) might have helped to perpetuate the British Empire before 1900.

In S3, **the correct answer is (A).** The last two sentences of the reading passage indicate that the folk in distant places might have been suitably impressed decades ago, but they are not impressed now.

In S4, **the correct answer is (E).** The "upper class" English accent might have been of value in maintaining the British Empire nine or ten decades ago (or before 1900).

Sample Items (four options)

For each of the following sample four-option questions, select the choice that best completes the statement or answers the question.

S5. The view is widely held that butter is more digestible and better absorbed than other fats because of its low melting point. There is little scientific authority for such a view. As margarine is made today, its melting point is close to that of butter, and tests show only the slightest degree of difference in digestibility of fats of equally low melting points.

The paragraph best supports the statement that

(A) butter is more easily digested than margarine.

(B) the concept that butter has a lower melting point than other fats is a common misconception, disproved by scientists.

(C) there is not much difference in the digestibility of butter and margarine.

(D) most people prefer butter to margarine.

The correct answer is (C). The passage states that the melting points of butter and margarine are similar and that therefore they are about equally digestible.

Answer the following two sample questions on the basis of the information contained in the passage below.

Science made its first great contribution to war with gunpowder. But because gunpowder can be used effectively only in suitable firearms, science also had to develop the iron and steel that were required to manufacture muskets and cannon on a huge scale. To this day, metallurgy receives much inspiration from war. Bessemer steel was the direct outcome of the deficiencies of artillery as they were revealed by the Crimean War. Concern with the expansion and pressure of gases in guns and combustibility of powder aroused interest in the laws of gases and other matters that seemingly have no relation whatever to war.

S6. The title below that best expresses the ideas of this passage is

(A) "Gunpowder, the First Great Invention."

(B) "How War Stimulates Science."

(C) "Improvement of Artillery."

(D) "The Crimean War and Science."

S7. An outcome of the Crimean War was the

(A) invention of gunpowder.

(B) origin of metallurgy.

(C) study of the laws of gases.

(D) use of muskets and cannon.

In S6, **the correct answer is (B).** The basic theme of the reading passage is that science contributes to the war effort and that war stimulates science research.

In S7, **the correct answer is (C).** The last sentence in the reading passage indicates that interest in the laws of gases arose as a direct outcome of artillery deficiencies revealed by the Crimean War.

S8. We find many instances in early science of "a priori" scientific reasoning. Scientists thought it proper to carry generalizations from one field to another. It was assumed that the planets revolved in circles because of the geometrical simplicity of the circle. Even Newton assumed that there must be seven primary colors corresponding to the seven tones of the musical scale.

The paragraph best supports the statement that

(A) Newton sometimes used the "a priori" method of investigation.

(B) scientists no longer consider it proper to uncritically carry over generalizations from one field to another.

(C) the planets revolve about the earth in ellipses rather than in circles.

(D) even great men like Newton sometimes make mistakes.

The correct answer is (B). The tone of the passage and the choice of illustrations showing the fallacy of "a priori" reasoning make it evident that scientists no longer carry generalizations automatically from one field to another. Choices (A) and (D) are true statements, but they are only illustrative points. Choice (B) carries the real message of the passage.

Sentence Comprehension

Sample Items (five options)

Question S9 consists of a sentence with a blank space, indicating that a word has been omitted. Beneath the sentence are five lettered options. Select the option that, when inserted in the sentence, best fits in with the meaning of the sentence as a whole.

S9. If the weather report forecasts fog and smoke, we can anticipate having _____.

(A) rain

(B) sleet

(C) smog

(D) snow

(E) thunder

The correct answer is (C). A mixture of fog and smoke is called smog.

Question S10 consists of a sentence with two blank spaces, each blank indicating that a word has been omitted. Beneath the sentence are five lettered sets of words. Choose the set of words that, when inserted in the sentence, best fits in with the meaning of the sentence as a whole.

S10. Although the publicity has been _____, the film itself is intelligent, well-acted, handsomely produced, and altogether _____.

(A) extensive . . . arbitrary

(B) tasteless . . . respectable

(C) sophisticated . . . amateurish

(D) risqué . . . crude

(E) perfect . . . spectacular

The correct answer is (B). The correct answer should involve two words that are more or less opposite in meaning, as the word *although* suggests that the publicity was not representative of the film. Another clue to the correct answer is that the second word should have the same connotations as the words "intelligent, well-acted, handsomely produced." Choices (A), (D), and (E) are not opposites. Choice (C) cannot be the correct answer even though the words in it are nearly opposites, because if the film is intelligent, well-acted, and handsomely produced, it is not amateurish. Only choice (B), when inserted in the sentence, produces a logical statement.

Question S11 consists of a quotation that contains one word that is incorrectly used, because it is not in keeping with the meaning that the quotation is intended to convey. Determine which word is incorrectly used. Then select from the lettered options the word that, when substituted for the incorrectly used word, would best convey the intended meaning of the quotation.

S11. "College placement officials have frequently noted the contradiction that exists between the public statements of the company president who questions the value of a liberal arts background in the business world and the practice of his recruiters who seek specialized training for particular jobs."

    (A) admissions

    (B) praises

    (C) reject

    (D) science

    (E) technical

The correct answer is (B). A careful reading of the passage shows no inconsistency until the word *questions* is reached. If a contradiction exists and the recruiters seek specialized training, the company president would accept, endorse, or praise rather than question the value of a liberal arts background. Choice (B) appears to be the proper substitute that would best convey the intended meaning of the quotation. *Contradiction* is used properly, as none of the options can be substituted for it. Although *reject* might appear to be an appropriate substitution for *seek*, it does not help convey the intended meaning of the quotation.

Sample Items (four options)

Question S12 consists of a sentence in which one word is omitted. Select the lettered option that best completes the thought expressed in the sentence.

S12. Although her argument was logical, her conclusion was _____.

    (A) illegible

    (B) natural

    (C) positive

    (D) unreasonable

The correct answer is (D). When a subordinate clause begins with *although*, the thought expressed in the main clause will not be consistent with that contained in the subordinate clause. If the argument was *logical*, the conclusion would be illogical. Of the options given, *unreasonable* is the only opposite to *logical*.

Question S13 consists of a sentence with two blank spaces, each blank indicating that a word or figure has been omitted. Select one of the lettered options that, when inserted in the sentence, best completes the thought expressed in the sentence as a whole.

S13. The height of a 5-foot, 10-inch person in the _____ system would be approximately _____ meters.

    (A) English . . . 1.78

    (B) English . . . 2.00

    (C) metric . . . 1.78

    (D) metric . . . 2.00

    The correct answer is (C). Feet and inches are used in the English system; meters are used in the metric system. Accordingly, choices (A) and (B) are eliminated immediately. A meter is equivalent to a little less than 40 inches, so the correct answer must be around 1.75. The only choice in this range is (C).

Question S14 consists of a quotation that contains one word that is incorrectly used, because it is not in keeping with the meaning that the quotation is intended to convey. Determine which word is used incorrectly. Then select from the lettered options the word that, when substituted for the incorrectly used word, would best help convey the intended meaning of the quotation.

S14. "In manufacturing a fabric-measuring device, it is advisable to use a type of cloth whose length is highly susceptible to changes of temperature, tension, etc."

    (A) decreases

    (B) increases

    (C) instrument

    (D) not

    The correct answer is (D). A careful reading of the passage shows no inconsistency until the word *highly* appears. To give a true measure, the device's length should not change with temperature or tension but should be constant.

For Question S15, select the option that best completes the statement or answers the question.

S15. "Look before you leap."

    The statement means most nearly that you should

    (A) always be alert.

    (B) always be carefree.

    (C) move quickly but carefully.

    (D) proceed rapidly when directed.

    The correct answer is (C). This proverb does not state or imply that you should always be alert or carefree or that you should proceed quickly when directed. It says that you should move quickly but carefully.

ARITHMETIC REASONING

Questions on arithmetic reasoning appear as five-option items in the AFOQT subtest and in the Math Skills Test of the Navy and Marine Corps Aviation Selection Test Battery (ASTB). They also appear as four-option items in the Armed Services Vocational Aptitude Battery subtest.

Arithmetic reasoning is concerned with solving mathematical problems. It requires the recognition and application of basic mathematical processes and operations in problems encountered in everyday life. Processes or operations required for solution rather than computational complexity are generally emphasized.

The following samples illustrate the types of arithmetic reasoning questions found on military tests.

Sample Items (five options)

S1. Which of the following amounts of money has the greatest value?

(A) 3 quarters

(B) 8 dimes

(C) 15 nickels

(D) 1 quarter, 3 dimes, and 4 nickels

(E) 4 dimes, 7 nickels, and 4 pennies

The correct answer is (B). Computing the value of the coins in each option proves that choice (B) has the greatest value.

$3 \times 25¢ = 75¢$

$8 \times 10¢ = 80¢$

$15 \times 5¢ = 75¢$

$25¢ + 30¢ + 20¢ = 75¢$

$40¢ + 35¢ + 4¢ = 79¢$

S2. Subtract 1 foot, 6 inches from 2 feet, 4 inches.

(A) 8 inches

(B) 10 inches

(C) 1 foot

(D) 1 foot, 2 inches

(E) 1 foot, 4 inches

The correct answer is (B). Two feet, 4 inches is equal to 1 foot, 16 inches. This amount minus 1 foot, 6 inches equals 10 inches.

S3. It costs $1.00 per square yard to waterproof canvas. What will it cost to waterproof a canvas truck cover that is 15′ × 24′?

(A) $20.00

(B) $36.00

(C) $40.00

(D) $360.00

(E) $400.00

The correct answer is (C). 15′ × 24′ = 5 yards × 8 yards = 40 square yards; 40 square yards × $1.00 = $40.00.

S4. Mr. Johnson earns $500 per week. If he spends 20% of his income for rent, 25% for food, and puts 10% in savings, how much is left each week for other expenses?

(A) $225

(B) $240

(C) $250

(D) $260

(E) $275

The correct answer is (A). Fifty-five percent goes for rent, food, and savings; 45 percent is left for other expenses; $500 × 0.45 = $225.

S5. A vessel left a port and sailed west at an average rate of 25 mph. Two hours later, a second vessel left the same port and traveled in the same direction at an average rate of 30 mph. In how many hours did the second vessel overtake the first vessel?

(A) 8 hours

(B) $8\frac{1}{2}$ hours

(C) 9 hours

(D) $9\frac{1}{2}$ hours

(E) 10 hours

The correct answer is (E). In 2 hours, the first vessel would be 50 miles out. Difference in rate is 5 mph. $\frac{50}{5}$ = 10 hours to overtake the first vessel.

Sample Items (four options)

S6. Of the 36 students registered in a class, $\frac{2}{3}$ are females. How many males are registered in the class?

(A) 12

(B) 18

(C) 24

(D) 30

The correct answer is (A). Two-thirds of 36 is 24, the number of females. This number subtracted from 36 gives the number of males.

S7. A team played 24 games, of which it won 18. What percent of the games played did it lose?

(A) 25%

(B) 42%

(C) 50%

(D) 75%

The correct answer is (A). If it won 18 games, it lost 6 games. $\frac{6}{24} = \frac{1}{4} = 0.25$ = 25 percent.

S8. A $75 fund is available for a holiday party. If 75% of the available money is spent for food and beverages, how much is left for other expenses?

(A) $18.75

(B) $28.75

(C) $46.25

(D) $56.25

The correct answer is (A). The amount of money spent is 0.75 times $75, which equals $56.25. $75.00 − $56.25 = $18.75.

S9. A certain employee is paid at the rate of $6.74 per hour with time-and-a-half for overtime. The regular work week is 40 hours. During the past week, the employee put in 44 working hours. What was the employee's gross wages for that week?

(A) $269.60

(B) $296.56

(C) $310.04

(D) $444.84

$$1\tfrac{1}{2} \times \$6.74 = \$\ \ 10.11$$
$$\$6.74 \times 40 = \$269.60$$
$$\$10.11 \times 4 = \underline{\ \ \ \ 40.44}$$
$$\$310.04$$

The correct answer is (C).

S10. If one quart of floor wax covers 400 square feet, how many gallons of wax are needed to wax the floor of a 6,400-sq.-ft. office?

(A) 4 gals.

(B) 8 gals.

(C) 12 gals.

(D) 16 gals.

$1:400 :: x:6400$

$400\,x = 6400$

$\quad x = 16$ (16 quarts of wax are needed.)

The correct answer is (A). There are four quarts to a gallon. Therefore, 16 quarts divided by 4 equals 4 gallons.

MATH KNOWLEDGE

Questions on math knowledge appear as five-option items in the AFOQT subtest and in the Math Skills Test of the Navy and Marine Corps ASTB. Mathematics knowledge questions also appear as four-option items in the ASVAB subtest.

Math knowledge involves the application of mathematical principles and measures the ability to use learned mathematical relationships. The content area may include equation solving; plane/solid geometry; exponents, roots, and powers; conversion of common fractions, decimals, and percents; least common denominators, greatest common factor, and smallest common multiple; prime numbers and factorials; linear equations; and transforming verbal problems into algebraic symbols.

The review of some basic mathematical concepts that follows should be helpful in reinforcing your math knowledge.

Factors of a Product

When two or more numbers are multiplied to produce a certain product, each of the numbers is known as a factor of the product.

$1 \times 8 = 8$ (1 and 8 are factors of the product)
$2 \times 4 = 8$ (2 and 4 are factors of the product)

Base

A base is a number used as a factor two or more times. $2 \times 2 \times 2$ may be written 2^3, which is read "2 cubed" or "2 to the third power." In the equation $2^3 = 8$, 2 is called the base.

Exponent

An exponent is a number that shows how many times the base is to be used as a factor. 10^2 is a short way of writing 10×10. 10 is called the base in 10^2; 2 is called the exponent.

$a^4 = a \times a \times a \times a$ (a is the base, 4 is the exponent)
$5^3 = 5 \times 5 \times 5$ (5 is the base; 3 is the exponent)

Power

A power is a number that can be expressed as a product of equal factors. 3^2 is the second power of 3 (3×3) and is equal to 9. 2^4 is the fourth power of 2 ($2 \times 2 \times 2 \times 2$) and is equal to 16.

Reciprocal

If the product of two numbers is 1, either number is called the reciprocal of the other number. $4 \times \frac{1}{4} = 1$. Therefore, 4 is the reciprocal of $\frac{1}{4}$, and $\frac{1}{4}$ is the reciprocal of 4. $\frac{3}{5} \times \frac{5}{3} = 1$. Therefore, $\frac{3}{5}$ is the reciprocal of $\frac{5}{3}$, and $\frac{5}{3}$ is the reciprocal of $\frac{3}{5}$.

Factorial

The factorial of a natural or counting number is the product of that number and all of the natural numbers less than it. 4 factorial, written as $4! = 4 \times 3 \times 2 \times 1 = 24$.

Prime Number

A prime number is a natural or counting number that is not divisible by any other number except 1 and itself. Examples of prime numbers are 2, 3, 5, 7, 11, 13, and 17.

Roots

A couple types of roots you will encounter are square roots and cube roots.

- **Square Root:** The square root of a number is a number that, when raised to the second power, produces the given number. For example, the square root of 16 is 4 because $4^2 = 16$. $\sqrt{}$ is the symbol for square root.

- **Cube Root:** Cube root is the procedural inverse of raising to a cube. If $2^3 = 8$, then $\sqrt[3]{8} = 2$. The cube root of 27 = 3; $3^3 = 27$.

Algebraic Equations

An equation is an equality. The values on either side of the equal sign in an equation must be equal. To learn the value of an unknown in an equation, do the same thing to both sides of the equation so as to leave the unknown on one side of the equal sign and its value on the other side. Here are three examples:

❶ $X - 2 = 8$

Add 2 to both sides of the equation.

$X - 2 + 2 = 8 + 2; X = 10$

$5X = 25$

Divide both sides of the equation by 5.

$$\frac{^1\!5X}{5_1} = \frac{25}{5}; X = 5$$

❷ $Y + 9 = 15$

Subtract 9 from both sides of the equation.

$Y + 9 - 9 = 15 - 9; Y = 6$

$A \div 4 = 48$

Multiply both sides of the equation by 4.

$$\frac{^1\!4A}{_1 4} = 48 \times 4; A = 192$$

❸   Sometimes more than one step is required to solve an equation.

$6A \div 4 = 48$

First, multiply both sides of the equation by 4.

$$\frac{6A}{_14} \times \frac{4^1}{1} = 48 \times 4; \ 6A = 192$$

Then, divide both sides of the equation by 6.

$$\frac{^16A}{_16} \times \frac{192}{6}; \ A = 32$$

Angles

An angle is a geometric figure made by two lines that intersect. The symbol for an angle is ∠. The two lines are called sides of the angle.

A *right angle* is an angle of 90° and is formed by one fourth of a complete revolution ($\frac{1}{4}$ of 360°).

A *straight angle* is an angle of 180° and is formed by one half of a complete revolution ($\frac{1}{2}$ of 360°).

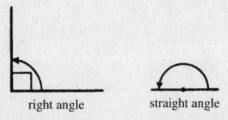

right angle   straight angle

An *acute angle* is an angle that is greater than 0° but less than 90°.

An *obtuse angle* is an angle that is greater than 90° but less than 180°.

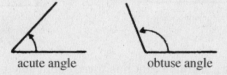

acute angle   obtuse angle

Complementary angles are two angles whose sum is 90°. Each angle is the complement of the other. If an angle contains 30°, its complement contains 60°. If an angle contains $x°$, its complement contains $(90 - x)°$.

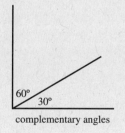

complementary angles

Supplementary angles are two angles whose sum is 180°. Each angle is the supplement of the other. If an angle contains 140°, its supplement contains 40°. If an angle contains x°, its supplement contains $(180 - x)$°.

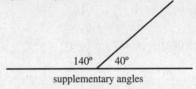

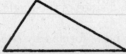
supplementary angles

Triangles

A triangle is a plane figure consisting of three points not on a straight line and the line segments connecting these points.

A *scalene triangle* is a triangle with no two sides equal.

An *isosceles triangle* is a triangle that has two equal sides. The equal sides are called legs or arms. The remaining side is called the base. The base angles of an isosceles triangle are equal.

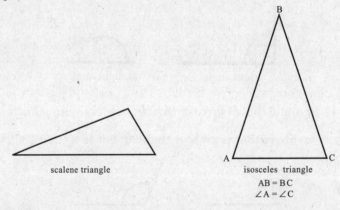

scalene triangle   isosceles triangle
$AB = BC$
$\angle A = \angle C$

An *equilateral triangle* is a triangle that has three equal sides. An equilateral triangle is also equiangular.

A *right triangle* is a triangle that has a right angle. The side opposite the right angle is called the hypotenuse.

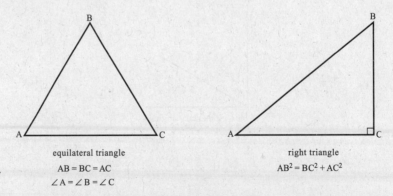

equilateral triangle   right triangle
$AB = BC = AC$ $AB^2 = BC^2 + AC^2$
$\angle A = \angle B = \angle C$

Pythagorean Theorem

In a right triangle, the square of the length of the hypotenuse is equal to the sum of the squares of the lengths of the other two sides: $a^2 + b^2 = c^2$.

Area, Perimeter, and Volume

Area is the space enclosed by a plane (flat) figure. A rectangle is a plane figure with four right angles. Opposite sides of a rectangle are of equal length and are parallel to each other. To find the area of a rectangle, multiply the length of the base of the rectangle by the length of its height. Area is *always* expressed in square units.

$$A = bh$$
$$A = 9\,\text{ft.} \times 3\,\text{ft.}$$
$$A = 27\,\text{sq. ft.}$$

A square is a rectangle in which all four sides are the same length. You can find the area of a square by squaring the length of one side, which is exactly the same as multiplying the square's length by its height.

$$A = S^2$$
$$A = 4\,\text{in.} \times 4\,\text{in.}$$
$$A = 16\,\text{sq. in.}$$

A triangle is a three-sided plane figure. You can find the area of a triangle by multiplying the base by the altitude (height) and dividing by two.

$$A = \frac{1}{2}\,bh$$
$$A = \frac{1}{2}\,(9\,\text{in.})(5\,\text{in.}) = \frac{45}{2}$$
$$A = 22\tfrac{1}{2}\,\text{sq. in.}$$

A circle is a perfectly round plane figure. The distance from the center of a circle to its rim is its radius. The distance from one edge to the other through the center is its diameter. The diameter is twice the length of the radius.

Pi (π) is a mathematical value equal to approximately 3.14, or $\frac{22}{7}$. Pi is frequently used in calculations involving circles. To find the area of a circle, square the radius and multiply it by π.

$$A = \pi r^2$$
$$A = \pi\,(4\,\text{cm.})^2$$
$$A = 16\pi\,\text{sq. cm.}$$

You may leave the area in terms of pi unless you are told what value to assign π.

The perimeter of a plane figure is the distance around the outside. To find the perimeter of a polygon (a plane figure bounded by straight lines), just add the lengths of the sides.

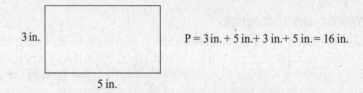

$P = 3 \text{ in.} + 5 \text{ in.} + 3 \text{ in.} + 5 \text{ in.} = 16 \text{ in.}$

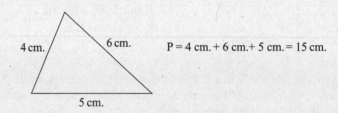

$P = 4 \text{ cm.} + 6 \text{ cm.} + 5 \text{ cm.} = 15 \text{ cm.}$

The perimeter of a circle is called the circumference. The formula for the circumference of a circle is πd or $2\pi r$, which are, of course, the same thing.

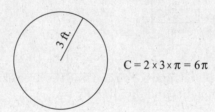

$C = 2 \times 3 \times \pi = 6\pi$

The volume of a solid figure is the measure of the space within. To determine the volume of a solid figure, multiply the area by the height or depth.

The volume of a rectangular solid is length × width × height. Volume is always expressed in cubic units.

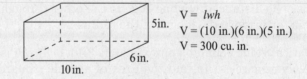

$V = lwh$
$V = (10 \text{ in.})(6 \text{ in.})(5 \text{ in.})$
$V = 300 \text{ cu. in.}$

The volume of a cube is the cube of one side.

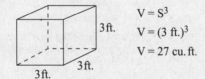

$V = S^3$
$V = (3 \text{ ft.})^3$
$V = 27 \text{ cu. ft.}$

The volume of a cylinder is π times the square of the radius of the base times the height.

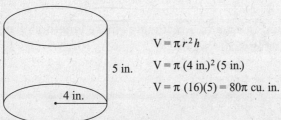

$$V = \pi r^2 h$$
$$V = \pi (4 \text{ in.})^2 (5 \text{ in.})$$
$$V = \pi (16)(5) = 80\pi \text{ cu. in.}$$

The following sample questions illustrate some of the types of questions on math knowledge found on military tests. Solutions to these sample questions are provided to show how you can obtain the correct answers.

Sample Items (five options)

S1. If 20% of a number is 8, what is 25% of the number?

(A) 10

(B) 11

(C) 12

(D) 14

(E) 15

The correct answer is (A). $0.20 \times x = 8$. $x = 40$. $0.25 \times 40 = 10$.

S2. Which of the following has the greatest value?

(A) $\dfrac{1}{2}$

(B) $\sqrt{2}$

(C) 0.2

(D) $(0.2)^2$

(E) $(0.02)^2$

The correct answer is (A). Choice (A) = 0.5. Choice (B) = more than 0.4 but less than 0.5. Choice (C) = 0.2. Choice (D) = 0.04. Choice (E) = 0.0004.

S3. Henry needs M hours to mow the lawn. After working for X hours, what part of the job remains to be done?

(A) $M - X$

(B) $X - M$

(C) $\dfrac{M - X}{M}$

(D) $\dfrac{X}{M}$

(E) $\dfrac{M - X}{X}$

The correct answer is (C). M hours to mow lawn; $M - X$ = time still needed to complete lawn. $\dfrac{M - X}{M}$ = part still to be done.

S4. A square is equal in area to a rectangle whose length is 9 and whose width is 4. Find the perimeter of the square.

(A) 24

(B) 26

(C) 30

(D) 34

(E) 36

The correct answer is (A). Area of rectangle = $9 \times 4 = 36$; area of square = 36. Each side = 6. Perimeter of square = $6 + 6 + 6 + 6 = 24$.

S5. The circumference of a circle whose area is 9π is

(A) 3

(B) 3π

(C) 6

(D) 6π

(E) 9

The correct answer is (D). If area is 9π, the radius is 3 and the diameter is 6. Circumference = πd or 6π.

Sample Items (four options)

S6. 80 is $12\frac{1}{2}$ % of what number?

(A) 10

(B) 64

(C) 100

(D) 640

The correct answer is (D). $12\frac{1}{2}\% = \frac{1}{8}$. $80 = \frac{1}{8} \times x$; $x = 640$.

S7. If $a = 5b$, then $\frac{3}{5} a =$

(A) $\frac{5}{3} b$

(B) $\frac{3}{5} b$

(C) $3b$

(D) $\frac{b}{3}$

The correct answer is (C). $\frac{3}{5} \times 5b = 3b$.

S8. A purse contains 28 coins in nickels and dimes. The ratio of nickels to dimes is 3:4. What is the value of the dimes?

(A) 20¢

(B) 60¢

(C) $1.00

(D) $1.60

The correct answer is (D). Let $3x$ = number of nickels, and $4x$ = number of dimes. $3x + 4x = 7x$. $7x = 28$. $x = 4$. $4x = 4 \times 4 = 16$ dimes, worth $1.60.

S9. Which of the following sets of angles can be the three angles of a triangle?

(A) 30°, 40°, 50°

(B) 30°, 45°, 90°

(C) 30°, 60°, 80°

(D) 30°, 65°, 85°

The correct answer is (D). The three angles of the triangle must add up to 180°. 30° + 65° + 85° = 180°.

S10. Water is poured into a cylindrical tank at the rate of 9 cubic inches a minute. How long will it take to fill the tank if its radius is 3 inches and its height is 14 inches?

(A) 41 minutes

(B) 44 minutes

(C) 47 minutes

(D) 50 minutes

The correct answer is (B). $\pi r^2 \times$ height = volume. $\pi \times 3^2 \times 14$ = volume. volume $= \frac{22 \times 9 \times 14}{7} = 396$. 396 cubic inches divided by 9 cubic inches per minute = 44 minutes.

GENERAL SCIENCE

Questions on general science appear as four-option items in the ASVAB subtest. Most of the questions deal with life science and physical science. There are also a few questions on earth science.

The life science items deal with basic biology, human nutrition, and health. The physical science items cover elementary chemistry and physics. Fundamentals of geology, meteorology, and astronomy are included in the earth science area.

Sample questions below illustrate some of the types of questions that appear in the general science subtest. Solutions to these sample questions show how you might determine the correct answers.

Sample Items (four options)

S1. Organisms that sustain their life cycles by feeding off other live organisms are known as

(A) parasites.

(B) saprophytes.

(C) bacteria.

(D) viruses.

The correct answer is (A). Organisms that live on or in the body of other live organisms from which food is obtained are called parasites.

S2. Lack of iodine is often related to which of the following diseases?

(A) Beriberi

(B) Scurvy

(C) Rickets

(D) Goiter

The correct answer is (D). Goiter is a disease of the thyroid gland, the body's storehouse for iodine. It may be caused by insufficient iodine in the diet.

S3. When two or more elements combine to form a substance that has properties different from those of the component elements, that new substance is known as a(n)

(A) mixture.

(B) solution.

(C) alloy.

(D) compound.

The correct answer is (D). A compound is a substance composed of two or more different elements that are chemically combined.

S4. Photosynthesis is the process by which green plants manufacture carbohydrates from

(A) oxygen and nitrogen.

(B) carbon dioxide and water.

(C) oxygen and water.

(D) glucose and water.

The correct answer is (B). Photosynthesis is the process by which green plants manufacture carbohydrates from carbon dioxide and water in the presence of sunlight and chlorophyll.

S5. The primary reason designers seek to lower the center of gravity in automobiles is to

(A) reduce wind resistance.

(B) provide smoother riding.

(C) increase stability.

(D) reduce manufacturing costs.

The correct answer is (C). The primary reason for lowering the center of gravity in automobiles is to give the car greater stability.

S6. A thermometer that indicates the freezing point of water at 0 degrees and the boiling point of water at 100 degrees is called the

(A) Celsius thermometer.

(B) Fahrenheit thermometer.

(C) Reaumer thermometer.

(D) Kelvin thermometer.

The correct answer is (A). With the Celsius or centigrade scale, the fixed points are the freezing and the boiling points of water. The interval is divided into 100 parts, so the freezing point of water is 0°C and the boiling point is 100°C.

S7. "Shooting stars" are

(A) exploding stars.

(B) cosmic rays.

(C) planetoids.

(D) meteors.

The correct answer is (D). Meteors, or "shooting stars," come into the earth's atmosphere from outer space with high velocity. The resistance offered by the earth's atmosphere makes these meteors incandescent in flight.

S8. A body in space that orbits around another body is known as a

(A) moon.

(B) planet.

(C) satellite.

(D) comet.

The correct answer is (B). A satellite is a small body that revolves around a planet. The moon is a satellite that revolves around the planet Earth.

ELECTRONICS INFORMATION

Questions on electronics information appear as four-option items in the ASVAB. They are designed to ascertain your knowledge of electrical, radio, and electronics information.

Sample questions to illustrate some of the types of questions that appear in the electronics information subtest follow. Solutions to these sample questions are also given.

Sample Items (four options)

S1. The safest way to run an extension cord to a lamp is

(A) under a rug.

(B) along a baseboard.

(C) under a sofa.

(D) behind a sofa.

The correct answer is (B). The safest way would be to run it along a baseboard where there would be little likelihood of it being tampered with.

S2. What does the abbreviation AC stand for?

(A) Additional charge

(B) Alternating coil

(C) Alternating current

(D) Ampere current

The correct answer is (C). AC is a standard electrical abbreviation and stands for alternating current.

S3. Most electrical problems involving voltage, resistance, and current are solved by applying

(A) Ohm's law.

(B) Watt's law.

(C) Coulomb's law.

(D) Kirchoff's voltage and current laws.

The correct answer is (A). Ohm's law describes the relationship between the voltage, current, and resistance in a circuit: $V = IR$. The watts consumed by a circuit are the product of the voltage times the current. One ampere flowing for 1 second delivers 1 coulomb of electrical charge. Kirchoff's voltage and current laws concern the way voltages and currents around a circuit can be summed up.

S4. Electronic circuits designed to produce high-frequency alternating currents are usually known as

(A) oscillators.

(B) amplifiers.

(C) rectifiers.

(D) detectors.

The correct answer is (A). Oscillators capable of producing high-frequency AC might include crystals capable of producing particular frequencies, or they might involve electronic components, such as capacitors and inductors, capable of being tuned to various frequencies.

S5. Which one of the following devices converts heat energy directly into electrical energy?

(A) A piezoelectrical crystal

(B) A photoelectric cell

(C) A steam-driven generator

(D) A thermocouple

The correct answer is (D). Thermocouples usually consist of connections between wires of two dissimilar metals. They are frequently calibrated so that the amount of voltage produced can be directly related to the temperature. They are thus capable of measuring temperatures.

S6. One use of a coaxial cable is to

(A) ground a signal.

(B) pass a signal from the set to the antenna of a mobile unit.

(C) carry the signal from a ballast tube.

(D) carry grid signals in high-altitude areas.

The correct answer is (B). Coaxial cable consists of an inner conducting wire covered with insulation and run inside a concentric cylindrical outer conductor. TV antenna lead-in wires of the 75-ohm variety are examples of coaxial cables. Coaxial cables are used principally to minimize signal loss between antennas and either receiving or transmitting sets.

S7. Which of the following has the least resistance?

(A) Silver

(B) Aluminum

(C) Copper

(D) Steel

The correct answer is (A). All of the materials listed are conductors. Silver is the best, although it is not often used because of its high cost. The moving contacts in motor starters, however, are often made of silver, and it is widely used where low-resistance contacts are required.

S8. In electronic circuits, the symbol shown below usually represents a

(A) transformer.

(B) capacitor.

(C) transistor.

(D) diode.

The correct answer is (D). The symbol shows a semiconductor diode. These usually contain silicon and sometimes germanium. They conduct only in the direction shown by the arrow. Currents flowing in the opposite direction meet with high resistance and are effectively blocked. For these reasons, silicon diodes are often used to rectify AC to DC.

MECHANICAL COMPREHENSION

Questions on mechanical comprehension are widely used by the military. They appear as three-option items in the Mechanical Comprehension Test of the Navy and Marine Corps ASTB. Your results on the Mechanical Comprehension Test are combined with those of the Math Skills Test and Reading Skills Test to arrive at the Officer Aptitude Rating (OAR).

Mechanical comprehension test items require an understanding of mechanical principles that comes from observing the physical world, working with or operating mechanical devices, or reading and studying.

These sample questions illustrate some of the types of questions on mechanical comprehension that might be found in this test. Solutions to these sample questions show how you can determine the correct answers.

Sample Items (three options)

Study each diagram carefully and select the choice that best answers the question or completes the statement.

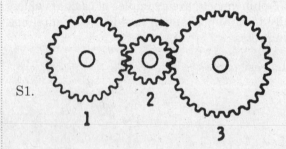

S1.

Which of the other gears is moving in the same direction as gear 2?

(A) Gear 1

(B) Gear 3

(C) Neither of the gears

The correct answer is (C). The arrow indicates that gear 2 is moving clockwise. This would cause both gear 1 and gear 3 to move counterclockwise.

S2.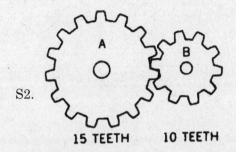

If gear A makes 30 revolutions, gear B will make

(A) 40

(B) 45

(C) 50

The correct answer is (B). For every revolution made by gear A, gear B will make $1\frac{1}{2}$ times as many. If gear A makes 30 revolutions, gear B will make 45.

S3.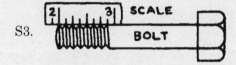

The number of threads per inch on the bolt is

(A) 7

(B) 8

(C) 10

The correct answer is (B). The bolt thread makes one revolution per $\frac{1}{8}$ inch. Accordingly, it has 8 threads in 1 inch.

S4.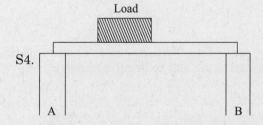

Which post holds up the greater part of the load?

(A) Post A

(B) Post B

(C) Both are equal

The correct answer is (A). The weight of the load is not centered but is closer to A. The distance from the center of the load to A is less than the distance from the center of the load to B. Therefore, post A would support the greater part of the load.

S5.

The convenience outlet that is known as a *polarized* outlet is number

(A) 1

(B) 2

(C) 3

The correct answer is (A). The plug can go into the outlet in only one way in a polarized outlet. In the other outlets, the plug can be reversed.

S6.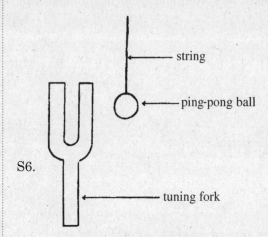

When the tuning fork is struck, the ping-pong ball will

(A) remain stationary.

(B) bounce up and down.

(C) swing away from the tuning fork.

The correct answer is (C). When a tuning fork vibrates, it moves currents of air. This vibrating air would cause the ping-pong ball to be pushed away.

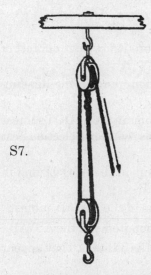

S7.

In the figure shown above, the pulley system consists of a fixed block and a movable block. The theoretical mechanical advantage is

(A) 2

(B) 3

(C) 4

The correct answer is (A). The number of parts of the rope going to and from the movable block indicates the mechanical advantage. In this case, it is 2.

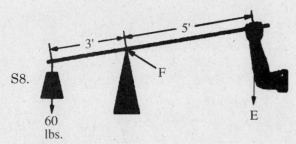

S8.

What effort must be exerted to lift a 60-pound weight in the figure of a first-class lever shown above? (Disregard weight of lever in your computation.)

(A) 36 pounds

(B) 45 pounds

(C) 48 pounds

Let x = effort that must be exerted.

$60 \times 3 = x \times 5$. $5x = 180$. $x = \frac{180}{5} = 36$.

The correct answer is (A).

SUMMING IT UP

- Synonym questions appear as five-option items in the Word Knowledge subtest of the Air Force Officer Qualifying Test.

- Paragraph comprehension questions appear as four-option items in the Reading Skills Test subtest of the ASVAB.

- Questions on arithmetic reasoning appear as five-option items in the AFOQT subtest and in the Math Skills Test of the Navy and Marine Corps Aviation Selection Test Battery (ASTB).

- Questions on math knowledge appear as five-option items in the AFOQT and in the Math Skills Test of the Navy and Marine Corps ASTB.

- Questions on general science appear as four-option items in the ASVAB subtest.

- Questions on electronics information appear as four-option items in the ASVAB.

- Mechanical comprehension questions are widely used by the military. They appear on the Navy and Marine Corps ASTB.

PART V

SUGGESTED STUDY PLAN FOR OFFICER CANDIDATE TEST PREPARATION

The Practice Tests and Officer Candidate Tests

OVERVIEW

- **U.S. Army**
- **U.S. Navy**
- **U.S. Air Force**
- **U.S. Marine Corps**
- **U.S. Coast Guard**
- **Summing it up**

This part contains basic information on the tests used by each branch of service in selecting officer candidates, followed by specific information as to which practice tests to review for each officer candidate test.

Based on the branch of service you are interested in and applying for, determine which practice tests and officer candidate tests are pertinent. Do these practice tests and take the officer candidate tests, recording your answers as directed in the spaces provided. Work carefully but quickly, simulating actual test conditions as much as possible.

After completing each practice test and officer candidate test, refer to the answer key and explanations to ascertain the number of questions you answered correctly and to note the questions you did not answer correctly and those you are still unsure of despite the fact that you selected the right answer.

Look these questions over carefully. Read the rationale. Be sure you fully understand why your answer was wrong, why the correct answer is the right answer, and the reasoning used to arrive at the correct answer. This is one of the most important benefits to be derived from doing these practice tests and taking these officer candidate tests. Practicing on these tests will increase your test-taking ability, improve your test sophistication, broaden your knowledge, and enable you to obtain a higher score on the real test.

Those interested in flight training should obtain a copy of *Peterson's Military Flight Aptitude Tests*.

chapter 11

U.S. ARMY

Test Areas	ASVAB General Technical Composite (GT)*
General Science	
Arithmetic Reasoning	X
Word Knowledge	X
Paragraph Comprehension	X
Mathematics Knowledge	
Electronics Information	
Auto and Shop Information	
Mechanical Comprehension	
Assembling Objects	

*Test requirements include an aptitude area General Technical (GT) score of 110 or higher. The GT aptitude area consists of Arithmetic Reasoning, Word Knowledge, and Paragraph Comprehension. It is derived from the Academic Ability composite on the Armed Services Vocational Aptitude Battery (ASVAB).

To prepare for the Army officer candidate test, complete the following practice tests:

Synonyms
Reading Comprehension
Arithmetic Reasoning

Take the following test sections from the Armed Services Vocational Aptitude Battery test on pages 299–313:

Arithmetic Reasoning
Word Knowledge
Paragraph Comprehension

U.S. NAVY

	ASTB Composites			
	Academic Qualification Rating (AQR)	Pilot Flight Aptitude Rating (PFAR)	Flight Officer Flight Aptitude Rating (FOFAR)	Officer Aptitude Rating (OAR)
Math Skills Test	X	X	X	X
Reading Skills Test	X	X	X	X
Mechanical Comprehension Test	X	X	X	X
Spatial Apperception Test	X	X	X	
Aviation and Nautical Information Test	X	X	X	
Aviation Supplemental Test	X	X	X	

To qualify for the Officer Candidate School, applicants must achieve a qualifying score on the Officer Aptitude Rating (OAR)—a composite formed from the scores received on the Math Skills Test, Reading Skills Test, and the Mechanical Comprehension Test of the Navy and Marine Corps Aviation Selection Test Battery.

The Math Skills Test measures quantitative aptitude (arithmetic reasoning, general mathematics, algebra, and plane geometry).

The Reading Skills Test measures reading aptitude (paragraph comprehension).

The Mechanical Comprehension Test measures mechanical aptitude (understanding of the principles involved in the operation of mechanical devices, basic physics, and so on).

Although applicants are encouraged by the Navy to take all test sectionss composing the Navy and Marine Corps Aviation Selection Test Battery, those interested in obtaining a commission only (and not in flight training) are permitted to take only the Math Skills Test, Reading Skills Test, and the Mechanical Comprehension Test. The Officer Aptitude Rating (OAR) is the relevant composite used in selecting individuals for the Officer Candidate School.

To prepare for the Navy officer candidate test, complete the following practice tests:

Reading Comprehension
Arithmetic Reasoning
Math Knowledge
Mechanical Comprehension

Take the following test sections on the Navy and Marine Corps Aviation Selection Test Battery on pages 339–357:

Math Skills Test
Reading Skills Test
Mechanical Comprehension Test

U.S. AIR FORCE

AFOQT Composites			
Subtests	Pilot	Navigator-Technical	Academic Aptitude
Verbal Analogies	X		X
Arithmetic Reasoning		X	X
Word Knowledge			X
Math Knowledge		X	X
Instrument Comprehension	X		
Block Counting	X	X	
Table Reading	X	X	
Aviation Information	X		
General Science		X	
Rotated Blocks		X	
Hidden Figures		X	

The AFOQT, published in several booklets, contains 250 cognitive test questions, excluding the self-description questions, and requires a total of 3½ hours of administrative and testing time. The test is administered on a monthly basis. Thousands of applicants are tested each year.

Although applicants are required to take all AFOQT test sections, the Academic Aptitude composite is the relevant composite used in selecting individuals for Officer Training School (OTS).

To prepare for the AFOQT Academic Aptitude composite, complete the following practice tests:

Synonyms
Verbal Analogies
Arithmetic Reasoning
Math Knowledge

Take the following test sections on the Air Force Officer Qualifying Test (AFOQT) test on pages 261–289:

Verbal Analogies
Arithmetic Reasoning
Word Knowledge
Math Knowledge

U.S. MARINE CORPS

Tests	Marine Corps ASVAB Composite
General Science	X
Arithmetic Reasoning	X
Mathematics Knowledge	X
Electronics Information	X

A bachelor's degree is required for a Marine Corps commission. In addition, applicants must have a minimum combined score of 1000 on the Critical Reading (Verbal) and Math sections of the SAT or a minimum combined Math and English (Verbal) score of 45 on the ACT or a minimum converted score of 120 (a waiver may be granted down to 115) on the composite of the ASVAB, derived from the scores received on the following ASVAB test sections:

General Science
Arithmetic Reasoning
Mathematics Knowledge
Electronics Information

Those who have the required minimum combined score in the SAT or ACT are not given the ASVAB.

To qualify on the basis of the above composite score on the Armed Services Vocational Aptitude Battery, complete the following practice tests:

Arithmetic Reasoning
Math Knowledge
General Science
Electronics Information

Take the following test sections from the Armed Services Vocational Aptitude Battery test on pages 293–333:

General Science
Arithmetic Reasoning
Mathematics Knowledge
Electronics Information

Only applicants for flight training are required by the Marine Corps to take the Navy and Marine Corps Aviation Selection Test Battery (ASTB). Those interested in flight training should refer to *Peterson's Military Flight Aptitude Tests.*

Tests	Officer Aptitude Rating (OAR)
Math Skills Test	X
Reading Skills Test	X
Mechanical Comprehension Test	X

Please refer to page 131 for more detailed information on the relevant practice tests and the ASTB Officer Aptitude Rating.

U.S. COAST GUARD

In order to qualify for the Officer Candidate School you must take the ASVAB General Technical composite and score 109 or higher.

Test Areas	ASVAB General Technical Composite (GT)*
Arithmetic Reasoning	X
Word Knowledge	X
Paragraph Comprehension	X

Please refer to page 131 for more detailed information on the relevant practice tests and the ASVAB General Technical aptitude area.

Tests	Officer Aptitude Rating (OAR)
Math Skills Test	X
Reading Skills Test	X
Mechanical Comprehension Test	X

To qualify for Officer Candidate School, applicants must achieve a qualifying score on the SAT or ACT. Those interested in obtaining a commission only and not in flight training should refer to *Peterson's Master the SAT* or *The Real ACT Prep Guide*.

Only applicants for flight training are required by the Coast Guard to take the Navy and Marine Corps Aviation Selection Test Battery. Those interested in flight training should refer to *Peterson's Military Flight Aptitude Tests*.

To prepare for the Navy and Marine Corps Aviation Selection Test Battery complete the following practice tests:

Reading Comprehension
Arithmetic Reasoning
Math Knowledge
Mechanical Comprehension

Take the following test sections on the Navy and Marine Corps Aviation Selection Test Battery test on pages 337–364:

Math Skills Test
Reading Skills Test
Mechanical Comprehension Test

SUMMING IT UP

- The U.S. Army requires a score of 110 or higher on the General Technical (GT) aptitude area. This test includes Arithmetic Reasoning, Word Knowledge, and Paragraph Comprehension.

- Applicants are encouraged by the U.S. Navy to take all test sections composing the Navy and Marine Corps Aviation Selection Test Battery; however the Officer Aptitude Rating (OAR) is the relevant composite used in selecting individuals for Officer Candidate School. This composite consists of the Math Skills Test, the Reading Skills Test, and the Mechanical Comprehension Test.

- The U.S. Air force requires all applicants to take all AFOQT test sections, however, the Academic Aptitude composite is the relevant composite used in selecting individuals for Officer Training School (OTS).

- Applicants for the U.S. Marines must have a minimum combined score of 1,000 on the Critical Reading (Verbal) and Math sections of the SAT or a minimum combined Math and English (Verbal) score of 45 on the ACT or a minimum converted score of 120 on the composite of the ASVAB.

- In order to qualify for the Coast Guard Officer Candidate School you must take the ASVAB General Technical composite and score 109 or higher.

- Only applicants for flight training are required by the Marine Corps and the Coast Guard to take the Navy and Marine Corps Aviation Selection Test Battery.

PART VI
EIGHT PRACTICE TESTS

Practice Test 1: Synonyms

Practice Test 2: Verbal Analogies

Practice Test 3: Reading Comprehension

Practice Test 4: Arithmetic Reasoning

Practice Test 5: Math Knowledge

Practice Test 6: General Science

Practice Test 7: Electronics Information

Practice Test 8: Mechanical Comprehension

ANSWER SHEET FOR PRACTICE TEST 1: SYNONYMS

1. Ⓐ Ⓑ Ⓒ Ⓓ Ⓔ	21. Ⓐ Ⓑ Ⓒ Ⓓ Ⓔ	41. Ⓐ Ⓑ Ⓒ Ⓓ Ⓔ	61. Ⓐ Ⓑ Ⓒ Ⓓ	81. Ⓐ Ⓑ Ⓒ Ⓓ
2. Ⓐ Ⓑ Ⓒ Ⓓ Ⓔ	22. Ⓐ Ⓑ Ⓒ Ⓓ Ⓔ	42. Ⓐ Ⓑ Ⓒ Ⓓ Ⓔ	62. Ⓐ Ⓑ Ⓒ Ⓓ	82. Ⓐ Ⓑ Ⓒ Ⓓ
3. Ⓐ Ⓑ Ⓒ Ⓓ Ⓔ	23. Ⓐ Ⓑ Ⓒ Ⓓ Ⓔ	43. Ⓐ Ⓑ Ⓒ Ⓓ Ⓔ	63. Ⓐ Ⓑ Ⓒ Ⓓ	83. Ⓐ Ⓑ Ⓒ Ⓓ
4. Ⓐ Ⓑ Ⓒ Ⓓ Ⓔ	24. Ⓐ Ⓑ Ⓒ Ⓓ Ⓔ	44. Ⓐ Ⓑ Ⓒ Ⓓ Ⓔ	64. Ⓐ Ⓑ Ⓒ Ⓓ	84. Ⓐ Ⓑ Ⓒ Ⓓ
5. Ⓐ Ⓑ Ⓒ Ⓓ Ⓔ	25. Ⓐ Ⓑ Ⓒ Ⓓ Ⓔ	45. Ⓐ Ⓑ Ⓒ Ⓓ Ⓔ	65. Ⓐ Ⓑ Ⓒ Ⓓ	85. Ⓐ Ⓑ Ⓒ Ⓓ
6. Ⓐ Ⓑ Ⓒ Ⓓ Ⓔ	26. Ⓐ Ⓑ Ⓒ Ⓓ Ⓔ	46. Ⓐ Ⓑ Ⓒ Ⓓ Ⓔ	66. Ⓐ Ⓑ Ⓒ Ⓓ	86. Ⓐ Ⓑ Ⓒ Ⓓ
7. Ⓐ Ⓑ Ⓒ Ⓓ Ⓔ	27. Ⓐ Ⓑ Ⓒ Ⓓ Ⓔ	47. Ⓐ Ⓑ Ⓒ Ⓓ Ⓔ	67. Ⓐ Ⓑ Ⓒ Ⓓ	87. Ⓐ Ⓑ Ⓒ Ⓓ
8. Ⓐ Ⓑ Ⓒ Ⓓ Ⓔ	28. Ⓐ Ⓑ Ⓒ Ⓓ Ⓔ	48. Ⓐ Ⓑ Ⓒ Ⓓ Ⓔ	68. Ⓐ Ⓑ Ⓒ Ⓓ	88. Ⓐ Ⓑ Ⓒ Ⓓ
9. Ⓐ Ⓑ Ⓒ Ⓓ Ⓔ	29. Ⓐ Ⓑ Ⓒ Ⓓ Ⓔ	49. Ⓐ Ⓑ Ⓒ Ⓓ Ⓔ	69. Ⓐ Ⓑ Ⓒ Ⓓ	89. Ⓐ Ⓑ Ⓒ Ⓓ
10. Ⓐ Ⓑ Ⓒ Ⓓ Ⓔ	30. Ⓐ Ⓑ Ⓒ Ⓓ Ⓔ	50. Ⓐ Ⓑ Ⓒ Ⓓ Ⓔ	70. Ⓐ Ⓑ Ⓒ Ⓓ	90. Ⓐ Ⓑ Ⓒ Ⓓ
11. Ⓐ Ⓑ Ⓒ Ⓓ Ⓔ	31. Ⓐ Ⓑ Ⓒ Ⓓ Ⓔ	51. Ⓐ Ⓑ Ⓒ Ⓓ	71. Ⓐ Ⓑ Ⓒ Ⓓ	91. Ⓐ Ⓑ Ⓒ Ⓓ
12. Ⓐ Ⓑ Ⓒ Ⓓ Ⓔ	32. Ⓐ Ⓑ Ⓒ Ⓓ Ⓔ	52. Ⓐ Ⓑ Ⓒ Ⓓ	72. Ⓐ Ⓑ Ⓒ Ⓓ	92. Ⓐ Ⓑ Ⓒ Ⓓ
13. Ⓐ Ⓑ Ⓒ Ⓓ Ⓔ	33. Ⓐ Ⓑ Ⓒ Ⓓ Ⓔ	53. Ⓐ Ⓑ Ⓒ Ⓓ	73. Ⓐ Ⓑ Ⓒ Ⓓ	93. Ⓐ Ⓑ Ⓒ Ⓓ
14. Ⓐ Ⓑ Ⓒ Ⓓ Ⓔ	34. Ⓐ Ⓑ Ⓒ Ⓓ Ⓔ	54. Ⓐ Ⓑ Ⓒ Ⓓ	74. Ⓐ Ⓑ Ⓒ Ⓓ	94. Ⓐ Ⓑ Ⓒ Ⓓ
15. Ⓐ Ⓑ Ⓒ Ⓓ Ⓔ	35. Ⓐ Ⓑ Ⓒ Ⓓ Ⓔ	55. Ⓐ Ⓑ Ⓒ Ⓓ	75. Ⓐ Ⓑ Ⓒ Ⓓ	95. Ⓐ Ⓑ Ⓒ Ⓓ
16. Ⓐ Ⓑ Ⓒ Ⓓ Ⓔ	36. Ⓐ Ⓑ Ⓒ Ⓓ Ⓔ	56. Ⓐ Ⓑ Ⓒ Ⓓ	76. Ⓐ Ⓑ Ⓒ Ⓓ	96. Ⓐ Ⓑ Ⓒ Ⓓ
17. Ⓐ Ⓑ Ⓒ Ⓓ Ⓔ	37. Ⓐ Ⓑ Ⓒ Ⓓ Ⓔ	57. Ⓐ Ⓑ Ⓒ Ⓓ	77. Ⓐ Ⓑ Ⓒ Ⓓ	97. Ⓐ Ⓑ Ⓒ Ⓓ
18. Ⓐ Ⓑ Ⓒ Ⓓ Ⓔ	38. Ⓐ Ⓑ Ⓒ Ⓓ Ⓔ	58. Ⓐ Ⓑ Ⓒ Ⓓ	78. Ⓐ Ⓑ Ⓒ Ⓓ	98. Ⓐ Ⓑ Ⓒ Ⓓ
19. Ⓐ Ⓑ Ⓒ Ⓓ Ⓔ	39. Ⓐ Ⓑ Ⓒ Ⓓ Ⓔ	59. Ⓐ Ⓑ Ⓒ Ⓓ	79. Ⓐ Ⓑ Ⓒ Ⓓ	99. Ⓐ Ⓑ Ⓒ Ⓓ
20. Ⓐ Ⓑ Ⓒ Ⓓ Ⓔ	40. Ⓐ Ⓑ Ⓒ Ⓓ Ⓔ	60. Ⓐ Ⓑ Ⓒ Ⓓ	80. Ⓐ Ⓑ Ⓒ Ⓓ	100. Ⓐ Ⓑ Ⓒ Ⓓ

answer sheet

Practice Test 1: Synonyms

Questions 1–50 are five-option items. For each question, select the option that means the same or most nearly the same as the capitalized word.

1. ABRIDGED
   - (A) alphabetized
   - (B) expanded
   - (C) linked
   - (D) researched
   - (E) shortened

2. ACUMEN
   - (A) caution
   - (B) inability
   - (C) keenness
   - (D) sarcasm
   - (E) strictness

3. ANARCHY
   - (A) chaos
   - (B) competition
   - (C) danger
   - (D) rule
   - (E) secrecy

4. APATHY
   - (A) aptness
   - (B) indifference
   - (C) poverty
   - (D) sickness
   - (E) sorrow

5. ASSIDUOUS
   - (A) amenable
   - (B) enthusiastic
   - (C) neglectful
   - (D) persistent
   - (E) sarcastic

6. BELLIGERENT
   - (A) artistic
   - (B) furious
   - (C) hostile
   - (D) loud
   - (E) worldly

7. BIZARRE
   - (A) accurate
   - (B) ancient
   - (C) fantastic
   - (D) market
   - (E) solvent

8. BUOYANT
   - (A) cautious
   - (B) conceited
   - (C) resilient
   - (D) resistant
   - (E) youthful

9. CAPITULATE
   - (A) destroy
   - (B) finance
   - (C) repeat
   - (D) retreat
   - (E) surrender

10. CENSURE
    (A) appraise
    (B) blame
    (C) count
    (D) pause
    (E) withhold

11. CHARLATAN
    (A) guest
    (B) official
    (C) quack
    (D) specialist
    (E) stranger

12. COLLATE
    (A) assemble
    (B) copy
    (C) mix
    (D) prepare
    (E) separate

13. COMPETENT
    (A) capable
    (B) caring
    (C) courteous
    (D) inept
    (E) informed

14. CONSTRUE
    (A) build
    (B) contradict
    (C) interpret
    (D) misrepresent
    (E) question

15. CREDIBLE
    (A) believable
    (B) correct
    (C) gullible
    (D) intelligent
    (E) obvious

16. CONTRITION
    (A) abrasion
    (B) controversy
    (C) insistence
    (D) intolerance
    (E) repentance

17. DELETE
    (A) complete
    (B) damage
    (C) delay
    (D) exclude
    (E) retain

18. DERISION
    (A) anger
    (B) disguise
    (C) fear
    (D) heredity
    (E) ridicule

19. DETERRENT
    (A) cleansing
    (B) concluding
    (C) deciding
    (D) defending
    (E) restraining

20. DISSEMINATE
    (A) disagree
    (B) slander
    (C) spread
    (D) strip
    (E) unite

21. DIVERGENCE
    (A) annoyance
    (B) difference
    (C) distraction
    (D) entertainment
    (E) revenge

22. ENERVATE

    (A) approximate
    (B) energize
    (C) exact
    (D) invite
    (E) weaken

23. EXCESS

    (A) exit
    (B) failure
    (C) inflation
    (D) luxury
    (E) surplus

24. EXTANT

    (A) destroyed
    (B) out-of-date
    (C) profound
    (D) still existing
    (E) widespread

25. FALLACIOUS

    (A) logical
    (B) misleading
    (C) obscene
    (D) reasonable
    (E) solemn

26. FUNDAMENTAL

    (A) accessible
    (B) difficult
    (C) essential
    (D) financial
    (E) serious

27. GHASTLY

    (A) breathless
    (B) frightening
    (C) furious
    (D) hasty
    (E) spiritual

28. ILLICIT

    (A) insignificant
    (B) overpowering
    (C) secret
    (D) unlawful
    (E) unreadable

29. INDIGENT

    (A) angry
    (B) crowded
    (C) foreign
    (D) natural
    (E) poor

30. INNATE

    (A) acquired
    (B) eternal
    (C) internal
    (D) native
    (E) prospective

31. INTREPID

    (A) complicated
    (B) cowardly
    (C) fanciful
    (D) fearless
    (E) willing

32. LIAISON

    (A) laziness
    (B) permission
    (C) satisfaction
    (D) scarf
    (E) tie

33. LUDICROUS

    (A) excessive
    (B) ridiculous
    (C) profitable
    (D) shallow
    (E) superior

34. MANDATORY
   (A) evident
   (B) insane
   (C) obligatory
   (D) strategic
   (E) undesirable

35. MOBILE
   (A) assembled
   (B) mechanical
   (C) movable
   (D) scornful
   (E) stationary

36. NEGOTIATE
   (A) bargain
   (B) exhaust
   (C) speak
   (D) suffer
   (E) think

37. NOXIOUS
   (A) gaseous
   (B) harmful
   (C) immoral
   (D) oily
   (E) repulsive

38. OFFICIOUS
   (A) arbitrary
   (B) brutal
   (C) meddlesome
   (D) unreasonable
   (E) vulgar

39. PLIGHT
   (A) conspiracy
   (B) departure
   (C) predicament
   (D) stamp
   (E) weight

40. PROFICIENCY
   (A) aptitude
   (B) expertness
   (C) sincerity
   (D) tolerance
   (E) wisdom

41. RECALCITRANT
   (A) defendant
   (B) obedient
   (C) obstinate
   (D) powder
   (E) unconcerned

42. REDUNDANT
   (A) concise
   (B) informed
   (C) reappearing
   (D) superfluous
   (E) unclear

43. REGALE
   (A) adjust
   (B) annoy
   (C) beat
   (D) delight
   (E) return

44. RELINQUISH
   (A) abandon
   (B) pursue
   (C) regret
   (D) secure
   (E) unite

45. SCRUPULOUS
   (A) careful
   (B) intricate
   (C) neurotic
   (D) persistent
   (E) unprincipled

46. SUBTERFUGE

    (A) confirmation

    (B) deception

    (C) excuse

    (D) flight

    (E) substitute

47. SURREPTITIOUS

    (A) complicated

    (B) magnificent

    (C) repetitive

    (D) stealthy

    (E) unbelievable

48. TURBID

    (A) clear

    (B) cloudy

    (C) flowing

    (D) swollen

    (E) twisted

49. VACILLATE

    (A) humiliate

    (B) inoculate

    (C) relinquish

    (D) waver

    (E) withdraw

50. VINDICTIVE

    (A) aggressive

    (B) boastful

    (C) impolite

    (D) revengeful

    (E) unconcerned

Questions 51–100 are four-option items. For each question, select the option that means the same or most nearly the same as the underlined word.

51. We were told to abandon the ship.

    (A) encompass

    (B) infiltrate

    (C) quarantine

    (D) relinquish

52. Acquired most nearly means

    (A) desired

    (B) obtained

    (C) plowed

    (D) sold

53. The door was left ajar.

    (A) blocked

    (B) locked

    (C) open

    (D) unlocked

54. Alias most nearly means

    (A) enemy

    (B) hero

    (C) other name

    (D) sidekick

55. Approximate most nearly means

    (A) mathematically correct

    (B) nearly exact

    (C) remarkable

    (D) worthless

56. Assemble most nearly means

    (A) bring together

    (B) examine carefully

    (C) fill

    (D) locate

57. The captive was treated kindly.
   (A) jailer
   (B) prisoner
   (C) savage
   (D) spy

58. Did the storm cease during the night?
   (A) change
   (B) continue
   (C) start
   (D) stop

59. Commended most nearly means
   (A) blamed
   (B) praised
   (C) promoted
   (D) reprimanded

60. Concisely most nearly means
   (A) accurately
   (B) briefly
   (C) fully
   (D) officially

61. The police officer consoled the weeping child.
   (A) carried home
   (B) comforted
   (C) found
   (D) scolded

62. The reply will be conveyed by messenger.
   (A) carried
   (B) damaged
   (C) guarded
   (D) refused

63. Customary most nearly means
   (A) common
   (B) curious
   (C) difficult
   (D) necessary

64. The foreman defended the striking workers.
   (A) delayed
   (B) informed on
   (C) protected
   (D) shot at

65. Deportment most nearly means
   (A) attendance
   (B) behavior
   (C) intelligence
   (D) neatness

66. The town will erect the bridge.
   (A) construct
   (B) design
   (C) destroy
   (D) paint

67. Fictitious most nearly means
   (A) easy to remember
   (B) imaginary
   (C) odd
   (D) well known

68. Flexible most nearly means
   (A) athletic
   (B) pliable
   (C) rigid
   (D) weak

69. Forthcoming events are published daily.
   (A) approaching
   (B) interesting
   (C) social
   (D) weekly

70. Frugal most nearly means
   (A) economical
   (B) expendable
   (C) musical
   (D) profitable

71. <u>Grimy</u> most nearly means
    (A) dirty
    (B) ill-fitted
    (C) poorly made
    (D) ragged

72. <u>Hollow</u> most nearly means
    (A) brittle
    (B) empty
    (C) rough
    (D) smooth

73. The judge ruled it to be <u>immaterial</u>.
    (A) not debatable
    (B) unclear
    (C) unimportant
    (D) unpredictable

74. <u>Impose</u> most nearly means
    (A) disguise
    (B) escape
    (C) prescribe
    (D) purchase

75. <u>Increment</u> most nearly means
    (A) an account
    (B) an improvision
    (C) an increase
    (D) a specification

76. <u>Insignificant</u> most nearly means
    (A) secret
    (B) thrilling
    (C) unimportant
    (D) unpleasant

77. The fog horn sounded <u>intermittently</u>.
    (A) annually
    (B) at irregular intervals
    (C) constantly
    (D) continuously

78. <u>Itinerant</u> most nearly means
    (A) aggressive
    (B) ignorant
    (C) shrewd
    (D) traveling

79. <u>Juvenile</u> most nearly means
    (A) delinquent
    (B) humorous
    (C) lovesick
    (D) youthful

80. The machine has <u>manual</u> controls.
    (A) handmade
    (B) hand-operated
    (C) self-acting
    (D) simple

81. We <u>misconstrued</u> what she had said.
    (A) followed directions
    (B) ignored
    (C) interpreted erroneously
    (D) strongly disagreed

82. <u>Pedestrian</u> most nearly means
    (A) passenger
    (B) street-crosser
    (C) traffic light
    (D) walker

83. The <u>preface</u> of the book was very interesting.
    (A) appendix
    (B) introduction
    (C) table of contents
    (D) title page

84. <u>Prior</u> most nearly means
    (A) earlier
    (B) more attractive
    (C) more urgent
    (D) personal

85. Punctual most nearly means
    (A) polite
    (B) prompt
    (C) proper
    (D) thoughtful

86. Resolve most nearly means
    (A) decide
    (B) forget
    (C) recall
    (D) understand

87. Revenue most nearly means
    (A) expenses
    (B) income
    (C) produce
    (D) taxes

88. Rudiments most nearly means
    (A) basic procedures
    (B) minute details
    (C) rough manners
    (D) ship's rudders

89. Self-sufficient most nearly means
    (A) clever
    (B) conceited
    (C) independent
    (D) stubborn

90. Solidity most nearly means
    (A) color
    (B) firmness
    (C) smoothness
    (D) unevenness

91. The classroom has stationary desks.
    (A) carved
    (B) heavy
    (C) not movable
    (D) written-upon

92. Stench most nearly means
    (A) dead animal
    (B) foul odor
    (C) pile of debris
    (D) puddle of slimy water

93. Sullen most nearly means
    (A) angrily silent
    (B) grayish yellow
    (C) soaking wet
    (D) very dirty

94. His answer was a superficial one.
    (A) cursory
    (B) excellent
    (C) official
    (D) profound

95. All service was suspended during the emergency.
    (A) checked carefully
    (B) regulated strictly
    (C) stopped temporarily
    (D) turned back

96. Terse most nearly means
    (A) concise
    (B) lengthy
    (C) oral
    (D) trivial

97. The cyclist pedaled at a uniform rate.
    (A) increasing
    (B) unchanging
    (C) unusual
    (D) very slow

98. Urgent most nearly means
    (A) exciting
    (B) pressing
    (C) startling
    (D) sudden

99. <u>Verdict</u> most nearly means
    (A) approval
    (B) arrival
    (C) decision
    (D) sentence

100. <u>Villainous</u> most nearly means
    (A) dignified
    (B) homely
    (C) untidy
    (D) wicked

ANSWER KEY AND EXPLANATIONS

1. (E)	21. (B)	41. (C)	61. (B)	81. (C)
2. (C)	22. (E)	42. (D)	62. (A)	82. (D)
3. (A)	23. (E)	43. (D)	63. (A)	83. (B)
4. (B)	24. (D)	44. (A)	64. (C)	84. (A)
5. (D)	25. (B)	45. (A)	65. (B)	85. (B)
6. (C)	26. (C)	46. (B)	66. (A)	86. (A)
7. (C)	27. (B)	47. (D)	67. (B)	87. (B)
8. (C)	28. (D)	48. (B)	68. (B)	88. (A)
9. (E)	29. (E)	49. (D)	69. (A)	89. (C)
10. (B)	30. (D)	50. (D)	70. (A)	90. (B)
11. (C)	31. (D)	51. (D)	71. (A)	91. (C)
12. (A)	32. (E)	52. (B)	72. (B)	92. (B)
13. (A)	33. (B)	53. (C)	73. (C)	93. (A)
14. (C)	34. (C)	54. (C)	74. (C)	94. (A)
15. (A)	35. (C)	55. (B)	75. (C)	95. (C)
16. (E)	36. (A)	56. (A)	76. (C)	96. (A)
17. (D)	37. (B)	57. (B)	77. (B)	97. (B)
18. (E)	38. (C)	58. (D)	78. (D)	98. (B)
19. (E)	39. (C)	59. (B)	79. (D)	99. (C)
20. (C)	40. (B)	60. (B)	80. (B)	100. (D)

Review those questions you did not answer correctly and those you did answer correctly but are unsure of. Refer to any good unabridged dictionary for the meaning of those words that are giving you trouble.

Developing your own list of words and their meanings will enable you to review these troublesome words periodically. Such practices will aid in increasing your vocabulary and raising your vocabulary scores.

Add to your vocabulary list whenever you come across a word whose meaning is unclear to you.

ANSWER SHEET FOR PRACTICE TEST 2: VERBAL ANALOGIES

1. Ⓐ Ⓑ Ⓒ Ⓓ Ⓔ
2. Ⓐ Ⓑ Ⓒ Ⓓ Ⓔ
3. Ⓐ Ⓑ Ⓒ Ⓓ Ⓔ
4. Ⓐ Ⓑ Ⓒ Ⓓ Ⓔ
5. Ⓐ Ⓑ Ⓒ Ⓓ Ⓔ
6. Ⓐ Ⓑ Ⓒ Ⓓ Ⓔ
7. Ⓐ Ⓑ Ⓒ Ⓓ Ⓔ
8. Ⓐ Ⓑ Ⓒ Ⓓ Ⓔ
9. Ⓐ Ⓑ Ⓒ Ⓓ Ⓔ
10. Ⓐ Ⓑ Ⓒ Ⓓ Ⓔ

11. Ⓐ Ⓑ Ⓒ Ⓓ Ⓔ
12. Ⓐ Ⓑ Ⓒ Ⓓ Ⓔ
13. Ⓐ Ⓑ Ⓒ Ⓓ Ⓔ
14. Ⓐ Ⓑ Ⓒ Ⓓ Ⓔ
15. Ⓐ Ⓑ Ⓒ Ⓓ Ⓔ
16. Ⓐ Ⓑ Ⓒ Ⓓ Ⓔ
17. Ⓐ Ⓑ Ⓒ Ⓓ Ⓔ
18. Ⓐ Ⓑ Ⓒ Ⓓ Ⓔ
19. Ⓐ Ⓑ Ⓒ Ⓓ Ⓔ
20. Ⓐ Ⓑ Ⓒ Ⓓ Ⓔ

21. Ⓐ Ⓑ Ⓒ Ⓓ Ⓔ
22. Ⓐ Ⓑ Ⓒ Ⓓ Ⓔ
23. Ⓐ Ⓑ Ⓒ Ⓓ Ⓔ
24. Ⓐ Ⓑ Ⓒ Ⓓ Ⓔ
25. Ⓐ Ⓑ Ⓒ Ⓓ Ⓔ
26. Ⓐ Ⓑ Ⓒ Ⓓ Ⓔ
27. Ⓐ Ⓑ Ⓒ Ⓓ Ⓔ
28. Ⓐ Ⓑ Ⓒ Ⓓ Ⓔ
29. Ⓐ Ⓑ Ⓒ Ⓓ Ⓔ
30. Ⓐ Ⓑ Ⓒ Ⓓ Ⓔ

31. Ⓐ Ⓑ Ⓒ Ⓓ Ⓔ
32. Ⓐ Ⓑ Ⓒ Ⓓ Ⓔ
33. Ⓐ Ⓑ Ⓒ Ⓓ Ⓔ
34. Ⓐ Ⓑ Ⓒ Ⓓ Ⓔ
35. Ⓐ Ⓑ Ⓒ Ⓓ Ⓔ
36. Ⓐ Ⓑ Ⓒ Ⓓ Ⓔ
37. Ⓐ Ⓑ Ⓒ Ⓓ Ⓔ
38. Ⓐ Ⓑ Ⓒ Ⓓ Ⓔ
39. Ⓐ Ⓑ Ⓒ Ⓓ Ⓔ
40. Ⓐ Ⓑ Ⓒ Ⓓ Ⓔ

41. Ⓐ Ⓑ Ⓒ Ⓓ Ⓔ
42. Ⓐ Ⓑ Ⓒ Ⓓ Ⓔ
43. Ⓐ Ⓑ Ⓒ Ⓓ Ⓔ
44. Ⓐ Ⓑ Ⓒ Ⓓ Ⓔ
45. Ⓐ Ⓑ Ⓒ Ⓓ Ⓔ
46. Ⓐ Ⓑ Ⓒ Ⓓ Ⓔ
47. Ⓐ Ⓑ Ⓒ Ⓓ Ⓔ
48. Ⓐ Ⓑ Ⓒ Ⓓ Ⓔ
49. Ⓐ Ⓑ Ⓒ Ⓓ Ⓔ
50. Ⓐ Ⓑ Ⓒ Ⓓ Ⓔ

answer sheet

Practice Test 2: Verbal Analogies

Questions 1–20 consist of a pair of capitalized words and a third capitalized word that is related to one of the five options in the same way that the first capitalized word is related to the second capitalized word. Choose the option that, when paired with the third capitalized word, shows a relationship similar to the one shown by the first and second capitalized words.

1. ARTIST is to EASEL
   as WEAVER is to
   (A) cloth
   (B) garment
   (C) loom
   (D) pattern
   (E) yarn

2. AUTOMOBILE is to HIGHWAY
   as TRAIN is to
   (A) axles
   (B) cars
   (C) rails
   (D) schedule
   (E) wheels

3. BIOGRAPHY is to FACT
   as NOVEL is to
   (A) art
   (B) book
   (C) fiction
   (D) history
   (E) library

4. CROWD is to PERSONS
   as FLEET is to
   (A) convoy
   (B) firepower
   (C) guns
   (D) navy
   (E) ships

5. DARKNESS is to LIGHT
   as STILLNESS is to
   (A) health
   (B) illness
   (C) quietness
   (D) serenity
   (E) sound

6. EFFICIENCY is to REWARD
   as CARELESSNESS is to
   (A) error
   (B) experience
   (C) inefficiency
   (D) reprimand
   (E) training

7. FALL is to FALLEN as FLY is to
   (A) fled
   (B) flew
   (C) flied
   (D) flown
   (E) flying

153

8. PORK is to HOG as MUTTON is to
   (A) cattle
   (B) deer
   (C) fowl
   (D) rabbit
   (E) sheep

9. SANDAL is to FOOT as SHAWL is to
   (A) knees
   (B) shoulders
   (C) thighs
   (D) waist
   (E) wrist

10. THEATER is to RECREATION as SCHOOL is to
    (A) education
    (B) examination
    (C) experimentation
    (D) exposition
    (E) orientation

11. III is to XIV as 3 is to
    (A) 13
    (B) 14
    (C) 15
    (D) 16
    (E) 19

12. WHEN is to TIME as HOW is to
    (A) degree
    (B) gender
    (C) manner
    (D) number
    (E) person

13. CLOCK is to TIME as THERMOMETER is to
    (A) climate
    (B) degrees
    (C) hour
    (D) temperature
    (E) weather

14. GAVEL is to JUDGE as BATON is to
    (A) carpenter
    (B) conductor
    (C) dancer
    (D) lawyer
    (E) writer

15. 1 is to 1000 as GRAM is to
    (A) centigram
    (B) hectogram
    (C) kilogram
    (D) megagram
    (E) milligram

16. SENTENCE is to PARAGRAPH as CHAPTER is to
    (A) book
    (B) magazine
    (C) novel
    (D) poem
    (E) verse

17. SEPARATE is to DIVIDE as THAW is to
    (A) dissolve
    (B) freeze
    (C) melt
    (D) rain
    (E) solidify

18. SPARROW is to BIRD as WASP is to
    (A) fish
    (B) insect
    (C) mammal
    (D) reptile
    (E) worm

19. SUBMARINE is to FISH as KITE is to
    (A) bird
    (B) boy
    (C) limousine
    (D) park
    (E) train

20. WINTER is to SUMMER as COLD is to
    - (A) breezy
    - (B) hot
    - (C) humid
    - (D) mild
    - (E) warm

Questions 21–50 consist of a pair of capitalized words followed by five pairs of words. Choose the option that shows a relationship similar to the one shown by the original pair of capitalized words.

21. AFFIRM is to HINT as
    - (A) accused is to dismissed
    - (B) assert is to convince
    - (C) charge is to insinuate
    - (D) confirm is to reject
    - (E) say is to deny

22. CAUTIOUS is to PRUDENT as
    - (A) brave is to watchful
    - (B) carefree is to ruthless
    - (C) full is to summarized
    - (D) greedy is to cruel
    - (E) rash is to reckless

23. GLOVE is to BALL as
    - (A) game is to pennant
    - (B) hook is to fish
    - (C) skates is to ice
    - (D) stadium is to seats
    - (E) winter is to weather

24. INTIMIDATE is to FEAR as
    - (A) astonish is to wonder
    - (B) awaken is to tiredness
    - (C) feed is to hunger
    - (D) maintain is to satisfaction
    - (E) mirth is to sorrow

25. KICK is to FOOTBALL as
    - (A) break is to pieces
    - (B) kill is to bomb
    - (C) message is to envelope
    - (D) question is to team
    - (E) smoke is to pipe

26. MIAMI is to FLORIDA as
    - (A) Albany is to New York
    - (B) Chicago is to the United States
    - (C) Los Angeles is to San Francisco
    - (D) Minneapolis is to St. Paul
    - (E) Trenton is to Princeton

27. RACE is to FATIGUE as
    - (A) ant is to bug
    - (B) fast is to hunger
    - (C) laughter is to tears
    - (D) track is to athlete
    - (E) walking is to running

28. STOVE is to KITCHEN as
    - (A) pot is to pan
    - (B) sink is to bathroom
    - (C) sofa is to dinette
    - (D) television is to living room
    - (E) trunk is to attic

29. THROW is to BALL as
    - (A) hit is to run
    - (B) kill is to bullet
    - (C) question is to answer
    - (D) show is to tell
    - (E) shoot is to gun

30. TRIANGLE is to PYRAMID as
    - (A) cone is to circle
    - (B) corner is to angle
    - (C) pentagon is to hexagon
    - (D) square is to cube
    - (E) tube is to cylinder

31. WARM is to HOT as
    (A) bright is to genius
    (B) climate is to weather
    (C) enormous is to huge
    (D) glue is to paste
    (E) snow is to cold

32. WOODSMAN is to AX as
    (A) carpenter is to saw
    (B) draftsman is to ruler
    (C) mechanic is to wrench
    (D) soldier is to rifle
    (E) tailor is to needle

33. ASTUTE is to STUPID as
    (A) afraid is to ignorant
    (B) agile is to clumsy
    (C) cruel is to feeble
    (D) dislike is to despise
    (E) intelligent is to clever

34. BRICKLAYER is to CARPENTER as
    (A) dust is to sawdust
    (B) house is to apartment
    (C) mortar is to glue
    (D) saw is to lathe
    (E) trowel is to scalpel

35. BOAT is to DOCK as
    (A) airplane is to land
    (B) bicycle is to path
    (C) bus is to highway
    (D) ship is to sea
    (E) train is to depot

36. CENTURY is to DECADE as
    (A) day is to hour
    (B) decade is to year
    (C) month is to week
    (D) week is to day
    (E) year is to month

37. DECIBEL is to SOUND as
    (A) area is to distance
    (B) calorie is to weight
    (C) color is to light
    (D) temperature is to weather
    (E) volt is to electricity

38. DEFER is to PROCRASTINATE as
    (A) advance is to retreat
    (B) delay is to postpone
    (C) draft is to exempt
    (D) hesitate is to stutter
    (E) natural is to artificial

39. EYE is to HURRICANE as
    (A) hub is to spoke
    (B) hub is to wheel
    (C) rim is to spoke
    (D) spoke is to wheel
    (E) wheel is to rim

40. FISSION is to FUSION as
    (A) conservative is to liberal
    (B) hydrogen is to uranium
    (C) melt is to split
    (D) miscellaneous is to homogeneous
    (E) segregation is to integration

41. GOOD is to ANGELIC as
    (A) bad is to poor
    (B) correct is to incorrect
    (C) glad is to joyous
    (D) mean is to unkind
    (E) sweet is to sour

42. HARE is to HOUND as
    (A) cattle is to cow
    (B) duckling is to duck
    (C) lion is to lamb
    (D) mare is to horse
    (E) mouse is to cat

43. HERD is to CATTLE as
    (A) cage is to birds
    (B) den is to thieves
    (C) flock is to geese
    (D) pair is to lions
    (E) trap is to lobsters

44. INCARCERATE is to EMANCIPATE as
    (A) conserve is to liberate
    (B) free is to jail
    (C) indict is to exonerate
    (D) investigate is to convict
    (E) restrain is to release

45. KEEL is to SHIP as
    (A) engine is to car
    (B) head is to tail
    (C) sole is to shoe
    (D) soul is to body
    (E) starboard is to port

46. LION is to CARNIVOROUS as
    (A) bird is to aquatic
    (B) dog is to canine
    (C) frog is to amphibious
    (D) horse is to herbivorous
    (E) tiger is to ferocious

47. MARGARINE is to BUTTER as
    (A) cream is to milk
    (B) egg is to chicken
    (C) lace is to cotton
    (D) nylon is to silk
    (E) oak is to acorn

48. MILLIGRAM is to DECILITER as
    (A) mass is to distance
    (B) mass is to time
    (C) pint is to quart
    (D) weight is to pressure
    (E) weight is to volume

49. NEGLIGENT is to REQUIREMENT as
    (A) careful is to position
    (B) cautious is to injury
    (C) cogent is to task
    (D) easy is to difficult
    (E) remiss is to duty

50. ORANGE is to MARMALADE as
    (A) cake is to picnic
    (B) jelly is to jam
    (C) potato is to vegetable
    (D) sandwich is to cheese
    (E) tomato is to ketchup

ANSWER KEY AND EXPLANATIONS

1. (C)	11. (B)	21. (C)	31. (A)	41. (C)
2. (C)	12. (C)	22. (E)	32. (A)	42. (E)
3. (C)	13. (D)	23. (B)	33. (B)	43. (C)
4. (E)	14. (B)	24. (A)	34. (C)	44. (E)
5. (E)	15. (C)	25. (E)	35. (E)	45. (C)
6. (D)	16. (A)	26. (A)	36. (B)	46. (D)
7. (D)	17. (C)	27. (B)	37. (E)	47. (D)
8. (E)	18. (B)	28. (B)	38. (B)	48. (E)
9. (B)	19. (A)	29. (E)	39. (B)	49. (E)
10. (A)	20. (B)	30. (D)	40. (E)	50. (E)

1. **The correct answer is (C).** An *easel* is used by *an artist* to support the canvas; a *loom* is used by a *weaver* to hold the yarn that makes up the fabric.

2. **The correct answer is (C).** An *automobile* travels on a *highway*; a *train* moves on the *rails*.

3. **The correct answer is (C).** A *biography* deals with the *facts* of a person's life; a *novel* deals with imaginative narration or *fiction*.

4. **The correct answer is (E).** A *crowd* consists of a large number of *persons*; a *fleet* consists of a large number of *ships*.

5. **The correct answer is (E).** *Darkness* and *light* are antonyms; *stillness* and *sound* are antonyms.

6. **The correct answer is (D).** *Efficiency* generally leads to a *reward*; *carelessness* generally leads to a severe reproof or *reprimand*.

7. **The correct answer is (D).** *Fallen* is the past participle of the infinitive *to fall*; *flown* is the past participle of the infinitive to *fly*.

8. **The correct answer is (E).** *Pork* is obtained from the *hog*; *mutton* is obtained from *sheep*.

9. **The correct answer is (B).** A *sandal* is worn on the *foot*; a *shawl* is worn around the *shoulders*.

10. **The correct answer is (A).** A *theater* is a building expressly designed for special forms of *recreation*; a *school* is a building expressly designed for the *education* of students.

11. **The correct answer is (B).** *III* is the Roman numeral for *3*; *XIV* is the Roman numeral for *14*.

12. **The correct answer is (C).** *When* refers to *time*; *how* refers to *manner*.

13. **The correct answer is (D).** A *clock* is used to determine the *time*; a *thermometer* is used to determine the *temperature*.

14. **The correct answer is (B).** A *gavel* is used by a *judge* to signal for attention or order; a *baton* is used by a *conductor* for the same purpose.

15. **The correct answer is (C).** A *kilogram* consists of 1000 *grams*. Therefore, *1* is to *1000* as *gram* is to *kilogram*.

16. **The correct answer is (A).** A *sentence* is a major subdivision of a *paragraph*; a *chapter* is a major subdivision of a *book*.

17. **The correct answer is (C).** The first pair of words are synonyms. *Melt* and *thaw* are synonymous also.

18. **The correct answer is (B).** A *sparrow* is a type of *bird*; a *wasp* is a type of *insect*.

19. **The correct answer is (A).** *Submarines* and *fish* are generally found in water. *Kites* and *birds* are generally seen in the air.

20. **The correct answer is (B).** The first pair of words are antonyms. The antonym for *cold* is *hot*.

21. **The correct answer is (C).** *Affirm* is direct; *hint* is indirect or suggestive. *Charge* is direct; *insinuate* is indirect or suggestive.

22. **The correct answer is (E).** The first pair of words are synonyms; *rash* and *reckless* are synonymous also.

23. **The correct answer is (B).** This is a purpose relationship. The *glove* is used to catch a *ball*; the *hook* is used to catch *fish*.

24. **The correct answer is (A).** To *intimidate* is to inspire *fear*; to *astonish* is to inspire *wonder*.

25. **The correct answer is (E).** This is an action-to-object relationship. You *kick* a *football* and *smoke* a *pipe*.

26. **The correct answer is (A).** This is a city/state relationship. *Miami* is a city in *Florida*; *Albany* is a city in *New York*.

27. **The correct answer is (B).** This is a cause-and-effect relationship. *Fatigue* results from *racing*; *hunger* results from *fasting*.

28. **The correct answer is (B).** A *stove* is an essential piece of equipment for a *kitchen*; a *sink* is essential for a *bathroom*.

29. **The correct answer is (E).** This is an action-to-object relationship. You *throw* a *ball* and *shoot* a *gun*.

30. **The correct answer is (D).** A *triangle*, a three-sided plane figure, is the side of a *pyramid*; a *square*, a four-sided plane figure, is the side of a *cube*.

31. **The correct answer is (A).** The relationship is that of degree. *Hot* is excessively *warm*; a *genius* is very *bright*.

32. **The correct answer is (A).** A *woodsman* cuts lumber with an *ax*; a *carpenter* cuts lumber with a *saw*.

33. **The correct answer is (B).** *Astute* and *stupid* are antonyms. Of the options given, only choice (B) contains antonyms.

34. **The correct answer is (C).** A *bricklayer* uses *mortar* as an adhesive for bricks; a *carpenter* uses *glue* as an adhesive for wood.

35. **The correct answer is (E).** *Boats* are laid up in a *dock*; *trains* are laid up in a *depot*.

36. **The correct answer is (B).** There are ten *decades* in a *century* and ten *years* in a *decade*.

37. **The correct answer is (E).** *Decibel* is a measure of *sound*; a *volt* is a measure of *electricity*.

38. **The correct answer is (B).** The relationship is that of synonyms. *Delay* and *postpone* are synonyms.

39. **The correct answer is (B).** The *eye* of a *hurricane* is the circular region surrounding the center of the storm's rotation. The *hub* of a *wheel* surrounds the axle, which is the center of the wheel's rotation.

40. The correct answer is (E). The relationship of *fission* and *fusion* is that of splitting and merging. The only parallel relationship is found in choice (E).

41. The correct answer is (C). An extremely *good* person would be *angelic*. An extremely *glad* person would be *joyous*.

42. The correct answer is (E). The relationship of the capitalized words is that of an animal that is normally pursued by another animal. The only parallel relationship is found in choice (E).

43. The correct answer is (C). The relationship of the two capitalized words is that of the term used with a number of animals of one kind kept or living together and the individuals making up this number. The only parallel relationship is found in choice (C).

44. The correct answer is (E). *Incarcerate* means to *restrain*; *emancipate* means to *release*.

45. The correct answer is (C). *Keel* is the bottom of a *ship*; *sole* is the bottom of a *shoe*.

46. The correct answer is (D). *Lions* are meat-eaters *(carnivorous)*; *horses* are plant-eaters *(herbivorous)*.

47. The correct answer is (D). *Margarine* is a manufactured substitute for *butter*; *nylon* is a manufactured substitute for *silk*.

48. The correct answer is (E). The relationship of the two capitalized words is that of a unit of *weight* and a unit of *volume*.

49. The correct answer is (E). One is generally *negligent* in meeting a *requirement* or *remiss* in performing a *duty*.

50. The correct answer is (E). *Marmalade* is made from *oranges*; *ketchup* is made from *tomatoes*.

ANSWER SHEET FOR PRACTICE TEST 3: READING COMPREHENSION

1. Ⓐ Ⓑ Ⓒ Ⓓ Ⓔ	16. Ⓐ Ⓑ Ⓒ Ⓓ Ⓔ	31. Ⓐ Ⓑ Ⓒ Ⓓ	46. Ⓐ Ⓑ Ⓒ Ⓓ	61. Ⓐ Ⓑ Ⓒ Ⓓ
2. Ⓐ Ⓑ Ⓒ Ⓓ Ⓔ	17. Ⓐ Ⓑ Ⓒ Ⓓ Ⓔ	32. Ⓐ Ⓑ Ⓒ Ⓓ	47. Ⓐ Ⓑ Ⓒ Ⓓ	62. Ⓐ Ⓑ Ⓒ Ⓓ
3. Ⓐ Ⓑ Ⓒ Ⓓ Ⓔ	18. Ⓐ Ⓑ Ⓒ Ⓓ Ⓔ	33. Ⓐ Ⓑ Ⓒ Ⓓ	48. Ⓐ Ⓑ Ⓒ Ⓓ	63. Ⓐ Ⓑ Ⓒ Ⓓ
4. Ⓐ Ⓑ Ⓒ Ⓓ Ⓔ	19. Ⓐ Ⓑ Ⓒ Ⓓ Ⓔ	34. Ⓐ Ⓑ Ⓒ Ⓓ	49. Ⓐ Ⓑ Ⓒ Ⓓ	64. Ⓐ Ⓑ Ⓒ Ⓓ
5. Ⓐ Ⓑ Ⓒ Ⓓ Ⓔ	20. Ⓐ Ⓑ Ⓒ Ⓓ Ⓔ	35. Ⓐ Ⓑ Ⓒ Ⓓ	50. Ⓐ Ⓑ Ⓒ Ⓓ	65. Ⓐ Ⓑ Ⓒ Ⓓ
6. Ⓐ Ⓑ Ⓒ Ⓓ Ⓔ	21. Ⓐ Ⓑ Ⓒ Ⓓ Ⓔ	36. Ⓐ Ⓑ Ⓒ Ⓓ	51. Ⓐ Ⓑ Ⓒ Ⓓ	66. Ⓐ Ⓑ Ⓒ Ⓓ
7. Ⓐ Ⓑ Ⓒ Ⓓ Ⓔ	22. Ⓐ Ⓑ Ⓒ Ⓓ Ⓔ	37. Ⓐ Ⓑ Ⓒ Ⓓ	52. Ⓐ Ⓑ Ⓒ Ⓓ	67. Ⓐ Ⓑ Ⓒ Ⓓ
8. Ⓐ Ⓑ Ⓒ Ⓓ Ⓔ	23. Ⓐ Ⓑ Ⓒ Ⓓ Ⓔ	38. Ⓐ Ⓑ Ⓒ Ⓓ	53. Ⓐ Ⓑ Ⓒ Ⓓ	68. Ⓐ Ⓑ Ⓒ Ⓓ
9. Ⓐ Ⓑ Ⓒ Ⓓ Ⓔ	24. Ⓐ Ⓑ Ⓒ Ⓓ Ⓔ	39. Ⓐ Ⓑ Ⓒ Ⓓ	54. Ⓐ Ⓑ Ⓒ Ⓓ	69. Ⓐ Ⓑ Ⓒ Ⓓ
10. Ⓐ Ⓑ Ⓒ Ⓓ Ⓔ	25. Ⓐ Ⓑ Ⓒ Ⓓ Ⓔ	40. Ⓐ Ⓑ Ⓒ Ⓓ	55. Ⓐ Ⓑ Ⓒ Ⓓ	70. Ⓐ Ⓑ Ⓒ Ⓓ
11. Ⓐ Ⓑ Ⓒ Ⓓ Ⓔ	26. Ⓐ Ⓑ Ⓒ Ⓓ	41. Ⓐ Ⓑ Ⓒ Ⓓ	56. Ⓐ Ⓑ Ⓒ Ⓓ	71. Ⓐ Ⓑ Ⓒ Ⓓ
12. Ⓐ Ⓑ Ⓒ Ⓓ Ⓔ	27. Ⓐ Ⓑ Ⓒ Ⓓ	42. Ⓐ Ⓑ Ⓒ Ⓓ	57. Ⓐ Ⓑ Ⓒ Ⓓ	72. Ⓐ Ⓑ Ⓒ Ⓓ
13. Ⓐ Ⓑ Ⓒ Ⓓ Ⓔ	28. Ⓐ Ⓑ Ⓒ Ⓓ	43. Ⓐ Ⓑ Ⓒ Ⓓ	58. Ⓐ Ⓑ Ⓒ Ⓓ	73. Ⓐ Ⓑ Ⓒ Ⓓ
14. Ⓐ Ⓑ Ⓒ Ⓓ Ⓔ	29. Ⓐ Ⓑ Ⓒ Ⓓ	44. Ⓐ Ⓑ Ⓒ Ⓓ	59. Ⓐ Ⓑ Ⓒ Ⓓ	74. Ⓐ Ⓑ Ⓒ Ⓓ
15. Ⓐ Ⓑ Ⓒ Ⓓ Ⓔ	30. Ⓐ Ⓑ Ⓒ Ⓓ	45. Ⓐ Ⓑ Ⓒ Ⓓ	60. Ⓐ Ⓑ Ⓒ Ⓓ	75. Ⓐ Ⓑ Ⓒ Ⓓ

answer sheet

Practice Test 3: Reading Comprehension

Questions 1–25 are five-option items. For each question, select the option that best completes the statement or answers the question.

1. The mental attitude of the employee toward safety is exceedingly important in preventing accidents. All efforts designed to keep safety on the employee's mind and to keep accident prevention a live subject in the office will help substantially in a safety program. Although it might seem strange, it is common for people to be careless. Therefore, safety education is a continuous process.

   The reason given in the above passage for maintaining ongoing safety education is that

   (A) employees must be told to stay alert at all times.

   (B) office tasks are often dangerous.

   (C) people are often careless.

   (D) safety rules change frequently.

   (E) safety rules change infrequently.

2. One goal of law enforcement is the reduction of stress between one population group and another. When no stress exists between population groups, law enforcement can deal with other tensions or simply perform traditional police functions. However, when stress between population groups does exist, law enforcement, in its efforts to prevent disruptive behavior, becomes committed to reduce that stress.

   According to the above passage, during times of stress between population groups in the community, it is necessary for law enforcement to attempt to

   (A) continue traditional police functions.

   (B) eliminate tension resulting from social change.

   (C) punish disruptive behavior.

   (D) reduce intergroup stress.

   (E) warn disruptive individuals.

Questions 3–5 are based on the information contained in the following passage.

Microwave ovens use a principle of heating different from that employed by ordinary ovens.

The key part of a microwave oven is its magnetron, which generates the microwaves that then go into the oven. Some of these energy waves hit the food directly, while others bounce around the oven until they find their way into the food. Sometimes the microwaves intersect, strengthening their effect. Sometimes they cancel each other out. Parts of the food might be heavily saturated with energy, while other parts might receive very little. In conventional cooking, you select the oven temperature. In microwave cooking, you select the power level. The walls of the microwave oven are made of metal, which helps the microwaves bounce off them. However, this turns to a disadvantage for the cook who uses metal cookware.

3. Based on the information contained in this passage, it is easy to see some advantages and disadvantages of microwave ovens. The greatest disadvantage would probably be

(A) overcooked food.

(B) radioactive food.

(C) unevenly cooked food.

(D) the high cost of preparing food.

(E) cold food.

4. In a conventional oven, the temperature selection would be based upon degrees. In a microwave oven, the power selection would probably be based upon

(A) wattage.

(B) voltage.

(C) lumens.

(D) solar units.

(E) ohms.

5. The source of the microwaves in the oven is

(A) reflected energy.

(B) convection currents.

(C) the magnetron.

(D) short waves and bursts of energy.

(E) the food itself.

Questions 6 and 7 are based on the information contained in the following passage.

For the past six or seven years, a group of scientists has been attempting to make fortunes by breeding "bugs"—microorganisms that will manufacture valuable chemicals and drugs. This budding industry is called genetic engineering, and out of this young program, at least one company has induced a lowly bacterium to manufacture human interferon, a rare and costly substance that fights virus infections by "splicing" human genes into their natural hereditary material. But there are dangers in this activity, including the accidental development of a mutant bacterium that might change the whole life pattern on Earth. There are also legal questions about whether a living organism can be patented and what new products can be marketed from living matter. The congressional agency that oversees these new developments says that it will be about seven years before any new product developed by genetic engineering will be allowed to be placed on the market.

6. One of the potential problems of genetic engineering is the possibility of

(A) an oversupply of bacteria.

(B) dangerous mutations.

(C) overpopulation.

(D) excess food.

(E) too many engineers.

7. Human interferon can be used to fight viral infections. This means that it may be a tool in curing

(A) the common cold.

(B) diseases caused by drugs and alcohol.

(C) diseases that cause deformities.

(D) diseases that are genetic in origin.

(E) problems related to psychological stress.

Questions 8–10 are based on the information contained in the following passage.

Progress in human achievement is never straightforward. Sometimes, a simple attempt to build a road can do incredible damage to the environment. The Brazilian government, which has been attempting to link highways in that enormous country, has had to build roads through the Amazon River basin. In the process, this road-building program has inadvertently destroyed much valuable timberland. The basin, which originally occupied nearly two million square miles, has fallen victim in the past five years to destruction that has wiped out more than a quarter-million square miles of the world's largest forest surrounding the world's longest river. The Trans-Amazonian Highway caused the felling of millions of trees and drastically changed the forest ecology. Attempts were made to establish farms along its route where rice, other grains, and cattle would be raised. But the soil of the Amazon, which gave rise to this magnificent timber, is unsuitable to agriculture. Many of the farmers who attempted to work the forestland went bankrupt. As a result, the Brazilian government has diminished its interest in the network of auxiliary and connecting roads that would have joined with the Trans-Amazonian Highway, only part of which has yet been completed.

8. Although there has been a great deal of timberland destruction in the Amazon River basin, most of it still remains intact. The Brazilian government deliberately set out to build a highway through the basin in order to

(A) establish new farming areas.

(B) harvest crops of timber.

(C) create new cities in the basin.

(D) link remote parts of Brazil.

(E) conquer the Amazon River.

9. A good title for this paragraph might be

(A) "Progress Isn't Always Easy."

(B) "Changes in Brazil's Ecology."

(C) "Don't Fool with Mother Nature."

(D) "Governments Are Bunglers."

(E) "The Amazon—A Great River."

10. In this paragraph, the word "inadvertently" (line 10) means

(A) specifically.

(B) accidentally.

(C) cleverly.

(D) knowingly.

(E) aimlessly.

Questions 11–14 are based on the information contained in the following passage.

Modern cartography was born in royal France during the latter part of the seventeenth century when King Louis XIV offered a handsome prize for anyone who could devise a method for accurately determining longitude. For two thousand years, sailors had been trying to find an exact way to locate different places on Earth. The circumference of the Earth had been calculated by the Greek Eratosthenes four hundred years before the birth of Christ, but as late as 1650 it was still difficult to exactly locate any single position on a map, and particularly difficult to determine longitude on land or sea. Longitude is used to determine the distance of a place east or west of a point of reference. By the end of the seventeenth century, two instruments had been invented which would provide greater accuracy in calculating longitude. The two new instruments were the telescope and the accurate clock. One final instrument remained to be devised. It was perfected by John Harrison in the latter part of the eighteenth century. It was called a chronometer.

11. The benefit of modern cartography was

    (A) more accurate clocks.

    (B) the determination of the exact location of the North Pole.

    (C) newer and better maps.

    (D) the introduction of excellent telescopes.

    (E) the invention of the chronometer.

12. It can be inferred from this paragraph that

    (A) John Harrison was a Frenchman.

    (B) the French government was interested in accurate maps.

    (C) the clock was invented in the seventeenth century.

    (D) the Greeks had calculated the size of the earth.

    (E) None of the above is true.

13. One direct consequence of modern cartography was the adoption, in succeeding years, of

    (A) radar as a time measurement.

    (B) plutonium temperature-recording devices.

    (C) pollution control devices.

    (D) armaments by France.

    (E) universally accepted time zones.

14. A famous cartographer who helped determine the location of the New World but who is not mentioned in this paragraph is

    (A) Amerigo Vespucci.

    (B) Thomas Jefferson.

    (C) Christopher Columbus.

    (D) George Washington.

    (E) Robert Perry.

Questions 15–17 are based on the information contained in the following passage.

Many educators have asserted that one of the major problems of business today is the excess of specialists and the paucity of generalists. They decry the lack of broadly educated men and women in the ranks of business. According to this narrow view of reality, most business leaders demand, first, a specific vocational skill of job applicants and then, as an afterthought, accept persons with broad general knowledge. This alleged fixation of a trade school mentality reflects an important gap in information on the part of the people making the charges.

Today, most business officials believe that management is deeply involved in the art of communication because success and profit depend upon it. The ability to communicate generally reflects a wide range of education, not a narrow one. Most business officials believe that without the ability to read intelligently and to communicate coherently, the young man or woman starting out in the business world faces a difficult, perhaps impossible, task in climbing the ladder of financial success.

15. The preceding paragraphs are divided into two separate and distinct ideas. The first idea conveys the belief that business is looking for people

    (A) with the proper image.

    (B) with narrow vocational skills.

    (C) who will be loyal to the company.

    (D) who have years of experience.

    (E) who can bring in profit.

16. The author of this passage, however, does not agree with the concepts stated in the first paragraph. Two key words that show the author's disagreement with those ideas are

    (A) "narrow" and "alleged."
    (B) "difficult" and "impossible."
    (C) "specialist" and "generalist."
    (D) "excess" and "paucity."
    (E) "success" and "profit."

17. The author's point of view is that young people wishing to get ahead in business today should

    (A) have a specialty.
    (B) be related to management.
    (C) be able to read intelligently and write coherently.
    (D) graduate from a trade school.
    (E) understand the intricacies of business.

Questions 18–20 are based on the information contained in the following passage.

Men who live in democratic communities not only seldom indulge in meditation, but they naturally entertain very little esteem for it. A democratic state of society and democratic institutions keep the greater part of men in constant activity; and the habits of mind that are suited to an active life are not always suited to a contemplative one. The man of action is frequently obliged to content himself with the best he can get because he would never accomplish his purpose if he chose to carry out every detail to perfection. He has occasion to perpetually rely on ideas that he has not had leisure to search to the bottom; for he is much more frequently aided by the reasonableness of an idea than by its strict accuracy; and in the long run he risks less in making use of some false principles than in spending his time in establishing all his principles on the basis of truth.

—from Alexis de Tocqueville
Democracy in America

18. The author of this passage, a French aristocrat who toured the United States in the early nineteenth century, believed that the Americans he encountered during his travels were NOT

    (A) intellectual.
    (B) shrewd.
    (C) hardworking.
    (D) active.
    (E) pragmatic.

19. If what de Tocqueville says is acceptable as a description of modern America, then it would be reasonable to assume that Americans are most affected by

    (A) political authorities.
    (B) college professors.
    (C) science fiction.
    (D) rumors.
    (E) fads and advertising.

20. De Tocqueville believes that Americans are much more likely to make significant personal achievements because they are

    (A) introspective.
    (B) action-oriented.
    (C) passive.
    (D) sedentary.
    (E) phlegmatic.

Questions 21–23 are based on the information contained in the following passage.

Can the interpretation of an inkblot reveal personality traits? The Rorschach Test, which uses the inkblot, is still not fully accepted as a valuable diagnostic tool by professionals in the field of psychology. If properly interpreted, a Rorschach Test, in one hour, could provide personality data that would take weeks or months of ordinary interviews to reveal. The test consists of ten cards, each of which contains an inkblot intended to elicit a response from the subject. Test result analysis is a complex computation of many variables, including what colors, designs, and images are reported by the subject. Normal subjects usually respond to the whole design, while disturbed subjects are more likely to focus on individual details. Highly excitable subjects often show intense response to color, while depressed subjects may not mention color at all. Lack of reliability is the major reason for the limited use of the Rorschach Test.

21. The Rorschach Test is a

  (A) universally accepted method of diagnosing a state of mind.

  (B) psychological test with limited reliability.

  (C) set of fifteen inkblots that subjects are asked to describe.

  (D) quick and easy new test that is used to diagnose behavior.

  (E) series of puzzles.

22. The major value of the Rorschach Test is

  (A) its ability to distinguish between sane people and lunatics.

  (B) the ease with which the results can be analyzed.

  (C) the speed that the test can be given.

  (D) the total acceptance of the test as a useful form of diagnosis.

  (E) Both choices (A) and (D) are correct.

23. A highly emotional and excited person, according to Rorschach standards, is most likely to

  (A) respond to color.

  (B) respond to card size.

  (C) not respond at all.

  (D) see whole designs in the inkblots.

  (E) focus on details rather than designs.

Questions 24 and 25 are based on the information contained in the following passage.

Proteins in all forms of plant and animal life are constructed of the same basic set of twenty amino acids. Proteins are assembled within living organisms by a second set of building blocks called nucleotides. Nucleotides are substances joined together within every cell to form very long chains called nucleic acids. The most important of these nucleic acids is called deoxyribonucleic acid, or DNA. DNA is the largest molecule known, containing, in animals and man alike, as many as ten billion separate atoms. It is also the most important molecule in every living organism, even more important than protein, because it determines how proteins will be assembled. In other words, the DNA molecule contains the master plan that shapes the organism. It is believed that the very first living organisms on earth contained DNA.

24. From this paragraph, one can infer that DNA

  (A) is a protein.

  (B) is an organ.

  (C) is an organism.

(D) is found in every living plant or animal.

(E) was the first living creature.

25. Although all molecules contain a great many atoms, DNA is seen as

(A) the largest molecule in man.

(B) a structure that contains no carbon or hydrogen.

(C) a protein that contains many acids.

(D) a nucleotide that forms large chains.

(E) a result of the cooling of the earth.

Questions 26–50 are four-option items. Read the paragraph(s) and select one of the lettered choices that best completes the statement or answers the question.

26. Few drivers realize that steel is used to keep the road surface flat in spite of the weight of buses and trucks. Steel bars, deeply embedded in the concrete, are sinews to take the stresses so that the stresses cannot crack the slab or make it wavy.

The passage best supports the statement that a concrete road

(A) is expensive to build.

(B) usually cracks under heavy weights.

(C) looks like any other road.

(D) is reinforced with other material.

27. Blood pressure, the force that the blood exerts against the walls of the vessels through which it flows, is commonly meant to be the pressure in the arteries. The pressure in the arteries varies with contraction (work period) and the relaxation (rest period) of the heart. When the heart contracts, the blood in the arteries is at its greatest, or systolic, pressure. When the heart

relaxes, the blood in the arteries is at its lowest, or diastolic, pressure. The difference between the two pressures is called the pulse pressure.

According to the passage, which one of the following statements is most accurate?

(A) The blood in the arteries is at its greatest pressure during contraction.

(B) Systolic pressure measures the blood in the arteries when the heart is relaxed.

(C) The difference between systolic and diastolic pressure determines the blood pressure.

(D) Pulse pressure is the same as blood pressure.

28. More patents have been issued for inventions relating to transportation than for those in any other line of human activity. These inventions have resulted in a great financial savings to the people and have made possible a civilization that could not have existed without them.

The one of the following that is best supported by the passage is that transportation

(A) would be impossible without inventions.

(B) is an important factor in our civilization.

(C) is still to be much improved.

(D) is more important than any other activity.

29. The Supreme Court was established by Article 3 of the Constitution. Since 1869 it has been made up of nine members—the chief justice and eight associate justices—who are appointed for life. Supreme Court justices are named by the president and must be confirmed by the Senate.

The Supreme Court

(A) was established in 1869.

(B) consists of nine justices.

(C) consists of justices who are appointed by the Senate.

(D) changes with each presidential election.

30. With the exception of Earth, all the planets in our solar system are named for gods and goddesses in Greek or Roman legends. This is because the other planets were thought to be in heaven like the gods and our planet lay beneath, like the earth. All the planets except Earth

    (A) were part of Greek and Roman legends.

    (B) were thought to be in heaven.

    (C) are part of the same solar system.

    (D) were worshipped as gods.

31. Both the high school and the college should take the responsibility for preparing the student to get a job. Since the ability to write a good application letter is one of the first steps toward this goal, every teacher should be willing to do what he can to help the student learn to write such letters.

    The paragraph best supports the statement that

    (A) inability to write a good letter often reduces one's job prospects.

    (B) the major responsibility of the school is to obtain jobs for its students.

    (C) success is largely a matter of the kind of work the student applies for first.

    (D) every teacher should teach a course in the writing of application letters.

32. Many people think that only older men who have a great deal of experience should hold public office. These people lose sight of an important fact. Many of the founding fathers of our country were comparatively young men. Today more than ever, our country needs young, idealistic politicians.

    The best interpretation of what this author believes is that

    (A) only experienced men should hold public office.

    (B) only idealistic men should hold public office.

    (C) younger men can and should take part in politics.

    (D) young people don't like politics.

33. The X-ray has gone into business. Developed primarily to aid in diagnosing human ills, the machine now works in packing plants, foundries, service stations, and in a dozen ways contributes to precision and accuracy in industry. The X-ray

    (A) was first developed to aid business.

    (B) is being used to improve the functioning of industry.

    (C) is more accurate in packing plants than in foundries.

    (D) increases the output of such industries as service stations.

34. In large organizations some standardized, simple, inexpensive method of giving employees information about company policies and rules, as well as specific instructions regarding their duties, is practically essential. This is the purpose of all office manuals of whatever type.

    The paragraph best supports the statement that office manuals

(A) are all about the same.

(B) should be simple enough for the average employee to understand.

(C) are necessary to large organizations.

(D) act as constant reminders to the employee of his or her duties.

35. In the relationship of humankind to nature, the procuring of food and shelter is fundamental. With the migration of humans to various climates, ever new adjustments to the food supply and to the climate became necessary.

According to the passage, the means by which humans supply their material needs are

(A) accidental.

(B) inadequate.

(C) limited.

(D) varied.

Questions 36 and 37 are based on the following passage.

Many experiments on the effects of alcoholic beverages show that alcohol decreases alertness and efficiency. It decreases self-consciousness and at the same time increases confidence and feelings of ease and relaxation. It impairs attention and judgment. It destroys fear of consequences. Usual cautions are thrown to the winds. Drivers who use alcohol tend to disregard their usual safety practices. Their reaction time slows down; normally quick reactions are not possible for them. They cannot judge the speed of their car or any other car. They become highway menaces.

36. The above passage states that the drinking of alcohol makes drivers

(A) more alert.

(B) less confident.

(C) more efficient.

(D) less attentive.

37. It is reasonable to assume that drivers may overcome the bad effects of drinking by

(A) relying on their good driving habits to a greater extent than normally.

(B) waiting for the alcohol to wear off before driving.

(C) watching the road more carefully.

(D) being more cautious.

Questions 38–40 are based on the passage shown below.

Arsonists are persons who set fires deliberately. They don't look like criminals, but they cost the nation millions of dollars in property loss and sometimes loss of life. Arsonists set fires for many different reasons. Sometimes a shopkeeper sees no way out of losing his business and sets fire to it to collect the insurance. Another type of arsonist is one who wants revenge and sets fire to the home or shop of someone he feels has treated him unfairly. Some arsonists just like the excitement of seeing the fire burn and watching the firefighters at work; arsonists of this type have been known to help fight the fire.

38. According to the passage above, an arsonist is a person who

(A) intentionally sets a fire.

(B) enjoys watching fires.

(C) wants revenge.

(D) needs money.

39. Arsonists have been known to help fight fires because they

 (A) felt guilty.

 (B) enjoyed the excitement.

 (C) wanted to earn money.

 (D) didn't want anyone hurt.

40. According to the passage above, we may conclude that arsonists

 (A) would make good firefighters.

 (B) are not criminals.

 (C) are mentally ill.

 (D) are not all alike.

41. The lead-acid storage battery is used for storing energy in its chemical form. The battery does not actually store electricity but converts an electrical charge into chemical energy that is stored until the battery terminals are connected to a closed external circuit. When the circuit is closed, the battery's chemical energy is transformed back into electrical energy, and as a result, current flows through the circuit.

 According to this passage, a lead-acid battery stores

 (A) current.

 (B) electricity.

 (C) electric energy.

 (D) chemical energy.

42. A good or service has value only because people want it. Value is an extrinsic quality wholly created in the minds of people and is not intrinsic in the property itself.

 According to this passage, it is correct to say that an object will be valuable if it is

 (A) beautiful.

 (B) not plentiful.

 (C) sought after.

 (D) useful.

43. You can tell a frog from a toad by its skin. In general, a frog's skin is moist, smooth, and shiny, while a toad's skin is dry, dull, and rough or covered with warts. Frogs are also better at jumping than toads are.

 You can recognize a toad by its

 (A) great jumping ability.

 (B) smooth, shiny skin.

 (C) lack of warts.

 (D) dry, rough skin.

44. The speed of a boat is measured in knots. One knot is equal to a speed of one nautical mile an hour. A nautical mile is equal to 6,080 feet, while an ordinary mile is 5,280 feet.

 According to the passage, which of the following statements is true?

 (A) A nautical mile is longer than an ordinary mile.

 (B) A speed of 2 knots is the same as 2 miles per hour.

 (C) A knot is the same as a mile.

 (D) The distance a boat travels is measured in knots.

45. There are only two grooves on a record—one on each side. The groove is cut in a spiral on the surface of the record. For stereophonic sound, a different sound is recorded in each wall of the groove. The pickup produces two signals, one of which goes to the left-hand speaker and one to the right-hand speaker. Stereophonic sound is produced by

 (A) cutting extra grooves in a record.

 (B) recording different sounds in each wall of the groove.

 (C) sending the sound to two speakers.

 (D) having left- and right-hand speakers.

46. It is a common assumption that city directories are prepared and published by the cities concerned. However, the directory business is as much a private business as is the publishing of dictionaries and encyclopedias. The companies financing the publication make their profits through the sales of the directories themselves and through the advertising in them.

   The paragraph best supports the statement that

   (A) the publication of a city directory is a commercial enterprise.

   (B) the size of a city directory limits the space devoted to advertising.

   (C) many city directories are published by dictionary and encyclopedia concerns.

   (D) city directories are sold at cost to local residents and businessmen.

47. Although rural crime reporting is spottier and less efficient than city and town reporting, sufficient data has been collected to support the statement that rural crime rates are lower than those in urban communities.

   The paragraph best supports the statement that

   (A) better reporting of crime occurs in rural areas than in cities.

   (B) there appears to be a lower proportion of crime in rural areas than in cities.

   (C) cities have more crime than towns.

   (D) no conclusions can be drawn regarding crime in rural areas because of inadequate reporting.

48. Iron is used in making our bridges and skyscrapers, subways and steamships, railroads and automobiles, and nearly all kinds of machinery—besides millions of small articles, from the farmer's scythe to the tailor's needle.

   The paragraph best supports the statement that iron

   (A) is the most abundant of the metals.

   (B) has many different uses.

   (C) is the strongest of all metals.

   (D) is the only material used in building skyscrapers and bridges.

49. Most solids, like most liquids, expand when heated and contract when cooled. To allow for this, roads, sidewalks, and railroad tracks are constructed with spacings between sections so that they can expand during the hot weather.

   If roads, sidewalks, and railroad tracks were not constructed with spacings between sections,

   (A) nothing would happen to them when the weather changed.

   (B) they could not be constructed as easily as they are now.

   (C) they would crack or break when the weather changed.

   (D) they would not appear to be even.

50. Twenty-five percent of all household burglaries can be attributed to unlocked windows or doors. Crime is the result of opportunity plus desire. To prevent crime, it is each individual's responsibility to

   (A) provide the desire.

   (B) provide the opportunity.

   (C) prevent the desire.

   (D) prevent the opportunity.

Questions 51–75 are four-option items. Each of questions 51–59 consists of a sentence in which one word is omitted. Select the lettered option that best completes the thought expressed in each sentence.

51. The explanation by the teacher was so _____ that the students solved the problem with ease.

    (A) complicated

    (B) explicit

    (C) protracted

    (D) vague

52. A(n) _____ listener can distinguish fact from fiction.

    (A) astute

    (B) ingenuous

    (C) prejudiced

    (D) reluctant

53. Your young nephew is going to ring the doorbells of the neighbors and say, "Trick or treat." You should send him a(n) _____ card.

    (A) April Fool's

    (B) Halloween

    (C) Thanksgiving

    (D) Valentine

54. We applauded the able cheerleader who _____ her baton so skillfully.

    (A) twiddled

    (B) twirled

    (C) twisted

    (D) twitched

55. His hatred for his brother Abel was so intense that Cain committed _____.

    (A) fratricide

    (B) genocide

    (C) patricide

    (D) suicide

56. Because corn is _____ to the region, it is not expensive.

    (A) alien

    (B) exotic

    (C) indigenous

    (D) indigent

57. Our colleague was so _____ that we could not convince him that he was wrong.

    (A) capitulating

    (B) complaisant

    (C) light-hearted

    (D) obdurate

58. A lover of democracy has a(n) _____ toward totalitarianism.

    (A) antipathy

    (B) appreciation

    (C) empathy

    (D) proclivity

59. As the Declaration of Independence was signed in 1776, the United States held its _____ celebration in 1976.

    (A) biannual

    (B) bicentennial

    (C) biennial

    (D) centennial

Questions 60–64 consist of a sentence with two blank spaces, each blank indicating that a word or figure has been omitted. Select one of the lettered options that, when inserted in the sentence, best completes the thought expressed in the sentence as a whole.

60. Human behavior is far _____ variable, and therefore _____ predictable, than that of any other species.

    (A) less . . . as

    (B) less . . . not

    (C) more . . . not

    (D) more . . . less

61. The _____ limitation of this method is that the results are based _____ a narrow sample.

    (A) chief . . . with
    (B) chief . . . on
    (C) only . . . for
    (D) only . . . to

62. He is rather _____ and, therefore, easily _____.

    (A) caustic . . . hurt
    (B) dangerous . . . noticed
    (C) immature . . . deceived
    (D) worldly . . . misunderstood

63. _____ education was instituted for the purpose of preventing _____ of young children, and guaranteeing them a minimum of education.

    (A) Compulsory . . . exploitation
    (B) Free . . . abuse
    (C) Kindergarten . . . ignorance
    (D) Secondary . . . delinquency

64. Any person who is in _____ while awaiting trial is considered _____ until he or she has been declared guilty.

    (A) custody . . . innocent
    (B) jail . . . suspect
    (C) jeopardy . . . suspicious
    (D) prison . . . rehabilitated

Questions 65–72 consist of a quotation that contains one word that is incorrectly used, because it is not in keeping with the meaning that the quotation is intended to convey. Determine which word is incorrectly used. Then select from the lettered options the word that, when substituted for the incorrectly used word, would best help to convey the intended meaning of the quotation.

65. "Under a good personnel policy, the number of employee complaints and grievances will tend to be a number which is sufficiently great to keep the supervisory force on its toes and yet large enough to leave time for other phases of supervision."

    (A) complete
    (B) definite
    (C) limit
    (D) small

66. "One of the important assets of a democracy is an active, energetic local government, meeting local needs, and giving an immediate opportunity to legislators to participate in their own public affairs."

    (A) citizens
    (B) convenient
    (C) local
    (D) officials

67. "If the supervisor of a group of employees is to supply the necessary leadership to his or her subordinates, they will seek a leader outside the group for guidance and inspiration, because leadership must be supplied by someone whenever people work together for a common purpose."

    (A) fails
    (B) information
    (C) manager
    (D) plan

68. "The cost of wholesale food distribution in large urban centers is related to the cost of food to ultimate consumers, because they cannot pay for any added distribution costs."

    (A) eventually
    (B) sales
    (C) some
    (D) unrelated

69. "Why is it that in these times, when poetry brings in little prestige and more money, people are found who devote their lives to the unrewarding occupation of writing poetry?"

(A) art

(B) great

(C) less

(D) publicity

70. "In whatever form and at whatever intervals, the written report submitted by the operating unit can never adequately supplement personal, firsthand acquaintance with the work."

(A) expect

(B) experience

(C) objective

(D) replace

71. "Unless reasonable managerial control is exercised over office supplies, one can be certain that there will be extravagance, rejected items out of stock, excessive prices paid for some items, and obsolete material in the stockroom."

(A) instituted

(B) needed

(C) overlooked

(D) supervisory

72. "Consumer information and trade compliance cannot be emphasized in low income areas where language and education difficulties may exist."

(A) do

(B) must

(C) not

(D) whether

Questions 73–75 are based on different reading passages. Answer each question on the basis of the information contained in the passage.

73. "Although foreign ministries and their ministers exist for the purpose of explaining the viewpoints of one nation in terms understood by the ministries of another, honest people in one nation find it difficult to understand the viewpoints of honest people in another."

The passage best supports the statement that

(A) it is unusual for many people to share similar ideas.

(B) people of different nations may not consider matters in the same light.

(C) suspicion prevents understanding between nations.

(D) the people of one nation must sympathize with the viewpoints of the people of other nations.

74. "Personal appearance may be relevant if the job is one involving numerous contacts with the public or with other people, but in most positions it is a matter of distinctly secondary importance; other qualities that have no bearing on the job to be filled should also be discounted."

According to this quotation,

(A) in positions involving contact with the public, the personal appearance of the applicant is the most important factor to be considered.

(B) the personal appearance of a candidate should not be considered of primary importance when interviewing persons for most positions.

(C) the personal appearance of the candidate should never be considered during an interview.

(D) there are many factors that should be considered during an interview, even though they have no direct bearing on the job to be filled.

75. "No matter how carefully planned or how painstakingly executed a sales letter may be, it will be useless unless it is sent to people selected from a good mailing list consisting of the correct names and addresses of bona fide prospects or customers."

This quotation best supports the statement that

(A) a good mailing list is more important than the sales letter.

(B) a sales letter should not be sent to anyone who is not already a customer.

(C) carefully planned letters may be wasted on poor mailing lists.

(D) sales letters are more effective when sent to customers rather than bona fide prospects.

practice test

ANSWER KEY AND EXPLANATIONS

1. (C)	16. (A)	31. (A)	46. (A)	61. (B)
2. (D)	17. (C)	32. (C)	47. (B)	62. (C)
3. (C)	18. (A)	33. (B)	48. (B)	63. (A)
4. (A)	19. (E)	34. (C)	49. (C)	64. (A)
5. (C)	20. (B)	35. (D)	50. (D)	65. (D)
6. (B)	21. (B)	36. (D)	51. (B)	66. (A)
7. (A)	22. (C)	37. (B)	52. (A)	67. (A)
8. (D)	23. (A)	38. (A)	53. (B)	68. (A)
9. (A)	24. (D)	39. (B)	54. (B)	69. (C)
10. (B)	25. (A)	40. (D)	55. (A)	70. (D)
11. (C)	26. (D)	41. (D)	56. (C)	71. (B)
12. (B)	27. (A)	42. (C)	57. (D)	72. (B)
13. (E)	28. (B)	43. (D)	58. (A)	73. (B)
14. (A)	29. (B)	44. (A)	59. (B)	74. (B)
15. (B)	30. (B)	45. (B)	60. (D)	75. (C)

1. **The correct answer is (C).** Safety education must be a continuous process because it is common for people to be careless.

2. **The correct answer is (D).** During times of stress, law enforcement becomes committed to reducing that stress between population groups.

3. **The correct answer is (C).** The uneven saturation of energy would result in unevenly cooked food.

4. **The correct answer is (A).** The watt is a measure of electrical energy. Electrical power in the home is measured in watts or kilowatts.

5. **The correct answer is (C).** The magnetron within the microwave oven generates the energy.

6. **The correct answer is (B).** A danger is the possible development of a mutant bacteria that may change the life pattern on Earth.

7. **The correct answer is (A).** The common cold is considered to be a viral infection. Interferon may be used to cure the infection.

8. **The correct answer is (D).** The purpose of the highway was to link various parts of Brazil. This included parts that were relatively inaccessible.

9. **The correct answer is (A).** The intent of the Brazilian government was to do good rather than harm. Plans to achieve human progress are not always realized.

10. **The correct answer is (B).** *Inadvertently* is synonymous with *accidentally* or *unintentionally*.

11. **The correct answer is (C).** Cartography is the science of mapmaking. Improved cartography means better maps.

12. **The correct answer is (B).** Offering a prize for better maps indicates the French government's concern with the development of better maps.

13. **The correct answer is (E).** The only direct consequence of improved map-making was that it enabled nations to agree on clearly defined time zones.

14. **The correct answer is (A).** Amerigo Vespucci is the only one of those listed who was a famous cartographer and who gave his name to the New World in the early part of the sixteenth century.

15. **The correct answer is (B).** Educators believe that business is looking for people who have specific vocational skills.

16. **The correct answer is (A).** The two key words that show the author does not agree with the educators' arguments are *narrow* and *alleged*.

17. **The correct answer is (C).** The author believes that most business leaders are looking for well-educated personnel who are able to communicate.

18. **The correct answer is (A).** The first sentence in the passage states that they neither indulge in nor esteem meditation.

19. **The correct answer is (E).** " . . . he is much more frequently aided by the reasonableness of an idea than by its strict accuracy."

20. **The correct answer is (B).** "A democratic state of society and democratic institutions keep the greater part of men in constant activity."

21. **The correct answer is (B).** Lack of reliability is the major reason for the limited use of the Rorschach test.

22. **The correct answer is (C).** The major value of the test is the speed with which it can be administered (one hour)

23. **The correct answer is (A).** "Highly excitable subjects often show intense response to color. . . ."

24. **The correct answer is (D).** DNA is the most important molecule in every living organism.

25. **The correct answer is (A).** DNA is the largest known molecule in all animals, including man.

26. **The correct answer is (D).** The first three choices are not supported by the passage. The second sentence in the passage states that steel bars, deeply embedded in the concrete, are sinews to take the stresses.

27. **The correct answer is (A).** The third sentence in the passage states that when the heart contracts, the blood in the arteries is at its greatest pressure.

28. **The correct answer is (B).** The second sentence states that inventions relating to transportation have made possible a civilization that could not have existed without them. This supports the correct answer—transportation is an important factor in our civilization.

29. **The correct answer is (B).** One chief justice plus eight associate justices equals nine justices.

30. **The correct answer is (B).** The second sentence states that the other planets were thought to be in heaven.

31. **The correct answer is (A).** Step one in the job application process is often the application letter. If the letter is not effective, the applicant will not move on to the next step, and job prospects will be greatly lessened.

32. **The correct answer is (C).** The last sentence states that the country needs young, idealistic politicians.

33. **The correct answer is (B).** The passage states that the X-ray machine "contributes to precision and accuracy in industry."

34. The correct answer is (C). The passage states that office manuals are a necessity in large organizations.

35. The correct answer is (D). The first three choices are not supported by the passage. Choice (D) is supported by the second sentence, which states, "With the migration of humans to various climates, ever new adjustments to the food supply and to the climate became necessary."

36. The correct answer is (D). The first three choices are not supported by the passage. The third sentence in the passage states that the drinking of alcohol impairs attention, that is, it makes the driver less attentive.

37. The correct answer is (B). Drinking alcohol causes harmful effects on the driver. The implication is that these effects do not last forever but wear off in time.

38. The correct answer is (A). The first sentence in the passage states that arsonists set fires deliberately or intentionally.

39. The correct answer is (B). The last sentence in the passage states that some arsonists just like the excitement of seeing the fire burn and watching the firefighters at work, and even helping fight the fire.

40. The correct answer is (D). The first three choices are not supported by the passage. Different types of arsonists given in the passage lead to the conclusion that arsonists are not all alike.

41. The correct answer is (D). The second sentence in the passage states that the battery converts an electrical charge into chemical energy that is stored until the battery terminals are connected to a closed external circuit.

42. The correct answer is (C). The first sentence states that a good or service has value only because people want it.

43. The correct answer is (D). The second sentence states that a toad's skin is both dry and rough.

44. The correct answer is (A). The last sentence states that a nautical mile is equal to 6,080 feet, while a land mile is 5,280 feet. Accordingly, a nautical mile is longer than a land mile.

45. The correct answer is (B). The third sentence states that for stereophonic sound, a different sound is recorded in each wall of the groove.

46. The correct answer is (A). The business of publishing city directories is a private business operated for profit. As such, it is a commercial enterprise.

47. The correct answer is (B). The passage says that enough data have been collected to draw the conclusion that the rural crime rates are lower than those in urban communities.

48. The correct answer is (B). The passage lists many different uses for iron.

49. The correct answer is (C). The spaces allow roads, sidewalks, and railroad tracks to expand in the summer and contract in winter without cracking or breaking.

50. The correct answer is (D). The second sentence states that crime is the result of opportunity plus desire. Accordingly, to prevent crime, it is each individual's responsibility to prevent the opportunity.

51. The correct answer is (B). For the students to solve the problem with ease, the teacher's explanation must have been clearly expressed or explicit.

52. **The correct answer is (A).** To differentiate between fact and fiction requires that the listeners have keen discernment or be shrewd.

53. **The correct answer is (B).** On Halloween, the eve of All Saints' Day, it is customary for children to engage in "trick or treat" visitations.

54. **The correct answer is (B).** A baton can be rotated rapidly, whirled, or twirled by a trained and skilled cheerleader.

55. **The correct answer is (A).** Fratricide is the act of killing one's brother.

56. **The correct answer is (C).** If corn is native or indigenous to the region, it is readily available and is generally inexpensive as transportation costs are reduced or eliminated.

57. **The correct answer is (D).** It is difficult to change the mind of a stubborn or obdurate individual even when he is in error.

58. **The correct answer is (A).** A lover of democracy has a dislike or antipathy for totalitarianism.

59. **The correct answer is (B).** As the event occurred 200 years before the time of celebration, it would be the bicentennial celebration.

60. **The correct answer is (D).** A general characteristic of human behavior is that it is highly variable and somewhat unpredictable. The behavior of other species tends to be less variable and more predictable.

61. **The correct answer is (B).** Using a narrow sample reduces the validity of a statistical analysis. In general, there are several or many limitations to different methods. Choice (A) is incorrect because *with* is not grammatically acceptable.

62. **The correct answer is (C).** Of the choices given, the only one that gives the sentence meaning states that one who is immature can readily be deceived or deluded.

63. **The correct answer is (A).** Of the choices given, the only one that gives the sentence meaning states that compulsory education was established to prevent exploitation of young children and to give them a minimum of education.

64. **The correct answer is (A).** The only choice that provides a meaningful sentence states that a person in custody awaiting trial is considered innocent until found to be guilty.

65. **The correct answer is (D).** The word *large* appears to be inconsistent. Substituting *small* for *large* restores the intended meaning of the quotation.

66. **The correct answer is (A).** The word *legislators* appears to be inconsistent. Substituting *citizens* for *legislators* helps convey the meaning intended.

67. **The correct answer is (A).** The troublesome word appears to be *is* as it is inconsistent with the main clause of the sentence. Substituting *fails* for *is* furnishes the meaning intended.

68. **The correct answer is (A).** The word *cannot* appears to be the cause of confusion. By substituting *eventually* for *cannot*, the intended meaning of the sentence is restored.

69. **The correct answer is (C).** The words *little prestige* and *more money* are inconsistent, especially with *unrewarding occupation*. Substituting *less* for *more* restores the intended meaning of the sentence.

70. **The correct answer is (D).** The word *supplement* appears to be inconsistent. Substituting *replace* restores the intended meaning of the sentence.

71. **The correct answer is (B).** The word *rejected* appears to be inconsistent. Substituting *needed* for *rejected* makes the sentence meaningful.

72. **The correct answer is (B).** The word *cannot* appears to be the troublesome word. Substituting *must* for *cannot* restores the intended meaning of the sentence.

73. **The correct answer is (B).** There is no support for choices (A), (C), or (D) in the passage. Choice (B) is the only correct answer and is supported by the main clause of the sentence.

74. **The correct answer is (B).** If personal appearance is a matter of distinctly secondary importance in most positions, it should not be considered of primary importance when interviewing persons for most positions.

75. **The correct answer is (C).** Both carefully planned sales letters and a good mailing list are essential. Carefully planned letters would be wasted on poor mailing lists.

ANSWER SHEET FOR PRACTICE TEST 4: ARITHMETIC REASONING

1. Ⓐ Ⓑ Ⓒ Ⓓ Ⓔ 16. Ⓐ Ⓑ Ⓒ Ⓓ Ⓔ 31. Ⓐ Ⓑ Ⓒ Ⓓ Ⓔ 46. Ⓐ Ⓑ Ⓒ Ⓓ Ⓔ 61. Ⓐ Ⓑ Ⓒ Ⓓ
2. Ⓐ Ⓑ Ⓒ Ⓓ Ⓔ 17. Ⓐ Ⓑ Ⓒ Ⓓ Ⓔ 32. Ⓐ Ⓑ Ⓒ Ⓓ Ⓔ 47. Ⓐ Ⓑ Ⓒ Ⓓ Ⓔ 62. Ⓐ Ⓑ Ⓒ Ⓓ
3. Ⓐ Ⓑ Ⓒ Ⓓ Ⓔ 18. Ⓐ Ⓑ Ⓒ Ⓓ Ⓔ 33. Ⓐ Ⓑ Ⓒ Ⓓ Ⓔ 48. Ⓐ Ⓑ Ⓒ Ⓓ Ⓔ 63. Ⓐ Ⓑ Ⓒ Ⓓ
4. Ⓐ Ⓑ Ⓒ Ⓓ Ⓔ 19. Ⓐ Ⓑ Ⓒ Ⓓ Ⓔ 34. Ⓐ Ⓑ Ⓒ Ⓓ Ⓔ 49. Ⓐ Ⓑ Ⓒ Ⓓ Ⓔ 64. Ⓐ Ⓑ Ⓒ Ⓓ
5. Ⓐ Ⓑ Ⓒ Ⓓ Ⓔ 20. Ⓐ Ⓑ Ⓒ Ⓓ Ⓔ 35. Ⓐ Ⓑ Ⓒ Ⓓ Ⓔ 50. Ⓐ Ⓑ Ⓒ Ⓓ Ⓔ 65. Ⓐ Ⓑ Ⓒ Ⓓ
6. Ⓐ Ⓑ Ⓒ Ⓓ Ⓔ 21. Ⓐ Ⓑ Ⓒ Ⓓ Ⓔ 36. Ⓐ Ⓑ Ⓒ Ⓓ Ⓔ 51. Ⓐ Ⓑ Ⓒ Ⓓ 66. Ⓐ Ⓑ Ⓒ Ⓓ
7. Ⓐ Ⓑ Ⓒ Ⓓ Ⓔ 22. Ⓐ Ⓑ Ⓒ Ⓓ Ⓔ 37. Ⓐ Ⓑ Ⓒ Ⓓ Ⓔ 52. Ⓐ Ⓑ Ⓒ Ⓓ 67. Ⓐ Ⓑ Ⓒ Ⓓ
8. Ⓐ Ⓑ Ⓒ Ⓓ Ⓔ 23. Ⓐ Ⓑ Ⓒ Ⓓ Ⓔ 38. Ⓐ Ⓑ Ⓒ Ⓓ Ⓔ 53. Ⓐ Ⓑ Ⓒ Ⓓ 68. Ⓐ Ⓑ Ⓒ Ⓓ
9. Ⓐ Ⓑ Ⓒ Ⓓ Ⓔ 24. Ⓐ Ⓑ Ⓒ Ⓓ Ⓔ 39. Ⓐ Ⓑ Ⓒ Ⓓ Ⓔ 54. Ⓐ Ⓑ Ⓒ Ⓓ 69. Ⓐ Ⓑ Ⓒ Ⓓ
10. Ⓐ Ⓑ Ⓒ Ⓓ Ⓔ 25. Ⓐ Ⓑ Ⓒ Ⓓ Ⓔ 40. Ⓐ Ⓑ Ⓒ Ⓓ Ⓔ 55. Ⓐ Ⓑ Ⓒ Ⓓ 70. Ⓐ Ⓑ Ⓒ Ⓓ
11. Ⓐ Ⓑ Ⓒ Ⓓ Ⓔ 26. Ⓐ Ⓑ Ⓒ Ⓓ Ⓔ 41. Ⓐ Ⓑ Ⓒ Ⓓ Ⓔ 56. Ⓐ Ⓑ Ⓒ Ⓓ 71. Ⓐ Ⓑ Ⓒ Ⓓ
12. Ⓐ Ⓑ Ⓒ Ⓓ Ⓔ 27. Ⓐ Ⓑ Ⓒ Ⓓ Ⓔ 42. Ⓐ Ⓑ Ⓒ Ⓓ Ⓔ 57. Ⓐ Ⓑ Ⓒ Ⓓ 72. Ⓐ Ⓑ Ⓒ Ⓓ
13. Ⓐ Ⓑ Ⓒ Ⓓ Ⓔ 28. Ⓐ Ⓑ Ⓒ Ⓓ Ⓔ 43. Ⓐ Ⓑ Ⓒ Ⓓ Ⓔ 58. Ⓐ Ⓑ Ⓒ Ⓓ 73. Ⓐ Ⓑ Ⓒ Ⓓ
14. Ⓐ Ⓑ Ⓒ Ⓓ Ⓔ 29. Ⓐ Ⓑ Ⓒ Ⓓ Ⓔ 44. Ⓐ Ⓑ Ⓒ Ⓓ Ⓔ 59. Ⓐ Ⓑ Ⓒ Ⓓ 74. Ⓐ Ⓑ Ⓒ Ⓓ
15. Ⓐ Ⓑ Ⓒ Ⓓ Ⓔ 30. Ⓐ Ⓑ Ⓒ Ⓓ Ⓔ 45. Ⓐ Ⓑ Ⓒ Ⓓ Ⓔ 60. Ⓐ Ⓑ Ⓒ Ⓓ 75. Ⓐ Ⓑ Ⓒ Ⓓ

answer sheet

Practice Test 4: Arithmetic Reasoning

Questions 1–50 are five-option items. For each question, select the option that is most nearly correct.

1. If a car uses $1\frac{1}{2}$ gallons of gas every 30 miles, how many miles can be driven with 6 gallons of gas?
   - (A) 100
   - (B) 110
   - (C) 120
   - (D) 130
   - (E) 140

2. A car has a gasoline tank that holds 20 gallons. When the gauge reads $\frac{1}{4}$ full, how many gallons are needed to fill the tank?
   - (A) 16
   - (B) 15
   - (C) 10
   - (D) 5
   - (E) 4

3. An airplane flying a distance of 875 miles used 70 gallons of gasoline. How many gallons will it need to travel 3000 miles?
   - (A) 108
   - (B) 120
   - (C) 144
   - (D) 240
   - (E) 280

4. The *Mayflower* sailed from Plymouth, England, to Plymouth Rock, a distance of approximately 2800 miles, in 63 days. The average speed in miles per hour was closest to which one of the following?
   - (A) $\frac{1}{2}$
   - (B) 1
   - (C) 2
   - (D) 3
   - (E) 4

5. A man drives 60 miles to his destination at an average speed of 40 miles per hour and makes the return trip at an average rate of 30 miles per hour. His average speed in miles per hour for the entire trip is most nearly
   - (A) 34
   - (B) 36
   - (C) 38
   - (D) 40
   - (E) 42

6. A plane flies over Cleveland at 10:20 A.M. It passes over a community 120 miles away at 10:32 A.M. Find the plane's flight rate in miles per hour.
   - (A) 600
   - (B) 540
   - (C) 480
   - (D) 420
   - (E) 360

7. Two trains start from the same station at 10:00 A.M., one traveling east at 60 mph and the other traveling west at 70 mph. At what time will these trains be 455 miles apart?

(A) 12:30 P.M.

(B) 1:00 P.M.

(C) 1:30 P.M.

(D) 2:00 P.M.

(E) 2:30 P.M.

8. Two trains running on the same track travel at the rates of 25 and 30 mph, respectively. If the slower train starts out an hour earlier, how long will it take the faster train to catch up with it?

(A) $3\frac{1}{2}$ hours

(B) 4 hours

(C) $4\frac{1}{2}$ hours

(D) 5 hours

(E) $5\frac{1}{2}$ hours

9. On a map, $\frac{1}{2}$ inch = 10 miles. How many miles apart are two towns that are $2\frac{1}{4}$ inches apart on the map?

(A) 33

(B) 36

(C) 39

(D) 42

(E) 45

10. The total savings in purchasing 30 13-cent candies for a class party at a reduced rate of $1.38 per dozen is

(A) $0.35

(B) $0.40

(C) $0.45

(D) $0.50

(E) $0.55

11. Mr. Jackson takes his wife and two children to the circus. If the price of a child's ticket is half the price of an adult ticket and Mr. Jackson pays a total of $12.60, the price of a child's ticket is

(A) $2.10

(B) $2.60

(C) $3.10

(D) $3.60

(E) $4.10

12. What part of a day is 5 hours 15 minutes?

(A) $\frac{7}{16}$

(B) $\frac{9}{16}$

(C) $\frac{7}{32}$

(D) $\frac{9}{32}$

(E) $\frac{11}{32}$

13. A team lost 10 games in a 35-game season. Find the ratio of games won to games lost.

(A) 2 : 5

(B) 5 : 2

(C) 5 : 7

(D) 7 : 2

(E) 7 : 5

14. In a 3-hour examination of 350 questions, there are 50 mathematics problems. If twice as much time should be allowed for each mathematics problem as for each of the other questions, how many minutes should be spent on the mathematics problems?

(A) 45 minutes

(B) 52 minutes

(C) 60 minutes

(D) 72 minutes

(E) 80 minutes

15. The parts department's profit is 12 percent on a new magneto. How much did the magneto cost if the selling price is $145.60?

    (A) $120.00
    (B) $125.60
    (C) $130.00
    (D) $133.60
    (E) $136.00

16. A typewriter was listed at $120.00 and was bought for $96.00. What was the rate of discount?

    (A) 16%
    (B) 20%
    (C) 24%
    (D) 28%
    (E) 32%

17. A class of 198 recruits consists of three racial and ethnic groups. If $\frac{1}{3}$ are black and $\frac{1}{4}$ of the remainder are Hispanic, how many of the recruits in the class are white?

    (A) 198
    (B) 165
    (C) 132
    (D) 99
    (E) 66

18. One third of the students at Central High are seniors. Three fourths of the seniors will go to college next year. What percentage of the students at Central High will go to college next year?

    (A) 25%
    (B) $33\frac{1}{3}$%
    (C) 45%
    (D) 50%
    (E) 75%

19. If 2.5 centimeters = 1 inch, and 36 inches = 1 yard, how many centimeters are in 1 yard?

    (A) 14
    (B) 25
    (C) 70
    (D) 80
    (E) 90

20. A rectangular fuel tank measures 60 inches in length, 30 inches in width, and 12 inches in depth. How many cubic feet are within the tank?

    (A) 12.5
    (B) 15.0
    (C) 18.5
    (D) 21.0
    (E) 24.5

21. How many gallons of fuel will be contained in a rectangular tank that measures 2 feet in width, 3 feet in length, and 1 foot 8 inches in depth (7.5 gallons = 1 cubic foot)?

    (A) 110
    (B) 75
    (C) 66.6
    (D) 55
    (E) 45

22. A rectangular bin 4 feet long, 3 feet wide, and 2 feet high is solidly packed with bricks whose dimensions are 8 inches by 4 inches by 2 inches. The number of bricks in the bin is

    (A) 54
    (B) 324
    (C) 648
    (D) 1072
    (E) 1296

23. A resolution was passed by a ratio of 5:4. If 90 people voted for the resolution, how many voted against it?
    (A) 40
    (B) 50
    (C) 60
    (D) 66
    (E) 72

24. If 2.5 centimeters = 1 inch, how many centimeters are in 1 foot?
    (A) 5
    (B) 10
    (C) 15
    (D) 30
    (E) 60

25. A gasoline tank is $\frac{1}{4}$ full. After adding 10 gallons of gasoline, the gauge indicates that the tank is $\frac{2}{3}$ full. What is the capacity of the tank in gallons?
    (A) 20
    (B) 24
    (C) 28
    (D) 32
    (E) 36

26. The water level of a swimming pool, 75 feet by 42 feet, is to be raised 4 inches. How many gallons of water are needed (7.5 gallons = 1 cubic foot)?
    (A) 7875
    (B) 15,750
    (C) 23,625
    (D) 31,500
    (E) 63,000

27. If the outer diameter of a cylindrical oil tank is 54.28 inches and the inner diameter is 48.7 inches, the thickness of the wall of the tank, in inches, is
    (A) 2.79
    (B) 3.29

(C) 4.58
(D) 5.58
(E) 6.47

28. A person travels 30 miles at 6 mph, 20 miles at 10 mph, and 15 miles at 5 mph. What is the person's average rate for the complete distance?
    (A) 6 mph
    (B) $6\frac{1}{2}$ mph
    (C) 7 mph
    (D) $7\frac{1}{2}$ mph
    (E) 8 mph

29. Sue and Joe are on opposite sides of a circular lake that is 1260 feet in circumference. They walk around it, starting at the same time and walking in the same direction. Sue walks at the rate of 50 yards a minute, and Joe walks at the rate of 60 yards a minute. In how many minutes will Joe overtake Sue?
    (A) 14
    (B) 21
    (C) 28
    (D) 35
    (E) 42

30. Two ships are 1550 miles apart and sailing toward each other. One sails at the rate of 85 miles per day and the other at the rate of 65 miles per day. How far apart will they be at the end of 9 days?
    (A) 100 miles
    (B) 150 miles
    (C) 175 miles
    (D) 200 miles
    (E) 225 miles

31. A family drove from New York to San Francisco, a distance of 3000 miles. They covered $\frac{1}{10}$ of the distance the first day and $\frac{2}{9}$ of the remaining distance on the second day. How many miles were left to be driven?

    (A) 2000
    (B) 2100
    (C) 2300
    (D) 2400
    (E) 2500

32. Assuming that on a blueprint $\frac{1}{8}$ inch equals 12 inches of actual length, the actual length (in feet) of a steel bar represented on the blueprint by a line $3\frac{3}{4}$ inches long is

    (A) 30
    (B) 45
    (C) 75
    (D) 160
    (E) 360

33. If pencils are bought at 36 cents per dozen and sold at 3 for 10 cents, the total profit on 5 dozen is

    (A) 18¢
    (B) 20¢
    (C) 22¢
    (D) 24¢
    (E) 26¢

34. The tunnel toll is $1.25 for car and driver and $0.75 for each additional passenger. How many people were riding in a car for which the toll was $4.25?

    (A) 3
    (B) 4
    (C) 5
    (D) 6
    (E) 7

35. Pren and Wright invested $8000 and $6000, respectively, in a hardware business. At the end of the year, the profits were $3800. Each partner received 6% on his investment and the remainder was shared equally. What was the total that Pren received?

    (A) $1960
    (B) $2040
    (C) $2180
    (D) $2300
    (E) $2380

36. How much money is saved by buying a car priced at $12,000 with a single discount of 15% rather than buying the same car with discounts of 10% and 5%?

    (A) $60
    (B) $120
    (C) $180
    (D) $360
    (E) $720

37. The price of an article has been reduced 25%. In order to restore the original price, the price must be increased by

    (A) 15.5%
    (B) 20%
    (C) 25%
    (D) $33\frac{1}{3}$ %
    (E) 40%

38. A stationer buys books at $0.75 per dozen and sells them at 25 cents apiece. The gross profit based on the cost is

    (A) 50%
    (B) 100%
    (C) 150%
    (D) 200%
    (E) 300%

39. A, B, and C invested $8000, $7500, and $6500, respectively. Their profits were to be divided according to the ratio of their investment. If B uses his share of the firm's profit of $825 to pay a personal debt of $230, how much will he have left?

    (A) $51.25
    (B) $51.20
    (C) $51.10
    (D) $51.05
    (E) $51.00

40. A merchant who has debts totaling $43,250 has gone bankrupt and can pay off only 15¢ on the dollar. How much will his creditors receive?

    (A) $6287.00
    (B) $6387.00
    (C) $6387.50
    (D) $6487.50
    (E) $6587.00

41. If 15 cans of food are needed for 6 adults for 2 days, the number of cans needed for 4 adults for 5 days is

    (A) 10
    (B) 15
    (C) 20
    (D) 25
    (E) 30

42. The school enrollment is 1700. Eighteen percent of the students study French, 25% study Spanish, 12% study Italian, 15% study German, and the rest study no foreign language. Assuming that each student may study only one foreign language, how many students do not study any foreign language?

    (A) 510
    (B) 520
    (C) 530
    (D) 540
    (E) 550

43. Four men working together can dig a ditch in 42 days. They begin the job, but one man works only half days. How long will it take to complete the job?

    (A) 46 days
    (B) 48 days
    (C) 50 days
    (D) 52 days
    (E) 54 days

44. What part of an hour elapses between 6:45 P.M. and 7:09 P.M.?

    (A) $\dfrac{2}{5}$
    (B) $\dfrac{5}{12}$
    (C) $\dfrac{1}{24}$
    (D) $\dfrac{6}{25}$
    (E) $\dfrac{10}{30}$

45. If a distance estimated at 150 feet is really 140 feet, the percent of error in this estimate is

    (A) $6\dfrac{2}{3}\%$
    (B) $7\dfrac{1}{7}\%$
    (C) 8%
    (D) 9%
    (E) 10%

46. Jack sells appliances and receives a salary of $150 per week plus 5% commission on all sales over $750. How much does he earn in a week in which his sales amount to $2400?

    (A) $222.50
    (B) $225
    (C) $227.50
    (D) $230
    (E) $232.50

47. If the average weight of girls of Jane's age and height is 105 pounds and if Jane weighs 110% of average, then Jane's weight in pounds is

(A) 110

(B) 112.5

(C) 115.5

(D) 118.5

(E) 126

48. A man willed his property to his three children. To the youngest he gave $10,000; to the second, 2.5 times as much as to the youngest; and to the eldest, 1.5 times as much as to the second. What was the value of the estate?

(A) $72,000

(B) $72,500

(C) $73,000

(D) $73,500

(E) $74,000

49. A person wishing to borrow a certain sum of money for 4 months goes to a bank offering an interest rate of 12%. If the interest is $720, how much does the person borrow?

(A) $10,000

(B) $12,000

(C) $14,000

(D) $16,000

(E) $18,000

50. What is the ratio of 2 feet 3 inches to 1 yard?

(A) 2:3

(B) 3:4

(C) 1:1

(D) 4:3

(E) 3:2

Questions 51–75 are four-option items. For each question, select the option that is most nearly correct.

51. A woman's weekly salary is increased from $350 to $380. The percent of increase is most nearly

(A) 6%

(B) $8\frac{1}{2}$%

(C) 10%

(D) $12\frac{1}{2}$%

52. A clerk divided his 35-hour work week as follows: $\frac{1}{5}$ of his time in sorting mail; $\frac{1}{2}$ of his time in filing letters; and $\frac{1}{7}$ of his time in reception work. The rest of his time was devoted to messenger work. The percentage of time spent on messenger work by the clerk during the week was most nearly

(A) 6%

(B) 10%

(C) 14%

(D) 16%

53. Many American cars feature speedometers that show kilometers per hour. If you are required to drive 500 miles, and you know that 1 kilometer is approximately $\frac{5}{8}$ of a mile, how many kilometers would you cover in that journey?

(A) 625

(B) 800

(C) 850

(D) 1000

54. A stock clerk had 600 pads on hand. He then issued $\frac{3}{8}$ of his supply of pads to Division X, $\frac{1}{4}$ to Division Y, and $\frac{1}{6}$ to Division Z. The number of pads remaining in stock is
    (A) 48
    (B) 125
    (C) 240
    (D) 475

55. Two sailors traveled by bus from one point to another. The trip took 15 hours, and they left their point of origin at 8 A.M. What time did they arrive at their destination?
    (A) 11 A.M.
    (B) 10 P.M.
    (C) 11 P.M.
    (D) 12 A.M.

56. A man deposited a check for $1000 to open an account. Shortly after that, he withdrew $400.00 and then $541.20. How much did he have left in his account?
    (A) $56.72
    (B) $58.80
    (C) $59.09
    (D) $60.60

57. After an employer figures out an employee's weekly salary of $190.57, he deducts $13.05 for Social Security and $5.68 for pension. What is the amount of the check after these deductions?
    (A) $171.84
    (B) $171.92
    (C) $172.84
    (D) $172.99

58. A pole 12 feet high has a shadow 4 feet long. A nearby pole is 24 feet high. How long is its shadow?
    (A) 4 feet
    (B) 8 feet
    (C) 12 feet
    (D) 16 feet

59. A skier started a fire in the fireplace. Each log she put on burned for a half-hour. If she started with a supply of 10 logs, for how many hours could the fire burn?
    (A) 5 hours
    (B) 7 hours
    (C) $8\frac{1}{2}$ hours
    (D) 10 hours

60. Mrs. Jones wishes to buy 72 ounces of canned beans for the least possible cost. Which of the following should she buy?
    (A) Six 12-ounce cans at 39¢ per can
    (B) Seven 10-ounce cans at 34¢ per can
    (C) Three 24-ounce cans at 79¢ per can
    (D) Two 25-ounce cans at 62¢ per can

61. A carpenter needs four boards, each 2 feet 9 inches long. If wood is sold only by the foot, how many feet must he buy?
    (A) 9
    (B) 10
    (C) 11
    (D) 12

62. It costs 31¢ a square foot to lay linoleum. To lay 20 square yards of linoleum, it will cost
    (A) $16.20
    (B) $18.60
    (C) $55.80
    (D) $62.00

63. A piece of wood 35 feet, 6 inches long was used to make 4 shelves of equal length. The length of each shelf was most nearly

(A) 9 feet, $1\frac{1}{2}$ inches

(B) 8 feet, $10\frac{1}{2}$ inches

(C) 7 feet, $10\frac{1}{2}$ inches

(D) 7 feet, $1\frac{1}{2}$ inches

64. A change purse contained 3 half dollars, 8 quarters, 7 dimes, 6 nickels, and 9 pennies. Express in dollars and cents the total amount of money in the purse.

(A) $3.78
(B) $3.95
(C) $4.32
(D) $4.59

65. A champion runner ran the 100-yard dash in three track meets. The first time he ran it in 10.2 seconds; the second in 10.4 seconds; and the third in 10 seconds. What was his average time?

(A) 10.1 seconds
(B) 10.2 seconds
(C) 10.3 seconds
(D) 10.4 seconds

66. A crate containing a tool weighs 12 pounds. If the tool weighs 9 pounds, 9 ounces, how much does the crate weigh?

(A) 2 pounds, 1 ounce
(B) 2 pounds, 7 ounces
(C) 3 pounds, 1 ounce
(D) 3 pounds, 7 ounces

67. The daily almanac report for one day during the summer stated that the sun rose at 6:14 A.M. and set at 6:06 P.M. Find the number of hours and minutes in the time between the rising and setting of the sun on that day.

(A) 11 hours, 2 minutes
(B) 11 hours, 52 minutes
(C) 12 hours, 8 minutes
(D) 12 hours, 48 minutes

68. If $\frac{1}{2}$ cup of spinach contains 80 calories and the same amount of peas contains 300 calories, how many cups of spinach have the same caloric content as $\frac{2}{3}$ cup of peas?

(A) $\frac{2}{5}$
(B) $1\frac{1}{3}$
(C) 2
(D) $2\frac{1}{2}$

69. A night watchman must check a certain storage area every 45 minutes. If he first checks the area as he begins a 9-hour tour of duty, how many times will he have checked this storage area?

(A) 13
(B) 12
(C) 11
(D) 10

70. What is the fifth term in the series: $4\frac{1}{2}$; $8\frac{3}{4}$; 13; $17\frac{1}{4}$; _____?

(A) $21\frac{1}{2}$
(B) $21\frac{3}{4}$
(C) 22
(D) $22\frac{1}{4}$

71. Three workers assemble 360 switches per hour, but 5% of the switches are defective. How many good (nondefective) switches will these 3 workers assemble in an 8-hour shift?

    (A) 2736
    (B) 2880
    (C) 2944
    (D) 3000

72. The butcher made $22\frac{1}{2}$ pounds of beef into hamburger and wrapped it in $1\frac{1}{4}$-pound packages. How many packages did he make?

    (A) 15
    (B) 16
    (C) 17
    (D) 18

73. If a car-renting agency charges a fixed rate of $12 per day plus 17¢ per mile, what would the charge be for using a car for 6 days and traveling 421 miles?

    (A) $143.57
    (B) $153.57
    (C) $163.57
    (D) $173.57

74. If the area of the figure below, which consists of 5 equal squares, is 125, what is the perimeter of this figure?

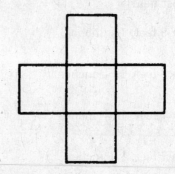

    (A) 125
    (B) 100
    (C) 80
    (D) 60

75. If the cost of digging a trench is $8.48 a cubic yard, what would be the cost of digging a trench 2 yards by 5 yards by 4 yards?

    (A) $93.28
    (B) $186.56
    (C) $237.44
    (D) $339.20

ANSWER KEY AND EXPLANATIONS

1. (C)	16. (B)	31. (B)	46. (E)	61. (C)
2. (B)	17. (D)	32. (A)	47. (C)	62. (C)
3. (D)	18. (A)	33. (B)	48. (B)	63. (B)
4. (C)	19. (E)	34. (C)	49. (E)	64. (D)
5. (A)	20. (A)	35. (A)	50. (B)	65. (B)
6. (A)	21. (B)	36. (A)	51. (B)	66. (B)
7. (C)	22. (C)	37. (D)	52. (D)	67. (B)
8. (D)	23. (E)	38. (E)	53. (B)	68. (D)
9. (E)	24. (D)	39. (A)	54. (B)	69. (A)
10. (C)	25. (B)	40. (D)	55. (C)	70. (A)
11. (A)	26. (A)	41. (D)	56. (B)	71. (A)
12. (C)	27. (A)	42. (A)	57. (A)	72. (D)
13. (B)	28. (B)	43. (B)	58. (B)	73. (A)
14. (A)	29. (B)	44. (A)	59. (A)	74. (D)
15. (C)	30. (D)	45. (B)	60. (A)	75. (D)

1. **The correct answer is (C).**
   $1\frac{1}{2} : 30 = 6 : x$; $\frac{3}{2} \times x = 180$; $x = \frac{2}{3} \times 180$ = 120 miles.

2. **The correct answer is (B).** $\frac{1}{4}$ of $20 = 5$ gallons in tank; $20 - 5 = 15$ gallons needed to fill tank.

3. **The correct answer is (D).**

   $\frac{875}{70} = \frac{3000}{x}$; $875x = 210,000$;

   $x = 240$ gallons

4. **The correct answer is (C).**

   $\frac{2800}{63 \times 24} = \frac{2800}{1512} = 1.85$, closest to 2 mph

5. **The correct answer is (A).**

   60 miles at 40 mph = $1\frac{1}{2}$ hours driving time

   60 miles at 20 mph = 2 hours driving time

   Total time = $3\frac{1}{2}$ hours

   Total distance = 120 miles

   Average speed = $\frac{120}{3\frac{1}{2}} = 120 \times \frac{2}{7} = \frac{240}{7}$

   $34\frac{2}{7}$ miles per hour

6. **The correct answer is (A).** $\frac{120}{12} = 10$ miles per minute; $10 \times 60 = 600$ mph.

7. **The correct answer is (C).** $60x$ traveling east; $70x$ traveling west; $60x + 70x = 455$; $130x = 455$; $x = \frac{455}{130} = 3\frac{1}{2}$ hours; 10:00 A.M. + $3\frac{1}{2}$ hours = 1:30 P.M.

8. **The correct answer is (D).** Train is 25 miles ahead in 1 hour. Difference in rate is 5 mph $\frac{25}{5} = 5$ hours.

9. **The correct answer is (E).**

$\frac{1}{2} : 10 = \frac{9}{4} : x; \frac{x}{2} = \frac{90}{4}; 4x = 180;$
$x = 45.$

10. **The correct answer is (C).** $0.13 \times 30 =$ $3.90, cost at regular rate. $1.38 \times 2.5 =$ $3.45, cost at reduced rate. $3.90 - $3.45 = $0.45.

11. **The correct answer is (A).** Two children's tickets cost the same as one adult ticket. $\frac{12.60}{3} =$ $4.20 for each adult ticket. $\frac{1}{2}$ of $4.20 = $2.10.

12. **The correct answer is (C).** 5 hours 15 minutes = 21 quarter-hours; 24 hours = 96 quarter-hours; $\frac{21}{96} = \frac{7}{32}$.

13. **The correct answer is (B).** $35 - 10 = 25$ games won; 10 games lost; $25 : 10 = 5 : 2$.

14. **The correct answer is (A).** 50 math problems; 300 other problems; let $x =$ minutes spent for each math problem.

$x \times 50 + \frac{x}{2} \times 300 = 180;$

$50x + 150x = 180;$

$200x = 180; x = \frac{180}{200};$

$50x = 50 \times \frac{180}{200} = 45 \text{ minutes.}$

15. **The correct answer is (C).**
$x + 0.12x = 145.60; 1.12x = 145.60;$

$x = \frac{145.60}{1.12} = \$130.00.$

16. **The correct answer is (B).** $120 - $96

$= $24 discount; $\frac{24}{120} = 20\%.$

17. **The correct answer is (D).** $\frac{1}{3}$ of 198 $= 66; 198 - 66 = 132; \frac{1}{4}$ of $132 = 33;$ $132 - 33 = 99.$

18. **The correct answer is (A).** $\frac{1}{3} \times \frac{3}{4} = \frac{3}{12}$ $= \frac{1}{4}$ or 25%.

19. **The correct answer is (E).**

$2.5 \times 36 = 90$

20. **The correct answer is (A).** 60 in. = 5 ft.; 30 in. = 2.5 ft.; 12 in. = 1 ft.; $5 \times 2.5 \times 1 = 12.5$ cubic feet.

21. **The correct answer is (B).** $2 \times 3 \times \frac{5}{3} = 10$ cubic feet; $10 \times 7.5 = 75$ gallons.

22. **The correct answer is (C).**

$\frac{48 \times 36 \times 24}{8 \times 4 \times 2} = 24 \times 27 = 648$

23. **The correct answer is (E).**

$5 : 4 = 90 : x; 360 = 5x; x = 72$

24. **The correct answer is (D).**

$2.5 : 1 = x : 12; x = 2.5 \times 12 = 30$

25. **The correct answer is (B).**

$\frac{2}{3}x - \frac{1}{4}x = 10; \frac{8}{12}x - \frac{3}{12}x = 10;$
$\frac{5}{12}x = 10; x = \frac{120}{5} = 24.$

26. **The correct answer is (A).**

$75 \times 42 \times \frac{1}{3} = 1050$ cu. ft.;
$7.5 : 1 = x : 1050;$
$x = 1050 \times 7.5 = 7875$

27. **The correct answer is (A).** $54.28 - 48.7$ $= 5.58$ for two thicknesses. $\frac{5.58}{2} = 2.79$-inch wall thickness.

28. **The correct answer is (B).**

5 hrs. at 6 mph	=	30 miles
2 hrs. at 10 mph	=	20 miles
3 hrs. at 5 mph	=	150 miles
10 hrs.	=	65 miles

$\frac{65}{10} = \quad 6.5 \text{ mph}$

29. **The correct answer is (B).** Joe must make up $\frac{1260}{2}$ feet, or $\frac{420}{2}$ yards, or 210 yards to meet. There is a 10-yard difference per minute in rate of travel. $\frac{210}{10} = 21$ minutes.

30. **The correct answer is (D).** Initially, the ships are 1550 miles apart. $85 \times 9 = 765$; $65 \times 9 = 585$; $1550 - (765 + 585) = 1550 - 1350 = 200$ miles.

31. **The correct answer is (B).**
$\frac{1}{10}$ of 3000 = 300; 3000 − 300 = 2700;

$\frac{2}{9}$ of 2700 = 600; 2700 − 600 = 2100

miles still to be driven.

32. **The correct answer is (A).** Let $x =$ length of bar in inches. $\frac{1}{8} : 12 = \frac{15}{4} : x$;

$\frac{1}{8}x = 12 \times \frac{15}{4}$; $x = 12 \times \frac{15}{4} \times 8 = 360$

inches. $\frac{360}{12} = 30$ feet.

33. **The correct answer is (B).** 36¢ × 5 = $1.80 for cost of 60 pencils; 3 : 0.10 = 60 : x; $3x = 6.00$; $x = \$2.00$ obtained from selling 60 pencils; $2.00 − $1.80 = $0.20.

34. **The correct answer is (C).** $4.25 − $1.25 = $3.00; $\frac{3.00}{0.75} = 4$ additional passengers; driver + 4 additional passengers = 5 people.

35. **The correct answer is (A).** $8000 × 0.06 = $480 = 6% of Pren's investment; $6000 × 0.06 = $360 = 6% of Wright's investment; $480 + $360 = $840; $3800 − $840 = $2960; $\frac{1}{2}$ of $2960 = $1480; Pren's total = $480 + $1480 = $1960.

36. **The correct answer is (A).** $12,000 × 0.15 = $1800; $12,000 × $1800 = $10,200 = Cost of car at 15% discount.

$12,000 × 0.10 = $1200; $12,000 − $1200 = $10,800

$10,800 × 0.05 = $540; $10,800 − $540 = $10,260 = Cost of car at successive discounts.

$10,260 − $10,200 = $60.

37. **The correct answer is (D).** 100 − 25 = 75; 75 + 25 = 100; $\frac{25}{75} = 33\frac{1}{3}$%.

38. **The correct answer is (E).** Cost = $0.75 per dozen; selling price is $0.25 each or $3.00 per dozen. $3.00 − 0.75 = $2.25 gross profit per dozen. $\frac{2.25}{0.75} \times 100 = 300$%.

39. **The correct answer is (A).** Total investment = $8000 + $7500 + $6500 = $22,000; B's share in profit = $\frac{7500}{22,000} \times 825 = \$281.25$. $281.25 − $230.00 = $51.25.

40. **The correct answer is (D).** $\frac{15}{100} = 0.15$; $43,250 × 0.15 = $6487.50.

41. **The correct answer is (D).** 15 : 12 = x : 20; $12x = 300$; $x = \frac{300}{12} = 25$.

42. **The correct answer is (A).** 18% + 25% + 12% + 15% = 70%; 30% study no foreign language; 1700 × 0.30 = 510.

43. **The correct answer is (B).** Let $x =$ time required to complete ditch with $3\frac{1}{2}$ men.
$4 \times 42 = 3\frac{1}{2} \times x$; $4 \times 42 = \frac{7}{2}x$;

$x = 4 \times 42 \times \frac{2}{7} = 48$ days

44. **The correct answer is (A).** 15 + 9 = 24 minutes; $\frac{24}{60} = \frac{2}{5}$.

45. **The correct answer is (B).** 150 − 140 = 10; $\frac{10}{140} = 0.0714$ or $7\frac{1}{7}$%.

46. **The correct answer is (E).** $2400 − $750 = $1650; $1650 × 0.05 = $82.50; $150 + $82.50 = $232.50.

47. The correct answer is (C). $\frac{110}{100}$ of 105 = 115.5 pounds.

48. The correct answer is (B).

Youngest	$10,000
Second	25,000
Eldest	37,500
	$72,500

49. The correct answer is (E).

Let x = amount borrowed.

$12x \times \frac{1}{3} = 720$; $0.04x = 720$; $x = \frac{720}{0.04} =$ $18,000.

50. The correct answer is (B).

$27'' : 36'' = 3 : 4$.

51. The correct answer is (B). To find percent of increase, subtract the original figure from the new figure. Then divide the amount of change by the original figure. $380 − $350 = $30; $30 ÷ $350 = .0857 (which is approximately $8\frac{1}{2}$%).

52. The correct answer is (D). The number of hours in the clerk's work week is irrelevant. Figure the percent of his time that he spent at the enumerated tasks. The difference between that percent and his full week (100%) is the percent of his time spent on messenger work.

$$\frac{1}{5} = \frac{14}{70}$$

$$\frac{1}{2} = \frac{35}{70}$$

$$\frac{1}{7} = \frac{10}{70}$$

$$\overline{\frac{59}{70}} = 0.84 = 84\%$$

$100\% − 84\% = 16\%$ on messenger work

53. The correct answer is (B). Convert the miles to kilometers by dividing them by $\frac{5}{8}$.

$$500 \text{ miles} \div \frac{5}{8} = \frac{\overset{100}{\cancel{500}}}{1} \times \frac{8}{\cancel{5}_1} =$$

800 kilometers.

54. The correct answer is (B).

$$\frac{3}{8} = \frac{9}{24}$$

$$\frac{1}{4} = \frac{6}{24}$$

$$\frac{1}{6} = \frac{4}{24}$$

$$\overline{\frac{19}{24}} = \text{ of the pads were issued;}$$

$\frac{5}{24}$ remained; $\frac{5}{\cancel{24}_1} \times \frac{\overset{25}{\cancel{600}}}{1} =$

125 pads remained

55. The correct answer is (C). 8 A.M. + 15 hours = 23 o'clock = 11 P.M.

56. The correct answer is (B). $1,000.00 − $941.20 = $58.80.

57. The correct answer is (A). $190.57 − $13.05 − $5.68 = $171.84.

58. The correct answer is (B). Let x = length of shadow of nearby pole. $12 : 4 = 24 : x$; $12x = 96$; $x = 8$ feet.

59. The correct answer is (A). $10 \times \frac{1}{2}$ hour = 5 hours.

60. The correct answer is (A). Only choices (A) and (C) represent 72 ounces. 6 × $0.39 = $2.34, which is less than 3 × $0.79 = $2.37.

61. The correct answer is (C). 2 ft 9 in. × 4 = 8 ft. 36 in. = 11 ft.

62. The correct answer is (C). It costs 31¢ per sq. ft., so it costs 31¢ × 9 = $2.79 per sq. yd. $2.79 × 20 sq. yds. = $55.80.

63. **The correct answer is (B).** First convert the feet to inches. 35 ft. 6 in. = 420 in. + 6 in. = 426 in. 426 ÷ 4 = 106.5 in. per shelf = 8 ft. $10\frac{1}{2}$ in. per shelf.

64. **The correct answer is (D).**

$0.50 \times 3 = \$1.50$

$0.25 \times 8 = \$2.00$

$0.10 \times 7 = \$0.70$

$0.05 \times 6 = \$0.30$

$\underline{0.01 \times 9 = \$0.09}$

$\$4.59$

65. **The correct answer is (B).** 10.2 + 10.4 + 10 = 30.6 ÷ 3 = 10.2 seconds.

66. **The correct answer is (B).** 11 lb., 16 oz. − 9 lb., 9 oz. = 2 lb., 7 oz.

67. **The correct answer is (B).** If you look at the entire problem, you will see that the time between sunrise and sunset was just 8 minutes short of 12 hours (14 − 6 = 8).

11 hrs 60 min.

$\underline{-\qquad 8 \text{ min.}}$

11 hrs 52 min.

68. **The correct answer is (D).**

$\frac{1}{2}$ c spinach = 80 calories

$\frac{1}{2}$ c peas = 300 calories

1 c peas = 600 calories

$\frac{2}{3}$ c peas = 400 calories

400 ÷ 80 = 5 cups of spinach

= $2\frac{1}{2}$ cups of spinach

69. **The correct answer is (A).** 9 hrs = 540 mins.; 540 ÷ 45 = 12.

The night watchman stops at the storage area 12 times during his tour plus once at the beginning of his tour of duty for a total of 13 times.

70. **The correct answer is (A).** The interval between each member of the series is $4\frac{1}{4}$. $17\frac{1}{4} + 4\frac{1}{4} = 21\frac{1}{2}$.

71. **The correct answer is (A).**

360 × 8 = 2880 switches in 8 hours

2880 × 0.05 = 144 defective switches

2880 − 144 = 2736 good switches

72. **The correct answer is (D).**

$22\frac{1}{2} + 1\frac{1}{4} = \frac{45}{2} \div \frac{5}{4} =$

$\frac{\overset{9}{\cancel{45}}}{\underset{1}{\cancel{2}}} \times \frac{\overset{2}{\cancel{4}}}{\underset{1}{\cancel{5}}} = 18 \text{ packages}$

73. **The correct answer is (A).** $12 × 6 = $72.00 for daily use:

421 × 0.17 = $71.57 for mileage charge;

$72.00 + $71.57 + $143.57

74. **The correct answer is (D).** Area of each square is 25; each side = 5; perimeter consists of 12 sides; 12 × 5 = 60.

75. **The correct answer is (D).** 2 yards × 5 yards × 4 yards = 40 cubic yards. $8.48 × 40 = $339.20.

answers practice test 4

ANSWER SHEET FOR PRACTICE TEST 5: MATH KNOWLEDGE

1. Ⓐ Ⓑ Ⓒ Ⓓ Ⓔ	16. Ⓐ Ⓑ Ⓒ Ⓓ Ⓔ	31. Ⓐ Ⓑ Ⓒ Ⓓ Ⓔ	46. Ⓐ Ⓑ Ⓒ Ⓓ Ⓔ	61. Ⓐ Ⓑ Ⓒ Ⓓ
2. Ⓐ Ⓑ Ⓒ Ⓓ Ⓔ	17. Ⓐ Ⓑ Ⓒ Ⓓ Ⓔ	32. Ⓐ Ⓑ Ⓒ Ⓓ Ⓔ	47. Ⓐ Ⓑ Ⓒ Ⓓ Ⓔ	62. Ⓐ Ⓑ Ⓒ Ⓓ
3. Ⓐ Ⓑ Ⓒ Ⓓ Ⓔ	18. Ⓐ Ⓑ Ⓒ Ⓓ Ⓔ	33. Ⓐ Ⓑ Ⓒ Ⓓ Ⓔ	48. Ⓐ Ⓑ Ⓒ Ⓓ Ⓔ	63. Ⓐ Ⓑ Ⓒ Ⓓ
4. Ⓐ Ⓑ Ⓒ Ⓓ Ⓔ	19. Ⓐ Ⓑ Ⓒ Ⓓ Ⓔ	34. Ⓐ Ⓑ Ⓒ Ⓓ Ⓔ	49. Ⓐ Ⓑ Ⓒ Ⓓ Ⓔ	64. Ⓐ Ⓑ Ⓒ Ⓓ
5. Ⓐ Ⓑ Ⓒ Ⓓ Ⓔ	20. Ⓐ Ⓑ Ⓒ Ⓓ Ⓔ	35. Ⓐ Ⓑ Ⓒ Ⓓ Ⓔ	50. Ⓐ Ⓑ Ⓒ Ⓓ Ⓔ	65. Ⓐ Ⓑ Ⓒ Ⓓ
6. Ⓐ Ⓑ Ⓒ Ⓓ Ⓔ	21. Ⓐ Ⓑ Ⓒ Ⓓ Ⓔ	36. Ⓐ Ⓑ Ⓒ Ⓓ Ⓔ	51. Ⓐ Ⓑ Ⓒ Ⓓ	66. Ⓐ Ⓑ Ⓒ Ⓓ
7. Ⓐ Ⓑ Ⓒ Ⓓ Ⓔ	22. Ⓐ Ⓑ Ⓒ Ⓓ Ⓔ	37. Ⓐ Ⓑ Ⓒ Ⓓ Ⓔ	52. Ⓐ Ⓑ Ⓒ Ⓓ	67. Ⓐ Ⓑ Ⓒ Ⓓ
8. Ⓐ Ⓑ Ⓒ Ⓓ Ⓔ	23. Ⓐ Ⓑ Ⓒ Ⓓ Ⓔ	38. Ⓐ Ⓑ Ⓒ Ⓓ Ⓔ	53. Ⓐ Ⓑ Ⓒ Ⓓ	68. Ⓐ Ⓑ Ⓒ Ⓓ
9. Ⓐ Ⓑ Ⓒ Ⓓ Ⓔ	24. Ⓐ Ⓑ Ⓒ Ⓓ Ⓔ	39. Ⓐ Ⓑ Ⓒ Ⓓ Ⓔ	54. Ⓐ Ⓑ Ⓒ Ⓓ	69. Ⓐ Ⓑ Ⓒ Ⓓ
10. Ⓐ Ⓑ Ⓒ Ⓓ Ⓔ	25. Ⓐ Ⓑ Ⓒ Ⓓ Ⓔ	40. Ⓐ Ⓑ Ⓒ Ⓓ Ⓔ	55. Ⓐ Ⓑ Ⓒ Ⓓ	70. Ⓐ Ⓑ Ⓒ Ⓓ
11. Ⓐ Ⓑ Ⓒ Ⓓ Ⓔ	26. Ⓐ Ⓑ Ⓒ Ⓓ Ⓔ	41. Ⓐ Ⓑ Ⓒ Ⓓ Ⓔ	56. Ⓐ Ⓑ Ⓒ Ⓓ	71. Ⓐ Ⓑ Ⓒ Ⓓ
12. Ⓐ Ⓑ Ⓒ Ⓓ Ⓔ	27. Ⓐ Ⓑ Ⓒ Ⓓ Ⓔ	42. Ⓐ Ⓑ Ⓒ Ⓓ Ⓔ	57. Ⓐ Ⓑ Ⓒ Ⓓ	72. Ⓐ Ⓑ Ⓒ Ⓓ
13. Ⓐ Ⓑ Ⓒ Ⓓ Ⓔ	28. Ⓐ Ⓑ Ⓒ Ⓓ Ⓔ	43. Ⓐ Ⓑ Ⓒ Ⓓ Ⓔ	58. Ⓐ Ⓑ Ⓒ Ⓓ	73. Ⓐ Ⓑ Ⓒ Ⓓ
14. Ⓐ Ⓑ Ⓒ Ⓓ Ⓔ	29. Ⓐ Ⓑ Ⓒ Ⓓ Ⓔ	44. Ⓐ Ⓑ Ⓒ Ⓓ Ⓔ	59. Ⓐ Ⓑ Ⓒ Ⓓ	74. Ⓐ Ⓑ Ⓒ Ⓓ
15. Ⓐ Ⓑ Ⓒ Ⓓ Ⓔ	30. Ⓐ Ⓑ Ⓒ Ⓓ Ⓔ	45. Ⓐ Ⓑ Ⓒ Ⓓ Ⓔ	60. Ⓐ Ⓑ Ⓒ Ⓓ	75. Ⓐ Ⓑ Ⓒ Ⓓ

answer sheet

Practice Test 5: Math Knowledge

Questions 1–50 are five-option items. For each question, select the option that is most nearly correct.

1. Which of the following fractions is the largest?

   (A) $\frac{1}{2}$

   (B) $\frac{3}{4}$

   (C) $\frac{5}{8}$

   (D) $\frac{11}{16}$

   (E) $\frac{23}{32}$

2. Arrange these fractions in order of size from largest to smallest: $\frac{1}{3}$, $\frac{2}{5}$, $\frac{4}{15}$.

   (A) $\frac{4}{15}, \frac{2}{5}, \frac{1}{3}$

   (B) $\frac{2}{5}, \frac{4}{15}, \frac{1}{3}$

   (C) $\frac{2}{5}, \frac{1}{3}, \frac{4}{15}$

   (D) $\frac{1}{3}, \frac{4}{15}, \frac{2}{5}$

   (E) $\frac{1}{3}, \frac{2}{5}, \frac{4}{15}$

3. Which of the following fractions is equal to $\frac{1}{4}$%?

   (A) $\frac{1}{4}$

   (B) $\frac{1}{25}$

   (C) $\frac{4}{25}$

   (D) $\frac{1}{40}$

   (E) $\frac{1}{400}$

4. What percent of 90 is 120?

   (A) $133\frac{1}{3}$

   (B) 125

   (C) 120

   (D) 75

   (E) $1\frac{1}{3}$

5. What number added to 40% of itself is equal to 84?

   (A) 64.0

   (B) 60.0

   (C) 50.4

   (D) 40.6

   (E) 33.6

6. Find the square of 212.

   (A) 40,144

   (B) 44,944

   (C) 45,924

   (D) 46,944

   (E) 47,924

7. If $2^{n-3} = 32$, then n equals
   - (A) 5
   - (B) 6
   - (C) 7
   - (D) 8
   - (E) 9

8. How many digits are there in the square root of a perfect square of 6 digits?
   - (A) 12
   - (B) 6
   - (C) 4
   - (D) 3
   - (E) 2

9. If $a = 4$, then $\sqrt{a^2 + 9} =$
   - (A) 1
   - (B) 5
   - (C) $\sqrt{5}$
   - (D) 25
   - (E) −25

10. Solve the following:
    $5[4 - (+3 - 4) + 13] - 6 =$
    - (A) −11
    - (B) 16
    - (C) 17
    - (D) 21
    - (E) 84

11. If x is less than 10, and y is less than 5, it follows that
    - (A) $x > y$
    - (B) $x - y = 5$
    - (C) $x = 2y$
    - (D) $x + y < 15$
    - (E) $x + y = 15$

12. If the length and width of a rectangle are each multiplied by 2, then the
    - (A) perimeter is multiplied by 4 and the area by 8.
    - (B) area is multiplied by 2 and the perimeter by 4.
    - (C) area is multiplied by 4 and the perimeter by 2.
    - (D) area and perimeter are both multiplied by 2.
    - (E) area and perimeter are both multiplied by 4.

13. The average of two numbers is A. If one of the numbers is x, the other number is
    - (A) $\dfrac{A}{2} - x$
    - (B) $\dfrac{A + x}{2}$
    - (C) $A - x$
    - (D) $x - A$
    - (E) $2A - x$

14. If p pencils cost $2D$ dollars, how many pencils can be bought for c cents?
    - (A) $\dfrac{pc}{2D}$
    - (B) $\dfrac{pc}{200D}$
    - (C) $\dfrac{2Dp}{c}$
    - (D) $\dfrac{50pc}{D}$
    - (E) $200\,pcD$

15. When −4 is subtracted from the sum of −3 and +5, the result is
    - (A) +12
    - (B) +6
    - (C) −6
    - (D) +2
    - (E) −2

16. Find the product of $(-6)(+5)(-4)$.
    (A) $+5$
    (B) -5
    (C) -34
    (D) -120
    (E) $+120$

17. When the product of (-10) and $(+\frac{1}{2})$ is divided by the product of (-15) and $(-\frac{1}{3})$, the quotient is
    (A) $+2$
    (B) -2
    (C) $+1$
    (D) -1
    (E) 0

18. If $r = 25 - s$, then $4r + 4s =$
    (A) 100
    (B) -100
    (C) 25
    (D) -25
    (E) 0

19. Solve for x: $\dfrac{2x}{3} = \dfrac{x+5}{4}$
    (A) 2
    (B) 3
    (C) 4
    (D) 5
    (E) 6

20. If $a = 7$, $b = 8$, and $c = 5$, solve for x:
    $$\frac{a-3}{x} = \frac{b+2}{4c}$$
    (A) 4
    (B) 5
    (C) 6
    (D) 7
    (E) 8

21. The difference between $\sqrt{144}$ and $\sqrt{36}$ is
    (A) 180
    (B) 108
    (C) 18
    (D) 6
    (E) 2

22. $\sqrt{150}$ is between which of the following consecutive integers?
    (A) 10 and 11
    (B) 11 and 12
    (C) 12 and 13
    (D) 13 and 14
    (E) 14 and 15

23. Simplify the expression $2\sqrt{50}$.
    (A) $7\sqrt{2}$
    (B) $10\sqrt{2}$
    (C) 14
    (D) $25\sqrt{2}$
    (E) $50\sqrt{2}$

24. The sum of $4\sqrt{8}$, $3\sqrt{18}$, and $2\sqrt{50}$ is
    (A) $9\sqrt{76}$
    (B) $17\sqrt{2}$
    (C) $17\sqrt{6}$
    (D) $27\sqrt{2}$
    (E) $27\sqrt{6}$

25. If $\dfrac{1}{a} + \dfrac{1}{b} = \dfrac{1}{c}$, then $c =$
    (A) ab
    (B) $a + b$
    (C) $\dfrac{1}{2}ab$
    (D) $\dfrac{ab}{b+a}$
    (E) $\dfrac{a+b}{ab}$

26. If $a + b = 9$ and $a - b = 3$, then $a^2 - b^2 =$

    (A) 12

    (B) 27

    (C) 36

    (D) 72

    (E) 75

27. Solve for x: $x + y = a$
    $x - y = b$

    (A) $a + b$

    (B) $a - b$

    (C) $\frac{1}{2}ab$

    (D) $\frac{1}{2}(a + b)$

    (E) $\frac{1}{2}(a - b)$

28. Solve for y: $7x - 2y = 2$
    $3x + 4y = 30$

    (A) −4

    (B) 1

    (C) 2

    (D) 6

    (E) 11

29. Mr. Mason is 24 years older than his son Mark. In 8 years, Mr. Mason will be twice as old as Mark. How old is Mr. Mason now?

    (A) 24

    (B) 32

    (C) 40

    (D) 48

    (E) 56

30. Samantha is one half as old as her father. Twelve years ago, Samantha was one third as old as her father was then. What is Samantha's present age?

    (A) 24

    (B) 30

(C) 36

(D) 42

(E) 48

31. How many ounces of a 75% acid solution must be mixed with 16 ounces of 30% acid solution to produce a 50% acid solution?

    (A) 12.8

    (B) 13.2

    (C) 13.6

    (D) 14.0

    (E) 14.4

32. $\frac{6!}{3!} =$

    (A) 2

    (B) 3

    (C) 63

    (D) 120

    (E) 200

33. Determine the pattern for the arrangement and then select the proper option to complete the following series of numbers: 2 4 8 10 20 22 __

    (A) 24

    (B) 28

    (C) 36

    (D) 44

    (E) 48

34. Determine the pattern for the arrangement and then select the proper option that gives the next two letters in the following series: C E H J M O __ __

    (A) Q T

    (B) Q S

    (C) Q R

    (D) R U

    (E) R T

35. The first term of an arithmetic progression is 3, and the sixth term is 23. The common difference is
    (A) 2
    (B) 4
    (C) 6
    (D) 8
    (E) 10

36. At 3:30 P.M., the angle between the hands of a clock is
    (A) 65°
    (B) 75°
    (C) 77.5°
    (D) 80°
    (E) 90°

37. In triangle *ABC*, *AB* = *BC* and *AC* is extended to *D*. If angle *BCD* contains 110°, find the number of degrees in angle *B*.

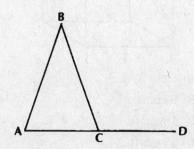

    (A) 20°
    (B) 40°
    (C) 50°
    (D) 60°
    (E) 80°

38. If one acute angle of a right triangle is 5 times as large as the other, the number of degrees in the smallest angle of the triangle is
    (A) 15°
    (B) 30°
    (C) 45°
    (D) 60°
    (E) 75°

39. If the angles of a triangle are in the ratio of 2 : 3 : 4, the triangle is
    (A) equilateral.
    (B) isosceles.
    (C) right.
    (D) obtuse.
    (E) acute.

40. If a base angle of an isosceles triangle is represented by $x°$, the number of degrees in the vertex angle is represented by
    (A) $180 - x$
    (B) $180 - 2x$
    (C) $90 - x$
    (D) $x - 180$
    (E) $2x - 180$

41. Find the area of the right triangle shown below.

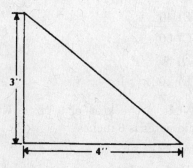

    (A) 5 sq. in.
    (B) 6 sq. in.
    (C) 9 sq. in.
    (D) 10 sq. in.
    (E) 12 sq. in.

42. A square lot has a diagonal path cut through it. If the path is 40 yards long, what is the area of the lot?
    (A) 400 square yards
    (B) 600 square yards
    (C) 800 square yards
    (D) 1200 square yards
    (E) 1600 square yards

43. If 140 feet of fencing is needed to enclose a rectangular field and the ratio of length to width in the field is 4 : 3, find the diagonal of the field.

    (A) 10 feet
    (B) 20 feet
    (C) 30 feet
    (D) 40 feet
    (E) 50 feet

44. In the figure shown below, if arc $AC = 80°$, then angle ABC is equal to

    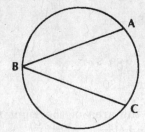

    (A) 20°
    (B) 40°
    (C) 60°
    (D) 80°
    (E) 100°

45. What is the area of a circle whose diameter is 6 inches?

    (A) 3π sq. in.
    (B) 6π sq. in.
    (C) 9π sq. in.
    (D) 12π sq. in.
    (E) 15π sq. in.

46. An automobile wheel has a diameter of 24 inches. How many revolutions will it make in covering one mile ($\pi = \frac{22}{7}$)?

    (A) 420
    (B) 630
    (C) 840
    (D) 1260
    (E) 1680

47. The area of circle O shown in the figure below is 16π. The perimeter of square $ABCD$ is

    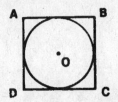

    (A) 4
    (B) 8
    (C) 16
    (D) 24
    (E) 32

48. The volume of the cube shown below is equal to

    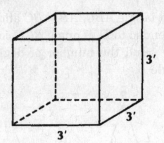

    (A) 3 cu. ft.
    (B) 9 cu. ft.
    (C) 18 cu. ft.
    (D) 27 cu. ft.
    (E) 54 cu. ft.

49. A cylindrical pail has a radius of 8 inches and a height of 10 inches. Approximately how many gallons will the pail hold? (There are 231 cubic inches to a gallon.)

    (A) 9
    (B) 11
    (C) 13
    (D) 15
    (E) 17

50. A circle graph shows that 30% of one year's immigrants were Hispanic, 28% were black, 20% were Asian, 17% were white, and the rest were classified as miscellaneous. How many degrees of the circle should be allocated to miscellaneous?

(A) 5°

(B) 9°

(C) 10°

(D) 14°

(E) 18°

Questions 51–75 are four-option items. For each question, select the option that is most nearly correct.

51.

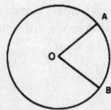

In the figure above, $\angle AOB = 60°$. If O is the center of the circle, then minor arc AB is what part of the circumference of the circle?

(A) $\frac{1}{2}$

(B) $\frac{1}{3}$

(C) $\frac{1}{6}$

(D) $\frac{1}{8}$

52. In a bag there are red, green, black, and white marbles. If there are 6 red, 8 green, 4 black, and 12 white, and one marble is to be selected at random, what is the probability it will be white?

(A) $\frac{1}{5}$

(B) $\frac{2}{5}$

(C) $\frac{4}{15}$

(D) $\frac{2}{15}$

53. 5 is what percent of 25?

(A) 5

(B) 20

(C) 80

(D) 125

54. If $a = 3$, then $a^a \cdot a =$

(A) 9

(B) 18

(C) 51

(D) 81

55. If $0.04y = 1$, then $y =$

(A) 0.025

(B) 25

(C) 0.25

(D) 250

56. A certain highway intersection has had A accidents over a ten-year period, resulting in B deaths. What is the yearly average death rate for the intersection?

(A) $A + B - 10$

(B) $\frac{B}{10}$

(C) $10 - \frac{A}{B}$

(D) $\frac{A}{10}$

57. $2.2 \times 0.00001 =$

   (A) 0.0022

   (B) 0.00022

   (C) 0.000022

   (D) 0.0000022

58. If T tons of snow fall in 1 second, how many tons fall in M minutes?

   (A) $60MT$

   (B) $MT + 60$

   (C) MT

   (D) $\dfrac{60M}{T}$

59. If $A^2 + B^2 = A^2 + X^2$, then B equals

   (A) $\pm X$

   (B) $X^2 - 2A^2$

   (C) A

   (D) $A^2 + X^2$

60. If $6 + x + y = 20$, and $x + y = k$, then $20 - k =$

   (A) 6

   (B) 0

   (C) 14

   (D) 20

61. $\sqrt{960}$ is a number between

   (A) 20 and 30

   (B) 60 and 70

   (C) 80 and 90

   (D) 30 and 40

62. If $x = y$, find the value of $8 + 5(x - y)$.

   (A) $8 + 5x - 5y$

   (B) $8 + 5xy$

   (C) $13x - 13y$

   (D) 8

63.

Triangle R is 3 times triangle S.
Triangle S is 3 times triangle T.
If triangle $S = 1$, what is the sum of the three triangles?

   (A) $2\dfrac{1}{3}$

   (B) $3\dfrac{1}{3}$

   (C) $4\dfrac{1}{3}$

   (D) 6

64. A boy has 5 pairs of slacks and 3 sport jackets. How many different combinations can he wear?

   (A) 3

   (B) 5

   (C) 8

   (D) 15

65. To find the radius of a circle whose circumference is 60 inches,

   (A) multiply 60 by π.

   (B) divide 60 by 2π.

   (C) divide 30 by 2π.

   (D) divide 60 by π and extract the square root of the result.

66. A is younger than B. With the passage of time,

   (A) the ratio of the ages of A and B remains unchanged.

   (B) the ratio of the ages of A and B increases.

   (C) the ratio of the ages of A and B decreases.

   (D) the difference in their ages varies.

67. If you multiply $x + 3$ by $2x + 5$, how many x's will there be in the product?

(A) 3

(B) 6

(C) 9

(D) 11

68. The area of a triangle ABC can be determined by the formula

(A) $AC \div B$

(B) $\frac{1}{2} bh$

(C) $BC \div A$

(D) bh^2

69. If psychological studies of college students show K percent to be emotionally unstable, the number of college students not emotionally unstable per 100 college students is

(A) $100 - K$

(B) $1 - K$

(C) $K - 1$

(D) $\frac{100}{K}$

70. If the circumference of a circle has the same numbered value as its area, then the radius of the circle must be

(A) 1

(B) 5

(C) 2

(D) 0

71.

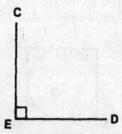

In the diagram above, $CE \perp ED$. If $CE = 7$ and $ED = 6$, what is the shortest distance from C to D?

(A) 6

(B) $4\sqrt{12}$

(C) 7

(D) $\sqrt{85}$

72. What is the correct time if the hour hand is exactly $\frac{2}{3}$ of the way between 5 and 6?

(A) 5:25

(B) 5:40

(C) 5:30

(D) 5:45

73. A square is changed into a rectangle by increasing its length 10% and decreasing its width 10%. Its area

(A) remains the same.

(B) decreases by 10%.

(C) increases by 1%.

(D) decreases by 1%.

74. If all P are S and no S are Q, it necessarily follows that

(A) all Q are S.

(B) all Q are P.

(C) no P are Q.

(D) no S are P.

75. The area of circle O is 64π. The perimeter of square $ABCD$ is

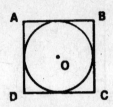

(A) 32

(B) 32π

(C) 64

(D) 16

ANSWER KEY AND EXPLANATIONS

1. (B)	16. (E)	31. (A)	46. (C)	61. (D)
2. (C)	17. (D)	32. (D)	47. (E)	62. (D)
3. (E)	18. (A)	33. (D)	48. (D)	63. (C)
4. (A)	19. (B)	34. (E)	49. (A)	64. (D)
5. (B)	20. (E)	35. (B)	50. (E)	65. (B)
6. (B)	21. (D)	36. (B)	51. (C)	66. (B)
7. (D)	22. (C)	37. (B)	52. (B)	67. (D)
8. (D)	23. (B)	38. (A)	53. (B)	68. (B)
9. (B)	24. (D)	39. (E)	54. (D)	69. (A)
10. (E)	25. (D)	40. (B)	55. (B)	70. (C)
11. (D)	26. (B)	41. (B)	56. (B)	71. (D)
12. (C)	27. (D)	42. (C)	57. (C)	72. (B)
13. (E)	28. (D)	43. (E)	58. (A)	73. (D)
14. (B)	29. (C)	44. (B)	59. (A)	74. (C)
15. (B)	30. (A)	45. (C)	60. (A)	75. (C)

1. **The correct answer is (B).**

$$\frac{1}{2} = \frac{16}{32}; \frac{3}{4} = \frac{24}{32}; \frac{5}{8} = \frac{20}{32}; \frac{11}{16} = \frac{22}{32}; \frac{23}{32}$$
$$= \frac{23}{32}$$

2. **The correct answer is (C).** $\frac{1}{3} = \frac{5}{15}$;

$$\frac{2}{5} = \frac{6}{15}; \frac{4}{15} = \frac{4}{15}.$$

3. **The correct answer is (E).** $\frac{1}{4}\% = \frac{1}{4} \times$

$$\frac{1}{100} = \frac{1}{400}.$$

4. **The correct answer is (A).** $\frac{120}{90} = \frac{4}{3}$;

$$\frac{4}{3} \times 100 = 133\frac{1}{3}\%.$$

5. **The correct answer is (B).** $x + 0.40x = 84$; $1.40x = 84$; $x = \frac{84}{1.40} = 60$.

6. **The correct answer is (B).** $212 \times 212 = 44,944$.

7. **The correct answer is (D).** $2^5 = 32$; $n - 3 = 5$; $n = 8$.

8. **The correct answer is (D).** There is one digit in the square root for every pair of digits in the whole number.

9. **The correct answer is (B).** $\sqrt{4^2 + 9} = \sqrt{25} = 5$.

10. **The correct answer is (E).** $5[4 - (-1) + 13] - 6 = 5[5 + 13] - 6 = 5 \times 18 - 6 = 90 - 6 = 84$.

11. **The correct answer is (D).** If x is less than 10 and y is less than 5, $x + y$ is less than 15.

12. **The correct answer is (C).** The area is multiplied by 2^2, or 4; the perimeter is doubled or multiplied by 2.

13. **The correct answer is (E).** Let $x =$ one of the numbers and $y =$ the other number; $\frac{x+y}{2} = A$; $x + y = 2A$; $y = 2A - x$.

14. **The correct answer is (B).**

$p : 200D = x : c$; $x \times 200D = pc$; $x = \dfrac{pc}{200D}$.

15. **The correct answer is (B).**

$(-3) + (+5) = +2$

$(+2) - (-4) = +6$

16. **The correct answer is (E).** An even number of negative signs when multiplying gives a positive product: $(-6)(+5)(-4) = +120$.

17. **The correct answer is (D).**

$(-10)(+\tfrac{1}{2}) = -5$; $(-15)(-\tfrac{1}{3}) = +5$;

-5 divided by $+5 = -1$

18. **The correct answer is (A).** $r + s = 25$; $4(r + s) = 100$.

19. **The correct answer is (B).** $8x = 3x + 15$; $5x = 15$; $x = 3$.

20. **The correct answer is (E).**

$\dfrac{7-3}{x} = \dfrac{8+2}{4 \times 5}$; $\dfrac{4}{x} = \dfrac{10}{20}$; $10x = 80$; $x = 8$

21. **The correct answer is (D).**

$\sqrt{144} = 12$; $\sqrt{36} = 6$; $12 - 6 = 6$

22. **The correct answer is (C).** $12 \times 12 = 144$; $13 \times 13 = 169$; thus, the square root of 150 is between 12 and 13.

23. **The correct answer is (B).**

$2\sqrt{50} = 2\sqrt{25 \times 2} = 2 \times 5\sqrt{2} = 10\sqrt{2}$.

24. **The correct answer is (D).** $4\sqrt{4 \times 2} + 3\sqrt{9 \times 2} + 2\sqrt{25 \times 2} = 8\sqrt{2} + 9\sqrt{2} + 10\sqrt{2} = 27\sqrt{2}$.

25. **The correct answer is (D).** Multiply by abc;

$bc + ac = ab$; $c(b + a) = ab$; $c = \dfrac{ab}{b+a}$.

26. **The correct answer is (B).**

$a^2 - b^2 = (a + b)(a - b) = 9 \times 3 = 27$

27. **The correct answer is (D).** Adding both equations: $2x = a + b$; $x = \dfrac{a+b}{2} = \dfrac{1}{2}(a + b)$.

28. **The correct answer is (D).** Multiply the first equation by 3 and the second equation by 7. $21x - 6y = 6$; $21x + 28y = 210$; subtracting, $34y = 204$; $y = \dfrac{204}{34} = 6$.

29. **The correct answer is (C).**

Person	Ages Now	Ages Then
Mr. Mason	x	$x + 8$
Mark	$x - 24$	$x - 24 + 8$

Let x = Mr. Mason's present age.

$x + 8 = 2(x - 16)$; $x + 8 = 2x - 32$; $x = 40$

30. **The correct answer is (A).**

Person	Ages Now	Ages Then
Samantha	x	$x - 12$
Father	$2x$	$2x - 12$

Let x = Samantha's age.

$x - 12 = \dfrac{1}{3}(2x - 12)$; $x - 12 = \dfrac{2}{3}x - 4$;

$\dfrac{1}{3}x = 8$; $x = 8 \times 3 = 24$

31. **The correct answer is (A).**

	No. of Ounces	Concentration	Ounces of Pure Substance
75% Solution	x	0.75	$0.75x$
30% Solution	16	0.30	4.80
50% Solution	$16 + x$	0.50	$0.50(16 + x)$

$0.75x + 4.80 = 8.00 + 0.50x$; $0.25x = 3.20$;

$x = \dfrac{3.20}{0.25} = 12.8$

32. **The correct answer is (D).**

$6! = 6 \times 5 \times 4 \times 3 \times 2 \times 1 = 720$;

$3! = 3 \times 2 \times 1 = 6$; $\dfrac{720}{6} = 120$.

33. **The correct answer is (D).** Add 2, multiply by 2; add 2, multiply by 2; etc.

34. **The correct answer is (E).**

C E H J M O R T
D FG I KL N PQ S
(Skip 1, skip 2; repeat.).

35. **The correct answer is (B).** There is a difference of 20 between the last term and the first term. There are 5 terms following the initial term. $\frac{20}{5} = 4$, the common difference (3, 7, 11, 15, 19, 23).

36. **The correct answer is (B).** At 3:30 P.M., the minute hand is at the 6 and the hour hand is midway between the 3 and the 4. $\frac{360°}{12} = 30°$ between numbers. $2\frac{1}{2} \times 30° = 75°$.

37. **The correct answer is (B).** If angle $BCD = 110°$, angle $BCA = 70°$, and angle $BAC = 70°$. Angle $ABC = 180° - 140°$ or $40°$.

38. **The correct answer is (A).** $x + 5x = 90°$; $6x = 90°$; $x = 15°$.

39. **The correct answer is (E).** $2x + 3x + 4x = 9x$; $9x = 180°$; $x = 20°$; the angles are $40°$, $60°$, and $80°$—all acute angles.

40. **The correct answer is (B).** The sum of the two base angles is $2x$. Therefore, the number of degrees in the vertex angle $= 180 - 2x$.

41. **The correct answer is (B).**

Area $= \frac{1}{2} \times$ base $\times$ altitude; Area $= \frac{1}{2}(4 \times 3) = \frac{1}{2}(12) = 6$ sq. in.

42. **The correct answer is (C).**

Area of square $= \frac{1}{2}$ of product of the diagonals.

$\frac{1}{2}(40 \times 40) = \frac{1}{2}(1600) = 800$

43. **The correct answer is (E).** Let $4x =$ length and $3x =$ width.

$4x + 3x + 4x + 3x = 140$; $14x = 140$; $x = 10$.

Length $= 40$ feet; width $= 30$ feet. If two sides of a right triangle are 40 and 30 feet, the hypotenuse or diagonal $= 50$ feet.

44. **The correct answer is (B).** An inscribed angle is equal in degrees to one half its intercepted arc. Angle ABC, an inscribed angle, is equal to one half of $80°$. Angle $ABC = 40°$.

45. **The correct answer is (C).** Area $= \pi r^2$. If diameter $= 6$ inches, radius $= 3$ inches; area $= \pi \times 3^2$; area $= 9\pi$.

46. **The correct answer is (C).** 24 inches $= 2$ feet; circumference $= 2\pi = \frac{44}{7}$; 5280 feet $= 1$ mile; 5280 divided by $\frac{44}{7} = 5280$ times $\frac{7}{44} = 840$.

47. **The correct answer is (E).** Area $= \pi r^2$; $r^2 = 16$; $r = 4$; diameter $= 8$; $4 \times 8 = 32$.

48. **The correct answer is (D).** The length, width, and height of a cube are all equal. The volume of a cube is equal to the cube of an edge. Each edge $= 3$ feet. Volume $= 3' \times 3' \times 3' = 27$ cubic feet.

49. **The correct answer is (A).** $\pi r^2 \times$ height $=$ volume; $\pi \times 8^2 \times 10 =$ volume; volume $= \frac{22 \times 64 \times 10}{7} = 2011.4$; 2011.4 cubic inches divided by 231 cubic inches $= 8.7$ gallons.

50. **The correct answer is (E).** $30 + 28 + 20 + 17 = 95$; $100 - 95 = 5$. The miscellaneous classification comprised 5% of the immigrants for that year. $360° \times 0.05 = 18°$.

51. **The correct answer is (C).** A circle is $360°$; $60°$ is $\frac{1}{6}$ of $360°$.

52. The correct answer is (B). There are 6 + 8 + 4 + 12 = 30 marbles. 12 + 30 = 0.40 = $\frac{2}{5}$.

53. The correct answer is (B). $\frac{\cancel{5}^{1}}{\cancel{25}_{5}} = 0.2 = 20\%$.

54. The correct answer is (D). $3^3 \times 3 = 27 \times 3 = 81$

55. The correct answer is (B). $0.04y = 1$; $y = 1 \div 0.04 = 25$.

56. The correct answer is (B). The number of accidents is irrelevant to the question, so A has no place in the equation. B(total deaths) ÷ 10 years = $\frac{B}{10}$ average deaths per year.

57. The correct answer is (C). To place the decimal point in the product, add together the number of digits to the right of the decimal points in all of the multipliers. In this case, the answer requires 6 decimal places.

58. The correct answer is (A). To find how many tons fall in a given number of minutes, multiply the number of tons that fall in one minute by the number of minutes. There are 60 seconds in 1 minute, and T tons fall in 1 second. In M minutes, the amount of snow that falls is $60MT$.

59. The correct answer is (A). Subtract A^2 from both sides of the equation: $B^2 = X^2$, therefore $B = X$ or $-X$.

60. The correct answer is (A).
$6 + x + y = 20$
$x + y = 14 = k$; now substitute
$20 - 14 = 6$

61. The correct answer is (D). The first step in finding a square root is grouping the digits into pairs, starting at the decimal point. If necessary, place a 0 to the left of the first digit to create a pair. Each pair represents one digit in the square root. The square root of 960 is a two-digit

number in the 30s because the square root of 09 is 3.

62. The correct answer is (D). $8 + 5(x - y)$
$= 8 + 5x - 5y$

Since $x = y$, $5x = 5y$ and $5x - 5y = 0$
Substituting: $8 + 0 = 8$

63. The correct answer is (C).

$$\begin{array}{l} S = 1 \\ R = 3 \times 1 \\ T = \dfrac{1}{3} \\ \hline \quad 4\dfrac{1}{3} \end{array}$$

64. The correct answer is (D). Each sport jacket can be worn with 5 pairs of slacks. $3 \times 5 = 15$.

65. The correct answer is (B).

$C = 2\pi r$

$60 = 2\pi r$ (Divide both sides by 2π).

$r = 60 \div 2\pi$

66. The correct answer is (B). Pick a pair of ages and try for yourself. A is 2; B is 4; the ratio of their ages is 2 to 4 or 1 to 2. In two years, A is 4 and B is 6. The ratio of their ages is 4 to 6 or 2 to 3.

67. The correct answer is (D).

$$\begin{array}{r} x + 3 \\ \times\, 2x + 5 \\ \hline 2x^2 + 6x \\ 5x + 15 \\ \hline 2x^2 + 11x + 15 \end{array}$$

68. The correct answer is (B). The formula for the area of a triangle is $\frac{1}{2}$ the base times the height.

69. The correct answer is (A). "Percent" means out of 100. If K percent are emotionally unstable, then K out of 100 are emotionally unstable. The remainder, $100 - K$, is not unstable.

70. **The correct answer is (C).** The formula to find the circumference of a circle is $2\pi r$. The formula to find the area of a circle is πr^2. The only number that has the same value when multiplied by 2 or squared is 2.

71. **The correct answer is (D).** CD is a hypotenuse, so use the Pythagorean theorem:

$$CD = \sqrt{CE^2 + ED^2}$$
$$CD = \sqrt{7^2 + 6^2} = \sqrt{49 + 36} = \sqrt{85}$$

72. **The correct answer is (B).** $\frac{2}{3}$ of 60 min. = 40 min. 5:00 + 40 min. = 5:40.

73. **The correct answer is (D).** Assign arbitrary values to solve this problem:

A square 10 ft. × 10 ft. = 100 sq. ft.

A rectangle 9 ft. × 11 ft. = 99 sq. ft.

$100 - 99 = 1$; $\frac{1}{100} = 1\%$.

74. **The correct answer is (C).** Diagram this problem:

75. **The correct answer is (C).** The formula for the area of a circle is πr^2. In this problem, $r^2 = 64$, so $r = 8$. The circle is tangent with the square on all four sides; the radius is exactly $\frac{1}{2}$ the length of a side of the square. Each side, then, is 16 units long. The formula for the perimeter of a square is $P = 4s$, so $4 \times 16 = 64$.

ANSWER SHEET FOR PRACTICE TEST 6: GENERAL SCIENCE

1. Ⓐ Ⓑ Ⓒ Ⓓ
2. Ⓐ Ⓑ Ⓒ Ⓓ
3. Ⓐ Ⓑ Ⓒ Ⓓ
4. Ⓐ Ⓑ Ⓒ Ⓓ
5. Ⓐ Ⓑ Ⓒ Ⓓ
6. Ⓐ Ⓑ Ⓒ Ⓓ
7. Ⓐ Ⓑ Ⓒ Ⓓ
8. Ⓐ Ⓑ Ⓒ Ⓓ
9. Ⓐ Ⓑ Ⓒ Ⓓ
10. Ⓐ Ⓑ Ⓒ Ⓓ

11. Ⓐ Ⓑ Ⓒ Ⓓ
12. Ⓐ Ⓑ Ⓒ Ⓓ
13. Ⓐ Ⓑ Ⓒ Ⓓ
14. Ⓐ Ⓑ Ⓒ Ⓓ
15. Ⓐ Ⓑ Ⓒ Ⓓ
16. Ⓐ Ⓑ Ⓒ Ⓓ
17. Ⓐ Ⓑ Ⓒ Ⓓ
18. Ⓐ Ⓑ Ⓒ Ⓓ
19. Ⓐ Ⓑ Ⓒ Ⓓ
20. Ⓐ Ⓑ Ⓒ Ⓓ

21. Ⓐ Ⓑ Ⓒ Ⓓ
22. Ⓐ Ⓑ Ⓒ Ⓓ
23. Ⓐ Ⓑ Ⓒ Ⓓ
24. Ⓐ Ⓑ Ⓒ Ⓓ
25. Ⓐ Ⓑ Ⓒ Ⓓ
26. Ⓐ Ⓑ Ⓒ Ⓓ
27. Ⓐ Ⓑ Ⓒ Ⓓ
28. Ⓐ Ⓑ Ⓒ Ⓓ
29. Ⓐ Ⓑ Ⓒ Ⓓ
30. Ⓐ Ⓑ Ⓒ Ⓓ

31. Ⓐ Ⓑ Ⓒ Ⓓ
32. Ⓐ Ⓑ Ⓒ Ⓓ
33. Ⓐ Ⓑ Ⓒ Ⓓ
34. Ⓐ Ⓑ Ⓒ Ⓓ
35. Ⓐ Ⓑ Ⓒ Ⓓ
36. Ⓐ Ⓑ Ⓒ Ⓓ
37. Ⓐ Ⓑ Ⓒ Ⓓ
38. Ⓐ Ⓑ Ⓒ Ⓓ
39. Ⓐ Ⓑ Ⓒ Ⓓ
40. Ⓐ Ⓑ Ⓒ Ⓓ

41. Ⓐ Ⓑ Ⓒ Ⓓ
42. Ⓐ Ⓑ Ⓒ Ⓓ
43. Ⓐ Ⓑ Ⓒ Ⓓ
44. Ⓐ Ⓑ Ⓒ Ⓓ
45. Ⓐ Ⓑ Ⓒ Ⓓ
46. Ⓐ Ⓑ Ⓒ Ⓓ
47. Ⓐ Ⓑ Ⓒ Ⓓ
48. Ⓐ Ⓑ Ⓒ Ⓓ
49. Ⓐ Ⓑ Ⓒ Ⓓ
50. Ⓐ Ⓑ Ⓒ Ⓓ

answer sheet

Practice Test 6: General Science

Questions 1–50 are four-option items. For each question, select the option that best completes the statement or answers the question.

1. Citrus fruits include
   (A) apples.
   (B) bananas.
   (C) oranges.
   (D) peaches.

2. What temperature is shown on a Fahrenheit thermometer when a centigrade thermometer reads 0°?
   (A) −40°
   (B) −32°
   (C) 0°
   (D) + 32°

3. The major chemical constituent of a cell (by weight) is
   (A) protein.
   (B) ash.
   (C) water.
   (D) carbohydrates.

4. The Wassermann test may indicate the presence of
   (A) syphilis.
   (B) tuberculosis.
   (C) measles.
   (D) AIDS.

5. Alcoholic beverages contain
   (A) wood alcohol.
   (B) isopropyl alcohol.
   (C) glyceryl alcohol.
   (D) grain alcohol.

6. The air around us is composed mostly of
   (A) carbon.
   (B) nitrogen.
   (C) hydrogen.
   (D) oxygen.

7. The process that is responsible for the continuous removal of carbon dioxide from the atmosphere is
   (A) respiration.
   (B) oxidation.
   (C) metabolism.
   (D) photosynthesis.

8. Ringworm is caused by a(n)
   (A) alga.
   (B) fungus.
   (C) bacterium.
   (D) protozoan.

9. Light passes through the crystalline lens in the eye and focuses on the
   (A) cornea.
   (B) iris.
   (C) pupil.
   (D) retina.

10. Saliva contains an enzyme that acts on
    (A) carbohydrates.
    (B) proteins.
    (C) minerals.
    (D) vitamins.

11. The vitamin that helps coagulation of the blood is
    (A) C
    (B) E
    (C) D
    (D) K

12. Of the following, the part of a ship that gives it stability by lowering the center of gravity is the
    (A) bulkhead.
    (B) keel.
    (C) anchor.
    (D) prow.

13. To reduce soil acidity, a farmer should use
    (A) lime.
    (B) phosphate.
    (C) manure.
    (D) peat moss.

14. Which of the following minerals is restored to the soil by plants of the pea and bean family?
    (A) Sulfates
    (B) Carbonates
    (C) Nitrates
    (D) Phosphates

15. The greater the frequency of sound waves,
    (A) the louder the sound.
    (B) the higher the pitch of the sound.
    (C) the softer the sound.
    (D) the lower the pitch of the sound.

16. Of the following, the food that contains the largest amount of vitamin C is
    (A) carrots.
    (B) sweet potatoes.
    (C) lima beans.
    (D) tomatoes.

17. The cyclotron is used to
    (A) measure radioactivity.
    (B) measure the speed of the Earth's rotation.
    (C) split atoms.
    (D) store radioactive energy.

18. The Earth completes one trip around the sun approximately every
    (A) 24 hours.
    (B) 52 weeks.
    (C) 7 days.
    (D) 30 days.

19. A person is more buoyant when swimming in salt water than in fresh water because
    (A) he keeps his head out of salt water.
    (B) salt coats his body with a floating membrane.
    (C) salt water has great tensile strength.
    (D) salt water weighs more than an equal volume of fresh water.

20. A volcanic eruption is caused by
    (A) sunspots.
    (B) pressure inside the Earth.
    (C) nuclear fallout.
    (D) boiling lava.

21. The vitamin manufactured by the skin with the help of the sun is
    (A) A
    (B) B_6
    (C) B_{12}
    (D) D

22. A tumor is a
    - (A) cancer.
    - (B) growth.
    - (C) sore spot.
    - (D) kind of mushroom.

23. All types of steel contain
    - (A) iron.
    - (B) chromium.
    - (C) nickel.
    - (D) tungsten.

24. The *most important* provision for a hike in hot, dry countryside is
    - (A) dried meat.
    - (B) raisins.
    - (C) fresh fruit.
    - (D) water.

25. The moon is a
    - (A) star.
    - (B) satellite.
    - (C) planetoid.
    - (D) planet.

26. During a thunderstorm, we see a lightning bolt before we hear the sound of the accompanying thunder chiefly because
    - (A) the eye is more sensitive than the ear.
    - (B) the wind interferes with the sound of the thunder.
    - (C) the storm may be very far away.
    - (D) the speed of light is much greater than the speed of sound.

27. Of the following, a human blood disease that has been definitely shown to be due to a hereditary factor or factors is
    - (A) pernicious anemia.
    - (B) polyscythemia.
    - (C) sickle cell anemia.
    - (D) leukemia.

28. The number of degrees on the Fahrenheit thermometer between the freezing point and the boiling point of water is
    - (A) 100 degrees.
    - (B) 212 degrees.
    - (C) 180 degrees.
    - (D) 273 degrees.

29. An observer on Earth sees the phases of the moon because the
    - (A) moon revolves around the sun.
    - (B) moon revolves around the Earth.
    - (C) Earth revolves around the sun.
    - (D) moon rotates on its axis.

30. The temperature of the air falls at night because the Earth loses heat by
    - (A) radiation.
    - (B) conduction.
    - (C) convection.
    - (D) rotation.

31. The normal height of a mercury barometer at sea level is
    - (A) 15 inches.
    - (B) 32 feet.
    - (C) 30 inches.
    - (D) 34 feet.

32. Nitrogen-fixing bacteria are found in nodules on the roots of the
    - (A) beet.
    - (B) potato.
    - (C) carrot.
    - (D) clover.

33. The vascular system of the body is concerned with
    - (A) respiration.
    - (B) sense of touch.
    - (C) circulation of blood.
    - (D) enzymes.

34. Of the following substances, the one that is nonmagnetic is
    (A) iron.
    (B) aluminum.
    (C) nickel.
    (D) cobalt.

35. If you wish to cut down on saturated fats and cholesterol in your diet, which of the following foods should you avoid?
    (A) Fish
    (B) Dry beans and peas
    (C) Cheese
    (D) Spaghetti

36. Which one of the following is NOT a fruit?
    (A) Potato
    (B) Tomato
    (C) Cucumber
    (D) Green pepper

37. The hammer, anvil, and stirrup bones lie in the
    (A) knee.
    (B) hip.
    (C) ear.
    (D) elbow.

38. Of the following, a condition NOT associated with heavy cigarette smoking is
    (A) shorter life span.
    (B) slowing of the heartbeat.
    (C) cancer of the lung.
    (D) heart disease.

39. You are most likely to develop hypothermia when
    (A) it is very hot and you have nothing to drink.
    (B) you are bitten by a rabid dog.
    (C) you fall asleep in the sun.
    (D) it is very cold and your clothes are wet.

40. Of the following, the gas that is needed for burning is
    (A) carbon dioxide.
    (B) nitrogen.
    (C) oxygen.
    (D) argon.

41. Of the following, the only safe blood transfusion would be
    (A) Group A blood into a Group O person.
    (B) Group B blood into a Group A person.
    (C) Group O blood into a Group AB person.
    (D) Group AB blood into a Group B person.

42. Of the following, the statement that best describes a "high" on a weather map is
    (A) the air extends farther up than normal.
    (B) the air pressure is greater than normal.
    (C) the air temperature is higher than normal.
    (D) the air moves faster than normal.

43. The smallest particle of gold that still retains the characteristics of gold is
    (A) a molecule.
    (B) a proton.
    (C) an electron.
    (D) an atom.

44. Narcotics may be dangerous if used without supervision, but they are useful in medicine because they
    (A) increase production of red blood cells.
    (B) kill bacteria.
    (C) relieve pain.
    (D) stimulate the heart.

45. The primary reason why fungi are often found growing in abundance deep in the forest is that there
    (A) it is cooler.
    (B) it is warmer.
    (C) they have little exposure to sunlight for photosynthesis.
    (D) they have a plentiful supply of organic matter.

46. The presence of coal deposits in Alaska shows that at one time Alaska
    (A) had a tropical climate.
    (B) was covered with ice.
    (C) was connected to Asia.
    (D) was formed by volcanic action.

47. If a person has been injured in an accident and damage to the back and neck is suspected, it is best to
    (A) roll the person over so that he does not lie on his back.
    (B) rush the person to the nearest hospital.
    (C) force the person to drink water to replace body fluids.
    (D) wait for professional help.

48. A 1,000-ton ship must displace a weight of water equal to
    (A) 500 tons.
    (B) 1,500 tons.
    (C) 1,000 tons.
    (D) 2,000 tons.

49. Vitamin C is also known as
    (A) citric acid.
    (B) ascorbic acid.
    (C) lactic acid.
    (D) glutamic acid.

50. If you are caught away from home during a thunderstorm, the safest place to be is
    (A) in a car.
    (B) under a tree.
    (C) in an open field.
    (D) at the top of a small hill.

practice test

ANSWER KEY AND EXPLANATIONS

1. (C)	11. (D)	21. (D)	31. (C)	41. (C)
2. (D)	12. (B)	22. (B)	32. (D)	42. (B)
3. (C)	13. (A)	23. (A)	33. (C)	43. (D)
4. (A)	14. (C)	24. (D)	34. (B)	44. (C)
5. (D)	15. (B)	25. (B)	35. (C)	45. (D)
6. (B)	16. (D)	26. (D)	36. (A)	46. (A)
7. (D)	17. (C)	27. (C)	37. (C)	47. (D)
8. (B)	18. (B)	28. (C)	38. (B)	48. (C)
9. (D)	19. (D)	29. (B)	39. (D)	49. (B)
10. (A)	20. (B)	30. (A)	40. (C)	50. (A)

1. **The correct answer is (C).** Citrus fruits include lemons, limes, oranges, and grapefruit.

2. **The correct answer is (D).** Water freezes at 0° on a centigrade or Celsius thermometer. Water freezes at 32° Fahrenheit.

3. **The correct answer is (C).** The major chemical constituent of a cell by importance is protein, but by weight it is water.

4. **The correct answer is (A).** The Wassermann test, developed by a German bacteriologist in 1906, is a blood test for syphilis.

5. **The correct answer is (D).** Wood alcohol is methyl alcohol, which is extremely toxic; drinking it may cause blindness. Isopropyl alcohol is rubbing alcohol. Glyceryl alcohol is an industrial solvent.

6. **The correct answer is (B).** Nitrogen constitutes about four fifths of the Earth's atmosphere, by volume.

7. **The correct answer is (D).** By the process of photosynthesis, green plants remove carbon dioxide from the atmosphere and replace it with oxygen.

8. **The correct answer is (B).** Ringworm is a skin disease caused by a fungus.

9. **The correct answer is (D).** Light enters the eye through the pupil (the opening in the center of the iris), travels through the transparent crystalline lens, then travels through the vitreous humor (eyeball), and finally is focused on the retina.

10. **The correct answer is (A).** The salivary glands secrete the enzyme ptyalin, which acts on carbohydrates.

11. **The correct answer is (D).** Vitamin K is useful in the coagulation of blood. Vitamin C prevents scurvy; vitamin E maintains muscle tone and aids in fertility; vitamin D prevents rickets.

12. **The correct answer is (B).** A bulkhead is a wall; the anchor keeps the ship from moving; and the prow is the front of the ship.

13. **The correct answer is (A).** Lime is highly alkaline.

14. **The correct answer is (C).** Bacteria on the roots of legumes, plants that include peas and beans, serve to fixate free nitrogen and return it to the soil as nitrates.

15. **The correct answer is (B).** Frequency is directly related to pitch. The higher pitched a sound is, the greater its frequency is. Low-pitched sounds have low frequencies.

16. **The correct answer is (D).** Most vegetables contain some vitamin C, and yellow vegetables contain more vitamin C than green ones. Tomatoes, however, are actually fruits and contain far more vitamin C than any vegetables.

17. **The correct answer is (C).** The cyclotron is an accelerating device that splits atoms.

18. **The correct answer is (B).** It takes the Earth 1 year to complete an orbit of the sun. A year contains 365 days, or 52 weeks.

19. **The correct answer is (D).** The weight of the salt water displaced by a human body is greater than the weight of fresh water displaced by that same body. Since the water displaced is heavier, the body is proportionally lighter and is more buoyant.

20. **The correct answer is (B).** Boiling lava erupts from a volcano. The force that causes the eruption is pressure inside the Earth.

21. **The correct answer is (D).** Vitamin D can be found in fish-liver oils and egg yolks. It can also be manufactured within skin that is exposed to sunlight.

22. **The correct answer is (B).** A tumor is a growth. A malignant tumor or growth is a cancer.

23. **The correct answer is (A).** Steel is a compound of iron and carbon.

24. **The correct answer is (D).** The greatest danger during exercise under hot, dry conditions is dehydration. A person can survive for a relatively long period of time without food, but for only a short

time without water. Hot, dry conditions make the need for water more urgent.

25. **The correct answer is (B).** The moon is a satellite of the Earth.

26. **The correct answer is (D).** The speed of light is about a million times that of sound.

27. **The correct answer is (C).** While the hereditary components of most diseases are still under study, the hereditary nature of sickle cell anemia is documented and well understood. Sickle cell anemia is most common among black people.

28. **The correct answer is (C).** Water boils at 212°F and freezes at 32°F. 212° − 32° = 180°.

29. **The correct answer is (B).** As viewed from space, one half of the moon is always illuminated by the sun. However, as the moon changes its position in its orbit around the Earth, different amounts of the illuminated side are visible from the Earth.

30. **The correct answer is (A).** Radiation is the process by which energy is transferred in space.

31. **The correct answer is (C).** Barometric pressure is expressed in inches. The range is generally from 28 to 31 inches.

32. **The correct answer is (D).** Clover serves to return nitrates to the soil through the action of nitrogen-fixing bacteria in nodules on its roots.

33. **The correct answer is (C).** The vascular system is the system of vessels for the circulation of blood. The respiratory system is concerned with respiration (breathing) and the endocrine system with enzymes.

34. **The correct answer is (B).** Aluminum is not magnetic. Cobalt and nickel are somewhat magnetic, while iron is highly magnetic.

35. **The correct answer is (C).** Milk and milk products such as cheese and butter are high in saturated fat and cholesterol.

36. **The correct answer is (A).** Fruits have seeds. Tomatoes, cucumbers, and green peppers have seeds. A potato is a tuber.

37. **The correct answer is (C).** The hammer, anvil, and stirrup are the three tiny bones that connect the eardrum with the inner ear.

38. **The correct answer is (B).** Cigarette smoking can speed up the heartbeat.

39. **The correct answer is (D).** The prefix *hypo* means *below* or *abnormally deficient. Hypo*thermia is a condition in which the body's temperature falls well below the normal 98.6°F. If it is very hot and you have nothing to drink, you may become dehydrated and might develop *hyper*thermia, overheating. Another name for rabies is hydrophobia.

40. **The correct answer is (C).** Combustion cannot occur in the absence of oxygen.

41. **The correct answer is (C).** Antigens and antibodies are hostile to one another. If antigens of a factor are introduced into a person who has antibodies toward that factor, a severe reaction and even possible death will result. Group A blood contains A antigens and B antibodies. Group B blood contains B antigens and A antibodies. Group AB blood contains A and B antigens but no antibodies. Group AB persons can receive any group blood; they are called "universal recipients." Group O blood contains no antigens but A and B antibodies. Group O persons are called "universal donors."

42. **The correct answer is (B).** The "highs" on a weather map are based on barometric pressure. The greater the air pressure, the higher the mercury in the barometer.

43. **The correct answer is (D).** An atom is the smallest part of an element that retains all the properties of the element.

44. **The correct answer is (C).** The action of narcotics is to deaden pain.

45. **The correct answer is (D).** Fungi do not contain chlorophyll so they cannot produce their own food through photosynthesis. Since fungi must rely for their food upon decaying organic matter, the forest is a hospitable home.

46. **The correct answer is (A).** Coal is formed by the partial decomposition of vegetable matter under the influence of moisture, pressure, and temperature, and in the absence of air. If there is coal in Alaska, there must once have been abundant vegetation in Alaska.

47. **The correct answer is (D).** Damage to the neck and back is especially dangerous because the spinal cord is so vulnerable. Once the spinal cord is severed, paralysis is inevitable and irreversible, so if there is any question of back or neck injury, the person should be moved only by a skilled professional.

48. **The correct answer is (C).** Like displaces like.

49. **The correct answer is (B).** Vitamin C, contained in citrus fruits, tomatoes, and green vegetables, is also known as ascorbic acid.

50. **The correct answer is (A).** Lightning is most likely to strike the highest object in an area. If you are standing in an open field or at the top of a small hill, you are likely to be the highest object and a good target. If you stand under a tree, lightning might hit the tree and cause it to fall on you. A car is grounded. If you are inside a car that is hit by lightning, the lightning will be transmitted into the ground by the car.

ANSWER SHEET FOR PRACTICE TEST 7: ELECTRONICS INFORMATION

1. Ⓐ Ⓑ Ⓒ Ⓓ
2. Ⓐ Ⓑ Ⓒ Ⓓ
3. Ⓐ Ⓑ Ⓒ Ⓓ
4. Ⓐ Ⓑ Ⓒ Ⓓ
5. Ⓐ Ⓑ Ⓒ Ⓓ
6. Ⓐ Ⓑ Ⓒ Ⓓ
7. Ⓐ Ⓑ Ⓒ Ⓓ
8. Ⓐ Ⓑ Ⓒ Ⓓ
9. Ⓐ Ⓑ Ⓒ Ⓓ
10. Ⓐ Ⓑ Ⓒ Ⓓ

11. Ⓐ Ⓑ Ⓒ Ⓓ
12. Ⓐ Ⓑ Ⓒ Ⓓ
13. Ⓐ Ⓑ Ⓒ Ⓓ
14. Ⓐ Ⓑ Ⓒ Ⓓ
15. Ⓐ Ⓑ Ⓒ Ⓓ
16. Ⓐ Ⓑ Ⓒ Ⓓ
17. Ⓐ Ⓑ Ⓒ Ⓓ
18. Ⓐ Ⓑ Ⓒ Ⓓ
19. Ⓐ Ⓑ Ⓒ Ⓓ
20. Ⓐ Ⓑ Ⓒ Ⓓ

21. Ⓐ Ⓑ Ⓒ Ⓓ
22. Ⓐ Ⓑ Ⓒ Ⓓ
23. Ⓐ Ⓑ Ⓒ Ⓓ
24. Ⓐ Ⓑ Ⓒ Ⓓ
25. Ⓐ Ⓑ Ⓒ Ⓓ
26. Ⓐ Ⓑ Ⓒ Ⓓ
27. Ⓐ Ⓑ Ⓒ Ⓓ
28. Ⓐ Ⓑ Ⓒ Ⓓ
29. Ⓐ Ⓑ Ⓒ Ⓓ
30. Ⓐ Ⓑ Ⓒ Ⓓ

31. Ⓐ Ⓑ Ⓒ Ⓓ
32. Ⓐ Ⓑ Ⓒ Ⓓ
33. Ⓐ Ⓑ Ⓒ Ⓓ
34. Ⓐ Ⓑ Ⓒ Ⓓ
35. Ⓐ Ⓑ Ⓒ Ⓓ
36. Ⓐ Ⓑ Ⓒ Ⓓ
37. Ⓐ Ⓑ Ⓒ Ⓓ
38. Ⓐ Ⓑ Ⓒ Ⓓ
39. Ⓐ Ⓑ Ⓒ Ⓓ
40. Ⓐ Ⓑ Ⓒ Ⓓ

41. Ⓐ Ⓑ Ⓒ Ⓓ
42. Ⓐ Ⓑ Ⓒ Ⓓ
43. Ⓐ Ⓑ Ⓒ Ⓓ
44. Ⓐ Ⓑ Ⓒ Ⓓ
45. Ⓐ Ⓑ Ⓒ Ⓓ
46. Ⓐ Ⓑ Ⓒ Ⓓ
47. Ⓐ Ⓑ Ⓒ Ⓓ
48. Ⓐ Ⓑ Ⓒ Ⓓ
49. Ⓐ Ⓑ Ⓒ Ⓓ
50. Ⓐ Ⓑ Ⓒ Ⓓ

answer sheet

Practice Test 7:
Electronics Information

Questions 1–50 are four-option items on electrical, radio, and electronics information. Select the correct response from the options given.

1. In lights controlled by three-way switches, the switches should be treated and put in as
   (A) flush switches.
   (B) single-pole switches.
   (C) three double-pole switches.
   (D) three-pole switches.

2. When working on live 600-volt equipment where rubber gloves might be damaged, an electrician should
   (A) work without gloves.
   (B) carry a spare pair of rubber gloves.
   (C) reinforce the fingers of the rubber gloves with rubber tape.
   (D) wear leather gloves over the rubber gloves.

3. A "mil" measures a(n)
   (A) eighth of an inch.
   (B) millionth of an inch.
   (C) thousandth of an inch.
   (D) ten-thousandth of an inch.

4.

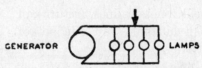

EACH LAMP TAKES 1 AMPERE

The current in the wire at the point indicated by the arrow above is
   (A) 1 ampere.
   (B) 2 amperes.
   (C) 3 amperes.
   (D) 4 amperes.

5. If a fuse of higher than the required current rating is used in an electrical circuit,
   (A) better protection will be afforded.
   (B) the fuse will blow more often since it carries more current.
   (C) serious damage may result to the circuit from overload.
   (D) maintenance of the large fuse will be higher.

6. The electrical contacts in the tuner of a television set are usually plated with silver. Silver is used to
   (A) avoid tarnish.
   (B) improve conductivity.
   (C) improve appearance.
   (D) avoid arcing.

7. The following equipment is required for a "2-line return-can" electric bell circuit:

(A) 2 bells, 2 metallic lines, 2 ordinary push buttons, and one set of batteries.

(B) 2 bells, 2 metallic lines, 2 return-call push buttons, and 2 sets of batteries.

(C) 2 bells, 2 metallic lines, 2 return-call push buttons, and one set of batteries.

(D) 2 bells, 2 metallic lines, one ordinary push button, one return-call push button, and one set of batteries.

8.

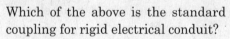

Which of the above is the standard coupling for rigid electrical conduit?

(A) 1

(B) 2

(C) 3

(D) 4

9. Metal cabinets used for lighting circuits are grounded to

(A) eliminate electrolysis.

(B) assure that the fuse in a defective circuit will blow.

(C) reduce shock hazard.

(D) simplify wiring.

10. Low Potential is a trade term that refers to

(A) 700 volts.

(B) 600 volts or less.

(C) 1,200 volts.

(D) 900 volts.

11. The purpose of having a rheostat in the field circuit of a DC shunt motor is to

(A) control the speed of the motor.

(B) minimize the starting current.

(C) limit the field current to a safe value.

(D) reduce sparking at the brushes.

12. A polarized plug generally has

(A) two parallel prongs of the same size.

(B) prongs at an angle with each other.

(C) magnetized prongs.

(D) prongs marked plus and minus.

13.

The reading of the above kilowatt-hour meter is

(A) 7972

(B) 1786

(C) 2786

(D) 6872

14. Commutators are found on

(A) mercury rectifiers.

(B) DC motors.

(C) circuit breakers.

(D) alternators.

15. Neutral wire can be quickly recognized by the

(A) greenish color.

(B) bluish color.

(C) natural or whitish color.

(D) black color.

16. The term that is NOT applicable in describing the *construction* of a microphone is
    (A) dynamic.
    (B) carbon.
    (C) crystal.
    (D) feedback.

17.

The fitting shown above is used in electrical construction to
    (A) clamp two adjacent junction boxes together.
    (B) act as a ground clamp for the conduit system.
    (C) attach a flexible metallic conduit to a junction box.
    (D) protect exposed wires where they pass through a wall.

18. A good magnetic material is
    (A) copper.
    (B) iron.
    (C) tin.
    (D) brass.

19. Rosin is a material generally used
    (A) in batteries.
    (B) for high-voltage insulation.
    (C) as a dielectric.
    (D) as a soldering flux.

20. The letters RHW when applied to electrical wire indicate the wire
    (A) has a solid conductor.
    (B) has rubber insulation.
    (C) is insulated with paper.
    (D) has lead sheath.

21. Boxes and fittings intended for outdoor use should be of
    (A) weatherproof type.
    (B) stamped steel of not less than No. 16.
    (C) standard gauge.
    (D) stamped steel plated with cadmium.

22. A direct-current supply may be obtained from an alternating-current source by means of
    (A) a frequency changer set.
    (B) an inductance-capacitance filter.
    (C) a silicon diode rectifier.
    (D) none of the devices mentioned above.

23. Fuses protecting motor circuits have to be selected to permit a momentary surge of
    (A) voltage when the motor starts.
    (B) voltage when the motor stops.
    (C) current when the motor starts.
    (D) current when the motor stops.

24. When working near lead acid storage batteries, extreme care should be taken to guard against sparks, essentially to avoid
    (A) overheating the electrolyte.
    (B) an electric shock.
    (C) a short circuit.
    (D) an explosion.

25. The voltage that will cause a current of 5 amperes to flow through a 20-Ohm resistance is
    (A) $\frac{1}{4}$ volt.
    (B) 4 volts.
    (C) 20 volts.
    (D) 100 volts.

26. Receptacles in a house-lighting system are regularly connected in
    (A) parallel.
    (B) series.
    (C) diagonal.
    (D) perpendicular.

27. The electronic symbol shown below usually represents a(n)

    (A) resistor.
    (B) inductor.
    (C) capacitor.
    (D) transformer.

28. If a live conductor is contacted accidentally, the severity of the electrical shock is determined primarily by
    (A) the size of the conductor.
    (B) the current of the conductor.
    (C) whether the current is AC or DC.
    (D) the contact resistance.

29. Locknuts are frequently used in making electrical connections on terminal boards. The purpose of the locknuts is to
    (A) eliminate the use of flat washers.
    (B) prevent unauthorized personnel from tampering with the connections.
    (C) keep the connections from loosening through vibration.
    (D) increase the contact area at the connection point.

30. If a condenser is connected across the make-and-break contact of an ordinary electric bell, the effect will be to
    (A) speed up the action of the clapper.
    (B) reduce the amount of arcing at the contact.

(C) slow down the action of the clapper.
(D) reduce the load on the bell transformer or battery.

31. A material NOT used in the makeup of lighting wires or cables is
    (A) rubber.
    (B) paper.
    (C) lead.
    (D) cotton.

32.

VOLTMETER

GOOD LAMPS   GOOD LAMPS

BURNED OUT LAMP

600 VOLTS

The reading of the voltmeter above should be
    (A) 600
    (B) 300
    (C) 120
    (D) 0

33. Silver is a better conductor of electricity than copper; however, copper is generally used for electrical conductors. The main reason for using copper instead of silver is its
    (A) cost.
    (B) weight.
    (C) strength.
    (D) melting point.

34. Direct-current arcs are "hotter" and harder to extinguish than alternating-current arcs, so electrical appliances that include a thermostat are frequently marked for use on "AC only."

One appliance that might be so marked because it includes a thermostat is a

(A) soldering iron.

(B) floor waxer.

(C) vacuum cleaner.

(D) household iron.

35. An alternator is a(n)

(A) AC generator.

(B) frequency meter.

(C) ground detector device.

(D) choke coil.

36. Operating an incandescent electric lightbulb at less than its rated voltage will result in

(A) shorter life and brighter light.

(B) brighter light and longer life.

(C) longer life and dimmer light.

(D) dimmer light and shorter life.

37.

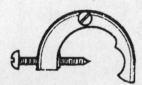

The device shown above is a

(A) C-clamp.

(B) test clip.

(C) battery connector.

(D) ground clamp.

38. When the electric refrigerator in a certain household kitchen starts up, the kitchen light at first dims considerably and then it increases somewhat in brightness while the refrigerator motor is running; the light finally returns to full brightness when the refrigerator shuts off. This behavior of the light shows that most likely the

(A) circuit wires are too small.

(B) refrigerator motor is defective.

(C) circuit fuse is too small.

(D) kitchen lamp is too large.

39. A circular mil is a measure of electrical conductor

(A) length.

(B) area.

(C) volume.

(D) weight.

40. The instrument by which electric power may be measured is a(n)

(A) rectifier.

(B) scanner drum.

(C) ammeter.

(D) watt-meter.

41. The most likely cause of a burned-out fuse in the primary circuit of a transformer in a rectifier is

(A) grounding of the electrostatic shield.

(B) an open circuit in a bleeder resistor.

(C) an open circuit in the secondary winding.

(D) a short-circuit filter capacitor.

42. The primary coil of a power transformer has 100 turns, and the secondary coil has 50 turns. The voltage across the secondary will be

(A) four times that of the primary.

(B) twice that of the primary.

(C) half that of the primary.

(D) one fourth that of the primary.

43. The best electrical connection between two wires is obtained when

(A) the insulations are melted together.

(B) all insulation is removed and the wires bound together with friction tape.

(C) both are wound on a common binding post.

(D) they are soldered together.

44. Excessive resistance in the primary circuit will lessen the output of the ignition coil and cause the
    (A) battery to short out and the generator to run down.
    (B) battery to short out and the plugs to wear out prematurely.
    (C) generator to run down and the timing mechanism to slow down.
    (D) engine to perform poorly and be hard to start.

45. During a "short circuit," the
    (A) current flow becomes very large.
    (B) resistance becomes very large.
    (C) voltage applied becomes very small.
    (D) power input becomes very small.

46. The main reason for making wire stranded is
    (A) to make it easier to insulate.
    (B) so that the insulation will not come off.
    (C) to decrease its weight.
    (D) to make it more flexible.

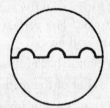

47. The oscilloscope image shown above represents
    (A) steady DC.
    (B) resistance in a resistor.
    (C) AC.
    (D) pulsating DC.

48. Voltage drop in a circuit is usually due to
    (A) inductance.
    (B) capacitance.
    (C) resistance.
    (D) conductance.

49. Which of the following sizes of electric heaters is the largest one that can be used in a 120-volt circuit protected by a 15-ampere circuit breaker?
    (A) 1000 watts
    (B) 1300 watts
    (C) 2000 watts
    (D) 2600 watts

50. The one of the following devices that will store an electric charge is the
    (A) capacitor.
    (B) inductor.
    (C) thyristor.
    (D) resistor.

ANSWER KEY AND EXPLANATIONS

1. (B)	11. (A)	21. (A)	31. (B)	41. (D)
2. (D)	12. (B)	22. (C)	32. (A)	42. (C)
3. (C)	13. (D)	23. (C)	33. (A)	43. (D)
4. (B)	14. (B)	24. (D)	34. (D)	44. (D)
5. (C)	15. (C)	25. (D)	35. (A)	45. (A)
6. (B)	16. (D)	26. (A)	36. (C)	46. (D)
7. (B)	17. (C)	27. (C)	37. (D)	47. (D)
8. (A)	18. (B)	28. (D)	38. (A)	48. (C)
9. (C)	19. (D)	29. (C)	39. (B)	49. (B)
10. (B)	20. (B)	30. (B)	40. (D)	50. (A)

1. **The correct answer is (B).** A three-way switch is a single-pole double-throw switch or two single-pole switches.

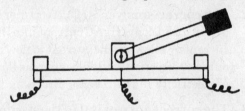

2. **The correct answer is (D).** Leather gloves offer the best protection over the rubber gloves. The leather can withstand severe conditions before it will tear. The rubber acts as insulation.

3. **The correct answer is (C).** A "mil" is short for milli or $\frac{1}{1,000}$ of an inch.

4. **The correct answer is (B).** The formula for determining the current in a parallel circuit is: It = I1 + I2 + I3 + . . . In. The current going through the lamps is 1 amp + 1 amp = 2 amps.

5. **The correct answer is (C).** Never use a fuse having a higher rating than that specifically called for in the circuit. A fuse is a safety device used to protect a circuit from serious damage caused by too high a current.

6. **The correct answer is (B).** Silver is a much better conductor of electricity than copper. However, gold is also used for tuner contacts because it will not tarnish. Silver can tarnish.

7. **The correct answer is (B).** A "2-line return-call" electric bell circuit would have 2 bells, 2 metallic lines, 2 return-call push buttons, and 2 sets of batteries. It might look like this:

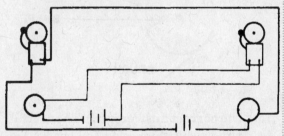

8. **The correct answer is (A).** Figure 1, a connector, is used to join two sections of aluminum pipe conduit.

9. **The correct answer is (C).** Grounding a fixture is a safety precaution used to lessen the chance of shock.

10. **The correct answer is (B).** In electrical terms, potential or E.M.F. is the voltage. Electricians consider any voltage of 600 volts or less to be Low Potential.

11. **The correct answer is (A).** A rheostat regulates the amount of voltage to the motor. The more voltage to a motor, the faster it will turn.

12. **The correct answer is (B).** A polarized plug is used so that the plug can go into the receptacle in only one way. The prongs are at an angle to each other.

13. **The correct answer is (D).** When reading an electric meter, you read the lower number just before the pointer. This meter would show 6872 kilowatt hours.

14. **The correct answer is (B).** In a DC motor, the commutators are the metal contact points that the brushes come into contact with.

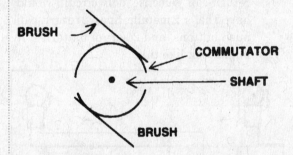

15. **The correct answer is (C).** The neutral wire is whitish in color; the hot lead is black; and the ground wire is green.

16. **The correct answer is (D).** Carbon, crystal, and dynamic are all types of microphones. Feedback is a condition caused when sound coming from a speaker is fed back into a microphone, causing noise.

17. **The correct answer is (C).** This type of connector will join a flexible metallic conduit to a junction box. The wire is secured by tightening the compression screw. The locknut is tightened to secure the connector to the junction box.

18. **The correct answer is (B).** Good magnetic metals are iron, steel, nickel, and cobalt. Iron is the only one mentioned here.

19. **The correct answer is (D).** Rosin is used to remove copper oxide from wires so that the solder can join the copper wires.

20. **The correct answer is (B).** In the letters RHW, R stands for rubber insulation, H stands for heat resistant, and W stands for waterproof.

21. **The correct answer is (A).** Outdoor boxes and fittings must be weatherproof to withstand any problems caused by moisture.

22. **The correct answer is (C).** A rectifier is a device that converts AC current into DC current by allowing the current to flow in only one direction while blocking the flow of electricity in the reverse direction.

23. **The correct answer is (C).** The starting current of a motor is normally six times greater than its running current.

24. **The correct answer is (D).** Lead acid batteries give off highly explosive hydrogen gas. This is a normal product of the acid reacting with the lead plates when electricity is made. A single spark can explode the gas.

25. **The correct answer is (D).** According to Ohm's law:

$$V = IR; V = 5 \times 20; V = 100 \text{ volts}$$

26. **The correct answer is (A).** Receptacles in a house are connected in parallel. In parallel circuits, the current increases as more appliances are added but the voltage remains the same. $Et = E1 = E2 \ldots En \ It = I1 + I2 + \ldots In.$

27. **The correct answer is (C).** The symbol is a standard one and shows the two conducting surfaces of a capacitor.

28. **The correct answer is (D).** An electric shock is determined by the contact resistance. If a person is standing in water while being shocked, the shock will be very severe because water reduces the amount of resistance and the electricity will flow freely through his body.

29. **The correct answer is (C).** Locknuts are bent so that their metal edges will bite into the terminal board and will require the use of a wrench to loosen them.

30. **The correct answer is (B).** A condenser or capacitor is an electrical device that will store and discharge an electrical charge. When the bell is off, the condenser will store electricity. When the circuit is on, the condenser will discharge. This will eliminate arcing.

31. **The correct answer is (B).** Paper is not used in the makeup of a lighting wire because a small electrical charge could set it on fire.

32. **The correct answer is (A).** No electricity flows through a burned out bulb. However, the voltmeter acts as a bypass around the burned out bulb and is therefore connected in series. It measures all of the voltage in the circuit. The voltage is 600 volts.

33. **The correct answer is (A).** Silver is a much better conductor than copper. It is not used in wires because it is very expensive.

34. **The correct answer is (D).** A household iron is the only device that depends on a thermostat to control its use. An over-heated iron will damage the clothing that it is supposed to press.

35. **The correct answer is (A).** An alternator is a device found in automobiles. It is used to produce AC in a car; the electronic circuitry changes AC to DC.

36. **The correct answer is (C).** An incandescent electric light bulb is a typical light bulb found in the home. When the incandescent bulb, which is rated for 110 volts, is run at 90 volts, it will not burn as brightly. Since the 110-volt capacity is not being used, it will last longer.

37. **The correct answer is (D).** This object is a ground clamp. It will be tightened around a cold water pipe. A grounding wire will be attached to the screw and thus stray electricity will be grounded.

38. **The correct answer is (A).** When a refrigerator motor starts up, it draws considerable current. This takes current away from the bulb. Thicker wires would allow more electricity to pass through, but they would be too expensive and impractical.

39. **The correct answer is (B).** A mil is [1/1,000] of an inch. A circular mil is the area of the cross-section of a wire.

40. **The correct answer is (D).** Electric power is measured in units called watts. A watt is calculated by multiplying voltage by amperage. Watts are measured by a watt-meter.

41. **The correct answer is (D).** Consider the following filtered rectifier circuit with a short circuit across capacitor A:

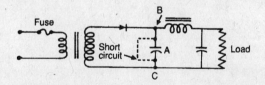

The current at point, B, which would ordinarily flow through the load resistor, will now flow through the short circuit to C and back through the transformer. The short circuit has virtually no resistance, causing large currents to flow in both the primary and secondary windings of the transformer. These large currents cause the fuse to burn out.

42. **The correct answer is (C).** Voltages are transformed directly as the ratio of the secondary to the primary turns:

$$\frac{\text{VOLTAGE}_{\text{Secondary}}}{\text{VOLTAGE}_{\text{Primary}}} = \frac{\text{TURNS}_{\text{Secondary}}}{\text{TURNS}_{\text{Primary}}}$$

$$\frac{V_S}{V_P} = \frac{T_S}{T_P}; V_S = \frac{T_S}{T_P} \times V_P; V_S = \frac{50}{100} V_P = \frac{1}{2} V_P$$

43. **The correct answer is (D).** A good electrical connection has as low a resistance as possible. Soldering provides a low resistance path through the connection. It is also a mechanically secure connection.

44. **The correct answer is (D).** Resistance in the primary will reduce the current flow and reduce the voltage and current available at the spark plug. A "hot" spark with as high a voltage and current as possible is necessary for easy starting and smooth performance.

45. **The correct answer is (A).** The resistance of a short circuit usually consists of little more than the resistance of the circuit's copper wires since the load has been "shorted" or bypassed. This very low resistance results in very high current flow.

46. **The correct answer is (D).** Wires larger than No. 10 AWG are usually stranded because a solid wire of that diameter is too stiff to make good connections or to "fish" readily through raceways.

47. **The correct answer is (D).** The image shows the current rising and falling from some minimum value indicated by the straight-line portions of the image. The current, therefore, pulses without changing direction. AC involves a reversal of direction.

48. **The correct answer is (C).** Ohm's law, V = IR, gives the voltage drop across a resistor. Inductance and capacitance do not produce a voltage drop. Conductance is the reciprocal of resistance. A high resistance has a low conductance.

49. **The correct answer is (B).** Maximum wattage that will cause a 15-ampere breaker to trip is (15 amps) (120 volts) = 1800 watts. Accordingly, 1300 watts is the largest heater that will operate without causing the circuit breaker to trip.

50. **The correct answer is (A).** A capacitor contains two conducting surfaces separated by an insulator and can, therefore, store static electrical charges. Caution should be exercised before touching capacitors. They should have their terminals "shorted" before being handled.

ANSWER SHEET FOR PRACTICE TEST 8: MECHANICAL COMPREHENSION

1. Ⓐ Ⓑ Ⓒ	11. Ⓐ Ⓑ Ⓒ	21. Ⓐ Ⓑ Ⓒ	31. Ⓐ Ⓑ Ⓒ	41. Ⓐ Ⓑ Ⓒ
2. Ⓐ Ⓑ Ⓒ	12. Ⓐ Ⓑ Ⓒ	22. Ⓐ Ⓑ Ⓒ	32. Ⓐ Ⓑ Ⓒ	42. Ⓐ Ⓑ Ⓒ
3. Ⓐ Ⓑ Ⓒ	13. Ⓐ Ⓑ Ⓒ	23. Ⓐ Ⓑ Ⓒ	33. Ⓐ Ⓑ Ⓒ	43. Ⓐ Ⓑ Ⓒ
4. Ⓐ Ⓑ Ⓒ	14. Ⓐ Ⓑ Ⓒ	24. Ⓐ Ⓑ Ⓒ	34. Ⓐ Ⓑ Ⓒ	44. Ⓐ Ⓑ Ⓒ
5. Ⓐ Ⓑ Ⓒ	15. Ⓐ Ⓑ Ⓒ	25. Ⓐ Ⓑ Ⓒ	35. Ⓐ Ⓑ Ⓒ	45. Ⓐ Ⓑ Ⓒ
6. Ⓐ Ⓑ Ⓒ	16. Ⓐ Ⓑ Ⓒ	26. Ⓐ Ⓑ Ⓒ	36. Ⓐ Ⓑ Ⓒ	46. Ⓐ Ⓑ Ⓒ
7. Ⓐ Ⓑ Ⓒ	17. Ⓐ Ⓑ Ⓒ	27. Ⓐ Ⓑ Ⓒ	37. Ⓐ Ⓑ Ⓒ	47. Ⓐ Ⓑ Ⓒ
8. Ⓐ Ⓑ Ⓒ	18. Ⓐ Ⓑ Ⓒ	28. Ⓐ Ⓑ Ⓒ	38. Ⓐ Ⓑ Ⓒ	48. Ⓐ Ⓑ Ⓒ
9. Ⓐ Ⓑ Ⓒ	19. Ⓐ Ⓑ Ⓒ	29. Ⓐ Ⓑ Ⓒ	39. Ⓐ Ⓑ Ⓒ	49. Ⓐ Ⓑ Ⓒ
10. Ⓐ Ⓑ Ⓒ	20. Ⓐ Ⓑ Ⓒ	30. Ⓐ Ⓑ Ⓒ	40. Ⓐ Ⓑ Ⓒ	50. Ⓐ Ⓑ Ⓒ

answer sheet

Practice Test 8: Mechanical Comprehension

Questions 1–50 are three-option items. Study each diagram carefully and select the choice that best answers the question or completes the statement.

1.

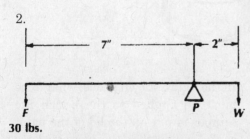

Shown above is a second-class lever. A common example of a second-class lever is

(A) a crowbar.

(B) a nutcracker.

(C) pliers.

2.

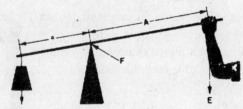

30 lbs.

The weight on the lever being balanced by the force of 30 pounds, shown in the diagram above, is most nearly

(A) 42 lbs.

(B) 84 lbs.

(C) 105 lbs.

3.

The force *F* required to balance the weight of 40 pounds on the lever shown in the diagram above is most nearly

(A) 8 lbs.

(B) 10 lbs.

(C) 11 lbs.

4.

The mechanical advantage of the lever shown above is

(A) $\dfrac{a}{A}$

(B) $\dfrac{A}{a}$

(C) $a \times A$

5.

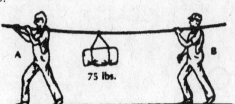

The weight is being carried entirely on the shoulders of the two persons shown above. Which person bears more weight on the shoulder?

(A) A

(B) B

(C) Both are carrying the same weight.

6.

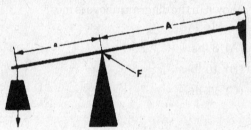

What effort must be exerted to lift a 60-pound weight in the figure of a lever shown above (disregard weight of lever in your computation)?

(A) 30 lbs.

(B) 32 lbs.

(C) 34 lbs.

7.

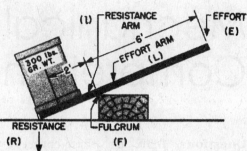

In the figure shown above, what effort must be exerted on the iron bar to raise a 300-pound crate off the floor (disregard weight of bar in your computation)?

(A) 50 lbs.

(B) 100 lbs.

(C) 150 lbs.

8.

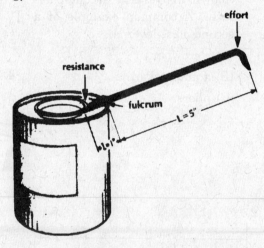

In the figure shown above, what force must be applied to the 6-inch file scraper to pry up the lid of the paint can? Assume that the average force holding the lid is 50 pounds (disregard weight of the scraper).

(A) 10 lbs.

(B) 20 lbs.

(C) 30 lbs.

9.

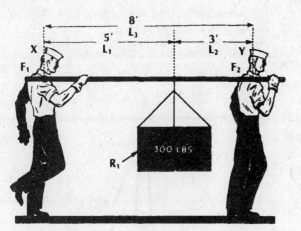

In the figure above, two sailors are carrying a 300-pound crate slung on a 10-foot pole. On the basis of the data shown in the figure,

(A) each sailor is carrying 150 pounds.

(B) sailor X is carrying approximately 188 pounds.

(C) sailor Y is carrying approximately 188 pounds.

10.

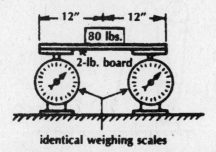

In the figure shown above, the weight held by the board and placed on the two identical scales will cause *each* scale to read

(A) 40 lbs.

(B) 41 lbs.

(C) 42 lbs.

11.

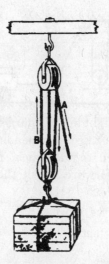

The crate shown in the figure above weighs 300 pounds. Neglecting block friction, the weight of the movable block, and the weight of the line, what pull is necessary to raise the crate?

(A) 50 pounds

(B) 100 pounds

(C) 150 pounds

12.

The theoretical mechanical advantage of the pulley system shown above is

(A) 3

(B) 4

(C) 5

13.

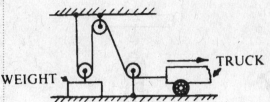

The weight in the figure shown above is to be raised by means of the rope attached to the truck. If the truck moves forward 10 feet, the weight will rise

(A) $2\frac{1}{2}$ feet.

(B) 5 feet.

(C) 10 feet.

Answer questions 14 and 15 on the basis of the pulley system shown below.

300 lbs.

14. Neglecting friction and the weight of the pulley system, what effort is needed to lift the 300-pound weight?

(A) 75 pounds

(B) 100 pounds

(C) 150 pounds

15. If 12 feet of rope was pulled by the person exerting the effort, how high was the weight raised?

(A) 3 feet

(B) 4 feet

(C) 5 feet

16.

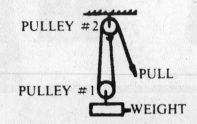

The block and tackle shown has two pulleys of equal diameter. While the weight is being raised, pulley #1 will rotate at

(A) twice the speed of pulley #2.

(B) the same speed as pulley #2.

(C) one half the speed of pulley #2.

17.

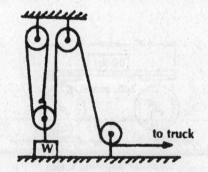

The tank "W" is to be raised as shown by attaching the pull rope to a truck. If the tank is to be raised six feet, the truck will have to move

(A) 12 feet.

(B) 15 feet.

(C) 18 feet.

18.

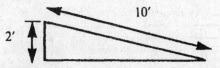

What is the ideal mechanical advantage of the incline shown in the above diagram?

(A) 5

(B) 4

(C) 3

19.

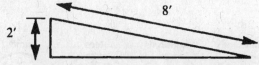

Neglecting friction, what effort is needed to roll a barrel weighing 400 pounds up the incline shown in the above diagram?

(A) 200 pounds

(B) 100 pounds

(C) 50 pounds

20.

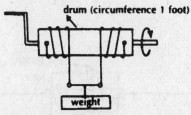

In the figure shown above, one complete revolution of the windlass drum will move the weight up

(A) 12 inches.

(B) 18 inches.

(C) 24 inches.

21.

A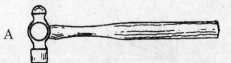

B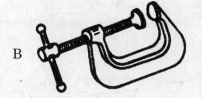

C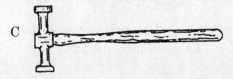

To smooth out a dent in a piece of formed sheet metal, use tool

(A) A

(B) B

(C) C

22.

A

B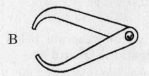

C

To lay out a horizontal line in the center of the wall, use tool

(A) A

(B) B

(C) C

23.

A

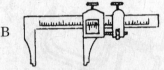

B

C

To determine the exact inside diameter of a metal tube, use tool

(A) A

(B) B

(C) C

24.

The tool shown above is properly called a

(A) depth gauge.

(B) screw pitch gauge.

(C) thickness gauge.

Refer to the circuit diagram below in answering **questions 25 and 26.**

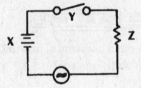

25. X is a

(A) battery.

(B) capacitor.

(C) motor.

26. Y is a

(A) fuse.

(B) rheostat.

(C) switch.

27.

The symbol given above is the standard circuit symbol for a

(A) capacitor.

(B) fixed resistor.

(C) variable resistor.

28.

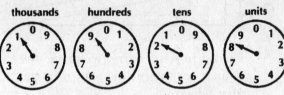

In the figure above, the reading of the kilowatt-hour meter, as shown by the dials, is

(A) 0918

(B) 1928

(C) 8190

29.

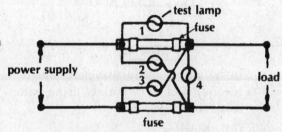

In the diagram shown above, if the upper fuse is good and the lower fuse is burned out, the test lamp that will be lighted is

(A) 1

(B) 2

(C) 3

Questions 30 and 31 are based on the following diagram of circuits numbered 1, 2, and 3.

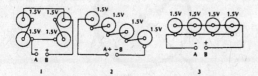

30. Which one of the circuits shown is a parallel circuit?

    (A) 1
    (B) 2
    (C) 3

31. Which one of the circuits shown is a series-parallel circuit?

    (A) 1
    (B) 2
    (C) 3

32.

The correct reading on the voltmeter shown above is

    (A) 26 volts.
    (B) 32 volts.
    (C) 36 volts.

Questions 33 and 34 are based on the ohmmeter scale shown below. Note that zero is at the right end of the scale.

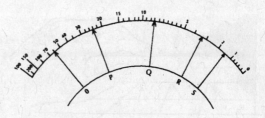

33. Point O has a value of

    (A) 57
    (B) 60
    (C) 63

34. Point S lies midway between 1 and 2. 1.5 lies

    (A) to the left of point S.
    (B) at point S.
    (C) to the right of point S.

Question 35 is based on the sketch of a portion of a multimeter (V-O-M) scale shown below. The selector switch on the meter can be set to several different resistance ranges, as well as a number of different DC voltage and milliampere ranges.

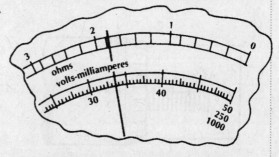

35. If the selector switch is set on the ohms × 100 range, the resistance value indicated is

    (A) 175 ohms.
    (B) 17.5 ohms.
    (C) 1.75 ohms.

Questions 36 and 37 are based on the diagram given below pertaining to the measuring with and reading of a common rule.

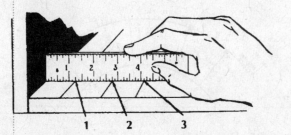

36. The reading at point 1 is

(A) $1\frac{1}{8}''$

(B) $1\frac{1}{4}''$

(C) $1\frac{3}{8}''$

37. The distance between point 2 and point 3 is

(A) $1\frac{3}{8}''$

(B) $1\frac{1}{2}''$

(C) $1\frac{5}{8}''$

38.

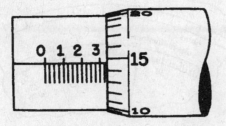

In the figure shown above, the micrometer reading to three decimal places is

(A) 0.338

(B) 0.339

(C) 0.340

39.

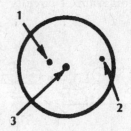

The figure above represents a revolving wheel. The numbers 1 and 2 indicate two fixed points on the wheel. The number 3 indicates the center of the wheel. Of the following, the most accurate statement is that

(A) point 1 traverses a greater linear distance than point 2.

(B) point 2 traverses a greater linear distance than point 1.

(C) all three points traverse the same linear distance.

40.

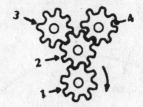

Four gears are shown in the figure above. If gear 1 turns as shown, then the gear turning in a counterclockwise direction is gear

(A) 2

(B) 3

(C) 4

41.

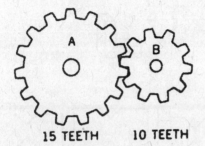

15 TEETH   10 TEETH

If the larger gear is revolving at 200 revolutions per minute, at how many revolutions per minute is the smaller gear revolving?

(A) 100

(B) 250

(C) 300

42.

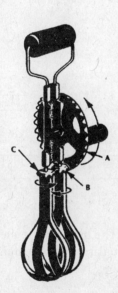

In the figure above, a simple gear arrangement is shown. If there are 32 teeth on the large vertical wheel A, 8 teeth on horizontal wheel B, and 8 teeth on horizontal wheel C, one complete revolution of wheel A results in

(A) two complete revolutions of gear C.

(B) three complete revolutions of gear C.

(C) four complete revolutions of gear C.

43.

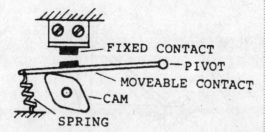

If the contacts come together twice every second, the cam is rotating at

(A) 30 RPM.

(B) 60 RPM.

(C) 120 RPM.

44.

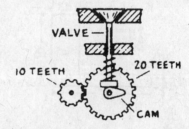

The figure above shows a cam that actuates a valve. If the 10-tooth gear makes six revolutions, the valve will open

(A) 6 times.

(B) 4 times.

(C) 3 times.

45.

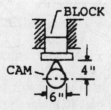

In the figure above, rotation of the cam will permit the block to drop a maximum of

(A) 1″

(B) 2″

(C) 4″

46.

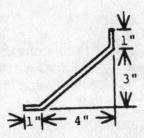

The length of the sheet metal strap before bending was most nearly

(A) 7 inches.

(B) 8 inches.

(C) 9 inches.

47.

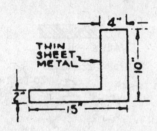

The maximum number of rectangular pieces, each two inches by eight inches, that can be cut from the thin metal sheet shown above is

(A) two.

(B) three.

(C) four.

48.

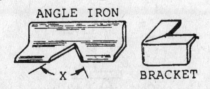

A piece is to be cut out of the angle iron in order to make the right angle bracket. Angle X should be

(A) 45 degrees.

(B) 60 degrees.

(C) 90 degrees.

49.

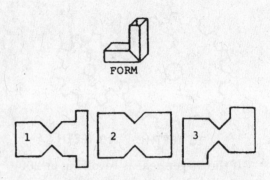

The form shown above, which is open at both ends, can be shaped from sheet metal number

(A) 1

(B) 2

(C) 3

50.

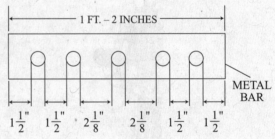

If all of the holes in the metal bar are to be equal in size, then their diameters should be

(A) $\frac{1}{2}$ inch.

(B) $\frac{3}{4}$ inch.

(C) 1 inch.

ANSWER KEY AND EXPLANATIONS

1. (B)	11. (B)	21. (C)	31. (A)	41. (C)
2. (C)	12. (C)	22. (A)	32. (B)	42. (C)
3. (C)	13. (B)	23. (B)	33. (B)	43. (B)
4. (B)	14. (A)	24. (B)	34. (A)	44. (C)
5. (A)	15. (A)	25. (A)	35. (A)	45. (A)
6. (B)	16. (C)	26. (C)	36. (B)	46. (A)
7. (B)	17. (C)	27. (C)	37. (A)	47. (B)
8. (A)	18. (A)	28. (A)	38. (C)	48. (C)
9. (C)	19. (B)	29. (C)	39. (B)	49. (C)
10. (B)	20. (A)	30. (C)	40. (A)	50. (B)

1. **The correct answer is (B).** The second-class lever has the fulcrum at one end; the effort is applied at the other end. The resistance is somewhere between these points. A nutcracker is a good example of a second-class lever.

2. **The correct answer is (C).** $30 \times 7 = 2 \times W$; $2W = 210$; $W = 105$ lbs.

3. **The correct answer is (C).** $40 \times 3 = 11 \times F$; $11F = 120$; $F = \frac{120}{11}$; $F = 10\frac{10}{11}$.

4. **The correct answer is (B)**

   Mechanical Advantage =

   $\frac{\text{Effort Arm}}{\text{Resistance Arm}}$; M.A. $= \frac{A}{a}$

5. **The correct answer is (A).** B has a greater effort arm; therefore, A would bear the most weight on the shoulder.

6. **The correct answer is (B).** $60 \times 8 = 15 \times E$; $15E = 480$; $E = \frac{480}{15} = 32$ lbs.

7. **The correct answer is (B).** $300 \times 2 = 6 \times E$; $6E = 600$; $E = \frac{600}{6}$; $E = 100$ lbs.

8. **The correct answer is (A).** $E \times 5 = 1 \times 50$; $5E = 50$; $E = \frac{50}{5}$; $E = 10$ lbs.

9. **The correct answer is (C).** As the weight is closer to sailor Y, sailor Y has the shorter effort arm and is therefore carrying the greater weight.

10. **The correct answer is (B).** The weight is equally distributed. $80 + 2 = 82$ lbs. $\frac{82}{2} = 41$ lbs.

11. **The correct answer is (B).** The number of the parts of rope going to and from the movable block determines the mechanical advantage. With a mechanical advantage of 3, a 100-pound pull is necessary to lift a 300-pound weight.

12. **The correct answer is (C).** There are five parts of rope going to and from the movable blocks. The MA is 5.

13. **The correct answer is (B).** The TMA of the pulley system is 2.

    TMA $= \frac{d_E}{d_R}$; $2 = \frac{10}{d_R}$; $2 \times d_R = 10$; $d_R = \frac{10}{2}$ $= 5$ feet

14. **The correct answer is (A).** There are four parts of rope going to and from the movable blocks.

    TMA $= 4$. $\frac{300}{4} = 75$ lbs.

15. **The correct answer is (A).**

$$\text{TMA} = \frac{d_E}{d_R}; \; 4 = \frac{12}{d_R}; \; 4d_R = 12; \; d_R = \frac{12}{4} =$$

3 feet

16. **The correct answer is (C).** Pulley #2 is a fixed pulley; pulley #1 is a movable one. Both are of equal diameter. If the rope is pulled a distance equal to the circumference of pulley #2 (one full turn), pulley #1 would move up only half that distance making only a half turn.

17. **The correct answer is (C).** The theoretical mechanical advantage is 3.

$$\frac{d_E}{d_R} = 3; \; \frac{d_E}{6} = 3; \; d_E = 3 \times 6 = 18 \text{ feet}$$

18. **The correct answer is (A).**

Theoretical Mechanical Advantage =
$\frac{\text{Length of Slope}}{\text{Height}}$; $\text{TMA} = \frac{10}{2} = 5$.

19. **The correct answer is (B).**

$$\text{TMA} = \frac{8}{2} = 4; \; 4 = \frac{W}{E}; \; 4 = \frac{400}{E}; \; 4E = 400;$$

E = 100 pounds.

20. **The correct answer is (A).** As the circumference of the drum is one foot, or 12 inches, one complete revolution of the windlass will pull each strand up one foot and will pull the weight up 12 inches.

21. **The correct answer is (C).** Tool C is a hammer that is generally used to smooth out dents in formed sheet metal.

22. **The correct answer is (A).** Tool A is a level used to ascertain whether a plane is true horizontal or true vertical.

23. **The correct answer is (B).** Tool B is a slide caliper used for measuring both inside and outside dimensions.

24. **The correct answer is (B).** The tool is a screw pitch gauge used to determine the pitch and number of threads per inch of threaded fasteners.

25. **The correct answer is (A).** The standard symbol for a battery is ⊣⊢⊢⊢.

26. **The correct answer is (C).** The standard symbol for a switch is ⊸⌒∘⊸.

27. **The correct answer is (C).** The standard symbol for a variable resistor is ⟋⟋.

28. **The correct answer is (A).** 0 thousands + 9 hundreds + 1 ten + 8 units = 0918.

29. **The correct answer is (C).** Although the lower fuse is burned out, lamp 3 will be lighted as it is in a complete circuit.

30. **The correct answer is (C).** Note that there are two paths for the flow of electrons in circuit 3 and that the resistors are connected in parallel.

31. **The correct answer is (A).** Note that circuit 1 contains resistors in parallel and in series.

32. **The correct answer is (B).** Note that the pointer is on the first mark above the 30 mark. As each mark is a 2-volt increment, the proper reading is 32 volts.

33. **The correct answer is (B).** Point O is directly on the mark having a value of 60 on this nonlinear scale.

34. **The correct answer is (A).** This is a nonlinear scale increasing in value from right to left. The midpoint has a value less than 1.5; therefore, 1.5 lies to the left of point S.

35. **The correct answer is (A).** The value on the basic scale is 1.75. On the ohms × 100 range, the resistance value would be 1.75 × 100 = 175 ohms.

36. **The correct answer is (B).** The point 1 reading is exactly $1\frac{1}{4}''$.

37. **The correct answer is (A).** Point 3 reading is $4\frac{1}{8}''$; point 2 reading is $2\frac{3}{4}''$.

$$4\frac{1}{8}'' - 2\frac{3}{4}'' = 3\frac{9}{8}'' - 2\frac{6}{8}'' = 1\frac{3}{8}''.$$

38. The correct answer is (C). 0.300 + 0.025 + 0.015 = 0.340

39. The correct answer is (B). Point 2 is a greater distance away from the center of the wheel than is point 1. Accordingly, point 2 will traverse a greater linear distance than would point 1.

40. The correct answer is (A). If gear 1 turns clockwise, gear 2 will turn counterclockwise. Gears 3 and 4 will turn clockwise.

41. The correct answer is (C). Let x = revolutions per minute of smaller gear. $15 \times 200 = 10x$; $10x = 3000$; $x = \frac{3000}{10} = 300$ revolutions per minute.

42. The correct answer is (C). One complete revolution of wheel A with 32 teeth will result in 4 complete revolutions of wheel B with 8 teeth; wheel C will also make 4 complete revolutions.

43. The correct answer is (B). Every complete revolution results in two contacts. Two contacts every second results from one complete revolution per second or 60 revolutions per minute.

44. The correct answer is (C). If the 10-tooth gear makes 6 revolutions, the 20-tooth gear will make 3 revolutions, causing the cam to activate the valve 3 times.

45. The correct answer is (A). The radius of the 6″ wheel is 3″. Therefore, the cam extends 1″ beyond the wheel's circumference. This permits the block to drop a maximum of 1″.

46. The correct answer is (A). According to the Pythagorean theorem, the hypotenuse of the right triangle is 5″. 1″ + 5″ + 1″ = 7″.

47. The correct answer is (B). Two 2″ × 8″ rectangular pieces can be cut from the vertical section. One 2″ × 8″ rectangular piece can be cut from the horizontal section. 2 + 1 = 3.

48. The correct answer is (C). To make the right angle bracket, the angle iron must be bent 90°. The two sides of a 90° angle X would then meet to form the bracket shown.

49. The correct answer is (C). Careful analysis will show that only sheet metal number 3 can be shaped to make the form that is open at both ends.

50. The correct answer is (B).

$$1\frac{1}{2}''+1\frac{1}{2}''+2\frac{1}{8}''+2\frac{1}{8}''+1\frac{1}{2}''+1\frac{1}{2}''=10\frac{1}{4}'';$$

$$14''-10\frac{1}{4}''=3\frac{3}{4}'';$$

$$\frac{3\frac{3}{4}}{5}=\frac{15}{4\times5}=\frac{3}{4}''$$

PART VII

THREE OFFICER CANDIDATE TESTS

Air Force Officer Qualifying Test (AFOQT)

Armed Services Vocational Aptitude Battery (ASVAB)

Navy and Marine Corps Aviation Selection Test Battery (ASTB)

ANSWER SHEET FOR U.S. AIR FORCE OFFICER QUALIFYING TEST

Part 1: Verbal Analogies

1. Ⓐ Ⓑ Ⓒ Ⓓ Ⓔ   6. Ⓐ Ⓑ Ⓒ Ⓓ Ⓔ   11. Ⓐ Ⓑ Ⓒ Ⓓ Ⓔ   16. Ⓐ Ⓑ Ⓒ Ⓓ Ⓔ   21. Ⓐ Ⓑ Ⓒ Ⓓ Ⓔ
2. Ⓐ Ⓑ Ⓒ Ⓓ Ⓔ   7. Ⓐ Ⓑ Ⓒ Ⓓ Ⓔ   12. Ⓐ Ⓑ Ⓒ Ⓓ Ⓔ   17. Ⓐ Ⓑ Ⓒ Ⓓ Ⓔ   22. Ⓐ Ⓑ Ⓒ Ⓓ Ⓔ
3. Ⓐ Ⓑ Ⓒ Ⓓ Ⓔ   8. Ⓐ Ⓑ Ⓒ Ⓓ Ⓔ   13. Ⓐ Ⓑ Ⓒ Ⓓ Ⓔ   18. Ⓐ Ⓑ Ⓒ Ⓓ Ⓔ   23. Ⓐ Ⓑ Ⓒ Ⓓ Ⓔ
4. Ⓐ Ⓑ Ⓒ Ⓓ Ⓔ   9. Ⓐ Ⓑ Ⓒ Ⓓ Ⓔ   14. Ⓐ Ⓑ Ⓒ Ⓓ Ⓔ   19. Ⓐ Ⓑ Ⓒ Ⓓ Ⓔ   24. Ⓐ Ⓑ Ⓒ Ⓓ Ⓔ
5. Ⓐ Ⓑ Ⓒ Ⓓ Ⓔ   10. Ⓐ Ⓑ Ⓒ Ⓓ Ⓔ   15. Ⓐ Ⓑ Ⓒ Ⓓ Ⓔ   20. Ⓐ Ⓑ Ⓒ Ⓓ Ⓔ   25. Ⓐ Ⓑ Ⓒ Ⓓ Ⓔ

Part 2: Arithmetic Reasoning

1. Ⓐ Ⓑ Ⓒ Ⓓ Ⓔ   6. Ⓐ Ⓑ Ⓒ Ⓓ Ⓔ   11. Ⓐ Ⓑ Ⓒ Ⓓ Ⓔ   16. Ⓐ Ⓑ Ⓒ Ⓓ Ⓔ   21. Ⓐ Ⓑ Ⓒ Ⓓ Ⓔ
2. Ⓐ Ⓑ Ⓒ Ⓓ Ⓔ   7. Ⓐ Ⓑ Ⓒ Ⓓ Ⓔ   12. Ⓐ Ⓑ Ⓒ Ⓓ Ⓔ   17. Ⓐ Ⓑ Ⓒ Ⓓ Ⓔ   22. Ⓐ Ⓑ Ⓒ Ⓓ Ⓔ
3. Ⓐ Ⓑ Ⓒ Ⓓ Ⓔ   8. Ⓐ Ⓑ Ⓒ Ⓓ Ⓔ   13. Ⓐ Ⓑ Ⓒ Ⓓ Ⓔ   18. Ⓐ Ⓑ Ⓒ Ⓓ Ⓔ   23. Ⓐ Ⓑ Ⓒ Ⓓ Ⓔ
4. Ⓐ Ⓑ Ⓒ Ⓓ Ⓔ   9. Ⓐ Ⓑ Ⓒ Ⓓ Ⓔ   14. Ⓐ Ⓑ Ⓒ Ⓓ Ⓔ   19. Ⓐ Ⓑ Ⓒ Ⓓ Ⓔ   24. Ⓐ Ⓑ Ⓒ Ⓓ Ⓔ
5. Ⓐ Ⓑ Ⓒ Ⓓ Ⓔ   10. Ⓐ Ⓑ Ⓒ Ⓓ Ⓔ   15. Ⓐ Ⓑ Ⓒ Ⓓ Ⓔ   20. Ⓐ Ⓑ Ⓒ Ⓓ Ⓔ   25. Ⓐ Ⓑ Ⓒ Ⓓ Ⓔ

Part 3: Word Knowledge

1. Ⓐ Ⓑ Ⓒ Ⓓ Ⓔ   6. Ⓐ Ⓑ Ⓒ Ⓓ Ⓔ   11. Ⓐ Ⓑ Ⓒ Ⓓ Ⓔ   16. Ⓐ Ⓑ Ⓒ Ⓓ Ⓔ   21. Ⓐ Ⓑ Ⓒ Ⓓ Ⓔ
2. Ⓐ Ⓑ Ⓒ Ⓓ Ⓔ   7. Ⓐ Ⓑ Ⓒ Ⓓ Ⓔ   12. Ⓐ Ⓑ Ⓒ Ⓓ Ⓔ   17. Ⓐ Ⓑ Ⓒ Ⓓ Ⓔ   22. Ⓐ Ⓑ Ⓒ Ⓓ Ⓔ
3. Ⓐ Ⓑ Ⓒ Ⓓ Ⓔ   8. Ⓐ Ⓑ Ⓒ Ⓓ Ⓔ   13. Ⓐ Ⓑ Ⓒ Ⓓ Ⓔ   18. Ⓐ Ⓑ Ⓒ Ⓓ Ⓔ   23. Ⓐ Ⓑ Ⓒ Ⓓ Ⓔ
4. Ⓐ Ⓑ Ⓒ Ⓓ Ⓔ   9. Ⓐ Ⓑ Ⓒ Ⓓ Ⓔ   14. Ⓐ Ⓑ Ⓒ Ⓓ Ⓔ   19. Ⓐ Ⓑ Ⓒ Ⓓ Ⓔ   24. Ⓐ Ⓑ Ⓒ Ⓓ Ⓔ
5. Ⓐ Ⓑ Ⓒ Ⓓ Ⓔ   10. Ⓐ Ⓑ Ⓒ Ⓓ Ⓔ   15. Ⓐ Ⓑ Ⓒ Ⓓ Ⓔ   20. Ⓐ Ⓑ Ⓒ Ⓓ Ⓔ   25. Ⓐ Ⓑ Ⓒ Ⓓ Ⓔ

Part 4: Math Knowledge

1. Ⓐ Ⓑ Ⓒ Ⓓ Ⓔ   6. Ⓐ Ⓑ Ⓒ Ⓓ Ⓔ   11. Ⓐ Ⓑ Ⓒ Ⓓ Ⓔ   16. Ⓐ Ⓑ Ⓒ Ⓓ Ⓔ   21. Ⓐ Ⓑ Ⓒ Ⓓ Ⓔ
2. Ⓐ Ⓑ Ⓒ Ⓓ Ⓔ   7. Ⓐ Ⓑ Ⓒ Ⓓ Ⓔ   12. Ⓐ Ⓑ Ⓒ Ⓓ Ⓔ   17. Ⓐ Ⓑ Ⓒ Ⓓ Ⓔ   22. Ⓐ Ⓑ Ⓒ Ⓓ Ⓔ
3. Ⓐ Ⓑ Ⓒ Ⓓ Ⓔ   8. Ⓐ Ⓑ Ⓒ Ⓓ Ⓔ   13. Ⓐ Ⓑ Ⓒ Ⓓ Ⓔ   18. Ⓐ Ⓑ Ⓒ Ⓓ Ⓔ   23. Ⓐ Ⓑ Ⓒ Ⓓ Ⓔ
4. Ⓐ Ⓑ Ⓒ Ⓓ Ⓔ   9. Ⓐ Ⓑ Ⓒ Ⓓ Ⓔ   14. Ⓐ Ⓑ Ⓒ Ⓓ Ⓔ   19. Ⓐ Ⓑ Ⓒ Ⓓ Ⓔ   24. Ⓐ Ⓑ Ⓒ Ⓓ Ⓔ
5. Ⓐ Ⓑ Ⓒ Ⓓ Ⓔ   10. Ⓐ Ⓑ Ⓒ Ⓓ Ⓔ   15. Ⓐ Ⓑ Ⓒ Ⓓ Ⓔ   20. Ⓐ Ⓑ Ⓒ Ⓓ Ⓔ   25. Ⓐ Ⓑ Ⓒ Ⓓ Ⓔ

answer sheet

Air Force Officer Qualifying Test (AFOQT)

Tests

Part 1: Verbal Analogies
Part 2: Arithmetic Reasoning
Part 3: Word Knowledge
Part 4: Math Knowledge

This part contains an answer sheet for use in answering the questions on the first four tests of the Air Force Officer Qualifying Test (AFOQT), the tests, and answer keys and explanations for determining your scores on these tests.

Remove (cut out) the answer sheet on page 259 for use in recording your answers to the test questions. These tests are similar in format and content to the tests given in the actual Air Force Officer Qualifying Test. Take these tests under "actual" test conditions. Time each test carefully.

Use the answers to obtain your test scores and to evaluate your performance on each test. Record the number of items you answered correctly, as well as the number of each item you answered incorrectly or wish to review, in the space provided below the answers for each test.

Be certain to review carefully and understand the explanations for the answers to all questions you answered incorrectly and for each of the questions you answered correctly but are unsure of. This is absolutely essential in order to acquire the knowledge and expertise necessary to obtain the maximum scores possible on the tests of the real Air Force Officer Qualifying Test.

practice test

PART 1: VERBAL ANALOGIES

Directions: This part of the test has 25 questions designed to measure your ability to reason and see relationships between words. Each question begins with a pair of capitalized words. You are to choose the option that best completes the analogy developed at the beginning of each question. That is, select the option that shows a relationship similar to the one shown by the original pair of capitalized words. Then mark the space on your answer form that has the same number and letter as your choice.

Sample Items

S1. FINGER is to HAND as TOOTH is to
- (A) tongue
- (B) lips
- (C) nose
- (D) mouth
- (E) molar

The correct answer is (D). A *finger* is part of the *hand*; a *tooth* is part of the *mouth*.

S2. RACQUET is to COURT as
- (A) tractor is to field
- (B) blossom is to bloom
- (C) stalk is to prey
- (D) plan is to strategy
- (E) moon is to planet

The correct answer is (A). A *racquet* is used by a tennis player on the *court*; a *tractor* is used by a farmer on the *field*.

Your score on this test will be based on the number of questions you answer correctly. You should try to answer every question. You will not lose points or be penalized for guessing. Do not spend too much time on any one question.

When you begin, be sure to start with question 1 of Part 1 of your test booklet and 1 of Part 1 on your answer form.

DO NOT TURN PAGE UNTIL TOLD TO DO SO.

TIME: 8 Minutes—25 Questions

Choose the answer that best completes the analogy developed at the beginning of each question.

1. PROSPECTOR is to GOLD as
   (A) carpenter is to wood
   (B) detective is to clue
   (C) doctor is to medicine
   (D) machinist is to lathe
   (E) preacher is to prayer

2. QUARRY is to MARBLE as
   (A) game is to preserve
   (B) igneous is to metamorphic
   (C) iron is to ore
   (D) mine is to coal
   (E) timber is to forest

3. RAM is to LAMB as
   (A) buck is to doe
   (B) bull is to calf
   (C) cat is to kitten
   (D) chicken is to hen
   (E) ewe is to sheep

4. GENERAL is to ADMIRAL as
   (A) squadron is to platoon
   (B) commander is to follower
   (C) soldier is to sailor
   (D) captain is to officer
   (E) leader is to manager

5. ROBIN is to SPARROW as
   (A) dog is to terrier
   (B) bluejay is to finch
   (C) mosquito is to insect
   (D) rodent is to rat
   (E) tree is to flower

6. SCRAWNY is to LEAN as BRAWNY is to
   (A) fat
   (B) slim
   (C) strong
   (D) tall
   (E) thin

7. SHY is to BASHFUL as INQUIRE is to
   (A) ask
   (B) conceal
   (C) frighten
   (D) suggest
   (E) tell

8. STALLION is to GELDING as BULL is to
   (A) boar
   (B) buck
   (C) mare
   (D) rooster
   (E) steer

9. TOIL is to STRIFE as WORK is to
   (A) arbitrate
   (B) labor
   (C) maneuver
   (D) struggle
   (E) suffer

10. VALID is to FALLACIOUS as VERACIOUS is to
    (A) delinquent
    (B) illegal
    (C) reliable
    (D) unsupportive
    (E) untrue

11. SHOOT is to SHOT as
   (A) bend is to bent
   (B) bleed is to bled
   (C) build is to built
   (D) feel is to felt
   (E) keep is to kept

12. AD LIB is to REHEARSAL as
   (A) random is to foresight
   (B) accidental is to preparation
   (C) unnecessary is to intention
   (D) improvised is to logic
   (E) aleatory is to plan

13. PAINT is to DAUB as
   (A) sculpt is to carve
   (B) pluck is to strum
   (C) sing is to caterwaul
   (D) versify is to compose
   (E) dance is to perform

14. 36 is to 4 as
   (A) 3 is to 2
   (B) 3 is to 24
   (C) 9 is to 1
   (D) 9 is to 4
   (E) 9 is to 6

15. TRUMPET is to INSTRUMENT as
   (A) barrel is to pistol
   (B) compass is to protractor
   (C) pliers is to tool
   (D) scissors is to shears
   (E) weapon is to bomb

16. DRIFT is to SNOW as DUNE is to
   (A) hail
   (B) hill
   (C) desert
   (D) rain
   (E) sand

17. MOON is to EARTH as EARTH is to
   (A) galaxy
   (B) ground
   (C) Mars
   (D) sky
   (E) sun

18. NECKLACE is to ADORNMENT as MEDAL is to
   (A) bravery
   (B) bronze
   (C) jewel
   (D) metal
   (E) decoration

19. PULP is to PAPER as HEMP is to
   (A) baskets
   (B) cotton
   (C) rope
   (D) sweaters
   (E) yarn

20. REGRESSIVE is to REGRESS as STERILE is to
   (A) sterilely
   (B) sterility
   (C) sterilization
   (D) sterilize
   (E) sterilizer

GO ON TO THE NEXT PAGE

21. WAVE is to CREST as
    (A) breaker is to swimming
    (B) island is to archipelago
    (C) levee is to dike
    (D) mountain is to peak
    (E) sea is to ocean

22. WITCH is to WIZARD as
    (A) duck is to drake
    (B) filly is to foal
    (C) gander is to goose
    (D) mare is to horse
    (E) ram is to sheep

23. ENIGMA is to MYSTIFIED as
    (A) problem is to apathetic
    (B) deception is to misinterpreted
    (C) mistake is to worried
    (D) dilemma is to undecided
    (E) threat is to irritated

24. WRING is to WRUNG as
    (A) bring is to brang
    (B) go is to went
    (C) lay is to laid
    (D) rang is to rung
    (E) think is to thank

25. ZINC is to SULFURIC ACID as
    (A) atom is to molecule
    (B) copper is to brass
    (C) element is to compound
    (D) metal is to salt
    (E) molecule is to mixture

STOP! DO NOT CONTINUE ON UNTIL TOLD TO DO SO. IF YOU FINISH BEFORE THE TIME IS UP, YOU MAY CHECK OVER YOUR WORK ON THIS PART ONLY.

PART 2: ARITHMETIC REASONING

Directions: This part of the test measures arithmetic reasoning or your ability to arrive at solutions to mathematical problems. Each problem is followed by five possible answers. Decide which one of the five options is most nearly correct. Then mark the space on your answer form that has the same number and letter as your choice. Use the scratch paper that has been given to you to do any figuring that you wish.

Sample Items

S1. A field with an area of 420 square yards is twice as large in area as a second field. If the second field is 15 yards long, how wide is it?

(A) 7 yards

(B) 14 yards

(C) 28 yards

(D) 56 yards

(E) 90 yards

The correct answer is (B). The second field has an area of 210 square yards. If one side is 15 yards, the other side must be 14 yards ($15 \times 14 = 210$).

S2. A typist took three typing tests. The average typing speed on these three tests was 48 words per minute. If the typist's speed on two of these tests was 52 words per minute, what was the typist's speed on the third test?

(A) 46 words per minute

(B) 44 words per minute

(C) 42 words per minute

(D) 40 words per minute

(E) 38 words per minute

The correct answer is (D). The total time for the three tests is 144 minutes (48×3). The time for two tests is 104 minutes. Therefore, the time on the third test is 40 minutes ($144 - 104 = 40$).

Your score on this test will be based on the number of questions you answer correctly. You should try to answer every question. You will not lose points or be penalized for guessing. Do not spend too much time on any one question.

When you begin, be sure to start with question 1 of Part 2 of your test booklet and 1 of Part 2 on your answer sheet.

DO NOT TURN PAGE UNTIL TOLD TO DO SO.

TIME: 29 Minutes—25 Questions

1. Assume that a musical instrument depreciates by 20% of its value each year. What would be the value of a piano purchased new for $2400 after 2 years?

   (A) $1350

   (B) $1536

   (C) $1692

   (D) $1824

   (E) $2304

2. A room 27 feet by 32 feet is to be carpeted wall to wall. The width of the carpet is 27 inches. The length, in yards, of the carpet needed for this room is

   (A) 128

   (B) 256

   (C) 384

   (D) 648

   (E) 1188

3. The cost of 4 rolls, 6 muffins, and 3 loaves of bread is $9.10. The cost of 2 rolls, 3 muffins, and a loaf of bread is $3.90. What is the cost of a loaf of bread?

   (A) $1.05

   (B) $1.10

   (C) $1.20

   (D) $1.25

   (E) $1.30

4. Maximum engine life is 900 hours. Recently, 27 engines were removed with an average life of 635.30 hours. What percent of the maximum engine life has been achieved?

   (A) 71%

   (B) 72%

   (C) 73%

   (D) 74%

   (E) 75%

5. Nicholas receives a basic weekly salary of $180 plus a 5% commission. In a week in which his sales amounted to $1800, the ratio of his basic salary to his commission was

   (A) 3 : 1

   (B) 2 : 1

   (C) 3 : 2

   (D) 1 : 1

   (E) 1 : 2

6. Mrs. Norton spent $\frac{2}{3}$ of the family income one year and divided the remainder among 4 different savings accounts. If she put $2000 into each account, what was the amount of her family income that year?

   (A) $8000

   (B) $16,000

   (C) $24,000

   (D) $32,000

   (E) $40,000

7. What is the tax rate per $1000 if a base of $338,555 would yield $616.07?

   (A) $1.82

   (B) $1.86

   (C) $1.90

   (D) $1.95

   (E) $2.00

8. The ratio of Democrats to Republicans in a certain state legislature is 5 : 7. If the legislature has 156 members, all of whom are either Democrats or Republicans (but not both), what is the difference between the number of Republicans and the number of Democrats?

   (A) 14

   (B) 26

   (C) 35

   (D) 37

   (E) 46

9. What part of a dime is a quarter?

   (A) $\dfrac{5}{2}$

   (B) $\dfrac{3}{2}$

   (C) $\dfrac{2}{5}$

   (D) $\dfrac{2}{3}$

   (E) $\dfrac{3}{4}$

10. A pole 24 feet high has a shadow 8 feet long. A nearby pole is 72 feet high. How long is its shadow?

   (A) 16 feet
   (B) 24 feet
   (C) 32 feet
   (D) 40 feet
   (E) 56 feet

11. If 15 cans of food are needed for 7 adults for 2 days, the number of cans needed for 4 adults for 7 days is

   (A) 15
   (B) 20
   (C) 25
   (D) 30
   (E) 35

12. The school enrollment is 1400. Twenty percent of the students study French, 25% study Spanish, 15% study Italian, 10% study German, and the rest study no foreign language. Assuming that each student may study only one foreign language, how many students do not study any foreign language?

   (A) 42
   (B) 280
   (C) 420
   (D) 480
   (E) 565

13. How many liters of 50% antifreeze must be mixed with 80 liters of 20% antifreeze to get a mixture that is 40% antifreeze?

   (A) 160
   (B) 140
   (C) 120
   (D) 100
   (E) 80

14. Eight hundred persons are employed by the Metropolitan Transit Authority. One quarter of the employees are college graduates; $\dfrac{5}{6}$ of the remainder are high school graduates. What part of the total number of employees never graduated from high school?

   (A) $\dfrac{1}{8}$

   (B) $\dfrac{1}{6}$

   (C) $\dfrac{1}{4}$

   (D) $\dfrac{5}{6}$

   (E) $\dfrac{7}{8}$

GO ON TO THE NEXT PAGE

15. Two children weighing 60 pounds and 80 pounds, respectively, balance a seesaw. How many feet from the fulcrum must the heavier child sit if the lighter child is 8 feet from the fulcrum?

(A) $4\frac{1}{2}$

(B) 6

(C) $7\frac{1}{2}$

(D) 9

(E) $10\frac{1}{2}$

16. A pole 63 feet long was broken into two unequal parts so that $\frac{3}{5}$ of the longer piece equaled $\frac{3}{5}$ of the shorter piece. Find the length of the longer piece.

(A) 33 feet

(B) $33\frac{1}{2}$ feet

(C) 34 feet

(D) $34\frac{1}{2}$ feet

(E) 35 feet

17. A rectangular flower bed whose dimensions are 16 yards by 12 yards is surrounded by a walk 3 yards wide. The area of the walk is

(A) 93 square yards.

(B) 96 square yards.

(C) 144 square yards.

(D) 204 square yards.

(E) 244 square yards.

18. The temperatures reported at hourly intervals on a winter evening were +6°, +3°, 0°, –4°, and –10°. What was the average temperature for this period of time?

(A) +5°

(B) –5°

(C) 0°

(D) +1°

(E) –1°

19. A purse contains $2.20 in dimes and quarters. If the number of dimes is $\frac{1}{4}$ the number of quarters, how many dimes are there?

(A) 2

(B) 4

(C) 6

(D) 8

(E) 10

20. Two trains are 630 miles apart. At 9:00 a.m., they start traveling toward each other at average rates of 50 and 55 mph, respectively. At what time will they pass each other?

(A) 1:00 P.M.

(B) 1:30 P.M.

(C) 2:00 P.M.

(D) 2:30 P.M.

(E) 3:00 P.M.

21. At 12:00 noon, two vessels started sailing toward each other from ports that are 450 miles apart. They traveled at average rates of 22 and 28 mph, respectively. How many miles apart will the vessels be at 8 P.M.?

(A) 125

(B) 100

(C) 75

(D) 50

(E) 25

22. Two planes left at the same time from two airports that are 6000 miles apart and flew toward each other. They passed each other in five hours. The rate of the fast plane was twice the rate of the slow plane. What was the speed of the fast plane?

    (A) 400 mph

    (B) 500 mph

    (C) 600 mph

    (D) 700 mph

    (E) 800 mph

23. Harvey paid $400 for a used car that travels 28 miles per gallon on the highway and 20 miles per gallon in the city. If he drove twice as many highway miles as city miles last month while using 34 gallons of gasoline, how many miles did he drive altogether?

    (A) 1,000

    (B) 840

    (C) 400

    (D) 340

    (E) 280

24. How much water must be evaporated from 120 pounds of a 3% saline solution to make it an 8% saline solution?

    (A) 36 pounds

    (B) 45 pounds

    (C) 75 pounds

    (D) 105 pounds

    (E) 120 pounds

25. One printing press can do a job in 8 hours. Another printing press can do the same job in 12 hours. How long would it take both presses, working together, to do the job?

    (A) 4 hours 12 minutes

    (B) 4 hours 24 minutes

    (C) 4 hours 36 minutes

    (D) 4 hours 48 minutes

    (E) 5 hours

practice test

STOP! DO NOT TURN THIS PAGE UNTIL TOLD TO DO SO. IF YOU FINISH BEFORE THE TIME IS UP, YOU MAY CHECK OVER YOUR WORK ON THIS PART ONLY.

PART 3: WORD KNOWLEDGE

Directions: This part of the test is designed to measure verbal comprehension involving your ability to understand written language. For each question, you are to select the option that means the same or most nearly the same as the capitalized word. Then mark the space on your answer form that has the same number and letter as your choice.

Sample Items

S1. CRIMSON
- (A) bluish
- (B) colorful
- (C) crisp
- (D) lively
- (E) reddish

The correct answer is (E). *Crimson* means "a deep purple red." Choice (E) has almost the same meaning. None of the other choices has the same or a similar meaning.

S2. CEASE
- (A) continue
- (B) fold
- (C) start
- (D) stop
- (E) transform

The correct answer is (D). *Cease* means "to stop."

Your score on this test will be based on the number of questions you answer correctly. You should try to answer every question. You will not lose points or be penalized for guessing. Do not spend too much time on any one question.

When you begin, be sure to start with question 1 of Part 3 of your test booklet and 1 of Part 3 on your answer form.

DO NOT TURN PAGE UNTIL TOLD TO DO SO.

TIME: 5 Minutes—25 Questions

For each question, select the choice that means the same or most nearly the same as the capitalized word.

1. ACCENTUATE
   (A) emphasize
   (B) hasten
   (C) modify
   (D) pronounce
   (E) sustain

2. ANCILLARY
   (A) genuine
   (B) lawful
   (C) obligatory
   (D) primary
   (E) subsidiary

3. CALUMNY
   (A) anxiety
   (B) calmness
   (C) chemical
   (D) journalism
   (E) slander

4. COHERENT
   (A) brief
   (B) detailed
   (C) impressive
   (D) logical
   (E) obvious

5. CONTRAVENE
   (A) appease
   (B) disassemble
   (C) oppose
   (D) postpone
   (E) proceed

6. CORROBORATION
   (A) compilation
   (B) confirmation
   (C) consternation
   (D) cooperation
   (E) coordination

7. CREDENCE
   (A) belief
   (B) claim
   (C) payment
   (D) surprise
   (E) understanding

8. DIFFIDENCE
   (A) awareness
   (B) confidence
   (C) dissimilarity
   (D) emotion
   (E) shyness

9. FLAUNT
   (A) display
   (B) insult
   (C) notify
   (D) praise
   (E) punish

10. FOMENT
   (A) spoil
   (B) torture
   (C) terrify
   (D) incite
   (E) release

11. GERMANE
   (A) budding
   (B) contemporary
   (C) essential
   (D) relevant
   (E) trivial

12. IMPLICATE
    (A) authorize
    (B) detain
    (C) dismiss
    (D) involve
    (E) mediate

13. INSIDIOUS
    (A) insincere
    (B) knowledgeable
    (C) rampant
    (D) treacherous
    (E) unimportant

14. IRRESOLUTE
    (A) impudent
    (B) insolvable
    (C) insubordinate
    (D) unobservant
    (E) vacillating

15. MALINGER
    (A) curse
    (B) deteriorate
    (C) loiter
    (D) shirk
    (E) slander

16. OBSTREPEROUS
    (A) childlike
    (B) delightful
    (C) hazardous
    (D) unruly
    (E) unyielding

17. PALTRY
    (A) adequate
    (B) dismal
    (C) fowl
    (D) petty
    (E) weakened

18. PERVERSE
    (A) contrary
    (B) persistent
    (C) secret
    (D) unconcerned
    (E) unfortunate

19. PRECISE
    (A) exact
    (B) expensive
    (C) long
    (D) short
    (E) trivial

20. PRISTINE
    (A) brilliant
    (B) captive
    (C) inexpensive
    (D) unspoiled
    (E) valuable

21. REPRISAL
    (A) denial
    (B) reevaluation
    (C) retaliation
    (D) upheaval
    (E) warning

GO ON TO THE NEXT PAGE

practice test

22. STRIDENT
    (A) angry
    (B) domineering
    (C) harsh
    (D) swaggering
    (E) vigorous

23. UNSCRUPULOUS
    (A) careless
    (B) disagreeable
    (C) disorganized
    (D) inefficient
    (E) unprincipled

24. VESTIGE
    (A) blessing
    (B) design
    (C) garment
    (D) strap
    (E) trace

25. VICARIOUS
    (A) courageous
    (B) injurious
    (C) sparkling
    (D) substituted
    (E) ugly

STOP! DO NOT CONTINUE ON UNTIL TOLD TO DO SO. IF YOU FINISH BEFORE THE TIME IS UP, YOU MAY CHECK OVER YOUR WORK ON THIS PART ONLY.

PART 4: MATH KNOWLEDGE

> **Directions:** This part of the test has 25 questions designed to measure your ability to use learned mathematical relationships. Each problem is followed by five possible answers. Decide which one of the five options is most nearly correct. Then mark the space on your answer form that has the same number and letter as your choice. Use scratch paper to do any figuring that you wish.

Sample Items

S1. The reciprocal of 5 is

    (A) 0.1

    (B) 0.2

    (C) 0.5

    (D) 1.0

    (E) 2.0

The correct answer is (B). The reciprocal of 5 is $\frac{1}{5}$, or 0.2.

S2. The expression "3 factorial" equals

    (A) $\frac{1}{9}$

    (B) $\frac{1}{6}$

    (C) 6

    (D) 9

    (E) 27

The correct answer is (C). "3 factorial" or 3! equals $3 \times 2 \times 1 = 6$.

S3. The logarithm to the base 10 of 1,000 is

    (A) 1

    (B) 1.6

    (C) 2

    (D) 2.7

    (E) 3

The correct answer is (E). $10 \times 10 \times 10 = 1,000$. The logarithm of 1,000 is the exponent 3 to which the base 10 must be raised.

Your score on this test will be based on the number of questions you answer correctly. You should try to answer every question. You will not lose points or be penalized for guessing. Do not spend too much time on any one question.

When you begin, be sure to start with question 1 of Part 4 of your test booklet and 1 of Part 4 on your answer form.

DO NOT TURN PAGE UNTIL TOLD TO DO SO.

TIME: 22 Minutes—25 Questions

1. The square root of 250 is between

    (A) 15 and 16
    (B) 14 and 15
    (C) 13 and 14
    (D) 12 and 13
    (E) 11 and 12

2. $5\sqrt{12} - 2\sqrt{27} =$

    (A) $3\sqrt{4}$
    (B) $3\sqrt{5}$
    (C) $4\sqrt{3}$
    (D) $5\sqrt{2}$
    (E) $5\sqrt{3}$

3. The numerical value of $\dfrac{5!}{3!}$ is

    (A) 1.67
    (B) 2
    (C) 15
    (D) 20
    (E) None of the above

4. The logarithm to the base 10 of 10,000 is

    (A) 2
    (B) 3
    (C) 4
    (D) 5
    (E) None of the above

5. $10^3 \times 10^5 =$

    (A) 10^2
    (B) 10^8
    (C) 10^{15}
    (D) 10^{35}
    (E) None of the above

6. The relationship between .01% and .1% is

    (A) 1 to 1
    (B) 1 to 10
    (C) 1 to 100
    (D) 1 to 1000
    (E) 1 to 10,000

7. Which of the following is equal to 16,300?

    (A) 1.63×10^2
    (B) 1.63×10^3
    (C) 1.63×10^4
    (D) 1.63×10^5
    (E) 1.63×10^6

8. 3.47×10^{-2} is equal to

    (A) 347
    (B) 34.7
    (C) 3.47
    (D) 0.347
    (E) 0.0347

9. If a is greater than 2, which of the following is the smallest?

    (A) $\dfrac{2}{a}$

    (B) $\dfrac{a}{2}$

    (C) $\dfrac{2}{a-1}$

    (D) $\dfrac{a+1}{2}$

    (E) $\dfrac{2}{a+1}$

10. Which of the following has the greatest value?

(A) $\dfrac{3}{5}$

(B) $\left(\dfrac{2}{3}\right)\left(\dfrac{3}{4}\right)$

(C) $\sqrt{25}$

(D) $(0.9)^2$

(E) $\dfrac{2}{0.3}$

11. If r varies directly as s and if $r = 3$ when $s = 8$, find r when $s = 12$.

(A) 4

(B) $4\dfrac{1}{2}$

(C) 5

(D) $5\dfrac{1}{2}$

(E) 6

12. The Spencers took t dollars in traveler's checks with them on a trip. During the first week, they spent $\dfrac{1}{5}$ of their money. During the second week, they spent $\dfrac{1}{3}$ of the remainder. How much did they have left at the end of the second week?

(A) $\dfrac{t}{15}$

(B) $\dfrac{4t}{15}$

(C) $\dfrac{7t}{15}$

(D) $\dfrac{8t}{15}$

(E) $\dfrac{11t}{15}$

13. If r planes carry p passengers, how many planes are needed to carry m passengers?

(A) $\dfrac{m}{rp}$

(B) $\dfrac{p}{rm}$

(C) $\dfrac{rm}{p}$

(D) $\dfrac{rp}{m}$

(E) $\dfrac{pm}{r}$

14. If $a = b$ and $\dfrac{1}{c} = b$, then $c =$

(A) $\dfrac{1}{a}$

(B) a

(C) $-a$

(D) b

(E) $-b$

15. If $x^2 - y^2 = 100$ and $x - y = 20$, then $x + y =$

(A) 4

(B) 5

(C) 25

(D) 50

(E) 80

16. Find the average of four consecutive odd integers whose sum is 104.

(A) 24

(B) 25

(C) 26

(D) 27

(E) 28

GO ON TO THE NEXT PAGE

17. If x is less than 0 and y is less than 0, then
    (A) xy is less than 0
    (B) $x = y$
    (C) x is greater than y
    (D) $x + y$ is greater than 0
    (E) xy is greater than 0

18. When the fractions $\frac{2}{3}$, $\frac{5}{7}$, $\frac{8}{11}$, and $\frac{9}{13}$ are arranged in ascending order of size, the result is
    (A) $\frac{2}{3}, \frac{9}{13}, \frac{5}{7}, \frac{8}{11}$
    (B) $\frac{2}{3}, \frac{8}{11}, \frac{5}{7}, \frac{9}{13}$
    (C) $\frac{5}{7}, \frac{8}{11}, \frac{2}{3}, \frac{9}{13}$
    (D) $\frac{5}{7}, \frac{9}{13}, \frac{2}{3}, \frac{8}{11}$
    (E) $\frac{8}{11}, \frac{2}{3}, \frac{9}{13}, \frac{5}{7}$

19. Points P, Q, and R are placed on line segment XY so that $XP = PQ = QR = RY$. What percent of PR is PY?
    (A) $66\frac{2}{3}\%$
    (B) 75%
    (C) 125%
    (D) 150%
    (E) 200%

20. If five triangles are constructed with sides of the lengths given below, which triangle will be a right triangle?
    (A) 2, 3, 4
    (B) 3, 4, 5
    (C) 5, 12, 15
    (D) 8, 9, 17
    (E) 12, 15, 18

21. At 6:00 A.M., the angle between the hands of a clock is
    (A) 45°
    (B) 90°
    (C) 120°
    (D) 180°
    (E) 360°

22. Find the number of degrees in the sum of the interior angles of a hexagon.
    (A) 360
    (B) 540
    (C) 720
    (D) 900
    (E) 1080

23. The radius of a wheel is 2 feet. What is the number of feet covered by this wheel in 10 revolutions?
    (A) 10
    (B) 10π
    (C) 20
    (D) 40
    (E) 40π

24. What is the appropriate number that should be inserted in the following series of numbers arranged in a logical order? 6 5 10 8 __ 9 12 8 10
    (A) 10
    (B) 11
    (C) 12
    (D) 13
    (E) 14

25. A round trip in a helicopter lasted 4 hours. If the helicopter flew away from the airport at 90 mph and returned at the rate of 45 mph, what was its greatest distance from the airport?

(A) 100 miles

(B) 105 miles

(C) 110 miles

(D) 115 miles

(E) 120 miles

IF YOU FINISH BEFORE THE TIME IS UP, YOU MAY CHECK OVER YOUR WORK ON THIS PART ONLY. END OF TEST.

ANSWER KEYS AND EXPLANATIONS

Use these key answers to determine the number of questions you answered correctly on each test and to list those questions that you answered incorrectly or that you are unsure of how to arrive at the correct answer.

Be certain to review carefully and understand the rationale for arriving at the correct answer for all items you answered incorrectly, as well as those you answered correctly but are unsure of.

Part 1: Verbal Analogies

1. (B)	6. (C)	11. (B)	16. (E)	21. (D)
2. (D)	7. (A)	12. (E)	17. (E)	22. (A)
3. (B)	8. (E)	13. (C)	18. (E)	23. (D)
4. (C)	9. (D)	14. (C)	19. (C)	24. (C)
5. (B)	10. (E)	15. (C)	20. (D)	25. (C)

1. **The correct answer is (B).** A *prospector* searches for *gold*; a *detective* searches for a *clue*.

2. **The correct answer is (D).** *Marble* is obtained from a *quarry*; *coal* is obtained from a *mine*.

3. **The correct answer is (B).** A *ram* is an adult male sheep; a *lamb* is a young sheep. A *bull* is an adult male bovine animal; a *calf* is the young of a cow.

4. **The correct answer is (C).** Whereas a *general* is a military leader of soldiers who operate mainly on land, an *admiral* is a military leader whose troops operate mainly on the sea. Similarly, a *soldier* is based mainly on land, while a *sailor* is based mainly on the sea.

5. **The correct answer is (B).** Both capitalized words are names of birds. The only parallel relationship is found in choice (B).

6. **The correct answer is (C).** *Scrawny* and *lean* are synonyms. The only other set of synonyms is *brawny* and *strong*.

7. **The correct answer is (A).** The first two capitalized words are synonymous. *Ask* is a synonym for *inquire*.

8. **The correct answer is (E).** A *stallion* is a male horse; a *gelding* is a castrated horse. A *steer* is a castrated *bull*.

9. **The correct answer is (D).** There is no apparent relationship between the first two capitalized words. However, *toil* is synonymous with *work* and *strife* is synonymous with *struggle*.

10. **The correct answer is (E).** *Valid* and *fallacious* are adjectives with opposite meanings. The only antonym for *veracious* is *untrue*.

11. **The correct answer is (B).** The past tense of *shoot* is formed by deleting a vowel from the present infinitive form. The past tense of *bleed* is also formed by deleting a vowel from the present infinitive form.

12. **The correct answer is (E).** Something that is *ad lib* is done without *rehearsal*—it's improvised. Something that is *aleatory* (meaning driven by chance, like the toss of a pair of dice) is done without a *plan*.

13. **The correct answer is (C).** To *daub* is to *paint* in a haphazard way, showing little care or talent for the art of painting. Similarly, to *caterwaul* is to *sing* without

care or talent, the way a cat in a back alley howls at the moon.

14. **The correct answer is (C).** This question pertains to a mathematical proportion: *36* is to *4* as *9* is to *1*.

15. **The correct answer is (C).** *Trumpet* is a type of *instrument*; *pliers* are a type of *tool*.

16. **The correct answer is (E).** *Drift* is a *snow* hill or ridge formed by the wind; *dune* is a *sand* hill or ridge formed by the wind.

17. **The correct answer is (E).** The *moon* revolves around the *earth*; the *earth* revolves around the *sun*.

18. **The correct answer is (E).** A *necklace* is an ornament or an *adornment*. A *medal* is a *decoration* for bravery or merit.

19. **The correct answer is (C).** *Paper* is made from *pulp*; *rope* is made from *hemp*.

20. **The correct answer is (D).** *Regressive* is the adjective form for *regress*; *sterile* is the adjective form for *sterilize*.

21. **The correct answer is (D).** The *crest* is the top of a *wave*; the *peak* is the top of a *mountain*.

22. **The correct answer is (A).** The relationship of the two capitalized words is that of the female and male. The only other parallel relationship is *duck* (female) and *drake* (male).

23. **The correct answer is (D).** An *enigma* (a difficult puzzle) is likely to leave you feeling *mystified*; a *dilemma* (a difficult choice) is likely to leave you feeling *undecided*.

24. **The correct answer is (C).** The past participle of *wring* is *wrung*; that of *lay* is *laid*.

25. **The correct answer is (C).** There is no apparent relationship between *zinc* and *sulfuric acid*. However, *zinc* is an *element* and *sulfuric acid* is a compound.

answers practice test

Part 2: Arithmetic Reasoning

1. (B)	6. (C)	11. (D)	16. (E)	21. (D)
2. (A)	7. (A)	12. (C)	17. (D)	22. (E)
3. (E)	8. (B)	13. (A)	18. (E)	23. (B)
4. (A)	9. (A)	14. (A)	19. (A)	24. (C)
5. (B)	10. (B)	15. (B)	20. (E)	25. (D)

1. **The correct answer is (B).** 20% of $2400 = 480;
2400 − 480 = $1920; 20% of $1920 = 384; 1920 − 384 = $1536.

2. **The correct answer is (A).** $27 \times 32 = 864$ square feet to be carpeted. Let $x =$ number of linear feet of carpeting needed.

27 inches $= \dfrac{9}{4}$ feet; $\dfrac{9}{4} \times x = 864$

$x = 864 \times \dfrac{4}{9} = 384$ feet; $\dfrac{384}{3} = 128$ yards.

3. **The correct answer is (E).** Let r, m, and b be the prices in cents of rolls, muffins, and bread, respectively. This yields two equations:

$4r + 6m + 3b = 910$

$2r + 3m + b = 390$

If we multiply the second equation by −2 and add the two together, we have: $b = 130$. Hence, the price of a loaf of bread is $1.30, which is choice (E).

4. **The correct answer is (A).**
$\dfrac{635.30}{900} = 0.7058 = 71\%$.

5. **The correct answer is (B).**

$1800 × 0.05 = $90.00; $\dfrac{180}{90} = \dfrac{2}{1}$.

6. **The correct answer is (C).** $\dfrac{1}{3}$ of family income, or $8000, was saved; $\dfrac{1}{3}$ of $x = 8000$; $x = $24,000$.

7. **The correct answer is (A).** Let $x =$ tax rate.

$338{,}555 \times x = 616.07$; $x = \dfrac{616.07}{338500} = 0.00182$;

$0.00182 \times 1000 = 1.82.

8. **The correct answer is (B).** Let the number of Democrats be $5m$ and the number of Republicans be $7m$, so that D : R :: $5m$: $7m = 5$: 7. The total is $5m + 7m = 12m$, which must be 156. Therefore, $12m = 156$, and $m = 13$. Of course, the difference is $7m − 5m = 2m = 2(13) = 26$. Hence the answer is choice (B).

9. **The correct answer is (A).**

$\dfrac{25}{10} = \dfrac{5}{2}$

10. **The correct answer is (B).**

$24 : 8 = 72 : x$; $3 : 1 = 72 : x$;

$x = \dfrac{72}{3} = 24$ feet

11. **The correct answer is (D).**

$15 : 14 = x : 28$; $x = \dfrac{28 \times 15}{14} = 30$

12. **The correct answer is (C).** 20% + 25% + 15% + 10% = 70%; 100% − 70% = 30% that do not study any foreign language; $1400 \times 0.30 = 420$.

13. **The correct answer is (A).** Let x be the unknown number of liters of 50% antifreeze. Now, the final mixture will have $(x + 80)$ liters, and the amount of antifreeze will be:

$$0.50x + 0.20(80) = 0.40(x + 80)$$
$$0.50x + 16 = 0.4x + 32$$
$$0.1x = 16$$
$$x = 160$$

14. **The correct answer is (A).**

$$\frac{1}{4} \times 800 = 200; \quad 800 - 200 = 600$$

$$\frac{5}{6} \times 600 = 500; \quad 600 - 500 = 100$$

There are 100 non-high school graduates employed; $\frac{100}{800} = \frac{1}{8}$.

15. **The correct answer is (B).**

$$60 \times 8 = 80 \times x; \quad 80x = 480; \quad x = \frac{480}{80} = 6$$

16. **The correct answer is (E).** Let x = length of longer piece; $63 - x$ = length of shorter piece.

$$\frac{3}{5x} = \frac{3}{4}(63 - x); \quad \frac{3}{5x} = \frac{189}{4} - \frac{3}{4}x; \quad \frac{3}{5x} +$$

$$\frac{3}{4}x = \frac{189}{4}; \quad \frac{12}{20}x + \frac{15}{20}x = \frac{189}{4}; \quad \frac{17}{20x} = \frac{189}{4};$$

$$x = \frac{189}{4} \times \frac{20}{27} = 35 \text{ feet.}$$

17. **The correct answer is (D).** Area of flower bed = 16 yards by 12 yards = 192 sq. yds.; area of bed and walk = (16 + 3 + 3) (12 + 3 + 3) = 22 × 18 = 396 sq. yds.; 396 − 192 = 204 sq. yds.

18. **The correct answer is (E).**

$$\frac{(+6) + (+3) + 0 + (-4) + (-10)}{5} = \frac{-5}{5} = -1$$

19. **The correct answer is (A).**

Let x = number of dimes. $0.10x + 0.25(4x) = 2.20$; $0.10x + x = 2.20$; $1.10x = 2.20$; $x = \frac{2.20}{1.10} = 2$.

20. **The correct answer is (E).**

Let x = time.

$50x + 55x = 630$; $105x = 630$; $x = \frac{630}{105} = 6$ hours. Trains left at 9:00 A.M. Six hours later, it would be 3:00 P.M.

21. **The correct answer is (D).** Noon to 8 P.M. = 8 hours

Distance covered = (22 × 8) + (28 × 8) = 176 + 224 = 400 miles. Total distance = 450 miles; 450 − 400 = 50 miles apart.

22. **The correct answer is (E).** Let x = rate of slower plane; $2x$ = rate of the faster plane. $5x + 10x = 6000$; $15x = 6000$; $x = 400$; $2x = 800$.

23. **The correct answer is (B).** Let x be the number of city miles Harvey drove, and let $2x$ be the number of highway miles. Miles divided by miles per gallon should give the number of gallons of gas used. Thus:

$$\frac{x}{20} = \frac{2x}{28} = 34$$

$$\frac{x}{20} = \frac{x}{14} = 34$$

Multiply the equation by the LCD 140 to get:

$$7x + 10x = 4760$$

$$17x = 4760; \quad x = 280$$

Since Harvey drove a total of $3x$ miles, the correct answer is 3(280) = 840.

24. **The correct answer is (C).** 3% of 120 pounds of saline = 3.6 pounds of pure salt; $\frac{3.6}{x} = 0.08$; $0.08x = 3.6$; $x = \frac{3.6}{0.08}$;

    $x = 45$ pounds of saline solution that is needed for an 8% solution; 120 pounds of solution must be reduced to 45 pounds. Therefore, $120 - 45$ or 75 pounds of water must be evaporated.

25. **The correct answer is (D).**

    First Press   **Second Press**

    $\dfrac{\text{Time actually needed}}{\text{Time needed to do job alone}}$ $\dfrac{x}{8} + \dfrac{x}{12} = 1$

    Multiply by 24 to clear fractions.

    $3x + 2x = 24$; $5x = 24$; $x = \frac{24}{5} = 4\frac{4}{5}$ hours or 4 hours 48 minutes.

Part 3: Word Knowledge

1. (A)	6. (B)	11. (D)	16. (D)	21. (C)
2. (E)	7. (A)	12. (D)	17. (D)	22. (C)
3. (E)	8. (E)	13. (D)	18. (A)	23. (E)
4. (D)	9. (A)	14. (E)	19. (A)	24. (E)
5. (C)	10. (D)	15. (D)	20. (D)	25. (D)

1. **The correct answer is (A).** *Accentuate* means to *emphasize*.

2. **The correct answer is (E).** *Ancillary* means *auxiliary* or *subsidiary*.

3. **The correct answer is (E).** *Calumny* means *false accusation* or *slander*.

4. **The correct answer is (D).** *Coherent* means *consistent* or *logical*.

5. **The correct answer is (C).** *Contravene* means to *oppose* or *infringe*.

6. **The correct answer is (B).** *Corroboration* and *confirmation* are synonymous.

7. **The correct answer is (A).** *Credence* and *belief* have similar meanings.

8. **The correct answer is (E).** *Diffidence*, *timidity*, and *shyness* have similar meanings.

9. **The correct answer is (A).** *Flaunt* means to *display*.

10. **The correct answer is (D).** *Foment* means to *stir up* or *incite*.

11. **The correct answer is (D).** *Germane* means *pertinent* or *relevant*.

12. **The correct answer is (D).** *Implicate* means to *involve*.

13. **The correct answer is (D).** *Insidious* and *treacherous* are synonymous.

14. **The correct answer is (E).** *Irresolute*, *uncertain*, and *vacillating* have similar meanings.

15. **The correct answer is (D).** *Malinger* and *shirk* have similar meanings.

16. **The correct answer is (D).** *Obstreperous* is synonymous with *unruly* and *boisterous*.

17. **The correct answer is (D).** *Paltry* is synonymous with *trifling* and *petty*.

18. **The correct answer is (A).** *Perverse* is synonymous with *stubborn* and *contrary*.

19. **The correct answer is (A).** *Precise* and *exact* have similar meanings.

20. **The correct answer is (D).** *Pristine*, *pure*, and *unspoiled* have similar meanings.

21. **The correct answer is (C).** *Reprisal*, *retaliation*, and *revenge* have similar meanings.

22. **The correct answer is (C).** *Strident*, *grating*, and *harsh* have similar meanings.

23. **The correct answer is (E).** *Unscrupulous* and *unprincipled* are synonymous.

24. **The correct answer is (E).** *Vestige* and *trace* are synonymous.

25. **The correct answer is (D).** *Vicarious* is a synonym for *substituted*.

answers practice test

Part 4: Math Knowledge

1. (A)	6. (B)	11. (B)	16. (C)	21. (D)
2. (C)	7. (C)	12. (D)	17. (E)	22. (C)
3. (D)	8. (E)	13. (C)	18. (A)	23. (E)
4. (C)	9. (E)	14. (A)	19. (D)	24. (C)
5. (B)	10. (E)	15. (B)	20. (B)	25. (E)

1. **The correct answer is (A).** $15^2 = 225$; $16^2 = 266$. 250 is between 225 and 266.

2. **The correct answer is (C).**

$$5\sqrt{12} = 5\sqrt{4 \times 3} = 5 \times 2\sqrt{3} = 10\sqrt{3}$$
$$2\sqrt{27} = 2\sqrt{9 \times 3} = 2 \times 3\sqrt{3} = 6\sqrt{3}$$
$$10\sqrt{3} - 6\sqrt{3} = 4\sqrt{3}$$

3. **The correct answer is (D).** The factorial of a natural number is the product of that number and all the natural numbers less than it.

$$5! = 5 \times 4 \times 3 \times 2 \times 1 = 120$$
$$3! = 3 \times 2 \times 1 = 6$$
$$\frac{120}{6} = 20$$

4. **The correct answer is (C).** The logarithm of a number is the exponent to which a base must be raised to produce the number. $10^2 = 100$; $10^3 = 1000$; $10^4 = 10,000$; $10^5 = 100,000$.

5. **The correct answer is (B).** When multiplying logarithms with the same base, add the exponents. $10^3 \times 10^5 = 10^8$.

6. **The correct answer is (B).**

$$0.01\% = \frac{0.01}{100} = 0.0001$$
$$0.1\% = \frac{0.1}{100} = 0.001$$
$$\frac{0.0001}{0.001} = \frac{1}{10}$$

7. **The correct answer is (C).** $16,300 = 1.63 \times 10,000 = 1.63 \times 10^4$.

8. **The correct answer is (E).** $10^{-2} = 0.01$; $3.47 \times 0.01 = 0.0347$.

9. **The correct answer is (E).** Choices (B) and (D) are greater than 1; other choices have the same numerator; however, choice (E) has the greatest denominator and, therefore, the smallest value, a value of less than 1.

10. **The correct answer is (E).** $A = 0.60$; $B = 0.50$; $C = 0.5$; $D = 0.81$; $E = 6.67$.

11. **The correct answer is (B).** $3 : 8 = x : 12$; $8x = 36$; $x = 4\frac{1}{2}$.

12. **The correct answer is (D).** $\frac{1}{5}t$ spent the first week; $t - \frac{t}{5}$ is left; $\frac{1}{3}(t - \frac{t}{5}) = \frac{1}{3}(\frac{5t}{5} - \frac{t}{5}) = \frac{1}{3} \times \frac{4}{5}t = \frac{4}{15}t$ spent the second week; $\frac{3}{15}t + \frac{4}{15}t = \frac{7}{15}t$ spent the first two weeks; $\frac{8}{15}t$ is left.

13. **The correct answer is (C).** Let x = number of planes needed to carry m passengers.

$$r : p = x : m; \quad px = rm; \quad x = \frac{rm}{p}$$

14. **The correct answer is (A).**

$$\frac{1}{c} = b = a; \quad c = \frac{1}{a}$$

15. **The correct answer is (B).**

$$x^2 - y^2 = (x + y)(x - y); \quad 100 = (x + y) \times 20$$
$$(x + y) = \frac{100}{20} = 5$$

16. **The correct answer is (C).** To find the average of any four numbers, divide the sum of the numbers by 4; $\frac{104}{4} = 26$.

17. **The correct answer is (E).** When two negative numbers are multiplied, the product is positive.

18. **The correct answer is (A).**

$\frac{2}{3} = 0.67$; $\frac{5}{7} = 0.71$; $\frac{8}{11} = 0.73$;

$\frac{9}{13} = 0.69$

19. **The correct answer is (D).**

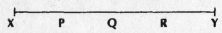

PR = 2 equal segments; PY = 3 equal

segments; $\frac{3}{2} = 150\%$.

20. **The correct answer is (B).** In a right triangle, the square of the hypotenuse = the sum of the squares of the other two sides. $3^2 + 4^2 = 5^2$; $9 + 16 = 25$.

21. **The correct answer is (D).** At 6:00 A.M., one hand is at the 6 and the other is at the 12, forming a straight angle, or 180°.

22. **The correct answer is (C).** A hexagon is a six-sided polygon. $180° (6 - 2) = x$; $180° \times 4 = x$; $x = 720°$.

23. **The correct answer is (E).** Radius = 2 feet; diameter = 4 feet; circumference = $\pi d = 4\pi$; $4\pi \times 10 = 40\pi$.

24. **The correct answer is (C).** Subtract 1, add 5; subtract 2, add 4; subtract 3, add 3; subtract 4, add 2.

25. **The correct answer is (E).** Let x = time flying out and $4 - x$ = time flying in.

$90x = 45(4 - x)$; $90x = 180 - 45x$; $135x = 180$

$x = \frac{180}{135} = \frac{4}{3}$; $\frac{4}{3} \times 90 = 120$ miles

answers practice test

ANSWER SHEET FOR ARMY AND COAST GUARD COMMISSIONING PROGRAM

Part 2: Arithmetic Reasoning

1. Ⓐ Ⓑ Ⓒ Ⓓ   7. Ⓐ Ⓑ Ⓒ Ⓓ   13. Ⓐ Ⓑ Ⓒ Ⓓ   19. Ⓐ Ⓑ Ⓒ Ⓓ   25. Ⓐ Ⓑ Ⓒ Ⓓ
2. Ⓐ Ⓑ Ⓒ Ⓓ   8. Ⓐ Ⓑ Ⓒ Ⓓ   14. Ⓐ Ⓑ Ⓒ Ⓓ   20. Ⓐ Ⓑ Ⓒ Ⓓ   26. Ⓐ Ⓑ Ⓒ Ⓓ
3. Ⓐ Ⓑ Ⓒ Ⓓ   9. Ⓐ Ⓑ Ⓒ Ⓓ   15. Ⓐ Ⓑ Ⓒ Ⓓ   21. Ⓐ Ⓑ Ⓒ Ⓓ   27. Ⓐ Ⓑ Ⓒ Ⓓ
4. Ⓐ Ⓑ Ⓒ Ⓓ   10. Ⓐ Ⓑ Ⓒ Ⓓ   16. Ⓐ Ⓑ Ⓒ Ⓓ   22. Ⓐ Ⓑ Ⓒ Ⓓ   28. Ⓐ Ⓑ Ⓒ Ⓓ
5. Ⓐ Ⓑ Ⓒ Ⓓ   11. Ⓐ Ⓑ Ⓒ Ⓓ   17. Ⓐ Ⓑ Ⓒ Ⓓ   23. Ⓐ Ⓑ Ⓒ Ⓓ   29. Ⓐ Ⓑ Ⓒ Ⓓ
6. Ⓐ Ⓑ Ⓒ Ⓓ   12. Ⓐ Ⓑ Ⓒ Ⓓ   18. Ⓐ Ⓑ Ⓒ Ⓓ   24. Ⓐ Ⓑ Ⓒ Ⓓ   30. Ⓐ Ⓑ Ⓒ Ⓓ

Part 3: Word Knowledge

1. Ⓐ Ⓑ Ⓒ Ⓓ   8. Ⓐ Ⓑ Ⓒ Ⓓ   15. Ⓐ Ⓑ Ⓒ Ⓓ   22. Ⓐ Ⓑ Ⓒ Ⓓ   29. Ⓐ Ⓑ Ⓒ Ⓓ
2. Ⓐ Ⓑ Ⓒ Ⓓ   9. Ⓐ Ⓑ Ⓒ Ⓓ   16. Ⓐ Ⓑ Ⓒ Ⓓ   23. Ⓐ Ⓑ Ⓒ Ⓓ   30. Ⓐ Ⓑ Ⓒ Ⓓ
3. Ⓐ Ⓑ Ⓒ Ⓓ   10. Ⓐ Ⓑ Ⓒ Ⓓ   17. Ⓐ Ⓑ Ⓒ Ⓓ   24. Ⓐ Ⓑ Ⓒ Ⓓ   31. Ⓐ Ⓑ Ⓒ Ⓓ
4. Ⓐ Ⓑ Ⓒ Ⓓ   11. Ⓐ Ⓑ Ⓒ Ⓓ   18. Ⓐ Ⓑ Ⓒ Ⓓ   25. Ⓐ Ⓑ Ⓒ Ⓓ   32. Ⓐ Ⓑ Ⓒ Ⓓ
5. Ⓐ Ⓑ Ⓒ Ⓓ   12. Ⓐ Ⓑ Ⓒ Ⓓ   19. Ⓐ Ⓑ Ⓒ Ⓓ   26. Ⓐ Ⓑ Ⓒ Ⓓ   33. Ⓐ Ⓑ Ⓒ Ⓓ
6. Ⓐ Ⓑ Ⓒ Ⓓ   13. Ⓐ Ⓑ Ⓒ Ⓓ   20. Ⓐ Ⓑ Ⓒ Ⓓ   27. Ⓐ Ⓑ Ⓒ Ⓓ   34. Ⓐ Ⓑ Ⓒ Ⓓ
7. Ⓐ Ⓑ Ⓒ Ⓓ   14. Ⓐ Ⓑ Ⓒ Ⓓ   21. Ⓐ Ⓑ Ⓒ Ⓓ   28. Ⓐ Ⓑ Ⓒ Ⓓ   35. Ⓐ Ⓑ Ⓒ Ⓓ

Part 4: Paragraph Comprehension

1. Ⓐ Ⓑ Ⓒ Ⓓ   4. Ⓐ Ⓑ Ⓒ Ⓓ   7. Ⓐ Ⓑ Ⓒ Ⓓ   10. Ⓐ Ⓑ Ⓒ Ⓓ   13. Ⓐ Ⓑ Ⓒ Ⓓ
2. Ⓐ Ⓑ Ⓒ Ⓓ   5. Ⓐ Ⓑ Ⓒ Ⓓ   8. Ⓐ Ⓑ Ⓒ Ⓓ   11. Ⓐ Ⓑ Ⓒ Ⓓ   14. Ⓐ Ⓑ Ⓒ Ⓓ
3. Ⓐ Ⓑ Ⓒ Ⓓ   6. Ⓐ Ⓑ Ⓒ Ⓓ   9. Ⓐ Ⓑ Ⓒ Ⓓ   12. Ⓐ Ⓑ Ⓒ Ⓓ   15. Ⓐ Ⓑ Ⓒ Ⓓ

answer sheet

ANSWER SHEET FOR MARINE CORPS COMMISSIONING PROGRAM

Part 1: General Science

1. Ⓐ Ⓑ Ⓒ Ⓓ	6. Ⓐ Ⓑ Ⓒ Ⓓ	11. Ⓐ Ⓑ Ⓒ Ⓓ	16. Ⓐ Ⓑ Ⓒ Ⓓ	21. Ⓐ Ⓑ Ⓒ Ⓓ
2. Ⓐ Ⓑ Ⓒ Ⓓ	7. Ⓐ Ⓑ Ⓒ Ⓓ	12. Ⓐ Ⓑ Ⓒ Ⓓ	17. Ⓐ Ⓑ Ⓒ Ⓓ	22. Ⓐ Ⓑ Ⓒ Ⓓ
3. Ⓐ Ⓑ Ⓒ Ⓓ	8. Ⓐ Ⓑ Ⓒ Ⓓ	13. Ⓐ Ⓑ Ⓒ Ⓓ	18. Ⓐ Ⓑ Ⓒ Ⓓ	23. Ⓐ Ⓑ Ⓒ Ⓓ
4. Ⓐ Ⓑ Ⓒ Ⓓ	9. Ⓐ Ⓑ Ⓒ Ⓓ	14. Ⓐ Ⓑ Ⓒ Ⓓ	19. Ⓐ Ⓑ Ⓒ Ⓓ	24. Ⓐ Ⓑ Ⓒ Ⓓ
5. Ⓐ Ⓑ Ⓒ Ⓓ	10. Ⓐ Ⓑ Ⓒ Ⓓ	15. Ⓐ Ⓑ Ⓒ Ⓓ	20. Ⓐ Ⓑ Ⓒ Ⓓ	25. Ⓐ Ⓑ Ⓒ Ⓓ

Part 2: Arithmetic Reasoning

1. Ⓐ Ⓑ Ⓒ Ⓓ	7. Ⓐ Ⓑ Ⓒ Ⓓ	13. Ⓐ Ⓑ Ⓒ Ⓓ	19. Ⓐ Ⓑ Ⓒ Ⓓ	25. Ⓐ Ⓑ Ⓒ Ⓓ
2. Ⓐ Ⓑ Ⓒ Ⓓ	8. Ⓐ Ⓑ Ⓒ Ⓓ	14. Ⓐ Ⓑ Ⓒ Ⓓ	20. Ⓐ Ⓑ Ⓒ Ⓓ	26. Ⓐ Ⓑ Ⓒ Ⓓ
3. Ⓐ Ⓑ Ⓒ Ⓓ	9. Ⓐ Ⓑ Ⓒ Ⓓ	15. Ⓐ Ⓑ Ⓒ Ⓓ	21. Ⓐ Ⓑ Ⓒ Ⓓ	27. Ⓐ Ⓑ Ⓒ Ⓓ
4. Ⓐ Ⓑ Ⓒ Ⓓ	10. Ⓐ Ⓑ Ⓒ Ⓓ	16. Ⓐ Ⓑ Ⓒ Ⓓ	22. Ⓐ Ⓑ Ⓒ Ⓓ	28. Ⓐ Ⓑ Ⓒ Ⓓ
5. Ⓐ Ⓑ Ⓒ Ⓓ	11. Ⓐ Ⓑ Ⓒ Ⓓ	17. Ⓐ Ⓑ Ⓒ Ⓓ	23. Ⓐ Ⓑ Ⓒ Ⓓ	29. Ⓐ Ⓑ Ⓒ Ⓓ
6. Ⓐ Ⓑ Ⓒ Ⓓ	12. Ⓐ Ⓑ Ⓒ Ⓓ	18. Ⓐ Ⓑ Ⓒ Ⓓ	24. Ⓐ Ⓑ Ⓒ Ⓓ	30. Ⓐ Ⓑ Ⓒ Ⓓ

Part 5: Mathematics Knowledge

1. Ⓐ Ⓑ Ⓒ Ⓓ	6. Ⓐ Ⓑ Ⓒ Ⓓ	11. Ⓐ Ⓑ Ⓒ Ⓓ	16. Ⓐ Ⓑ Ⓒ Ⓓ	21. Ⓐ Ⓑ Ⓒ Ⓓ
2. Ⓐ Ⓑ Ⓒ Ⓓ	7. Ⓐ Ⓑ Ⓒ Ⓓ	12. Ⓐ Ⓑ Ⓒ Ⓓ	17. Ⓐ Ⓑ Ⓒ Ⓓ	22. Ⓐ Ⓑ Ⓒ Ⓓ
3. Ⓐ Ⓑ Ⓒ Ⓓ	8. Ⓐ Ⓑ Ⓒ Ⓓ	13. Ⓐ Ⓑ Ⓒ Ⓓ	18. Ⓐ Ⓑ Ⓒ Ⓓ	23. Ⓐ Ⓑ Ⓒ Ⓓ
4. Ⓐ Ⓑ Ⓒ Ⓓ	9. Ⓐ Ⓑ Ⓒ Ⓓ	14. Ⓐ Ⓑ Ⓒ Ⓓ	19. Ⓐ Ⓑ Ⓒ Ⓓ	24. Ⓐ Ⓑ Ⓒ Ⓓ
5. Ⓐ Ⓑ Ⓒ Ⓓ	10. Ⓐ Ⓑ Ⓒ Ⓓ	15. Ⓐ Ⓑ Ⓒ Ⓓ	20. Ⓐ Ⓑ Ⓒ Ⓓ	25. Ⓐ Ⓑ Ⓒ Ⓓ

Part 6: Electronics Information

1. Ⓐ Ⓑ Ⓒ Ⓓ	5. Ⓐ Ⓑ Ⓒ Ⓓ	9. Ⓐ Ⓑ Ⓒ Ⓓ	13. Ⓐ Ⓑ Ⓒ Ⓓ	17. Ⓐ Ⓑ Ⓒ Ⓓ
2. Ⓐ Ⓑ Ⓒ Ⓓ	6. Ⓐ Ⓑ Ⓒ Ⓓ	10. Ⓐ Ⓑ Ⓒ Ⓓ	14. Ⓐ Ⓑ Ⓒ Ⓓ	18. Ⓐ Ⓑ Ⓒ Ⓓ
3. Ⓐ Ⓑ Ⓒ Ⓓ	7. Ⓐ Ⓑ Ⓒ Ⓓ	11. Ⓐ Ⓑ Ⓒ Ⓓ	15. Ⓐ Ⓑ Ⓒ Ⓓ	19. Ⓐ Ⓑ Ⓒ Ⓓ
4. Ⓐ Ⓑ Ⓒ Ⓓ	8. Ⓐ Ⓑ Ⓒ Ⓓ	12. Ⓐ Ⓑ Ⓒ Ⓓ	16. Ⓐ Ⓑ Ⓒ Ⓓ	20. Ⓐ Ⓑ Ⓒ Ⓓ

Armed Services Vocational Aptitude Battery (ASVAB)

Tests

Part 1: General Science
Part 2: Arithmetic Reasoning
Part 3: Word Knowledge
Part 4: Paragraph Comprehension
Part 5: Mathematics Knowledge
Part 6: Electronics Information

The answer sheet for the Army commissioning program should be used for answering the following:

    ASVAB Part 2: Arithmetic Reasoning
    ASVAB Part 3: Word Knowledge
    ASVAB Part 4: Paragraph Comprehension

The answer sheet for the Marine Corps commissioning program should be used for answering the following:

    ASVAB Part 1: General Science
    ASVAB Part 2: Arithmetic Reasoning
    ASVAB Part 5: Mathematics Knowledge
    ASVAB Part 6: Electronics Information

In addition to the pertinent tests required for both the Army and the Marine Corps commissioning programs, this section also contains answer keys and explanations for determining your scores on these tests.

When you take this test, try to simulate the test conditions you will encounter when taking the real test. That is, try to eliminate all possible distractions (like the radio or TV) and have each test carefully timed. Cut out the appropriate answer sheet and record your answers to the test questions.

After you finish, use the key answers to obtain your test scores and to evaluate your performance on each test. Place the number of items you answered correctly, as well as the number of each item you answered incorrectly or wish to review, in the space provided below the answers for each test.

Be certain to review carefully and understand the rationale for the answers for all questions you answered incorrectly and for each of the questions that you answered correctly but are unsure of. This is absolutely essential in order to acquire the knowledge and expertise necessary to obtain the maximum scores possible on the test.

practice test

PART 1: GENERAL SCIENCE

Directions: This is a test of 25 questions to find out how much you know about general science as usually covered in high school courses. Pick the best answer for each question, then blacken the space on your answer form that has the same number and letter as your choice.

Sample Items

S1. Water is an example of a

(A) solid.

(B) gas.

(C) liquid.

(D) crystal.

The correct answer is (C). Now do practice questions 2 and 3 by yourself. Find the correct answer to the question, then mark the space on your answer form that has the same letter as the answer you picked. Do this now.

S2. Lack of iodine is often related to which of the following diseases?

(A) Beriberi

(B) Scurvy

(C) Rickets

(D) Goiter

S3. An eclipse of the sun throws the shadow of the

(A) earth on the moon.

(B) moon on the earth.

(C) moon on the sun.

(D) earth on the sun.

The corect answers are (D) for question 2 and (B) for question 3. If you made any mistakes, erase your mark carefully and blacken the correct answer space. Do this now.

Your score on this test will be based on the number of questions you answer correctly. You should try to answer every question. Do not spend too much time on any one question.

When you begin, be sure to start with question 1 of Part 1 of your test booklet, and 1 in Part 1 on your answer form.

DO NOT TURN PAGE UNTIL TOLD TO DO SO.

TIME: 11 Minutes—25 Questions

1. Under natural conditions, large quantities of organic matter decay after each year's plant growth has been completed. As a result of such conditions,

   (A) many animals are deprived of adequate food supplies.

   (B) soil erosion is accelerated.

   (C) soils maintain their fertility.

   (D) earthworms are added to the soil.

2. The thin, clear layer that forms the outer coat of the eyeball is called the

   (A) pupil.

   (B) iris.

   (C) lens.

   (D) cornea.

3. The most likely reason why dinosaurs became extinct was that they

   (A) were killed by erupting volcanoes.

   (B) were eaten as adults by the advancing mammalian groups.

   (C) failed to adapt to a changing environment.

   (D) killed each other in combat.

4. Which of the following is a chemical change?

   (A) Magnetizing a rod of iron

   (B) Burning one pound of coal

   (C) Mixing flake graphite with oil

   (D) Vaporizing one gram of mercury in a vacuum

5. A person with high blood pressure should

   (A) take frequent naps.

   (B) avoid salt.

   (C) eat only iodized salt.

   (D) exercise vigorously.

6. One-celled animals belong to the group of living things known as

   (A) protozoa.

   (B) annelida.

   (C) porifera.

   (D) arthropoda.

7. Spiders can be distinguished from insects by the fact that spiders have

   (A) hard outer coverings.

   (B) large abdomens.

   (C) four pairs of legs.

   (D) biting mouth parts.

8. An important ore of uranium is called

   (A) hermatite.

   (B) chalcopyrite.

   (C) bauxite.

   (D) pitchblende.

9. Of the following, the lightest element known on Earth is

   (A) hydrogen.

   (B) oxygen.

   (C) helium.

   (D) air.

10. Of the following gases in the air, the most plentiful is

    (A) argon.

    (B) oxygen.

    (C) nitrogen.

    (D) carbon dioxide.

11. The time it takes for light from the sun to reach the earth is approximately

    (A) four years.

    (B) eight minutes.

    (C) four months.

    (D) sixteen years.

12. Of the following types of clouds, the ones that occur at the greatest altitude are called
    (A) cirrus.
    (B) nimbus.
    (C) cumulus.
    (D) stratus.

13. A new drug for treatment of tuberculosis was being tested in a hospital. Patients in Group A actually received doses of the new drug; those in Group B were given only sugar pills. Group B represents a(n)
    (A) scientific experiment.
    (B) scientific method.
    (C) experimental error.
    (D) experimental control.

14. The statement that carrots help one to see in the dark is
    (A) ridiculous.
    (B) reasonable because orange is a reflective color.
    (C) reasonable because carrots are high in vitamin A.
    (D) reasonable because rabbits see very well at night.

15. Radium is stored in lead containers because
    (A) the lead absorbs the harmful radiation.
    (B) radium is a heavy substance.
    (C) lead prevents the disintegration of the radium.
    (D) lead is cheap.

16. The type of joint that attaches the arm to the shoulder blade is known as a
    (A) hinge.
    (B) pivot.
    (C) immovable.
    (D) ball and socket.

17. Limes were eaten by British sailors in order to
    (A) justify their nickname, "limeys."
    (B) pucker their mouths to resist the wind.
    (C) satisfy their craving for something acid.
    (D) prevent scurvy.

18. The time that it takes for the Earth to rotate 45° is
    (A) 1 hour.
    (B) 4 hours.
    (C) 3 hours.
    (D) 10 hours.

19. Of the following glands, the one that regulates the metabolic rate is the
    (A) adrenal.
    (B) thyroid.
    (C) salivary.
    (D) thymus.

20. All of the following are amphibia EXCEPT the
    (A) salamander.
    (B) frog.
    (C) lizard.
    (D) toad.

practice test

GO ON TO THE NEXT PAGE

21. Of the following planets, the one that has the shortest revolutionary period around the sun is
    (A) Earth.
    (B) Jupiter.
    (C) Mercury.
    (D) Venus.

22. The term ft./sec. is a unit of
    (A) mass.
    (B) speed.
    (C) length.
    (D) density.

23. A circuit breaker is used in many homes instead of a
    (A) switch.
    (B) fire extinguisher.
    (C) fuse.
    (D) meter box.

24. What is the name of the negative particle that circles the nucleus of the atom?
    (A) Neutron
    (B) Meson
    (C) Proton
    (D) Electron

25. Which of the following rocks can be dissolved with a weak acid?
    (A) Sandstone
    (B) Gneiss
    (C) Granite
    (D) Limestone

STOP! DO NOT CONTINUE ON UNTIL TOLD TO DO SO. IF YOU FINISH BEFORE THE TIME IS UP, YOU MAY CHECK OVER YOUR WORK ON THIS PART ONLY.

PART 2: ARITHMETIC REASONING

Directions: This test has 30 questions on arithmetic reasoning. Each question is followed by four possible answers. Decide which answer is correct, then blacken the space on your answer form that has the same number and letter as your choice. Use your scratch paper for any figuring you wish to do.

Sample Items

S1. A person buys a sandwich for $2.90, soda for 75¢, and pie for 90¢. What is the total cost?

   (A) $3.85
   (B) $4.45
   (C) $4.55
   (D) $4.65

The correct answer is (C). The total cost is $4.55.

S2. If 8 workers are needed to run 4 machines, how many workers are needed to run 20 machines?

   (A) 16
   (B) 32
   (C) 36
   (D) 40

The correct answer is (D). The number needed is 40.

Your score on this test will be based on the number of questions you answer correctly. You should try to answer every question. Do not spend too much time on any one question.

Notice that Part 2 begins with question number 1. When you begin, be sure to start with question 1 in Part 2 of your test booklet and 1 in Part 2 on your answer form.

DO NOT TURN PAGE UNTIL TOLD TO DO SO.

practice test

TIME: 36 Minutes—30 Questions

1. A man owned 75 shares of stock worth $50 each. The corporation declared a dividend of 8%, payable in stock. How many shares did he then own?

    (A) 81 shares

    (B) 90 shares

    (C) 80 shares

    (D) 85 shares

2. A certain type of siding for a house costs $10.50 per square yard. What does it cost for the siding for a wall 4 yards wide and 60 feet long?

    (A) $800

    (B) $840

    (C) $2,520

    (D) $3,240

3. A gallon contains 4 quarts. A cartoning machine can fill 120 one-quart cartons a minute. How long will it take to put 600 gallons of orange juice into cartons?

    (A) 1 minute 15 seconds

    (B) 5 minutes

    (C) 10 minutes

    (D) 20 minutes

4. A typist uses lengthwise a sheet of paper 9 inches by 12 inches. She leaves a 1-inch margin on each side and a $1\frac{1}{2}$-inch margin on top and bottom. What fractional part of the page is used for typing?

    (A) $\dfrac{21}{22}$

    (B) $\dfrac{7}{12}$

    (C) $\dfrac{5}{9}$

    (D) $\dfrac{3}{4}$

5. A student deposited in her savings account the money she had saved during the week. Find the amount of her deposit if she had 10 one-dollar bills, 9 half dollars, 8 quarters, 16 dimes, and 25 nickels.

    (A) $16.20

    (B) $17.42

    (C) $18.60

    (D) $19.35

6. How many minutes are there in 1 day?

    (A) 60

    (B) 1,440

    (C) 24

    (D) 1,440 × 60

7. One year, the postage rate for sending 1 ounce of mail first class was increased from 25 cents to 29 cents. The percent of increase in the postage rate was most nearly

    (A) 12%

    (B) 14%

    (C) 16%

    (D) 18%

8. On a scale drawing, a line $\frac{1}{4}$ inch long represents a length of 1 foot. On the same drawing, what length represents 4 feet?

    (A) 1 inch

    (B) 2 inches

    (C) 3 inches

    (D) 4 inches

9. What is the greatest number of half-pint bottles that can be filled from a 10-gallon can of milk?

    (A) 160

    (B) 170

    (C) 16

    (D) 17

10. If 6 people can paint a fence in 2 days, how many people, working at the same uniform rate, can finish it in 1 day?

    (A) 2

    (B) 3

    (C) 12

    (D) 14

11. A team won 2 games and lost 10. The fraction of its games won is correctly expressed as

    (A) $\dfrac{1}{6}$

    (B) $\dfrac{1}{5}$

    (C) $\dfrac{4}{5}$

    (D) $\dfrac{5}{6}$

12. How much time is there between 8:30 A.M. today and 3:15 A.M. tomorrow?

    (A) $17\dfrac{3}{4}$ hrs.

    (B) $18\dfrac{2}{3}$ hrs.

    (C) $18\dfrac{1}{2}$ hrs.

    (D) $18\dfrac{3}{4}$ hrs.

13. A clerk is asked to file 800 cards. If he can file cards at the rate of 80 cards an hour, the number of cards remaining to be filed after 7 hours of work is

    (A) 140

    (B) 240

    (C) 250

    (D) 260

14. A telephone pole 60 feet high casts a shadow 80 feet long at the same time that a nearby tree casts a shadow 120 feet. What is the height of the tree?

    (A) 80 feet

    (B) 90 feet

    (C) 120 feet

    (D) 150 feet

15. A plane left New York at 3:30 P.M. EST and arrived in Los Angeles at 4:15 P.M. PST. How long did the flight take?

    (A) 7 hours 15 minutes

    (B) 6 hours 45 minutes

    (C) 3 hours 45 minutes

    (D) 3 hours 15 minutes

16. If a barrel has a capacity of 120 gallons, it will contain how many gallons when it is two-fifths full?

    (A) 36 gal.

    (B) 48 gal.

    (C) 60 gal.

    (D) 72 gal.

17. If a salary of $20,000 is subject to a 20 percent deduction, the net salary is

    (A) $14,000

    (B) $15,500

    (C) $16,000

    (D) $16,500

18. If $2,500 is the cost of repairing 100 square yards of pavement, the cost of repairing five square yards is

    (A) $125

    (B) $130

    (C) $135

    (D) $140

GO ON TO THE NEXT PAGE

19. A car can travel 24 miles on a gallon of gasoline. How many gallons will be used on a 192-mile trip?

    (A) 8 gal.

    (B) 9 gal.

    (C) 10 gal.

    (D) 11 gal.

20. If an annual salary of $21,600 is increased by a bonus of $720 and by a service increment of $1,200, the total pay rate is

    (A) $22,320

    (B) $22,800

    (C) $23,320

    (D) $23,520

21. A man takes out a $5,000 life insurance policy at a yearly rate of $29.62 per $1,000. What is the yearly premium?

    (A) $ 90.10

    (B) $100.10

    (C) $126.10

    (D) $148.10

22. On her maiden voyage, the *S.S. United States* made the trip from New York to England in 3 days, 10 hours and 40 minutes, beating the record set by the *R.M.S. Queen Mary* in 1938 by 10 hours and 2 minutes. How long did it take the *Queen Mary* to make the trip?

    (A) 3 days 20 hrs. 42 mins.

    (B) 3 days 15 hrs. 38 mins.

    (C) 3 days 12 hrs. 2 mins.

    (D) 3 days 8 hrs. 12 mins.

23. Gary bought a shirt for $15.00 and a tie for $3.95. He gave the clerk $20.00. How much change did Gary get?

    (A) $2.05

    (B) $1.95

    (C) $1.05

    (D) $ .05

24. If erasers cost 8¢ each for the first 250, 7¢ each for the next 250, and 5¢ for every eraser thereafter, how many erasers may be purchased for $50?

    (A) 600

    (B) 750

    (C) 850

    (D) 1000

25. An inch on a map represents 200 miles. On the same map, a distance of 375 miles is represented by

    (A) $1\frac{1}{2}$ inches.

    (B) $1\frac{7}{8}$ inches.

    (C) $2\frac{1}{4}$ inches.

    (D) $2\frac{3}{4}$ inches.

26. The library charges 5¢ for the first day and 2¢ for each additional day that a book is overdue. If a borrower paid 65¢ in late charges, for how many days was the book overdue?

    (A) 15

    (B) 21

    (C) 25

    (D) 31

27. A pile of magazines is 4 feet high. If each magazine is $\frac{3}{4}$ of an inch thick, the number of magazines is

    (A) 36

    (B) 48

    (C) 64

    (D) 96

28. Potatoes are selling at $1.59 for a 5-pound bag. The cost for 10 pounds is

    (A) $1.59 × 10

    (B) $1.59 × 2

    (C) $1.59 × 50

    (D) $1.59 × 5 ÷ 10

29. Don and Frank started from the same point and drove in opposite directions. Don's rate of travel was 50 miles per hour. Frank's rate of travel was 40 miles per hour. How many miles apart were they at the end of 2 hours?

    (A) 90
    (B) 140
    (C) 160
    (D) 180

30. A folding chair regularly sells for $29.50. How much money is saved if the chair is bought at a 20% discount?

    (A) $4.80
    (B) $5.90
    (C) $6.20
    (D) $7.40

STOP! DO NOT TURN THIS PAGE UNTIL TOLD TO DO SO. IF YOU FINISH BEFORE THE TIME IS UP, YOU MAY CHECK OVER YOUR WORK ON THIS PART ONLY.

PART 3: WORD KNOWLEDGE

Directions: This test has 35 questions about the meanings of words. Each question has an italicized word. You are to decide which one of the four words in the choices most nearly means the same as the italicized word, then mark the space on your answer form that has the same number and letter as your choice.

Sample Items

S1. *Mended* most nearly means

   (A) repaired.

   (B) torn.

   (C) clean.

   (D) tied.

The correct answer is (A). *Mended* means *fixed* or *repaired*.

S2. It was a *small* table.

   (A) sturdy

   (B) round

   (C) cheap

   (D) little

The correct answer is (D). *Little* means the same as *small*.

Your score on this test will be based on the number of questions you answer correctly. You should try to answer every question. Do not spend too much time on any one question.

When you begin, be sure to start with question 1 in Part 3 of your test booklet and 1 in Part 3 on your answer form.

DO NOT TURN PAGE UNTIL TOLD TO DO SO.

TIME: 11 Minutes—35 Questions

1. *Superiority* most nearly means
   (A) abundance
   (B) popularity
   (C) permanence
   (D) excellence

2. *Absurd* most nearly means
   (A) disgusting
   (B) foolish
   (C) reasonable
   (D) very old

3. Be careful, that liquid is *inflammable*!
   (A) poisonous
   (B) valuable
   (C) explosive
   (D) likely to give off fumes

4. *Conscious* most nearly means
   (A) surprised
   (B) afraid
   (C) disappointed
   (D) aware

5. *Exhibit* most nearly means
   (A) display
   (B) trade
   (C) sell
   (D) label

6. We *assumed* that Jack had been elected.
   (A) knew
   (B) wished
   (C) decided
   (D) supposed

7. *Counterfeit* most nearly means
   (A) mysterious
   (B) false
   (C) unreadable
   (D) priceless

8. *Expertly* most nearly means
   (A) awkwardly
   (B) quickly
   (C) skillfully
   (D) unexpectedly

9. *Marshy* most nearly means
   (A) swampy
   (B) sandy
   (C) wooded
   (D) rocky

10. The children pledged *allegiance* to the flag.
    (A) freedom
    (B) homeland
    (C) protection
    (D) loyalty

11. The cashier *yearned* for a vacation.
    (A) begged
    (B) longed
    (C) saved
    (D) applied

12. *Summit* most nearly means
    (A) face
    (B) top
    (C) base
    (D) side

13. The driver *heeded* the traffic signals.
    (A) worried about
    (B) ignored
    (C) disagreed with
    (D) took notice of

14. *Vigorously* most nearly means
    (A) sleepily
    (B) thoughtfully
    (C) energetically
    (D) sadly

15. *Imitate* most nearly means
    (A) copy
    (B) attract
    (C) study
    (D) appreciate

16. The *severity* of their criticism upset us.
    (A) harshness
    (B) suddenness
    (C) method
    (D) unfairness

17. *Incredible* most nearly means
    (A) thrilling
    (B) convincing
    (C) uninteresting
    (D) unbelievable

18. We made a very *leisurely* trip to California.
    (A) roundabout
    (B) unhurried
    (C) unforgettable
    (D) tiresome

19. *Gratitude* most nearly means
    (A) thankfulness
    (B) excitement
    (C) disappointment
    (D) sympathy

20. *Familiar* most nearly means
    (A) welcome
    (B) dreaded
    (C) rare
    (D) well-known

21. He had an *acute* pain in his back.
    (A) dull
    (B) slight
    (C) alarming
    (D) sharp

22. *Bewildered* most nearly means
    (A) worded
    (B) offended
    (C) puzzled
    (D) delighted

23. *Conclusion* most nearly means
    (A) theme
    (B) suspense
    (C) end
    (D) beginning

24. She likes the *aroma* of fresh-brewed coffee.
    (A) flavor
    (B) warmth
    (C) fragrance
    (D) steam

25. *Nonessential* most nearly means
    (A) damaged
    (B) unnecessary
    (C) expensive
    (D) foreign-made

practice test

GO ON TO THE NEXT PAGE

26. *Amplified* most nearly means
    (A) expanded
    (B) summarized
    (C) analyzed
    (D) shouted

27. The vase remained *intact* after it was dropped.
    (A) unattended
    (B) undamaged
    (C) a total loss
    (D) unmoved

28. Penicillin is a *potent* drug.
    (A) harmless
    (B) possible
    (C) effective
    (D) drinkable

29. *Terminate* most nearly means
    (A) continue
    (B) go by train
    (C) begin
    (D) end

30. The prisoner is a *notorious* bank robber.
    (A) convicted
    (B) dangerous
    (C) well-known
    (D) escaped

31. *Fatal* most nearly means
    (A) accidental
    (B) deadly
    (C) dangerous
    (D) beautiful

32. *Indigent* people are entitled to food stamps.
    (A) poor
    (B) lazy
    (C) angry
    (D) homeless

33. *Technique* most nearly means
    (A) computed
    (B) engineered
    (C) calculation
    (D) method

34. *Vocation* most nearly means
    (A) school
    (B) examination
    (C) occupation
    (D) carpentry

35. One should eat only *mature* fruits.
    (A) edible
    (B) washed
    (C) ripe
    (D) sprayed

STOP! DO NOT CONTINUE ON UNTIL TOLD TO DO SO. IF YOU FINISH BEFORE THE TIME IS UP, YOU MAY CHECK OVER YOUR WORK ON THIS PART ONLY.

PART 4: PARAGRAPH COMPREHENSION

Directions: This test contains 15 items measuring your ability to obtain information from written passages. You will find one or more paragraphs of reading material followed by incomplete statements or questions. You are to read the paragraph(s) and select the one of the lettered choices that best completes the statement or answers the question.

Sample Items

S1. From a building designer's standpoint, three things that make a home livable are the client, the building site, and the amount of money the client has to spend. According to the passage, to make a home livable

(A) the prospective piece of land makes little difference.

(B) it can be built on any piece of land.

(C) the design must fit the owner's income and the building site.

(D) the design must fit the designer's income.

The correct answer is (C). The design must fit the owner's income and the building site.

S2. In certain areas, water is so scarce that every attempt is made to conserve it. For instance, on one oasis in the Sahara Desert the amount of water necessary for each date palm tree has been carefully determined.
How much water is each tree given?

(A) No water at all

(B) Exactly the amount required

(C) Water only if it is healthy

(D) Water on alternate days

The correct answer is (B). The correct answer is exactly the amount required.

Your score on this test will be based on the number of questions you answer correctly. You should try to answer every question. Do not spend too much time on any one question.

When you begin, be sure to start with question 1 in Part 4 of your test booklet and 1 in Part 4 on your answer form.

DO NOT TURN PAGE UNTIL TOLD TO DO SO.

TIME: 13 Minutes—15 Questions

1. Numerous benefits to the employer as well as to the worker have resulted from physical examinations of employees. Such examinations are intended primarily as a means of increasing efficiency and production, and they have been found to accomplish these ends.

   The passage best supports the statement that physical examinations

   (A) may serve to increase output.

   (B) are required in some plants.

   (C) often reveal serious defects previously unknown.

   (D) always are worth more than they cost.

2. Examination of traffic accident statistics reveals that traffic accidents are frequently the result of violations of traffic laws—and usually the violations are the result of illegal and dangerous driving behavior rather than the result of mechanical defects or poor road conditions.

   According to this passage, the majority of dangerous traffic violations are caused by

   (A) poor driving.

   (B) bad roads.

   (C) unsafe cars.

   (D) unwise traffic laws.

3. Complaints from the public are no longer regarded by government officials as mere nuisances. Instead, complaints are often welcomed because they frequently bring into the open conditions and faults in operation and service that should be corrected.

   This passage most nearly means that

   (A) government officials now realize that complaints from the public are necessary.

   (B) faulty operations and services are not brought into the open except by complaints from the public.

   (C) government officials now realize that complaints from the public are in reality a sign of a well-run agency.

   (D) complaints from the public can be useful in indicating needs for improvement in operation and service.

4. In a pole-vaulting competition, the judge decides on the minimum height to be jumped. The vaulter may attempt to jump any height above the minimum. Using flexible fiberglass poles, vaulters have jumped as high as 18 feet $8\frac{1}{4}$ inches.

   According to the passage, pole vaulters

   (A) may attempt to jump any height in competition.

   (B) must jump higher than 18' $8\frac{1}{4}$ " to win.

   (C) must jump higher than the height set by the judge.

   (D) must use fiberglass poles.

5. When gas is leaking, any spark or sudden flame can ignite it. This can create a "flashback," which burns off the gas in a quick puff of smoke and flame. But the real danger is in a large leak, which can cause an explosion.

   According to the passage, the real danger from leaking gas is a(n)

   (A) flashback.

   (B) puff of smoke and flame.

   (C) explosion.

   (D) spark.

6. A year—the time it takes the Earth to go exactly once around the sun—is not 365 days. It is actually 365 days 6 hours 9 minutes $9\frac{1}{2}$ seconds, or $365\frac{1}{4}$ days. Leap years make up for this discrepancy by adding an extra day once every four years.

The purpose of leap year is to

(A) adjust for the fact that it takes $365\frac{1}{4}$ days for the Earth to circle the sun.

(B) make up for time lost in the work year.

(C) occur every four years.

(D) allow for differences in the length of a year in each time zone.

7. Any business not provided with capable substitutes to fill all important positions is a weak business. Therefore, a foreman should train each man not only to perform his own particular duties but also to do those of two or three positions.

The paragraph best supports the statement that

(A) dependence on substitutes is a sign of a weak organization.

(B) training will improve the strongest organization.

(C) the foreman should be the most expert at any particular job under him.

(D) vacancies in vital positions should be provided for in advance.

8. In the business districts of cities, collections from street letter boxes are made at stated hours, and collectors are required to observe these hours exactly. Anyone using these boxes can rely with certainty upon the time of the next collection.

The paragraph best supports the statement that

(A) mail collections in business districts are more frequent during the day than at night.

(B) mail collectors are required to observe safety regulations exactly.

(C) mail collections are made often in business districts.

(D) mail is collected in business districts on a regular schedule.

9. The increasing size of business organizations has resulted in less personal contact between superior and subordinate. Consequently, business executives today depend more upon records and reports to secure information and exercise control over the operations of various departments.

The increasing size of business organizations

(A) has caused a complete cleavage between employer and employee.

(B) has resulted in less personal contact between superior and subordinate.

(C) has tended toward class distinctions in large organizations.

(D) has resulted in a better means of controlling the operations of various departments.

10. Kindling temperature is the lowest temperature at which a substance catches fire and continues to burn. Different fuels have different kindling temperatures. Paper catches fire easily because it has a low kindling temperature. Coal, because of its high kindling temperature, requires much heat before it will begin to burn. Matches are tipped with phosphorus, or some

GO ON TO THE NEXT PAGE

other low-kindling material, to permit the small amount of heat produced by friction to ignite the match.

The property of phosphorus that makes it ideal for use on matches is

(A) its light color.

(B) its high kindling temperature.

(C) its low kindling temperature.

(D) the fact that it contains carbon.

Questions 11 and 12 are based on the following passage.

Racketeers are primarily concerned with business affairs, legitimate or otherwise, and preferably those that are close to the margin of legitimacy. They get their best opportunities from business organizations that meet the needs of large sections of the public for goods and services that are defined as illegitimate by the same public, such as gambling, illicit drugs, etc. In contrast to the thief, the racketeer and the establishments he or she controls deliver goods and services for money received.

11. According to the above passage, racketeering, unlike theft, involves

(A) payment for goods received.

(B) unlawful activities.

(C) organized gangs.

(D) objects of value.

12. It can be deduced that suppression of racketeering is difficult because

(A) many people want services that are not obtainable through legitimate sources.

(B) racketeers are generally engaged in fully legitimate enterprises.

(C) victims of racketeers are not guilty of violating the law.

(D) laws prohibiting gambling are unenforceable.

Questions 13–15 are based on the passage shown below.

The two systems of weights and measures are the English system and the Metric system. The English system uses units such as foot, pound, and quart; the Metric system uses meter, gram, and liter.

The Metric system was first adopted in France in 1795 and is now used by most countries in the world. In the Metric system, the unit of length is the meter, which is one ten-millionth of the distance from the Equator to the North Pole.

The British have changed their system of weights and measures to the Metric system; however, in the United States, there has been much opposition to this change. It would cost billions of dollars to change all our weights and measures to the Metric system.

13. According to the passage above, the Metric system is used

(A) in all of Europe except Great Britain.

(B) in almost all countries of the world.

(C) in only a few countries.

(D) mostly in Europe.

14. The United States has not changed to the Metric system because

(A) the system is too complicated.

(B) the change would be costly.

(C) the system is not accurate.

(D) it is difficult to learn.

15. The meter is equal to

(A) the distance from the Equator to the North Pole.

(B) $\dfrac{1}{1,000,000}$ of the distance from the Equator to the North Pole.

(C) $\dfrac{1}{10,000,000}$ of the distance from the Equator to the North Pole.

(D) $\dfrac{1}{100,000,000}$ of the distance from the Equator to the North Pole.

practice test

STOP! DO NOT TURN THIS PAGE UNTIL TOLD TO DO SO. IF YOU FINISH BEFORE THE TIME IS UP, YOU MAY CHECK OVER YOUR WORK ON THIS PART ONLY.

PART 5: MATHEMATICS KNOWLEDGE

Directions: This is a test of your ability to solve 25 general mathematical problems. You are to select the correct response from the choices given. Then mark the space on your answer form that has the same number and letter as your choice. Use the scratch paper that has been given to you to do any figuring that you need.

Sample Items

S1. If $x + 6 = 7$, then x is equal to

(A) 0

(B) 1

(C) −1

(D) $\dfrac{7}{6}$

The correct answer is (B). The correct answer is 1.

S2. What is the area of the square shown below?

(A) 1 square

(B) 5 square feet

(C) 10 square feet

(D) 25 square feet

The correct answer is (D). The correct answer is 25 square feet.

Your score on this test will be based on the number of questions you answer correctly. You should try to answer every question. Do not spend too much time on any one question.

When you are told to begin, be sure to start with question 1 in Part 5 of your test booklet and 1 in Part 5 on your answer form.

DO NOT TURN PAGE UNTIL TOLD TO DO SO.

TIME: 24 Minutes—25 Questions

1. If you subtract $6a - 4b + 3c$ from a polynomial, you get $4a + 9b - 5c$. What is the polynomial?

   (A) $10a - 5b + 2c$

   (B) $10a + 5b - 2c$

   (C) $24 + 13b - 8c$

   (D) $2a + 5b + 8c$

2. If 50% of $x = 66$, then $x =$

   (A) 33

   (B) 99

   (C) 122

   (D) None of the above

3. If $3x = -5$, then x equals

   (A) $\frac{3}{5}$

   (B) $-\frac{5}{3}$

   (C) $-\frac{3}{5}$

   (D) -2

4. The first digit of the square root of 59043 is

   (A) 2

   (B) 4

   (C) 5

   (D) 7

5. A square is equal in area to a rectangle whose length is 9 and whose width is 4. Find the perimeter of the square.

   (A) 24

   (B) 26

   (C) 34

   (D) 36

6. The value of $\frac{27}{8} \times \frac{24}{9} \div \frac{3}{2} =$

   (A) 6

   (B) $7\frac{2}{9}$

   (C) $8\frac{1}{4}$

   (D) $9\frac{5}{8}$

7. If the perimeter of an equilateral triangle is $6n - 12$, what is the length of the base?

   (A) $3(2n - 4)$

   (B) $2(3n - 6)$

   (C) $3n - 6$

   (D) $2n - 4$

8. Which one of the following is a polygon?

   (A) Circle

   (B) Ellipse

   (C) Star

   (D) Parabola

9. The sum of the inside angles of a regular hexagonal (six-sided) field is

   (A) 360°

   (B) 540°

   (C) 630°

   (D) 720°

10. The area of a rectangle 12 feet by 18 feet is equal to

   (A) 8 square yards.

   (B) 24 square yards.

   (C) 36 square yards.

   (D) 72 square yards.

11. Given the formulas $d = rt$ and $A = r + \dfrac{d}{t}$, which formula below correctly expresses the value of A without using t?

(A) $A = dr$

(B) $A = r + \dfrac{2d}{r}$

(C) $A = 2r + d$

(D) $A = 2r$

12. R is what percent of 1,000?

(A) $0.001R$

(B) $0.01R$

(C) $0.1R$

(D) $1R$

13. The distance in miles around a circular course that has a radius of 35 miles is (use $\pi = \frac{22}{7}$)

(A) 156

(B) 220

(C) 440

(D) 880

14. The expression "3 factorial" equals

(A) $\dfrac{1}{9}$

(B) $\dfrac{1}{6}$

(C) 6

(D) 9

15. If $a = 2b$ and $4b = 6c$, then $a =$

(A) $3c$

(B) $4c$

(C) $9c$

(D) $12c$

16. Solve for x: $\dfrac{2x}{7} = 2x^2$

(A) $\dfrac{1}{7}$

(B) $\dfrac{2}{7}$

(C) 2

(D) 7

17. Solve the following equation for C:

$$A^2 = \frac{B^2}{C + D}$$

(A) $C = \dfrac{B^2 - A^2 D}{A^2 B}$

(B) $C = \dfrac{A^2}{B^2} - D$

(C) $C = \dfrac{A^2 + D}{B^2 - D}$

(D) $C = \dfrac{B^2}{A^2} - D$

18. The expression $-1(3 - 2)$ is equal to

(A) $-3 + 2$

(B) $-3 - 2$

(C) $3 - 2$

(D) $3 + 2$

19. The reciprocal of 5 is

(A) 1.0

(B) 0.5

(C) 0.2

(D) 0.1

GO ON TO THE NEXT PAGE

20. What is the area, in square inches, of a circle whose radius measures 7 inches? (use $\pi = \frac{22}{7}$)

   (A) 22

   (B) 44

   (C) 154

   (D) 616

21. Evaluate the expression $5a - 4x - 3y$ if $a = -2$, $x = -10$, and $y = 5$.

   (A) + 15

   (B) +25

   (C) −65

   (D) −35

22. If one book costs c dollars, what is the cost, in dollars, of m books?

   (A) $m + c$

   (B) mc

   (C) $\dfrac{c}{m}$

   (D) $\dfrac{m}{c}$

23. A purse contains 16 coins in dimes and quarters. If the value of the coins is $2.50, how many dimes are there?

   (A) 6

   (B) 8

   (C) 9

   (D) 10

24. Solve for x: $\dfrac{x}{2} - \dfrac{x}{5} = 3$

   (A) 2

   (B) 3

   (C) 5

   (D) 10

25. If the radius of a circle is increased by 3, the circumference is increased by

   (A) 3

   (B) 3π

   (C) 6π

   (D) 6

STOP! DO NOT CONTINUE ON UNTIL TOLD TO DO SO. IF YOU FINISH BEFORE THE TIME IS UP, YOU MAY CHECK OVER YOUR WORK ON THIS PART ONLY.

PART 6: ELECTRONICS INFORMATION

Directions: This is a test of your knowledge of electrical, radio, and electronics information. There are 20 questions. You are to select the correct response from the choices given. Then mark the space on your answer form that has the same number and letter as your choice.

Sample Items

S1. What does the abbreviation AC stand for?
   (A) Additional charge
   (B) Alternating coil
   (C) Alternating current
   (D) Ampere current

The correct answer is (C). The correct answer is alternating current.

S2. Which of the following has the least resistance?
   (A) Wood
   (B) Silver
   (C) Rubber
   (D) Iron

The correct answer is (B). The correct answer is silver.

Your score on this test will be based on the number of questions you answer correctly. You should try to answer every question. Do not spend too much time on any one question.

When you are told to begin, be sure to start with question 1 in Part 6 of your test booklet and 1 in Part 6 on your answer form.

DO NOT TURN PAGE UNTIL TOLD TO DO SO.

TIME: 9 Minutes—20 Questions

1. The core of an electromagnet is usually
   (A) aluminum.
   (B) brass.
   (C) lead.
   (D) iron.

2. An electrician should consider all electrical equipment "alive" unless he definitely knows otherwise. The main reason for this practice is to avoid
   (A) doing unnecessary work.
   (B) energizing the wrong circuit.
   (C) personal injury.
   (D) de-energizing a live circuit.

3. If *voltage* is represented by V, *current* by I, and *resistance* by R, then the one of the following that correctly states Ohm's law is
   (A) $R = V \times I$
   (B) $R = \dfrac{I}{V}$
   (C) $V = I \times R$
   (D) $V = \dfrac{I}{R}$

4. The device used to change AC to DC is a
   (A) frequency changer.
   (B) transformer.
   (C) regulator.
   (D) rectifier.

5.

The reading of the kilowatt-hour meter is
   (A) 9672
   (B) 1779
   (C) 2770
   (D) 0762

6. The device that is often used to change the voltage in alternating current circuits is the
   (A) contactor.
   (B) converter.
   (C) rectifier.
   (D) transformer.

7. Electrical contacts are opened or closed when the electrical current energizes the coils of a device called a
   (A) reactor.
   (B) transtat.
   (C) relay.
   (D) thermostat.

8. To determine directly whether finished wire installations possess resistance between conductors and ground, use
   (A) clamps.
   (B) set screws.
   (C) shields.
   (D) a megger.

9.

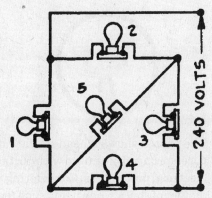

The five lamps shown are each rated at 120 volts, 60 watts. If all are good lamps, lamp 5 will be

(A) much brighter than normal.

(B) about its normal brightness.

(C) much dimmer than normal.

(D) completely dark.

10. Microfarads are units of measurement usually associated with

(A) sockets.

(B) switches.

(C) capacitors.

(D) connectors.

11. The three elements of a transistor are the

(A) collector, base, and emitter.

(B) collector, grid, and cathode.

(C) plate, grid, and emitter.

(D) plate, base, and cathode.

12. Is it proper procedure to ground the frame of a portable motor?

(A) No

(B) No, if it is AC

(C) Yes, unless the tool is specifically designed for use without a ground

(D) Yes, if the operation takes place only at less than 150 volts

13. In comparing Nos. 00, 8, 12, and 6 A.W.G. wires, the smallest of the group is

(A) No. 00.

(B) No. 8.

(C) No. 12.

(D) No. 6.

14.

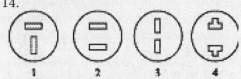

The convenience outlet that is known as a *polarized* outlet is number

(A) 1

(B) 2

(C) 3

(D) 4

15. In a house bell circuit, the push button for ringing the bell is generally connected in the secondary of the transformer feeding the bell. One reason for doing this is to

(A) save power.

(B) keep line voltage out of the push button circuit.

(C) prevent the bell from burning out.

(D) prevent arcing of the vibrator contact points in the bell.

GO ON TO THE NEXT PAGE

16.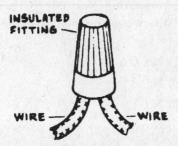

Wires are often spliced by the use of a fitting like the one shown above. The use of this fitting does away with the need for

(A) skinning.

(B) cleaning.

(C) twisting.

(D) soldering.

17. In order to control a lamp from two different positions, it is necessary to use

(A) two single-pole switches.

(B) one single-pole switch and one four-way switch.

(C) two three-way switches.

(D) one single-pole switch and two four-way switches.

18. In electronic circuits, the symbol shown below usually represents a

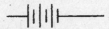

(A) resistor.

(B) battery.

(C) capacitor.

(D) transformer.

19.

The sketch shows a head-on view of a three-pronged plug used with portable electrical power tools. Considering the danger of shock when using such tools, it is evident that the function of the U-shaped prong is to

(A) ensure that the other two prongs enter the outlet with the proper polarity.

(B) provide a half-voltage connection when doing light work.

(C) prevent accidental pulling of the plug from the outlet.

(D) connect the metallic shell of the tool motor to ground.

20. A compound motor usually has

(A) only a shunt field.

(B) both a shunt and a series field.

(C) only a series field.

(D) no brushes.

IF YOU FINISH BEFORE THE TIME IS UP, YOU MAY CHECK OVER YOUR WORK ON THIS PART ONLY. END OF FIRST SIX SUBTESTS.

ANSWER KEYS AND EXPLANATIONS

Part 1: General Science

1. (C)	6. (A)	11. (B)	16. (D)	21. (C)
2. (D)	7. (C)	12. (A)	17. (D)	22. (B)
3. (C)	8. (D)	13. (D)	18. (C)	23. (C)
4. (B)	9. (A)	14. (C)	19. (B)	24. (D)
5. (B)	10. (C)	15. (A)	20. (C)	25. (D)

1. **The correct answer is (C).** When organic matter decays, it decomposes into its constituent elements. These elements are returned to the soil, thus increasing its fertility.

2. **The correct answer is (D).** The cornea, a transparent tissue, forms the outer coat of the eyeball covering the iris and pupil.

3. **The correct answer is (C).** The extinction of all sizes and varieties of dinosaurs all over the world can be explained neither by local phenomena nor on a one-by-one basis. The most reasonable assumption is that the dinosaurs failed to adapt and were unable to survive as climatic conditions changed radically.

4. **The correct answer is (B).** Combustion is a chemical process.

5. **The correct answer is (B).** Salt contributes to high blood pressure. The critical element in the action of salt upon the blood pressure is sodium. Iodine, or the lack of it, plays no role in raising blood pressure.

6. **The correct answer is (A).** Protozoa are one-celled animals. Annelida are worms; porifera are sponges; arthropoda are spiders and crustaceans.

7. **The correct answer is (C).** All spiders have four pairs of legs. True insects have three pairs of legs.

8. **The correct answer is (D).** Uranium is found in pitchblende and other rare metals. Hematite is a source of iron; chalcopyrite is an ore of copper; bauxite is a source of aluminum.

9. **The correct answer is (A).** The atomic weight of hydrogen is 1.0080, that of helium 4.003, and of oxygen 16.00. Air is not an element but a mixture of gases.

10. **The correct answer is (C).** Nitrogen constitutes about four fifths of the atmosphere by volume.

11. **The correct answer is (B).** Light travels at the rate of 186,300 miles per second. The sun is 92,900,000 miles from the Earth, so its light arrives here in just over 8 minutes.

12. **The correct answer is (A).** Cirrus clouds occur at 20,000 to 40,000 feet and are made up of ice crystals. Nimbus clouds are gray rain clouds; cumulus clouds are fluffy white clouds; stratus clouds are long, low clouds, generally at altitudes of 2,000 to 7,000 feet.

13. **The correct answer is (D).** Group B served as the control group. If the condition of patients in Group A were to improve significantly more than that of patients in Group B, scientists might have reason to believe in the effectiveness of the drug.

14. **The correct answer is (C).** Vitamin A deficiency leads to poor night vision. Since carrots are high in vitamin A, they should have a positive effect upon night vision, although eating large quantities of carrots will not in itself ensure perfect night vision.

15. **The correct answer is (A).** Radiation cannot pass through lead.

16. **The correct answer is (D).** Ball-and-socket joints permit movement in almost all directions.

17. **The correct answer is (D).** Scurvy is a disease caused by a vitamin C deficiency. Limes are rich in vitamin C.

18. **The correct answer is (C).** The Earth rotates 360° in 24 hours; therefore, it rotates 45° in 3 hours.

19. **The correct answer is (B).** The thyroid gland regulates the metabolic rate. The adrenal glands secrete hormones that regulate one's reaction to emergencies, among other things. Salivary glands secrete oral saliva. The thymus gland influences growth and development.

20. **The correct answer is (C).** A lizard is a reptile.

21. **The correct answer is (C).** Mercury is closest to the sun; therefore, it has the shortest revolutionary period around the sun.

22. **The correct answer is (B).**

$$\frac{\text{Distance}}{\text{Time}} = \text{Speed}$$

23. **The correct answer is (C).** Circuit breakers serve exactly the same function as fuses. Should wires become overheated for any reason, the circuit breaker will "trip," thus breaking the circuit and interrupting the flow of electricity. Fuse burnout creates the same protective interruption of current.

24. **The correct answer is (D).** An electron is a negative particle. A proton is positively charged; a neutron is neutral and without charge; a meson has both positive and negative charges.

25. **The correct answer is (D).** Limestone, a sedimentary rock composed of calcium carbonate, can be dissolved with a weak acid.

Part 2: Arithmetic Reasoning

1. (A)	7. (C)	13. (B)	19. (A)	25. (B)
2. (B)	8. (A)	14. (B)	20. (D)	26. (D)
3. (D)	9. (A)	15. (C)	21. (D)	27. (C)
4. (B)	10. (C)	16. (B)	22. (A)	28. (B)
5. (D)	11. (A)	17. (C)	23. (C)	29. (D)
6. (B)	12. (D)	18. (A)	24. (B)	30. (B)

1. **The correct answer is (A).** 8% of 75 = 6 shares; 75 shares + 6 shares = 81 shares.

2. **The correct answer is (B).** 60 ft. = 20 yd. The wall is 4 yd. × 20 yd. = 80 sq. yd. $10.50 × 80 = $840.

3. **The correct answer is (D).**

   600 gallons = 2400 quarts;

   $\frac{2400}{120} = 20$ minutes.

4. **The correct answer is (B).** The whole paper is 9 in. × 12 in. = 108 in.^{2} Subtract the margin:

   9 in. – 1 in. – 1 in. = 7 in.;

   12 in. – $1\frac{1}{2}$ in. – $1\frac{1}{2}$ in. = 9 in.

   The paper she uses is 7 in. × 9 in. = 63 in.^{2}

   $\frac{63}{108} = \frac{7}{12}$ is used for typing.

5. **The correct answer is (D).**

10 ×	$1.00	=	$10.00
9 ×	0.50	=	4.50
8 ×	0.25	=	2.00
16 ×	0.10	=	1.60
25 ×	0.05	=	1.25
			$19.35

6. **The correct answer is (B).** 60 minutes in one hour; 24 hours in one day; 60 × 24 = 1,440 minutes.

7. **The correct answer is (C).** To find the percent of increase, subtract the original figure from the new figure. Then divide the amount of change by the original figure.

   $$\frac{29-25}{25} = \frac{4}{25} = 0.16 = 16\%$$

8. **The correct answer is (A).** $4 \times \frac{1}{4}$ inch = 1 inch

9. **The correct answer is (A).** 8 pts. in 1 gal.; 80 pts. in 10 gal.; 160 half-pints in 10 gal.

10. **The correct answer is (C).** Common sense will tell you that twice as many people will paint the fence in half the time.

11. **The correct answer is (A).** The team won 2 games and lost 10, so it played 12 games. $\frac{2}{12} = \frac{1}{6}$.

12. **The correct answer is (D).**

    From 8:30 A.M. until noon today:

    12:00 = 11:60
    – 8:30 = 8:30
    3 hrs. 30 min.

    From noon until midnight: 12 hrs.
    From midnight until 3:15 A.M.:

    + 3 hrs. 15 min.
    18 hrs. 45 min.

    $= 18\frac{3}{4}$ hours

13. **The correct answer is (B).** 80 cards × 7 hours = 560 cards filed; 800 − 560 = 240 cards remaining.

14. **The correct answer is (B).** Let x = height of tree. $\frac{60}{80} = \frac{x}{120}$; $80x = 7200$; $x = 90$ feet.

15. **The correct answer is (C).** Time difference between New York and Los Angeles is 3 hours. 4:15 P.M. − 3:30 P.M. = 45 minutes; 3 hours + 45 minutes = 3 hours 45 minutes for flight time.

16. **The correct answer is (B).**

$$\frac{2}{1\cancel{5}} \times \frac{\cancel{120}^{24}}{1} = 48 \text{ gal.}$$

17. **The correct answer is (C).** If 20% is deducted, the net salary is 80%. $20,000 × 80% = $20,000 × 0.80 = $16,000.

18. **The correct answer is (A).** $2,500 ÷ 100 = $25 per square yard; 25 × 5 = $125.

19. **The correct answer is (A).** 192 ÷ 24 = 8 gal.

20. **The correct answer is (D).** $21,600 + $720 + $1,200 = $23,520.

21. **The correct answer is (D).** $29.62 × 5 = $148.10.

22. **The correct answer is (A).**

```
  3 days 10 hrs. 40 min.
+        10 hrs.  2 min.
  3 days 20 hrs. 42 min.
```

23. **The correct answer is (C).** $15 + $3.95 = $18.95; $20.00 − $18.95 = $1.05.

24. **The correct answer is (B).** 250 × 0.08 = $20.00; 250 × 0.07 = $17.50; 500 erasers cost $37.50; $50.00 − $37.50 = $12.50. Let x = additional erasers purchased.

$0.05x = 12.50$; $x = \dfrac{12.50}{0.05} = 250$; 500 + 250 = 750 erasers.

25. **The correct answer is (B).** $1 : 200 = x : 375$; $200x = 375$; $x = 375 ÷ 200 = 1.875 = 1\frac{7}{8}$ inches.

26. **The correct answer is (D).** 65¢ − 5¢ for the first day = 60¢ for the other days. 60¢ ÷ 2¢ = 30 other days. The book was 31 days overdue.

27. **The correct answer is (C).**

4 feet = 48 inches; $48 ÷ \dfrac{3}{4} = \dfrac{\cancel{48}^{16}}{1} \times \dfrac{4}{\cancel{3}_1}$

= 64 magazines.

28. **The correct answer is (B).** 10 pounds = 2 × 5 pounds, so the cost of 10 pounds is 2 times the cost of 5 pounds.

29. **The correct answer is (D).** Don drove 50 miles × 2 hours = 100 miles. Frank drove 40 miles × 2 hours = 80 miles. Since they drove in opposite directions, add the two distances to learn that they were 180 miles apart.

30. **The correct answer is (B).** $29.50 × 20% = $29.50 × 0.20 = $5.90 saved.

Part 3: Word Knowledge

1. (D)	8. (C)	15. (A)	22. (C)	29. (D)
2. (B)	9. (A)	16. (A)	23. (C)	30. (C)
3. (C)	10. (D)	17. (D)	24. (C)	31. (B)
4. (D)	11. (B)	18. (B)	25. (B)	32. (A)
5. (A)	12. (B)	19. (A)	26. (A)	33. (D)
6. (D)	13. (D)	20. (D)	27. (B)	34. (C)
7. (B)	14. (C)	21. (D)	28. (C)	35. (C)

1. **The correct answer is (D).** *Superiority* is *excellence*.

2. **The correct answer is (B).** *Absurd* means irrational, unreasonable, or *foolish*.

3. **The correct answer is (C).** *Inflammable* means easily inflamed, hence *explosive*.

4. **The correct answer is (D).** *Conscious* means mentally awake or *aware*.

5. **The correct answer is (A).** To *exhibit* means to show publicly or to *display*. Often one exhibits goods that one hopes to subsequently trade or sell.

6. **The correct answer is (D).** To *assume* is to take for granted or to *suppose*.

7. **The correct answer is (B).** That which is *counterfeit* is an imitation made with intent to defraud, hence *false*.

8. **The correct answer is (C).** That which is done *expertly* is done *skillfully*. It might also be done quickly, but not necessarily so.

9. **The correct answer is (A).** *Marshy* means boggy or *swampy*.

10. **The correct answer is (D).** *Allegiance* means devotion or *loyalty*.

11. **The correct answer is (B).** To *yearn* is to have a great desire for or to be filled with *longing*.

12. **The correct answer is (B).** The *summit* is the *top*.

13. **The correct answer is (D).** To *heed* is to pay attention to or to *take notice of*.

14. **The correct answer is (C).** *Vigorously* means forcefully and *energetically*.

15. **The correct answer is (A).** To *imitate* is to *copy*.

16. **The correct answer is (A).** *Severity* means seriousness, extreme strictness, or *harshness*. It does not necessarily imply unfairness.

17. **The correct answer is (D).** That which is *incredible* is too improbable to believe.

18. **The correct answer is (B).** *Leisure* is freedom from pressure. A leisurely trip is an *unhurried* one.

19. **The correct answer is (A).** *Gratitude* is the state of being grateful or *thankfulness*.

20. **The correct answer is (D).** *Familiar* means *well-known*. (Think of the word *family*.)

21. **The correct answer is (D).** An *acute* pain may well be alarming, but what makes it acute is its *sharpness*.

22. **The correct answer is (C).** To be *bewildered* is to be confused or *puzzled*.

23. **The correct answer is (C).** The *conclusion* is the *end*.

24. **The correct answer is (C).** An *aroma* is a pleasing smell or *fragrance*.

25. **The correct answer is (B).** The prefix *non* means not. That which is not essential is *unnecessary*.

26. **The correct answer is (A).** To *amplify* is to enlarge by adding illustrations or details—in short, to *expand*.

27. **The correct answer is (B).** *Intact* means unimpaired, whole, or *undamaged*.

28. **The correct answer is (C).** *Potent* means powerful or *effective*. The word that means drinkable is "potable."

29. **The correct answer is (D).** To *terminate* is to *end*. The end of a train line is the terminus or terminal.

30. **The correct answer is (C).** *Notorious* means *well-known*, generally in an unfavorable sense.

31. **The correct answer is (B).** *Fatal* means causing death or *deadly*.

32. **The correct answer is (A).** *Indigent* means needy or *poor*. Indigent people might be lazy or homeless, but their indigence is their poverty.

33. **The correct answer is (D).** The *technique* is the *method* by which something is done.

34. **The correct answer is (C).** One's *vocation* is one's *occupation* or calling.

35. **The correct answer is (C).** That which is *mature* is fully aged or *ripe*.

Part 4: Paragraph Comprehension

1. (A)	4. (C)	7. (D)	10. (C)	13. (B)
2. (A)	5. (C)	8. (D)	11. (A)	14. (B)
3. (D)	6. (A)	9. (B)	12. (A)	15. (C)

1. **The correct answer is (A).** The passage states that physical examinations are intended to increase efficiency and production and that they do accomplish these ends.

2. **The correct answer is (A).** The passage states that traffic violations are usually the result of illegal and dangerous driving behavior.

3. **The correct answer is (D).** Complaints frequently bring into the open conditions and faults in operation and service that should be corrected.

4. **The correct answer is (C).** The vaulter may attempt to jump any height above the minimum, which is set by the judge.

5. **The correct answer is (C).** The last sentence in the passage states that the real danger is in a large leak that can cause an explosion.

6. **The correct answer is (A).** The time it takes the Earth to go around the sun is 365¼ days rather than 365 days. Leap years correct for this discrepancy by adding an extra day once every four years.

7. **The correct answer is (D).** The point of the passage is that a business should be prepared to fill unexpected vacancies with pretrained staff members.

8. **The correct answer is (D).** See the first sentence in the reading passage.

9. **The correct answer is (B).** See the first sentence in the reading passage.

10. **The correct answer is (C).** Phosphorus catches fire easily. Therefore, it has a low kindling temperature.

11. **The correct answer is (A).** See the last sentence in the reading passage.

12. **The correct answer is (A).** From the second sentence in the reading passage, it may be deduced that it is difficult to suppress racketeering because so many people want services that are not obtainable through legitimate sources.

13. **The correct answer is (B).** See the second paragraph in the reading passage.

14. **The correct answer is (B).** See the last paragraph in the reading passage.

15. **The correct answer is (C).** A meter is one ten-millionth of the distance from the Equator to the North Pole. One ten-millionth $= \frac{1}{10,000,000}$

Part 5: Mathematics Knowledge

1. (B)	6. (A)	11. (D)	16. (A)	21. (A)
2. (D)	7. (D)	12. (C)	17. (D)	22. (B)
3. (B)	8. (C)	13. (B)	18. (A)	23. (D)
4. (A)	9. (D)	14. (C)	19. (C)	24. (D)
5. (A)	10. (B)	15. (A)	20. (C)	25. (C)

1. **The correct answer is (B).** Add:

$$\begin{array}{r} 6a - 4b + 3c \\ 4a + 9b - 5c \\ \hline 10a + 5b - 2c \end{array}$$

2. **The correct answer is (D).**

$$\frac{1}{2} \text{ of } x = 66$$
$$x = 66 \times 2$$
$$x = 132$$

3. **The correct answer is (B).**

$$3x = -5$$
$$x = \frac{-5}{3}$$
$$x = -\frac{5}{3}$$

4. **The correct answer is (A).** The first step to finding the square root of a number is to pair the digits to each side of the decimal point. If necessary, place 0 to the left of the first digit to form a pair and then solve with a modified form of long division. $\sqrt{05\ 90\ 43}$.

As the square root of 05 is between 2 and 3, place 2 above the first pair. The first digit of the square root of 59043 is 2.

5. **The correct answer is (A).**

Area of rectangle = 9 × 4 = 36. Area of square = 36; each side = 6; perimeter of square = 6 + 6 + 6 + 6 = 24.

6. **The correct answer is (A).**

$$\frac{27}{8} \times \frac{24}{9} \div \frac{3}{2} = \frac{\overset{3}{\cancel{27}}}{\underset{1}{\cancel{8}}} \times \frac{\overset{\cancel{24}^{1}}{}}{9_1} \times \frac{2}{\cancel{3}_1} = 6$$

7. **The correct answer is (D).** An equilateral triangle has 3 equal sides.

$$\frac{6n - 12}{3} = 2n - 4$$

8. **The correct answer is (C).** Only the star is a closed plane figure bounded by straight lines.

9. **The correct answer is (D).** Sum of angles of a hexagon = 180°(6 − 2) = 180° × 4 = 720°.

10. **The correct answer is (B).** Area of rectangle = 12′ × 18′ = 4 yards × 6 yards = 24 square yards.

11. **The correct answer is (D).**

$$d = rt; A = r + \frac{d}{t}; A = r + \frac{rt}{t};$$
$$A = r + r; A = 2r$$

12. **The correct answer is (C).** To find what percent one number is of another number, create a fraction by putting the part over the whole. Then convert to a decimal by dividing the numerator by the denominator and change to a percent by multiplying by 100.

$$\frac{R}{1,000} = 0.001R = 0.1R\%$$

13. **The correct answer is (B).** If radius = 35 miles, diameter = 70 miles.

Circumference = $\pi d = \dfrac{22}{7} \times 70 =$ 220 miles.

14. **The correct answer is (C).**

$3! = 3 \times 2 \times 1 = 6$

15. **The correct answer is (A).**

$a = 2b$; $2a = 4b = 6c$; $a = \dfrac{6c}{2} = 3c$

16. **The correct answer is (A).**

$\dfrac{2x}{7} = 2x^2$; $14x^2 = 2x$; $\dfrac{14x^2}{2x} = 1$; $7x = 1$; $x = \dfrac{1}{7}$

17. **The correct answer is (D).**

$A^2 = \dfrac{B^2}{C+D}$; $A^2(C+D) = B^2$;

$C + D = \dfrac{B^2}{A^2}$; $C = \dfrac{B^2}{A^2} - D$

18. **The correct answer is (A).**

$-1(3-2) = -3 + 2$

19. **The correct answer is (C).** Reciprocal of $5 = \dfrac{1}{5} = 0.20 = 0.2$.

20. **The correct answer is (C).**

Area = $\pi r^2 = \dfrac{22}{7} \times 7^2 = \dfrac{22}{7} \times 49 = 154$ sq. in.

21. **The correct answer is (A).**

$5a - 4x - 3y = 5(-2) - 4(-10) - 3(5) = -10 + 40 - 15 = +15$

22. **The correct answer is (B).** 1 book costs c dollars; m books = $m \times c = mc$.

23. **The correct answer is (D).** Let $x = $ # of dimes; $16 - x = $ # of quarters.

$$0.10x + 0.25(16 - x) = 2.50$$
$$10x + 25(16 - x) = 250$$
$$10x + 400 - 25x = 250$$
$$-15x = -150$$
$$x = 10$$

24. **The correct answer is (D).**

$\dfrac{x}{2} - \dfrac{x}{5} = 3$; $\dfrac{5x}{10} - \dfrac{2x}{10} = 3$; $\dfrac{3x}{10} = 3$;

$3x = 30$; $x = 10$

25. **The correct answer is (C).** $C = \pi d = \pi 2r$; if radius is increased by 3, $C = \pi 2(r + 3)$; $C = \pi 2r + 6\pi$.

Part 6: Electronics Information

1. (D)	5. (A)	9. (D)	13. (C)	17. (C)
2. (C)	6. (D)	10. (C)	14. (A)	18. (B)
3. (C)	7. (C)	11. (A)	15. (B)	19. (D)
4. (D)	8. (D)	12. (C)	16. (D)	20. (B)

1. **The correct answer is (D).** Soft iron has the property of being easily magnetized or demagnetized. When the current is turned on in an electromagnet, it becomes magnetized. When the current is turned off, the iron loses its magnetism.

2. **The correct answer is (C).** This is a general safety question. Never assume that there is no current in a piece of electrical equipment; the results could be shocking.

3. **The correct answer is (C).** Using algebraic rules, Ohm's law can be written in three equivalent ways:
$$R = \frac{V}{I}; I = \frac{V}{R}; V = IR$$

4. **The correct answer is (D).** A rectifier, or diode, is a device that changes AC to DC.

5. **The correct answer is (A).** When a kilowatt-hour meter is read, the number that comes just before the indicator is the number that is important. The answer would then be 9672 KwHtt.

6. **The correct answer is (D).** Converters change DC to AC. Rectifiers change AC to DC. Contractors are remote controlled switches frequently used as part of elevator controls. Transformers change voltages in AC circuits in accordance with the ratio of the number of turns in the secondary winding to the number of turns in the primary winding.

7. **The correct answer is (C).** A relay works on the principle of an energized coil or an electromagnet. Another device that works by an electromagnet is a solenoid.

8. **The correct answer is (D).** A megger (megohmmeter) is a portable device that produces a voltage. It is used to check for high voltage breakdown of insulation. In this case, it uses a resistance measurement to determine continuity.

9. **The correct answer is (D).** This is the Wheatstone bridge circuit with balanced loads in each of its arms. As there is no voltage across lamp No. 5, it will not be lit.

10. **The correct answer is (C).** The farad is a unit of capacitance. Most capacitors used in electronics are small and their capacitance is only a tiny fraction of a farad. One microfarad is one millionth of a farad.

11. **The correct answer is (A).** Three common elements of the transistor are the emitter, base, and collector.

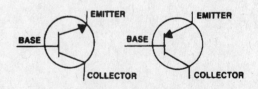

12. **The correct answer is (C).** This is proper safety procedure and should be followed.

13. **The correct answer is (C).** The number on the wires is in reverse order to the amount of current that they can carry. No. 12 is the smallest of the wires.

14. **The correct answer is (A).** The plug can go into the outlet in only one way in a polarized outlet. In the other outlets, the plug can be reversed.

15. **The correct answer is (B).** Connecting the bell to a 6- or 12-volt source on the secondary of a transformer is done as a safety precaution. Any other way would be dangerous.

16. **The correct answer is (D).** This is a mechanical or solderless connector. It does away with the need to solder wires and is found in house wiring.

17. **The correct answer is (C).** Two three-way switches will control a lamp from two different positions.

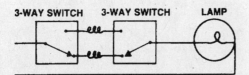

18. **The correct answer is (B).** A battery is an assembly of chemical cells. The common 9-volt battery found in transistor radios consists of six 1.5-volt cells connected in series to produce a total of six times 1.5 volts—or 9 volts.

19. **The correct answer is (D).** The third prong in the plug is the grounding wire.

20. **The correct answer is (B).** A compound motor has two sets of field coils. One is connected in series with the armature. The other is the shunt. It is connected in parallel across the armature.

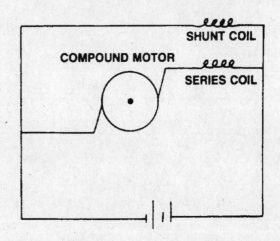

PART 1: MATH SKILLS TEST

1. Ⓐ Ⓑ Ⓒ Ⓓ	7. Ⓐ Ⓑ Ⓒ Ⓓ	13. Ⓐ Ⓑ Ⓒ Ⓓ	19. Ⓐ Ⓑ Ⓒ Ⓓ	25. Ⓐ Ⓑ Ⓒ Ⓓ
2. Ⓐ Ⓑ Ⓒ Ⓓ	8. Ⓐ Ⓑ Ⓒ Ⓓ	14. Ⓐ Ⓑ Ⓒ Ⓓ	20. Ⓐ Ⓑ Ⓒ Ⓓ	26. Ⓐ Ⓑ Ⓒ Ⓓ
3. Ⓐ Ⓑ Ⓒ Ⓓ	9. Ⓐ Ⓑ Ⓒ Ⓓ	15. Ⓐ Ⓑ Ⓒ Ⓓ	21. Ⓐ Ⓑ Ⓒ Ⓓ	27. Ⓐ Ⓑ Ⓒ Ⓓ
4. Ⓐ Ⓑ Ⓒ Ⓓ	10. Ⓐ Ⓑ Ⓒ Ⓓ	16. Ⓐ Ⓑ Ⓒ Ⓓ	22. Ⓐ Ⓑ Ⓒ Ⓓ	28. Ⓐ Ⓑ Ⓒ Ⓓ
5. Ⓐ Ⓑ Ⓒ Ⓓ	11. Ⓐ Ⓑ Ⓒ Ⓓ	17. Ⓐ Ⓑ Ⓒ Ⓓ	23. Ⓐ Ⓑ Ⓒ Ⓓ	29. Ⓐ Ⓑ Ⓒ Ⓓ
6. Ⓐ Ⓑ Ⓒ Ⓓ	12. Ⓐ Ⓑ Ⓒ Ⓓ	18. Ⓐ Ⓑ Ⓒ Ⓓ	24. Ⓐ Ⓑ Ⓒ Ⓓ	30. Ⓐ Ⓑ Ⓒ Ⓓ

PART 2: READING SKILLS TEST

1. Ⓐ Ⓑ Ⓒ Ⓓ	7. Ⓐ Ⓑ Ⓒ Ⓓ	13. Ⓐ Ⓑ Ⓒ Ⓓ	19. Ⓐ Ⓑ Ⓒ Ⓓ	25. Ⓐ Ⓑ Ⓒ Ⓓ
2. Ⓐ Ⓑ Ⓒ Ⓓ	8. Ⓐ Ⓑ Ⓒ Ⓓ	14. Ⓐ Ⓑ Ⓒ Ⓓ	20. Ⓐ Ⓑ Ⓒ Ⓓ	26. Ⓐ Ⓑ Ⓒ Ⓓ
3. Ⓐ Ⓑ Ⓒ Ⓓ	9. Ⓐ Ⓑ Ⓒ Ⓓ	15. Ⓐ Ⓑ Ⓒ Ⓓ	21. Ⓐ Ⓑ Ⓒ Ⓓ	27. Ⓐ Ⓑ Ⓒ Ⓓ
4. Ⓐ Ⓑ Ⓒ Ⓓ	10. Ⓐ Ⓑ Ⓒ Ⓓ	16. Ⓐ Ⓑ Ⓒ Ⓓ	22. Ⓐ Ⓑ Ⓒ Ⓓ	
5. Ⓐ Ⓑ Ⓒ Ⓓ	11. Ⓐ Ⓑ Ⓒ Ⓓ	17. Ⓐ Ⓑ Ⓒ Ⓓ	23. Ⓐ Ⓑ Ⓒ Ⓓ	
6. Ⓐ Ⓑ Ⓒ Ⓓ	12. Ⓐ Ⓑ Ⓒ Ⓓ	18. Ⓐ Ⓑ Ⓒ Ⓓ	24. Ⓐ Ⓑ Ⓒ Ⓓ	

PART 3: MECHANICAL COMPREHENSION TEST

1. Ⓐ Ⓑ Ⓒ	7. Ⓐ Ⓑ Ⓒ	13. Ⓐ Ⓑ Ⓒ	19. Ⓐ Ⓑ Ⓒ	25. Ⓐ Ⓑ Ⓒ
2. Ⓐ Ⓑ Ⓒ	8. Ⓐ Ⓑ Ⓒ	14. Ⓐ Ⓑ Ⓒ	20. Ⓐ Ⓑ Ⓒ	26. Ⓐ Ⓑ Ⓒ
3. Ⓐ Ⓑ Ⓒ	9. Ⓐ Ⓑ Ⓒ	15. Ⓐ Ⓑ Ⓒ	21. Ⓐ Ⓑ Ⓒ	27. Ⓐ Ⓑ Ⓒ
4. Ⓐ Ⓑ Ⓒ	10. Ⓐ Ⓑ Ⓒ	16. Ⓐ Ⓑ Ⓒ	22. Ⓐ Ⓑ Ⓒ	28. Ⓐ Ⓑ Ⓒ
5. Ⓐ Ⓑ Ⓒ	11. Ⓐ Ⓑ Ⓒ	17. Ⓐ Ⓑ Ⓒ	23. Ⓐ Ⓑ Ⓒ	29. Ⓐ Ⓑ Ⓒ
6. Ⓐ Ⓑ Ⓒ	12. Ⓐ Ⓑ Ⓒ	18. Ⓐ Ⓑ Ⓒ	24. Ⓐ Ⓑ Ⓒ	30. Ⓐ Ⓑ Ⓒ

answer sheet

Navy and Marine Corps Aviation Selection Test Battery (ASTB)

Subtests

Part 1: Math Skills Test
Part 2: Reading Skills Test
Part 3: Mechanical Comprehension Test

The answer sheet for the Navy and the Coast Guard commissioning programs should be used in answering the questions on the Math Skills Test, Reading Skills Test, and the Mechanical Comprehension Test of the Navy and Marine Corps Aviation Selection Test Battery. In addition, this section contains answer keys and explanations for determining your scores on these tests.

Remove (cut out) the answer sheet to record your answers to the test questions. The specimen Navy and Marine Corps Aviation Selection Test Battery is similar in format and content to the actual Navy and Marine Corps Aviation Selection Test Battery. Take these tests under real test conditions. Time each test carefully.

Use the key answers to obtain your test scores and to evaluate your performance on each test. Record the number of items you answered correctly, as well as the number of each question you answered incorrectly or wish to review, in the space provided below the answers for each test.

Be certain to review carefully and understand the explanations for the answers to all questions you answered incorrectly and for each of the questions that you answered correctly but are unsure of. This is absolutely essential in order to acquire the knowledge and expertise necessary to obtain the maximum score possible on the tests of the real Navy and Marine Corps Aviation Selection Test Battery.

practice test

PART 1: MATH SKILLS TEST

TIME: 25 Minutes—30 Questions

Questions 1–30 make up the math section of the test. Each of the math questions is followed by four possible answers. Decide which one of the four options is the correct answer. Then mark the space on your answer sheet that has the same number and letter as your choice.

1. A 6-foot-tall farmer wants to determine the height of his barn. He notices that his shadow is 10 feet long and that his barn casts a shadow 75 feet long. How high is the barn?

   (A) 30 feet
   (B) 35 feet
   (C) 40 feet
   (D) 45 feet

2. What is the square root of 16 raised to the fourth power?

   (A) 16
   (B) 64
   (C) 128
   (D) 256

3. If the sum of the edges of a cube is 48 inches, the volume of the cube is

   (A) 4 cubic inches.
   (B) 8 cubic inches.
   (C) 16 cubic inches.
   (D) 64 cubic inches.

4. If the tax rate is 3½% and the amount to be raised is $6440, what is the base?

   (A) $180,000
   (B) $181,000
   (C) $182,000
   (D) $184,000

5. Each corridor contains 8 to 10 classrooms and each classroom contains 20 to 24 students. If all classrooms are occupied, what is the minimum number of students on one corridor at a given time?

   (A) 160
   (B) 170
   (C) 180
   (D) 190

6. At 8:00 A.M., two trains started out from the same station. One traveled north at the rate of 60 mph; the other traveled south at the rate of 50 mph. At what time were the trains 550 miles apart?

   (A) Noon
   (B) 12:30 P.M.
   (C) 1:00 P.M.
   (D) 1:30 P.M.

7. How much pure acid must be added to 12 ounces of a 40% acid solution in order to produce a 60% acid solution?

   (A) 5 ounces
   (B) 6 ounces
   (C) 7 ounces
   (D) 8 ounces

8. If x varies directly as y^2 and if $x = 9$ when $y = 2$, what is the value of x when $y = 8$?

   (A) 32
   (B) 130
   (C) 144
   (D) 168

GO ON TO THE NEXT PAGE

9. The hour hand of a clock is 3 feet long. How many feet does the tip of this hand move between 1:00 P.M. and 5:00 P.M.?

(A) 2π

(B) 4π

(C) 6π

(D) 8π

10. Find the second of three consecutive integers if the sum of the first and third is 26.

(A) 9

(B) 10

(C) 11

(D) 13

11. Find the area of a square circumscribed about a circle whose radius is 10.

(A) $31\dfrac{3}{7}$

(B) $62\dfrac{6}{7}$

(C) 100

(D) 400

12. An island is defended by a battery of coastal guns placed at the easternmost point of the island and having a maximum range of 10 miles. A ship, sailing due north at 24 mph along a course that will bring it within 8 miles of these guns, is approaching the position where it will be 10 miles from these guns. Assuming that the ship will maintain a straight course and the same speed, for approximately how long will the ship be within range of the coastal guns?

(A) 15 minutes

(B) 20 minutes

(C) 25 minutes

(D) 30 minutes

13. A team won 25 games in a 40-game season. Find the ratio of games won to games lost.

(A) 3 : 5

(B) 5 : 3

(C) 3 : 8

(D) 8 : 3

14. If the entrance requirement of a certain college is 82, what mark must a student have in Geometry (weight 2) to be able to enter if his other marks are English 88 (weight 3), Spanish 78 (weight 2), and History 80 (weight 2)?

(A) 83

(B) 82

(C) 81

(D) 79

15. Two planes started at the same time from the same airport and flew in opposite directions. One flew 80 mph faster than the other. In four hours they were 2600 miles apart. What was the speed of the slower plane?

(A) 285 mph

(B) 305 mph

(C) 325 mph

(D) 345 mph

16. One recruit can complete a certain assignment in 40 minutes; another recruit can complete the same assignment in one hour. How long would it take to complete the assignment if the two recruits worked together?

(A) 12 minutes

(B) 18 minutes

(C) 24 minutes

(D) 30 minutes

17. If $(x - y)^2 = 40$ and $x^2 + y^2 = 60$, then $xy =$

(A) 40

(B) 20

(C) 12

(D) 10

18. If a triangle of base 6 has the same area as a circle of radius 6, what is the altitude of the triangle?

(A) 6π

(B) 8π

(C) 10π

(D) 12π

19. In the following series of numbers arranged in a logical order, ascertain the pattern or rule for the arrangement and then select the appropriate option to complete the series:

5 3 9 7 21 19 __

(A) 41

(B) 45

(C) 49

(D) 57

20. In the figure shown below, what is the measure of angle x?

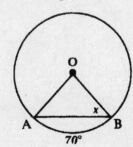

(A) 35°

(B) 45°

(C) 55°

(D) 70°

21. Two trains running on the same track travel at the rates of 30 and 35 mph, respectively. If the slower train starts out an hour earlier, how long will it take the faster train to catch up with it?

(A) 4 hours

(B) 5 hours

(C) 6 hours

(D) 7 hours

22. A naval detachment has enough rations to feed sixteen people for 10 days. If four more people join the detachment, for how many fewer days will the rations last?

(A) 1

(B) 2

(C) 3

(D) 4

23. A field can be plowed by 9 machines in 5 hours. If 3 machines are broken and cannot be used, how many hours will it take to plow the field?

(A) $7\frac{1}{2}$ hours

(B) $8\frac{1}{2}$ hours

(C) $9\frac{1}{2}$ hours

(D) $10\frac{1}{2}$ hours

24. What is the square root of 9 raised to the fourth power?

(A) 12

(B) 27

(C) 49

(D) 81

25. If $2^{n-2} = 32$, then n equals

(A) 5

(B) 7

(C) 8

(D) 12

GO ON TO THE NEXT PAGE

26. Jane received grades of 90, 88, and 75 on three tests. What grade must she receive on the next test so that her average for these four tests is 86?

    (A) 88
    (B) 89
    (C) 90
    (D) 91

27. A family drove from New York to San Francisco, a distance of 3,000 miles. They drove $\frac{1}{10}$ of the distance the first day and $\frac{1}{9}$ of the remaining distance the second day. How many miles were left to be driven?

    (A) 2,200 miles
    (B) 2,300 miles
    (C) 2,400 miles
    (D) 2,500 miles

28. In a 3-hour examination of 320 questions, there are 40 mathematics problems. If twice as much time should be allowed for each mathematics problem as for each of the other questions, how many minutes should be spent on the mathematics problems?

    (A) 40 minutes
    (B) 45 minutes
    (C) 50 minutes
    (D) 55 minutes

29. 100,000 may be represented as

    (A) 10^4
    (B) 10^5
    (C) 10^6
    (D) 10^7

30. If $a = 3b$ and $6b = 12c$, then $a =$

    (A) $6c$
    (B) $9c$
    (C) $12c$
    (D) $15c$

STOP! DO NOT CONTINUE ON UNTIL TOLD TO DO SO. IF YOU FINISH BEFORE THE TIME IS UP, YOU MAY CHECK OVER YOUR WORK ON THIS PART ONLY.

PART 2: READING SKILLS TEST

27 Questions—25 Minutes

Directions: Each item consists of a passage that you should assume to be true, followed by four possible answer choices. For each item, select the choice that can be inferred *only* from the passage itself. Some or all of the choices following the passage may be true and reasonable, but only one of them can be derived solely from the information in the passage.

1. In a pole-vaulting competition, the judge decides on the minimum height to be jumped. The vaulter may attempt to jump any height above the minimum. Using flexible fiberglass poles, vaulters have jumped as high as 18 feet, 8¼ inches.

   This passage means most nearly that

   (A) pole vaulters may attempt to jump any height in competition.

   (B) pole vaulters must jump higher than 18 feet, 8¼ inches to win.

   (C) pole vaulters must jump higher than the height set by the judge.

   (D) pole vaulters must use fiberglass poles.

2. Only about one tenth of an iceberg is visible above water. Eight to nine times as much ice is hidden below the waterline. In the Antarctic Ocean, near the South Pole, there are icebergs that rise as high as 300 feet above the water.

   The passage best supports the statement that icebergs in the Antarctic Ocean

   (A) are usually 300 feet high.

   (B) can be as much as 3,000 feet high.

   (C) are difficult to spot.

   (D) are hazards to navigation.

3. You can tell a frog from a toad by its skin. In general, a frog's skin is moist, smooth, and shiny, but a toad's skin is dry, dull, and rough or covered with warts. Frogs are also better at jumping than toads are.

   The passage best supports the statement that

   (A) you can recognize a toad by its great jumping ability.

   (B) you can recognize a toad by its smooth, shiny skin.

   (C) you can recognize a toad by its lack of warts.

   (D) you can recognize a toad by its dry, rough skin.

4. Thomas Edison was responsible for more than 1,000 inventions in his 84-year lifespan. Among the most famous of his inventions are the phonograph, the electric lightbulb, motion picture film, the electric generator, and the battery.

   This passage means most nearly that

   (A) Thomas Edison was the most famous inventor.

   (B) Thomas Edison was responsible for 84 inventions.

   (C) Thomas Edison invented many things in his short life.

   (D) Thomas Edison invented the phonograph and motion picture film.

GO ON TO THE NEXT PAGE

5. Amateur sportsmen and sportswomen are those who take part in sports purely for enjoyment, not for financial reward. Professional sportsmen and sportswomen are people who are paid to participate in sports. Most athletes who compete in the Olympic Games are amateurs.

The passage best supports the statement that

(A) an amateur sportsperson might be an Olympic champion.

(B) an amateur sportsperson might be a member of the Pittsburgh Steelers.

(C) an amateur sportsperson might be the holder of the heavyweight boxing crown.

(D) an amateur sportsperson might be a participant in the World Series.

6. A year—the time it takes Earth to go exactly once around the sun—is not 365 days. It is actually 365 days, 6 hours, 9 minutes, 9½ seconds—or 365¼ days. Leap years make up for this discrepancy by adding an extra day to the calendar once every four years.

This passage means most nearly that

(A) the purpose of leap years is to adjust for the fact that it takes 365¼ days for the Earth to circle the sun.

(B) the purpose of leap years is to make up for time lost in the work year.

(C) the purpose of leap years is to occur every four years.

(D) the purpose of leap years is to allow for differences in the length of a year in each time zone.

7. Scientists are taking a closer look at the recent boom in the use of wood for heating. Wood burning, it seems, releases high-level pollutants. It is believed that burning wood produces a thousand times more CO—carbon monoxide—than natural gas does when it burns.

The passage best supports the statement that

(A) CO is natural gas.

(B) CO is wood.

(C) CO is carbon monoxide.

(D) CO is heat.

8. The average American family makes a move every ten years. This means that family history becomes scattered. In some cases, a person searching for his or her family's past must hire a professional researcher to track down ancestors.

This passage means most nearly that

(A) every few years, somebody tries to trace his or her family's history.

(B) every few years, the average American family moves.

(C) every few years, family history becomes scattered.

(D) every few years, professional researchers are hired to track down ancestors.

9. When gas is leaking, any spark or sudden flame can ignite it. This can create a "flashback," which burns off the gas in a quick puff of smoke and flame. But the real danger is a large leak, which can cause an explosion.

   The passage best supports the statement that

   (A) the real danger from leaking gas is a flashback.

   (B) the real danger from leaking gas is a puff of smoke and flame.

   (C) the real danger from leaking gas is an explosion.

   (D) the real danger from leaking gas is a spark.

10. With the exception of Earth, all of the planets in our solar system are named for gods and goddesses in Greek or Roman mythology. This is because other planets were thought to be in heaven, like the gods, and our planet lay beneath, like the earth.

    The passage best supports the statement that

    (A) all the planets except Earth were part of Greek and Roman mythology.

    (B) all the planets except Earth were thought to be in heaven.

    (C) all the planets except Earth are part of the same solar system.

    (D) all the planets except Earth were worshipped as gods.

11. The Supreme Court was established by Article 3 of the Constitution. Since 1869, it has been made up of nine members—the Chief Justice and eight associate justices—who are appointed for life. Supreme Court justices are named by the President and must be confirmed by the Senate.

    This passage means most nearly that

    (A) the Supreme Court was established in 1869.

    (B) the Supreme Court consists of nine judges.

    (C) the Supreme Court consists of judges appointed by the Senate.

    (D) the Supreme Court changes with each presidential election.

12. The sport of automobile racing originated in France in 1894. There are five basic types of competition: (1) the grand prix, a series of races that leads to a world championship; (2) stock car racing, which uses specially equipped standard cars; (3) midget car racing; (4) sports car racing; and (5) drag racing. The best-known U.S. race is the Indianapolis 500, first held in 1911.

    The passage best supports the statement that

    (A) the sport of auto racing started with the Indianapolis 500 in 1911.

    (B) the sport of auto racing uses only standard cars, which are specially equipped.

    (C) the sport of auto racing holds its championship race in France.

    (D) the sport of auto racing includes five different types of competition.

GO ON TO THE NEXT PAGE

13. The brain controls both voluntary behavior such as walking and talking, and most involuntary behavior such as the beating of the heart and breathing. In higher animals, the brain is also the site of emotions, memory, self-awareness, and thought.

The passage best supports the statement that in higher animals,

(A) the brain controls emotion, memory, and thought.

(B) the brain controls voluntary behavior.

(C) the brain controls most involuntary behavior.

(D) the brain controls all of the above.

14. The speed of a boat is measured in knots. One knot is equal to a speed of one nautical mile per hour. A nautical mile is equal to 6,080 feet, while an ordinary mile is 5,280 feet.

This passage means most nearly that

(A) a nautical mile is longer than an ordinary mile.

(B) a speed of 2 knots is the same as 2 miles per hour.

(C) a knot is the same as a mile.

(D) the distance a boat travels is measured in knots.

15. It is recommended that the net be held by not more than 14 persons nor fewer than 10 persons, although under certain conditions it may become necessary to use fewer persons.

According to this passage, it is

(A) best to use between 10 and 14 persons on the net.

(B) better to use 10 persons on the net rather than 14.

(C) impossible to use a net unless at least 10 persons are available to hold it.

(D) sometimes advisable to use more than 14 persons on the net.

16. The overuse of antibiotics today represents a growing danger, according to many medical authorities. Patients everywhere, stimulated by reports of new wonder drugs, continue to ask their doctors for a shot to relieve a cold, flu, or any other viral infections that occur during the course of a bad winter. But, for the common cold and many other viral infections, antibiotics have no effect.

The passage best supports the statement that

(A) the use of antibiotics is becoming a health hazard.

(B) antibiotics are of no value in treating many viral infections.

(C) patients should ask their doctors for a shot of one of the new wonder drugs to relieve the symptoms of the flu.

(D) the treatment of colds and other viral infections by antibiotics will lessen their severity.

17. In examining the scene of a homicide, one should not only look for the usual, standard traces—fingerprints, footprints, etc.—but also take notice of details that at first glance may not seem to have any connection to the crime.

One may conclude from the above statement that at the scene of a homicide,

(A) one cannot tell in advance what will be important.

(B) only the usual, standard traces are important.

(C) sometimes one should not look for footprints.

(D) standard traces are not generally available.

18. Alertness and attentiveness are essential qualities for success as a telephone operator. The work the operator performs often requires careful attention under conditions of stress.

The passage best supports the statement that a telephone operator

(A) always works under stress.

(B) cannot be successful unless he or she memorizes many telephone numbers.

(C) must be trained before he or she can render good service.

(D) must be able to work under difficult conditions.

19. To prevent industrial accidents, safety devices must be used to guard exposed machinery, the light in the plant must be adequate, and mechanics should be instructed in safety rules that they must follow for their own protection.

The passage best supports the statement that industrial accidents

(A) are always avoidable.

(B) may be due to ignorance.

(C) usually result from inadequate machinery.

(D) cannot be entirely overcome.

20. The leader of an industrial enterprise has two principal functions. He or she must manufacture and distribute a product at a profit, and he or she must keep individuals and groups of individuals working effectively.

The passage best supports the statement that

(A) an industrial leader should increase the distribution of his or her plant's products.

(B) an industrial leader should introduce large-scale production methods.

(C) an industrial leader should coordinate the activities of employees.

(D) an industrial leader should profit by the experience of other leaders.

21. Genuine coins have an even and distinct corrugated outer edge; the corrugated outer edges of counterfeit coins are usually uneven, crooked, or missing.

The passage best supports the statement that

(A) counterfeit coins can rarely be distinguished from genuine coins.

(B) counterfeit coins never lose their corrugated outer edge.

(C) genuine coins never lose their uneven, corrugated outer edge.

(D) the quality of the outer edge of a coin may show that it is counterfeit.

GO ON TO THE NEXT PAGE

22. In most U.S. states, no crime is considered to have occurred unless there is a written law forbidding the act, and even though an act may not be exactly in harmony with public policy, such act is not a crime unless it is expressly forbidden by legislative enactment.

The passage best supports the statement that

(A) a crime is committed only with reference to a particular law.

(B) all acts not in harmony with public policy should be expressly forbidden by law.

(C) legislative enactments frequently forbid actions that are exactly in harmony with public policy.

(D) nothing contrary to public policy can be done without legislative authority.

23. Only one measure, but a quite obvious measure, of the merits of the personnel policies of an organization and of the adequacy and fairness of the wages and other conditions of employment prevailing in it is the rate at which replacements must be made in order to maintain the work force.

This passage means most nearly that

(A) maximum effectiveness in personnel management has been achieved when there is no employee turnover.

(B) organization policies should be based on both social and economic considerations.

(C) rate of employee turnover is one indicator of the effectiveness of personnel management.

(D) wages and working conditions are of prime importance to both union leaders and managers.

24. Education should not stop when the individual has been prepared to make a livelihood and to live in modern society; living would be mere existence were there no appreciation and enjoyment of the riches of art, literature, and science.

This passage best supports the statement that true education

(A) deals chiefly with art, literature, and science.

(B) disregards practical goals.

(C) prepares an individual for a full enjoyment of life.

(D) teaches a person to focus on the routine problems of life.

25. Just as the procedure of a collection department must be clear-cut and definite, the steps being taken with the sureness of a skilled chess player, so the various paragraphs of a collection letter must show clear organization, giving evidence of mind that, from the beginning, has had a specific end in view.

The passage means most nearly that a collection letter should always

(A) be carefully planned.

(B) be courteous but brief.

(C) be divided into several long paragraphs.

(D) show a spirit of sportsmanship.

26. The palest ink is better than the best memory.

This passage means most nearly that

(A) a good memory is very useful.

(B) a written record is more dependable than a good memory.

(C) records are worth more if they are made by a person with a good memory.

(D) records must never be made in pencil.

27. In almost every community, fortunately, there are certain people known to be public spirited; others, however, may be selfish and act only as their private interests seem to require.

This passage means most nearly that those citizens who disregard others are

(A) community minded.

(B) fortunate.

(C) not public spirited.

(D) unknown.

STOP! DO NOT TURN THIS PAGE UNTIL TOLD TO DO SO. IF YOU FINISH BEFORE THE TIME IS UP, YOU MAY CHECK OVER YOUR WORK ON THIS PART ONLY.

PART 3: MECHANICAL COMPREHENSION TEST

TIME: 15 Minutes—30 Questions

Questions 1–30 are designed to measure your ability to reason with mechanical terms. Each diagram is followed by a question or an incomplete statement. Study the diagram carefully and select the choice that best answers the question or completes the statement. Then mark the space on your answer sheet that has the same number and letter as your choice.

1.

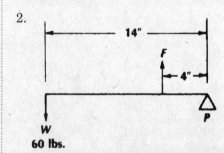

Shown above is a first-class lever. A common example of a first-class lever is

(A) a seesaw.

(B) a wheelbarrow.

(C) tongs.

2.

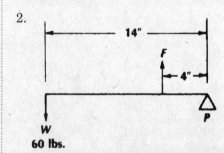

The force F required to balance the weight of 60 pounds on the lever, shown in the diagram above, is most nearly

(A) 210 lbs.

(B) 240 lbs.

(C) 672 lbs.

3.

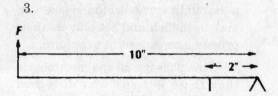

The mechanical advantage of the lever shown in the diagram above is

(A) 4

(B) 5

(C) 8

4.

What effort must be exerted to the handles of the wheelbarrow shown above carrying a load of 200 pounds (neglect the weight of the wheelbarrow in your computation)?

(A) 40 lbs.

(B) 50 lbs.

(C) 65 lbs.

5.

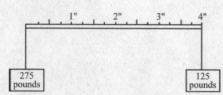

The bar above, which is exactly 4 inches in length, has a 275-pound weight on one end and a 125-pound weight on the opposite end.

For the bar to balance, the distance from the 275-pound weight to the fulcrum point should be (neglect the weight of the bar in your computation)

(A) $1\frac{1}{4}$ inches

(B) 1 inch

(C) $\frac{3}{4}$ inch

6.

Neglecting friction, what is the mechanical advantage in using a single fixed pulley as shown above?

(A) 1

(B) 2

(C) 3

7.

In the figure shown above, the pulley system consists of a fixed block and a movable block. Neglecting friction and the weight of the pulley system, what effort would be needed to lift a 100-pound weight?

(A) 100 pounds

(B) 75 pounds

(C) 50 pounds

8.

The weight W is to be raised as shown in the figure above by attaching the pull rope to the truck. If the weight is to be raised 8 feet, the truck will have to move

(A) 16 feet.

(B) 24 feet.

(C) 32 feet.

GO ON TO THE NEXT PAGE

9.

In the figure shown above, the serviceperson is using a plank to roll a 300-pound barrel up to the bed of the truck. The force that must be applied is most nearly

(A) 200 pounds.

(B) 150 pounds.

(C) 100 pounds.

10.

In the figure shown above, a bucket is being raised by a wheel-and-axle arrangement. If the distance from the center of the axle to the handle is 8 inches and the diameter of the drum around which the rope is wound is 4 inches, the theoretical mechanical advantage is

(A) 2

(B) 4

(C) 8

11.

A 

B 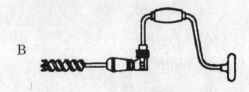

C 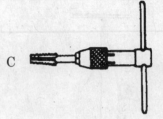

To make a ½" hole in a block of wood, use tool

(A) A

(B) B

(C) C

12.

A 

B 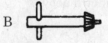

C 

To cut a thread on a ½" brass rod, use tool

(A) A

(B) B

(C) C

13.

The number 18 appearing on the tool shown above indicates

(A) depth of opening.

(B) size of opening.

(C) threads per inch.

14.

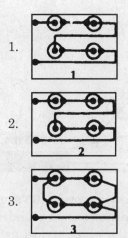

1.

2.

3.

Which one of the 1½-volt dry cell battery connections shown above will deliver 6 volts?

(A) 1

(B) 2

(C) 3

15.

In the figure given above, if the thickness of the wall of the pipe is $\frac{1}{2}''$, the inside diameter of the pipe is

(A) $3''$

(B) $3\frac{1}{8}''$

(C) $3\frac{1}{4}''$

16.

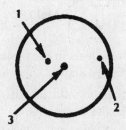

The figure above represents a revolving wheel. The numbers 1 and 2 indicate two fixed points on the wheel. The number 3 indicates the center of the wheel. Of the following, the most accurate statement is that

(A) point 1 makes more revolutions per minute than point 2.

(B) point 2 makes more revolutions per minute than point 1.

(C) points 1 and 2 make the same number of revolutions per minute.

17.

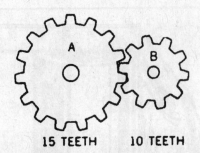

15 TEETH   10 TEETH

In the figure shown above, if gear A makes 14 revolutions, gear B will make

(A) 14

(B) 17

(C) 21

18.

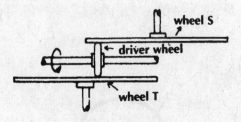

With the wheels in the position shown in the figure above,

(A) wheels S and T will rotate in opposite directions.

(B) wheels S and T will rotate in the same direction.

(C) wheels S and T will rotate at the same speed.

19.

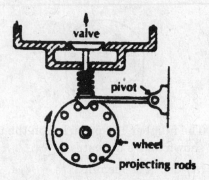

In order to open the valve four times every second, the wheel must rotate at

(A) 12 rpm.

(B) 18 rpm.

(C) 24 rpm.

20.

In the figure shown above, a 160-pound individual jumps off an 800-pound raft to a point in the water 10 feet away. Theoretically, the raft will move

(A) 2 feet in the opposite direction.

(B) 3 feet in the opposite direction.

(C) 4 feet in the opposite direction.

21.

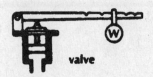

The figure above shows a lever-type safety valve. It will blow off at a lower pressure if weight W is

(A) increased.

(B) moved to the left.

(C) moved to the right.

22.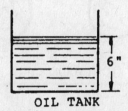

As shown in the figure above, four air reservoirs have been filled with air by the air compressor. If the main line air gauge reads 100 pounds, then the tank air gauge will read

(A) 25 pounds.

(B) 50 pounds.

(C) 100 pounds.

23.

In the figure above, the number of complete turns the vise handle must make to fully close the jaws is

(A) 16

(B) 18

(C) 20

24.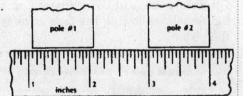

In the figure shown above, the center-to-center distance between the two poles is

(A) $1\dfrac{3}{4}''$

(B) $1\dfrac{15}{16}''$

(C) $1\dfrac{7}{8}''$

25.

If an 8″ level indicates 16 quarts of oil in the tank, then the number of quarts of oil to be added to raise the level from 6″ to 8″ is

(A) 2 quarts.

(B) 4 quarts.

(C) 6 quarts.

GO ON TO THE NEXT PAGE

Questions 26 and 27 are based on the figure below showing the four strokes of the piston.

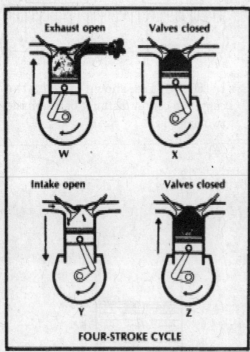

Exhaust open   Valves closed

W   X

Intake open   Valves closed

Y   Z

FOUR-STROKE CYCLE

26. Which illustration depicts the compression stroke?

   (A) X

   (B) Y

   (C) Z

27. What is the proper sequence of the four strokes of a piston in a gasoline engine?

   (A) W, X, Y, Z

   (B) X, Z, Y, W

   (C) Y, Z, X, W

28.

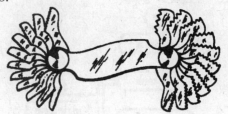

The gauge shown above is a

   (A) depth gauge.

   (B) feeler gauge.

   (C) thread gauge.

29.

The wrench shown above is generally used when

   (A) a definite force must be applied to a nut or bolt head.

   (B) a tight nut must be broken loose.

   (C) rapid turning of the nut or bolt is of prime importance.

30.

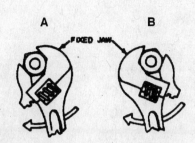

Which of the figures shown above is the proper procedure for pulling adjustable wrenches?

(A) A

(B) B

(C) Both are proper procedures.

STOP! DO NOT TURN THIS PAGE UNTIL TOLD TO DO SO. IF YOU FINISH BEFORE THE TIME IS UP, YOU MAY CHECK OVER YOUR WORK ON THIS PART ONLY.

ANSWER KEY AND EXPLANATIONS
Part 1: Math Skills Test

1. (D)	7. (B)	13. (B)	19. (D)	25. (B)
2. (D)	8. (C)	14. (D)	20. (C)	26. (D)
3. (D)	9. (A)	15. (A)	21. (C)	27. (C)
4. (D)	10. (D)	16. (C)	22. (B)	28. (A)
5. (A)	11. (D)	17. (D)	23. (A)	29. (B)
6. (C)	12. (D)	18. (D)	24. (D)	30. (A)

1. **The correct answer is (D).** $6 : 10 = x : 75; 10x = 450; x = 45$ feet.

2. **The correct answer is (D).**

   The square root of $16 = 4$;

   $4^4 = 4 \times 4 \times 4 \times 4 = 16 \times 16 = 256$.

3. **The correct answer is (D).** A cube has 12 edges.

   $\frac{48}{12}" = 4"; 4" \times 4" \times 4" = 64$ cubic inches.

4. **The correct answer is (D).** Let $x =$ base.

   $x \times .035 = 6440; x = \frac{6440}{.035} = $184,000$.

5. **The correct answer is (A).** There is a minimum of 20 students in a minimum of 8 classrooms; $8 \times 20 = 160$.

6. **The correct answer is (C).** Let $x =$ time. $60x + 50x = 550; 110x = 550; x = 5$. Trains left at 8:00 A.M. Five hours later, it would be 1:00 P.M.

7. **The correct answer is (B).**

	No. of Ounces	Parts Pure Acid	No. of Ounces of Pure Acid
Pure Acid	x	100	$100x$
40% Acid Solution	12	40	480
60% Acid Solution	$12 + x$	60	$60(12 + x)$

   $100x + 480 = 60(12 + x); 100x + 480 = 720 + 60x; 40x = 240; x = 6$.

8. **The correct answer is (C).**

   $9 : 4 = x : 64; 4x = 64 \times 9; x = \frac{64 \times 9}{4} = 144$.

9. **The correct answer is (A).** The hour hand traces a circle of radius 3. The circumference of that circle $= 2\pi r = 2\pi(3) = 6\pi$. A 4-hour interval is one third of a 12-hour period or one third of a full circle. $\frac{1}{3}$ of $6\pi = 2\pi$.

10. **The correct answer is (D).** Represent the integers as $x, x + 1$, and $x + 2$. $x + x + 2 = 26; 2x = 26 - 2; 2x = 24; x = 12$; therefore, $x + 1 = 13$.

11. **The correct answer is (D).**

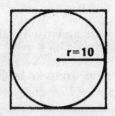

Diameter = 20 = side of square;

Area of square = 20 × 20 = 400.

12. **The correct answer is (D).**

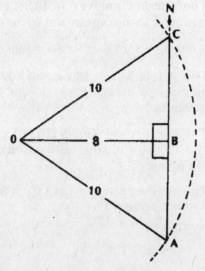

Referring to the sketch above, the ship will be within range of the coastal guns from point A to point C. Triangle OBA and triangle OBC are right triangles with one leg of 8 miles and a hypotenuse of 10 miles.

The time for the ship to travel from point A to point C must be determined. Let x = the distance from A to B; $2x$ = distance from A to C. $8^2 + x^2 = 10^2$; $64 + x^2 = 100$; $x^2 = 36$; $x = 6$ miles; $2x = 12$ miles.

Let t = time required to travel from A to C (in minutes).

$\frac{24}{60} = \frac{12}{t}$; $24t = 720$; $t = 30$ minutes.

13. **The correct answer is (B).** 25 games won: 15 games lost: $\frac{25}{15} = \frac{5}{3}$.

14. **The correct answer is (D).**

Eng   88 × 3 = 264

Span   78 × 2 = 156

Hist   80 × 2 = 160

Geom x × 2 = $\underline{2x}$

              9 =   580 + 2x

82 × 9 = 738 points needed

580 + 2x = 738

2x = 738 − 580 = 158

$x = \dfrac{158}{2} = 79$

15. **The correct answer is (A).** Let x = rate of slower plane; $x + 80$ = rate of faster plane.

$4x + 4(x + 80) = 2600$; $4x + 4x + 320 = 2600$; $8x = 2280$; $x = 285$.

16. **The correct answer is (C).**

	Recruit 1	Recruit 2
$\dfrac{\text{Time actually needed}}{\text{Time needed to do job alone}}$	$\dfrac{x}{40}$ +	$\dfrac{x}{60} = 1$

Multiply by 120 to clear fractions.

$3x + 2x = 120$; $5x = 120$; $x = \dfrac{120}{5} = 24$ minutes.

17. **The correct answer is (D).**

$(x - y)^2 = x^2 - 2xy + y^2$

$40 = 60 - 2xy$

$2xy = 20$

$xy = 10$

18. **The correct answer is (D).** The area of the circle is $\pi(6)^2$, or 36π. In the triangle,

$$\frac{1}{2}(6)(h) = 36\pi$$

$$3h = 36\pi$$

$$h = 12\pi$$

19. **The correct answer is (D).** Subtract 2, multiply by 3; subtract 2, multiply by 3; etc.

20. **The correct answer is (C).** Arc $AB = 70°$; therefore $AOB = 70°$.

The two radii are equal.

Angle $x = \frac{1}{2}(180° - 70°) = \frac{1}{2}(110°) = 55°$.

21. **The correct answer is (C).** Slower train is 30 miles ahead in one hour. Difference in rate is 5 mph. $\frac{30}{5} = 6$ hours.

22. **The correct answer is (B).** Let $x =$ number ration days for 20 persons. $16 \times 10 = 20 \times x$; $20x = 160$; $x = \frac{180}{20} = 8$ ration days for 20 persons. 10 days − 8 days = 2 days fewer.

23. **The correct answer is (A).** Let x = number of hours to plow with 6 machines.

$$9 \times 5 = 6 \times x$$

$$6x = 45$$

$$x = \frac{45}{8} = 7\frac{1}{2} \text{ hours}$$

24. **The correct answer is (D).** $\sqrt{9} = 3$; $3^4 = 3 \times 3 \times 3 \times 3 = 81$.

25. **The correct answer is (B).** $2^{n-2} = 32$; $2^5 = 32$; $n - 2 = 5$; $n = 7$.

26. **The correct answer is (D).** $86 \times 4 = 344$; $90 + 88 + 75 = 253$; $344 - 253 = 91$.

27. **The correct answer is (C).** $\frac{1}{10}$ of 3,000 $= 300$; $3,000 - 300 = 2,700$; $\frac{1}{9}$ of $2,700 = 300$; $2,700 - 300 = 2,400$ miles still to be driven.

28. **The correct answer is (A).** Let $x =$ minutes to be spent on each math problem, $x \times 40 + \frac{x}{2} \times 280 = 180$; $40x + 140x = 180$; $180x = 180$; $x = 1$; $40x = 40$ minutes to be spent on the 40 math problems.

29. **The correct answer is (B).** $10 \times 10 \times 10 \times 10 \times 10 = 100,000$ or 10 raised to the 5th power.

30. **The correct answer is (A).** $a = 3b$; $2a = 6b = 12c$; $2a = 12c$; $a = 6c$.

Part 2: Reading Skills Test

1. C	7. C	13. D	18. D	23. C
2. B	8. B	14. A	19. B	24. C
3. D	9. C	15. A	20. C	25. A
4. D	10. B	16. B	21. D	26. B
5. A	11. B	17. A	22. A	27. C
6. A	12. D			

1. **The correct answer is (C).** The judge decides on the minimum height to be jumped, so pole vaulters must jump higher than the height set by the judge.

2. **The correct answer is (B).** Since some icebergs in the Antarctic Ocean rise as high as 300 feet above the water, and since only one tenth of an iceberg is visible above the waterline, there are icebergs in the Antarctic Ocean that are as high as 3,000 feet altogether.

3. **The correct answer is (D).** A toad's skin is dry, dull, and rough or covered with warts.

4. **The correct answer is (D).** The phonograph and motion picture film are listed among Thomas Edison's inventions. While Edison may be in the running as the most famous inventor, such a statement is not supported by the paragraph, so choice (A) is incorrect. Choice (B) is incorrect because the passage specifically states that he was responsible for more than 1,000 inventions. Since Edison lived 84 years, his was not a short life, so choice (C) is incorrect.

5. **The correct answer is (A).** Since the other three answer choices involve monetary gain for the athlete, choice (A) can be the only correct answer.

6. **The correct answer is (A).** This is a restatement of the paragraph. The other answer choices have no relevance to the paragraph.

7. **The correct answer is (C).** This answer is stated in the last sentence of the passage.

8. **The correct answer is (B).** Although all four answer choices are somewhat supported by the passage, the one that *best* supports it is the statement that the average American family moves every few years.

9. **The correct answer is (C).** See the last sentence of the passage.

10. **The correct answer is (B).** Choice (B) restates the last sentence of the passage.

11. **The correct answer is (B).** The other three answer choices are incorrect statements. The date 1869 refers to the establishment of the current nine-member court, so answer choice (A) is incorrect. Justices are appointed by the president, so answer choice (C) is incorrect. And justices serve for life, so choice (D) is incorrect.

12. **The correct answer is (D).** Most of the passage is devoted to describing the five different types of competition.

13. **The correct answer is (D).** The word *also* in the last sentence is the key to the fact that in higher animals the brain controls voluntary behavior, involuntary behavior, emotions, memory, and thought.

14. **The correct answer is (A).** Because 6,080 feet is greater than 5,280 feet, choice (A) is correct.

15. **The correct answer is (A).** The recommendation to use not more than 14 persons nor fewer than 10 persons means that it is best to use between 10 and 14 persons on the net, even if fewer can be used.

16. **The correct answer is (B).** The paragraph may open by mentioning that there is a growing danger in the overuse of antibiotics; however, the paragraph does not expand on this theme. The passage mainly focuses on the ineffectiveness of antibiotics against viral infections. Because more than twice as much of the paragraph is devoted to the second theme, choice (B) is the best answer.

17. **The correct answer is (A).** Choices (B), (C), and (D) are not valid options. To take notice of details that at first glance may not seem to have any connection to the crime implies that one cannot tell in advance what will be important.

18. **The correct answer is (D).** The passage states that the work of the operator often requires careful attention under stress. This means that the operator must be able to work under difficult conditions. The passage does not state that the work must *always* be performed under stress.

19. **The correct answer is (B).** The answer to this question is implied in the statement that "mechanics be instructed in safety rules that they must follow for their own protection." If the mechanics must be instructed, then we can infer that accidents may occur if they have not been instructed (that is, if they are ignorant of the rules).

20. **The correct answer is (C).** Keeping individuals and groups of individuals working effectively is coordinating the activities of employees. This answer

choice is stated in the passage. The other choices require more interpretation. Introduction of large-scale production methods and increasing distribution of products may very well increase profits, but not necessarily.

21. **The correct answer is (D).** There is nothing in the passage to support choices (A), (B), or (C); only choice (D) summarizes the data given in the passage.

22. **The correct answer is (A).** There is nothing in the passage to support choices (B), (C), or (D). Choice (A) is supported by the excerpt "no crime is considered to occur unless there is a written law forbidding the act" at the beginning of the sentence.

23. **The correct answer is (C).** There is nothing in the passage to support answer choices (A), (B), or (D). Choice (C) is supported by this section: "Only one measure . . . is the rate at which replacements must be made in order to maintain the work force."

24. **The correct answer is (C).** There is nothing in the passage to support choices (A), (B), or (D). Choice (C) summarizes the ideas expressed in the quotation.

25. **The correct answer is (A).** There is nothing in the passage to support answer choices (B), (C), or (D). Choice (A) is clearly implied from the ideas expressed in the passage.

26. **The correct answer is (B).** Choice (B) is the only option that rephrases the sentence without changing the meaning.

27. **The correct answer is (C).** According to the quotation, citizens who are selfish and act only as their private interests seem to require are not public spirited. Those who disregard others are concerned principally with their own selfish interests. Choice (C) is therefore the correct answer.

Part 3: Mechanical Comprehension Test

1. (A)	7. (C)	13. (C)	19. (C)	25. (B)
2. (A)	8. (B)	14. (B)	20. (A)	26. (C)
3. (B)	9. (C)	15. (B)	21. (B)	27. (C)
4. (B)	10. (B)	16. (C)	22. (C)	28. (C)
5. (A)	11. (B)	17. (C)	23. (B)	29. (A)
6. (A)	12. (A)	18. (B)	24. (B)	30. (A)

1. **The correct answer is (A).** A seesaw is a good example of the first-class lever.

2. **The correct answer is (A).**
$F \times 4 = 60 \times 14$; $F = \frac{840}{4}$;
F = 210 pounds.

3. **The correct answer is (B).**
$MA = \frac{10}{2} = 5$

4. **The correct answer is (B).** This is a second-class lever with the fulcrum at the end, the effort being applied at the other end, and the resistance between these points. There is an ideal mechanical advantage of 4. The application of a 50-lb. effort to the handle of the wheelbarrow 4 feet from the fulcrum will lift a 200-lb. weight 1 foot from the fulcrum.

5. **The correct answer is (A).** Let x = distance from the 275-lb. weight to the fulcrum point.
275 lbs. $\times x$ = 125 lbs. $\times (4 - x)$;
$275x = 500 - 125x$;
$400x = 500$; $x = \frac{500}{400} = 1.25$ inches

6. **The correct answer is (A).** A single fixed pulley is actually a first-class lever with equal arms. The mechanical advantage, neglecting friction, is 1.

7. **The correct answer is (C).** The number of parts of the rope going to and from the movable block indicates the mechanical advantage. In this case, it is 2. Accordingly, a 50-pound effort would be needed.

8. **The correct answer is (B).** If the weight is to be raised 8 feet, each of the strands that either go around or are attached to the movable pulley must be shortened by 8 feet. 8 × 3 = 24 feet.

9. **The correct answer is (C).**
$TMA = \frac{9}{3} = 3$; $\frac{300}{3} = 100$ lbs.

10. **The correct answer is (B).** Diameter of drum = 4"; radius of drum = 2";
$TMA = \frac{8}{2} = 4$.

11. **The correct answer is (B).** Tool B is a bit and brace used for making holes in wood.

12. **The correct answer is (A).** Tool A is a die used to cut external threads.

13. **The correct answer is (C).** The number 18 indicates the number of threads per inch.

14. **The correct answer is (B).** Circuit 2 is in series. 1½ × 4 = 6 volts.

15. **The correct answer is (B).**
4⅛" − (2 × ½") = 4⅛" − 1" = 3⅛"

16. **The correct answer is (C).** The only correct choice is that points 1 and 2 make the same number of revolutions per minute.

17. **The correct answer is (C).** Gear A has 15 teeth; gear B has 10 teeth.

Let x = number of revolutions gear B will make.

$15 \times 14 = 10 \times x$; $10x = 15 \times 14$;
$x = \dfrac{15 \times 14}{10}$; $x = 21$.

18. **The correct answer is (B).** The top and the bottom of the driver wheel go in opposite directions. The driver wheel moves the left side of wheel S but the right side of wheel T, causing both wheels S and T to rotate in the same direction.

19. **The correct answer is (C).** Four times every second = 240 times a minute. With 10 projection rods on the wheel, the wheel must rotate at 24 rpm to make 240 rod contacts per minute.

20. **The correct answer is (A).** The raft will move in the opposite direction.

Let x = theoretical distance moved.
$10 \times 60 = x \times 800$; $800x = 1600$;
$x = \dfrac{1600}{800} = 2$.

21. **The correct answer is (B).** By reducing the length of the lever arm, you are reducing the effort and will permit the valve to blow off at a lower pressure.

22. **The correct answer is (C).** The pressure is uniform in the system given. If the main line air gauge reads 100 pounds, the tank air gauge will also read 100 pounds.

23. **The correct answer is (B).** Eight threads per inch indicates that 8 complete turns of the vise handle are required to close the jaws 1". 18 complete turns are needed to close the jaws 2¼".

24. **The correct answer is (B).** Careful scrutiny will indicate that the center-to-center distance is 2 inches minus $\frac{1}{16}$ inches, or $1\frac{15}{16}$".

25. **The correct answer is (B).** If an 8" level indicates 16 quarts, a 6" level would indicate 12 quarts. Four additional quarts would be needed.

26. **The correct answer is (C).** Z is the compression stroke. Both valves are closed and the piston is moving upward.

27. **The correct answer is (C).** The proper sequence is: intake (Y); compression (Z); power (X); exhaust (W).

28. **The correct answer is (C).** The thread or screw-pitch gauge is used to determine the pitch and number of threads per inch of threaded fasteners.

29. **The correct answer is (A).** The torque is read visually on a dial mounted on the handle of the wrench. It is used when a definite force must be applied.

30. **The correct answer is (A).** The handle of the adjustable wrench should be pulled toward the side having the adjustable jaw. This will prevent the adjustable jaw from springing open and slipping off the nut.

NOTES

NOTES

NOTES

NOTES

NOTES

NOTES

NOTES

NOTES

Peterson's
Book Satisfaction Survey

Give Us Your Feedback

Thank you for choosing Peterson's as your source for personalized solutions for your education and career achievement. Please take a few minutes to answer the following questions. Your answers will go a long way in helping us to produce the most user-friendly and comprehensive resources to meet your individual needs.

When completed, please tear out this page and mail it to us at:

> Publishing Department
> Peterson's, a Nelnet company
> 2000 Lenox Drive
> Lawrenceville, NJ 08648

You can also complete this survey online at **www.petersons.com/booksurvey**.

1. What is the ISBN of the book you have purchased? (The ISBN can be found on the book's back cover in the lower right-hand corner.) _____

2. Where did you purchase this book?
   - ❏ Retailer, such as Barnes & Noble
   - ❏ Online reseller, such as Amazon.com
   - ❏ Petersons.com
   - ❏ Other (please specify) _____

3. If you purchased this book on Petersons.com, please rate the following aspects of your online purchasing experience on a scale of 4 to 1 (4 = Excellent and 1 = Poor).

	4	3	2	1
Comprehensiveness of Peterson's Online Bookstore page	❏	❏	❏	❏
Overall online customer experience	❏	❏	❏	❏

4. Which category best describes you?
   - ❏ High school student
   - ❏ Parent of high school student
   - ❏ College student
   - ❏ Graduate/professional student
   - ❏ Returning adult student
   - ❏ Teacher
   - ❏ Counselor
   - ❏ Working professional/military
   - ❏ Other (please specify) _____

5. Rate your overall satisfaction with this book.

Extremely Satisfied	Satisfied	Not Satisfied
❏	❏	❏

6. **Rate each of the following aspects of this book on a scale of 4 to 1 (4 = Excellent and 1 = Poor).**

	4	3	2	1
Comprehensiveness of the information	❑	❑	❑	❑
Accuracy of the information	❑	❑	❑	❑
Usability	❑	❑	❑	❑
Cover design	❑	❑	❑	❑
Book layout	❑	❑	❑	❑
Special features (e.g., CD, flashcards, charts, etc.)	❑	❑	❑	❑
Value for the money	❑	❑	❑	❑

7. **This book was recommended by:**
   ❑ Guidance counselor
   ❑ Parent/guardian
   ❑ Family member/relative
   ❑ Friend
   ❑ Teacher
   ❑ Not recommended by anyone—I found the book on my own
   ❑ Other (please specify) _____

8. **Would you recommend this book to others?**

   Yes   Not Sure   No
    ❑   ❑   ❑

9. **Please provide any additional comments.**

   _____

   _____

   _____

   _____

Remember, you can tear out this page and mail it to us at:

   Publishing Department
   Peterson's, a Nelnet company
   2000 Lenox Drive
   Lawrenceville, NJ 08648

or you can complete the survey online at **www.petersons.com/booksurvey**.

Your feedback is important to us at Peterson's, and we thank you for your time!

If you would like us to keep in touch with you about new products and services, please include your e-mail address here: _____